ANNALS OF THE NEW YORK ACADEMY OF SCIENCES

Volume 929

EDITORIAL STAFF

Executive Editor
BARBARA M. GOLDMAN

Managing Editor
JUSTINE CULLINAN

The New York Academy of Sciences
2 East 63rd Street
New York, New York 10021

THE NEW YORK ACADEMY OF SCIENCES
(Founded in 1817)

BOARD OF GOVERNORS, September 2000 – September 2001

BILL GREEN, *Chairman of the Board*
TORSTEN WIESEL, *Vice Chairman of the Board*
RODNEY W. NICHOLS, *President and CEO* [ex officio]

Honorary Life Governors
WILLIAM T. GOLDEN JOSHUA LEDERBERG

JOHN T. MORGAN, *Treasurer*

Governors

ELEANOR BAUM	D. ALLAN BROMLEY	KAREN BURKE
	LAWRENCE B. BUTTENWIESER PRAVEEN CHAUDHARI	
JOHN H. GIBBONS	MICHAEL GOLDEN	RONALD L. GRAHAM
ROBERT G. LAHITA	JACQUELINE LEO	WILLIAM J. McDONOUGH
JOHN F. NIBLACK	SANDRA PANEM	RICHARD RAVITCH
RICHARD A. RIFKIND	SARA LEE SCHUPF	JAMES H. SIMONS

HELENE L. KAPLAN, *Counsel* [ex officio]   PETER H. KOHN, *V.P. & Secretary* [ex officio]

CAJAL AND CONSCIOUSN

Scientific Approaches to Consciousness on Centennial of Ramón y Cajal's *Textura*

ANNALS OF THE NEW YORK ACADEMY OF SCIENCES
Volume 929

CAJAL AND CONSCIOUSNESS
Scientific Approaches to Consciousness on the Centennial of Ramón y Cajal's *Textura*

Edited by Pedro C. Marijuán

The New York Academy of Sciences
New York, New York
2001

Copyright © 2001 by the New York Academy of Sciences. All rights reserved. Under the provisions of the United States Copyright Act of 1976, individual readers of the Annals are permitted to make fair use of the material in them for teaching or research. Permission is granted to quote from the Annals provided that the customary acknowledgment is made of the source. Material in the Annals may be republished only by permission of the Academy. Address inquiries to the Permissions Department (permissions@nyas.org) at the New York Academy of Sciences.

Copying fees: For each copy of an article made beyond the free copying permitted under Section 107 or 108 of the 1976 Copyright Act, a fee should be paid through the Copyright Clearance Center, Inc., 222 Rosewood Drive, Danvers, MA 01923 (www.copyright.com).

∞ The paper used in this publication meets the minimum requirements of the American National Standard for Information Sciences—Permanence of Paper for Printed Library Materials, ANSI Z39.48-1984.

Library of Congress Cataloging-in-Publication Data

Cajal and consciousness: scientific approaches to consciousness on the centennial of Ramón y Cajal's *Textura* / edited by Pedro C. Marijuán.
    p. cm. — (Annals of the New York Academy of Sciences, ISSN 0077-8923 ; v. 929)
"This volume is the result of a meeting entitled Cajal and Consciousness: International Centennial Conference Commemorating the publication of Textura del sistema nervioso del hombre y de los vertebrados organized by the government of Aragón and the University of Zaragoza and held November 29–December 1, 1999 in Zaragoza, Spain."
    Includes bibliographical references and indexes.
    ISBN 1-57331-304-1 (cloth : alk. paper) — ISBN 1-57331-305-X (pbk. : alk. paper)
    1. Consciousness—Congresses. I. Marijuán, Pedro C. II. Ramón y Cajal, Santiago, 1852–1934. Textura del sistema nervioso del hombre y de los vertebrados. III. Series.

Q11.N5 vol. 929
[QP411]
500 s—dc21
[612.8'2]   2001030422

GYAT/B-MP
Printed in the United States of America
ISBN 1-57331-304-1 (cloth)
ISBN 1-57331-305-X (paper)
ISSN 0077-8923

ANNALS OF THE NEW YORK ACADEMY OF SCIENCES
Volume 929
April 2001

CAJAL AND CONSCIOUSNESS
Scientific Approaches to Consciousness on the Centennial of Ramón y Cajal's *Textura*

Editor
PEDRO C. MARIJUÁN

Advisory Board
CONSTANTINO SOTELO, ALBERTO PORTERA, ALBERTO FERRÚS,
JUAN PÉREZ MERCADER, ANTONIO GARCÍA BELLIDO,
RICARD GUERRERO, CARLOS BELMONTE, ENRIC TRILLAS,
AND SANTIAGO RAMÓN Y CAJAL JUNQUERA

This volume is the result of a meeting entitled **Cajal and Consciousness: International Centennial Conference Commemorating the Publication of** *Textura del sistema nervioso del hombre y de los vertebrados* organized by the Government of Aragón and the University of Zaragoza and held November 29–December 1, 1999 in Zaragoza, Spain.

CONTENTS

Cajal and Consciousness: Introduction. *By* PEDRO C. MARIJUÁN 1

Part I. Consciousness, One Hundred Years after *Textura*

Progress in the Neural Sciences in the Century after Cajal (and the Mysteries That Remain). *By* THOMAS D. ALBRIGHT, THOMAS M. JESSELL, ERIC R. KANDEL, AND MICHAEL I. POSNER 11

Part II. Biological Complexity and the Emergence of Consciousness

Consciousness, Reduction, and Emergence: Some Remarks. *By* MURRAY GELL-MANN 41

The Epistemic Paradox of Mind and Matter. *By* HAROLD J. MOROWITZ 50

The Conscious Cell. *BY* LYNN MARGULIS 55

Complexity and Tinkering. *By* FRANÇOIS JACOB 71

Consciousness, the Brain, and Spacetime Geometry. *By* STUART HAMEROFF . 74

Consciousness, the Brain, and Spacetime Geometry: An Addendum—Some New Developments on the Orch OR Model for Consciousness. *By* ROGER PENROSE 105

Part III. From Primary to Higher-level Consciousness

Consciousness: The Remembered Present. *By* GERALD EDELMAN 111

Consciousness and the Binding Problem. *By* WOLF SINGER 123

Cajal on Neurons, Molecules, and Consciousness. *By* JEAN-PIERRE CHANGEUX . 147

A Neuronal Model of a Global Workspace in Effortful Cognitive Tasks. *By* STANISLAS DEHAENE, MICHEL KERSZBERG, AND JEAN-PIERRE CHANGEUX 152

Consciousness and the Brain: The Thalamocortical Dialogue in Health and Disease. *By* RODOLFO LLINÁS AND URS RIBARY 166

The Neuroanatomy of Phenomenal Vision: A Psychological Perspective. *By* PETRA STOERIG 176

Co-evolution of Human Consciousness and Language. *By* MICHAEL A. ARBIB 195

From Computing with Numbers to Computing with Words—From Manipulation of Measurements to Manipulations of Perceptions. *By* LOTFI A. ZADEH 221

Part IV. Closing Remarks

Who Was Cajal? *By* ALBERTO PORTERA-SÁNCHEZ 253

Index of Contributors 259

Subject Index 261

Financial assistance was received from:

- **Diputación General de Aragón**
- **IBERCAJA**
- **Caja de Ahorros Inmaculada**
- **Fundación Airtel**

The New York Academy of Sciences believes it has a responsibility to provide an open forum for discussion of scientific questions. The positions taken by the participants in the reported conferences are their own and not necessarily those of the Academy. The Academy has no intent to influence legislation by providing such forums.

Cajal and Consciousness

Introduction

PEDRO C. MARIJUÁN

Departamento de Ingeniería Electrónica y Comunicaciones, CPS, Universidad de Zaragoza, Zaragoza 50015, Spain

ABSTRACT: One hundred years after Santiago Ramón Cajal established the bases of modern neuroscience in his masterpiece *Textura del sistema nervioso del hombre y de los vertebrados*, the question is stated again: What is the status of consciousness today? The responses in this book, by contemporary leading figures of neuroscience, evolution, molecular biology, computer science, and quantum physics, collectively compose a fascinating conceptual landscape. Both the evolutionary emergence of consciousness and its development towards the highest level may be analyzed by a wealth of new theories and hypotheses, including Cajal's prescient ones. Some noticeable gaps remain, however. Celebrating the centennial of *Textura* is a timely occasion to reassess how close—and how far—our system of the sciences is to explaining consciousness.

KEYWORDS: Ramón y Cajal; *Textura*; Consciousness; Interdisciplinary problem; Biological complexity; Time granularities; Brain economy; Neurodynamic optimization principle

The conference **Cajal and Consciousness** was held in Zaragoza on November 29–December 1, 1999 to commemorate the centennial of Ramón y Cajal's masterwork *Textura del sistema nervioso del hombre y de los vertebrados*.[1] This solid work, almost 1,800 pages in the original edition and close to 2,000 in the French and English versions that followed,[2–4] was the fruit of more than twenty years of solitary effort by one of the most original and staunch scientists of that time. It was a monumental effort that paid off: *Textura* became not only the most important scientific work ever written by a Spaniard, but also served as the foundation of modern neuroscience. It can legitimately be included within that historical sequence of Great Books that have decisively contributed to configuring the fundamental disciplines of Western science over the last four centuries: natural (mathematical) science with Galileo's *Dialogo*, physics with Newton's *Principia*, chemistry with Lavoisier's *Traité*, biology with Darwin's *Origin*, and neuroscience with Cajal's *Textura*.

Address for communication: Departamento de Ingeniería Electrónica y Comunicaciones, Centro Politécnico Superior, Universidad de Zaragoza, Zaragoza 50015, Spain. Voice: 34-976-761927; fax: 34-976-762111.

marijuan@posta.unizar.es

Several contributions in this volume will refer to *Textura*'s contents and to Cajal's multifaceted achievements. Let us only mention *en passant* that both the artistic genius of the author and his insightful choice of drawings (close to 1,000 in the final version), and above all the clarity with which he expounded, one hundred years ago, most of the modern neuroscientific ideas of today, give this book an unmistakable contemporaneity.[5] Almost every contemporary subject in the neurosciences—including some sober theorizing on the neuronal basis of consciousness—can be found in the pages of *Textura*, be it the "doctrine of the neuron," the evolutionary origins of the nervous system, the general architecture of the central nervous system, structure of the neuronal cortex, interneuronal circuits, neurotropism of growing axons, plasticity of neuronal contacts, "trophic theory," advantages of decusation, or teleological economy principles of nervous system evolution. It is a book full of interesting nooks for neuroscientific readers to carefully explore, and is even useful for general educated readers. As a contributor to these proceedings, François Jaçob, points out, it is rare to find a book which, a hundred years after it was written, is still read by students. The passage of time has been kind to *Textura* compared with the other Great Books.[a]

The topic chosen for the centennial conference held in Zaragoza, the scientific approach to consciousness, is a *leit motiv* that somehow underlies *Textura*'s contents and even Cajal's global scientific enterprise. Explaining the phenomenon of consciousness is what initially attracted Cajal, as a young medical graduate, to phenomenology and psychology[7]—and to the practice of many other exciting fields, including first-class microbiology and pioneering medical experiences on hypnosis.[b] Later on he gradually realized the possibilities of the microscope and was able to improve on Golgi's silver impregnation method; thus armed with this powerful new "epistemological engine" he undertook a life-long exploration ultimately oriented to break into "...the utter darkness of the inner mechanism of psychic acts. The determination of the sequence of molecular processes that the neurons undergo...during the production of the concomitant phenomena of perception and thought, namely feelings, consciousness, and volition.*" But as he soberly confesses—we are in the final pages of *Textura* (p. 1,141)—"*This ideal is still very distant.*"

Since Cajal's seminal insights on the neuronal basis of consciousness—and let us not forget the work of his great contemporaries William James and Sigmund Freud—the scientific approach to this phenomenon has undergone pronounced ups, downs, and twists. But today, at the turn of the millennium, consciousness once again has become a focal point for interdisciplinary dialogue. Indeed, one of the perennial engines of scientific progress is the ambition to understand the nature of our own consciousness. And the ideal of its understanding seems to be far closer today than Cajal's realistic remarks one hundred years ago—or is it?

---

[a]Seemingly the Science Citations Index has also been very generous with *Textura*. Including its French version (the two English translations are only a few years old), the book has been leading the ranking of accumulated citations of recent classics during extended periods of the 20th century. See studies by historian López Piñero.[6]

[b]Cajal himself reported remarkable success in a practical case of hypnosis applied to childbirth. His own wife was the subject of the experience.[8]

CONSCIOUSNESS, ONE HUNDRED YEARS AFTER *TEXTURA*

Approaching the question of consciousness from the vantage points of the many different disciplines is the goal of this symposium. The covert premise, although it does not pass undiscussed, is that no single discipline contains the complete set of keys to understanding the phenomenon. The lion's share may reside in the neurosciences, but consciousness seems to have very rich areas of discussion outside that province of knowledge.

Philosophers A.N. Whitehead and Ortega y Gasset both were contemporaries of Cajal, and both wrote eloquently about the problem of integration left in the wake of the progressive specialization of scientific disciplines.[9,10] They understood how important it is to take account of the interdisciplinary dimensions of our knowledge. Otherwise the system of the sciences spontaneously produces *specialism* and loses most of its efficiency as an "illuminator" of knowledge in the service of helping society to resolve its most complex existential problems.[c] In the practice of science, the unavoidable fact is that individual disciplines do not contain internal logical cues to inform the specialized practitioner about the *relevance* of their respective contents concerning the multilevel explanation of complex organismic and social phenomena. And there is at least an *art* involved in combining the different scientific perspectives so as to maximize—optimize—comprehension by the limited subject.[13] This is not the place to discuss this issue, but further views on the *optimization* theme will appear later in this paper.

An interdisciplinary blend was chosen, thus, for presentation at this conference to properly represent the different views *a priori* most relevant to the occasion. These included those of the well-known polymaths and Nobel laureates, Murray Gell-Mann, Gerald Edelman, and François Jacob, as well as of such other leading figures in the neurosciencies, biology, physical chemistry, mathematics, and computing as Wolf Singer, Jean-Pierre Changeux, Rodolfo Llinás, Petra Stoerig, Stuart Hameroff, Lynn Margulis, Harold Morowitz, Michael Arbib, Roger Penrose, and Lotfi Zadeh. The philosopher David Chalmers participated too, and the neuroscientist Eric Kandel, who was unable to attend, is represented by a contribution to these proceedings.

Good science and good scientists always are a spectacle, and so more than 400 participants, from different countries and disciplinary backgrounds, were attracted to this conference in Zaragoza to watch the unfolding of an exciting, trendy—and, for some, a little bit eccentric—program. They were not disappointed. The presentations and debates were excellent, and involved substantial participation from the attendees. There were moments of heated discussions, and readers will easily discover the reason for the heat in the following pages. We hope that most of the inter-

---

[c]It may well be that an unsolved discussion on "causality boundaries" lies behind the whole interdisciplinary theme—yet would neatly affect consciousness too. To simplify: it is the dilemma of attributing either "causal impotence" or autonomous "causal efficacy" to the successive (biological, neuronal, social) realms that progressively emerge from the "simple" physicochemical interactions.[11,12] Unfortunately the successful claims of reductionism at downgrading the efficient causality of organisms exclusively towards the physicochemical realm are often contested under the banner of relativism (which does not consider the integrative or interdisciplinary problem at all), and the contemporary development of an interesting doctrine of perspectivism in science, implied by Whitehead and Ortega, represents almost uncharted waters.

est and excitement of the conference sessions have been conveyed, together with some more penetrating *a posteriori* reflections, in this book, the written record of the conference.

The contributions to this volume can be grouped into two thematic blocks: The first focuses on biological complexity and the emergence of consciousness, and the second concerns the transition from primary to higher-level consciousness. Together they provide a relevant sample of how the varying sciences contemplate the phenomenon of consciousness.

BIOLOGICAL COMPLEXITY AND THE EMERGENCE OF CONSCIOUSNESS

The book begins with a historical summary of the stunning progress that the neurosciences themselves have made during the century that has elapsed since Cajal, and particularly of the new perspectives gained during last two decades in physiological, imaging, and cognitive aspects of the question. The contributions of these new fields towards elucidating consciousness and the other mysteries that remain in the neurosciences are discussed, and a forecast is made of the breakthroughs to come, in a review by E.R. Kandel with his colleagues T.D. Albright, T.M. Jessell, and M.I. Posner. This is followed by a progression of concepts, predominantly across physics and biology, towards neuronal matters by M. Gell-Mann, H. Morowitz, L. Margulis, F. Jacob, and S. Hameroff and R. Penrose.

Emergence is the key concept for Murray Gell-Mann. Fundamental physical laws plus historical accidents, or special circumstances, are all we need in science to explain the emergence of complexity in the universe. This understanding embraces the origins of life, the growth of biological complexity, and the appearance of self-awareness (capable of discovering those basic probabilistic laws of nature: and here the loop is closed). Nature would conform to herself across the different levels: simplicity and elegance that stem from quantum mechanics and extend up to "complex adaptive systems." From a different perspective, Harold Morowitz's contribution also posits a conceptual loop—unavoidable circularity—between matter and mind. The quest for undiscovered principles in the evolution of nervous systems of the same epistemological status as the Pauli exclusion principle (which makes matter information-laden) is recommended. Homeotic genes and mappings from genes to nervous systems do indeed suggest such higher-order principles. We might be at the beginning of a new level of understanding about the operation of the nervous system.

Lynn Margulis argues about the evolutionary origins of eukaryotes and particularly about the neuronal cytoskeleton. Her idea is that the system of microtubules that became neurotubules has as its origin once-independent eubacteria of a very specific kind—spirochetes. In her view, the evolutionary antecedent of the nervous system is "microbial consciousness." Thus in the origins of the eukaryotic-cell-via bacterial-cell merger, the components fused by symbiogenesis are already "conscious" entities, that is, capable of sensing their environment and of producing adaptive responses. The ways and means by which evolution generates novelties is the focus of François Jacob's essay, in which he likens the work of evolution to that of a tinkerer, a *bricoleur*. In the process of producing new genes from available ones, it appears that the regulatory novelties are much more important evolutionarily than are all the other structural novelties. The evolutionary *bricolage* has been amazingly parsimonious in choosing the basic building blocks, but enormously creative in deploying these gene products in a variety of forms. The evolution of the vertebrate brain is a particular case in point.

Putting together physical, molecular-biological, and neurocomputational views, Stuart Hameroff and Roger Penrose (the latter in his Addendum) argue that neuronal systems perform noncomputable operations because they have evolutionarily explored and exploited quantum processing. The microtubule system of the neuronal cytoskeleton has been evolutionarily co-opted to exploit quantum effects (quantum superposition following Penrose's "Orch-OR" model), boosting the regular synaptic information-processing of pyramidal neurons. Coupled through gap junctions, assemblies of such cells would generate conscious brain states. The viability of this hypothesis depends on some controverted quantum mechanical and neurobiological assumptions—the crucial issue is the biological feasibility of sustaining quantum coherences. The authors respond here to recent criticisms[14,15] and add new arguments.

A bridge between the main conceptual paths of the foregoing contributions and the properly neuroscientific ones of the next section can be envisioned through some informational concepts. From the point of view of information, the living cell represents the emergence of a very special "complex adaptive system": a quasi-universal problem-solver based on the cytoplasm/genome interrelationship. By playing any conceivable kind of "genetic algorithm" (by structural and regulatory genetic alterations and also by symbiogenesis), the cellular system, or, even better, the communities of cells, continuously confront and solve the existential problems posed by their niches. The only inconvenience about the universality of such gene-based solutions—DNA computations—is their *time granularity,* as creation and testing of new adaptive knowledge are strictly generational. And that slow pace of processing operations completely precludes the immediate and precise cognitive coupling with the environment needed for motile multicellular life, at least until a new type of "electro-chemical" processor, the nervous system, stemmed from the unbounded creativity of the gene-based system. Out of obscure evolutionary (trophic?) origins,[16,17] nervous systems quickly specialized in informational functions and became the most important animal tool for climbing "Mount Fitness." The finer time granularity of the new system allowed infinitely faster problem-solving operations and, above all, the storage of a new type of inner, ontogenetic knowledge about the animal's coupling with the environment. As was emphasized during the conference debates, especially when encephalized nervous systems full of mappings and "memory surfaces" evolved in vertebrates a *remembered present* popped out into existence and primary consciousness was born.

FROM PRIMARY TO HIGHER-LEVEL CONSCIOUSNESS

The contributions that follow by G.E. Edelman, W. Singer, J.-P. Changeux, R. Llinás, P. Stoerig, M. Arbib, and L. Zadeh span a broad arch that goes from the primary consciousness common to most vertebrates, the special organization of human brains, and the origins of our language abilities up to the "computing with words" capabilities that might be implemented on machines soon. It is perhaps reassuring to discern an estimable nucleus of convergence among most of these contributions.

Gerald Edelman addresses the complexion of our own consciousness based on an evolutionary model of "primary consciousness." The latter, according to his views on "neuronal groups selection" and the phenomenon of *reentry*, helps an organism to abstract and organize complex changes in an environment involving multiple parallel signals. A scene of "remembered present" is continuously built, integrating the self and the non-self. The features are connected in terms of the saliency determined by the animal's past history and its values. A hypothesis of functional self-similarity (consistent with the Gell-Mann and Morowitz approaches) is at the center of Wolf Singer's scheme: phenomenal awareness, the ability to be aware of one's sensations and feelings, emerges from the capacity of evolved brains to reapply within themselves the very same cortical operations that they use for the interpretation of signals from the outer world. Dynamic binding processes are at the heart of both perception and self-perception operations. Consciousness becomes a graded phenomenon whereby the gradations are correlated with the phylogenetic and ontogenetic differentiation of the cerebral cortex.

Jean-Pierre Changeux's preface considers the "then" and "now" of Cajal's *doctrine of the neuron*. He reviews the fundamental ideas exposed in *Textura* about dynamic polarization, synaptic transmission and receptors, higher brain function, localization, etc. The second part of his contribution, with Stanislas Dehaene and Michel Kerszberg, deals with a cognitive model of the "conscious workspace" which implements selectionist views on the functional organization of the brain—the model would be coherent with Cajal's approach to higher mental function. They propose a minimal hypothesis concerning the brain processes underlying effortful tasks. Rodolfo Llinás and Urs Ribary also propose an approach *à la Cajal* to consciousness. For them, human consciousness is a phenomenon that requires coherence and that occurs in the brain by thalamocortical dialogue at certain frequencies. A basic cerebral circuit, capable of achieving low-granularity complex states, is absolutely necessary to support consciousness. When it malfunctions, many possible neurologic or psychiatric conditions may occur. We begin to understand that various ailments (depression, Parkinsonism, and others) are all part of the same thalamocortical syndrome. Not far from this neurophysiological pool of ideas, experimentalist Petra Stoerig combines clinical cases of lesions with neuroimaging methods to study the difference in activation patterns evoked by conscious as opposed to unconscious processes. Using functional magnetic resonance techniques in "blindsight" cases (cortically blind visual subjects, who nevertheless show localization and discrimination), she obtains a firmer hold on the conscious–unconscious activation patterns in different areas, which holds important implications for our understanding of such areas and of the neuronal correlates of consciousness.

Higher-order consciousness is fundamentally determined by language processes. In this regard, Michael Arbib presents an exciting convergence of several strands of thought—neurological, evolutionary, behavioral, and cognitive—about "the coevolution of human consciousness and language." His key hypothesis is that the origin of language must be located in a speech-manual-orofacial gesture complex that, working as a "communication plexus," actually restructures brain dynamics (both during the evolutionary process and during ontogenetic development) so that our higher-level awareness emerges endowed with its expression of thoughts in language and playing its dual role as an inner observer/controller. In the discussion he also reviews some of Cajal's tenets related to consciousness. Finally, an intriguing aspect related to the human use of language is the extent to which formal procedures, or computers for that matter, can capture its "meaning." Lotfi Zadeh presents a pathbreaking contribution (many readers will be reminded of his seminal paper creating the field of "fuzzy logic" in the 1960s) in which he argues that those aspects of consciousness that relate to reasoning and concept-formation may be linked to his new methodology of "computing with words." This may represent a foundational step for a *computational theory of perceptions*. In his view, the underachievements and failures underlying Artificial Intelligence reflect the unavailability of a methodology for reasoning and computing with "soft" perceptions rather than "hard" measurements.

Obviously there is much to add to this series of issues: the research and literature on consciousness have grown exponentially during recent years, and not only in the neurosciences. But the selection in this volume provides a fair representation of some of today's most relevant disciplinary approaches to consciousness. Nevertheless, two brief notes about what has not been included may be worth considering, the first about emotions and the second about the principles of brain evolution.

Emotions are important in the context of consciousness, not just in themselves, because of the fundamental role they play in inner life, but also because they reveal some persisting gaps in neuroscientific, psychological, and behavioral knowledge. In spite of all the growing interest and literature about emotions, what do we understand about *laughter*, for instance? Emotions may be characterized as highly influential neurodynamic events that the biological life-cycle has superimposed upon the relatively "free" cerebral processes in order to grant the advancement of the life-cycle itself—evolutionarily playing a sophisticated cognitive role. But how are they cognitively, neurodynamically and molecularly intertwined?[18,19] Emotions also need to be connected with the vast theme of social adaptation[20] and with ecological adaptations as well, such as *time cycles*.[21,22] This opens up new vistas since the richness of temporal granularities in the cognitive and behavioral realm is amazing. In this sense, if we look at one of the preferred vehicles for the transmission of our states of mind across time—the book—we can see it as a cyclical landscape of letters, syllables, words, phrases, clauses, sentences, paragraphs, full paragraphs, subsections, sections, chapters, parts, etc. We can bet that there is a correspondence between these cyclicities and structural, built-in time granularities of our own cerebral processes, and that some parallels can be drawn even at the level of synaptic events. Intriguingly, the concurrence within synapses of different molecular signaling pathways with very different time properties could represent a processing device to orchestrate at the cellular level such plethora of cognitive, emotional, and ecological timings. Notwithstanding, the basic problem with emotions, and their social and ecological retinue of complex adaptations, seems to be integrative: maybe we still lack a central theory of the neurosciences. In other words, we still lack an accepted theory about the "automation" of knowledge by the central nervous system that parallels the Darwinian theory about how the cytogenetic systems perform their problem-solving and knowledge-gathering operations.[23–27] "From Darwin to Cajal," we could summarize this theoretical absence reminding us of the intriguing *principles of economy* about brain evolution that Cajal tried to establish in *Textura* (pp. 95–106 [Vol.1] and pp. 1138–1152 [Vol.2]).

That reflection leads to the second brief note, about the principles of brain evolution (which is also present in Morowitz' contribution). In point of fact Cajal's illuminating discussion about such principles has been scarcely mentioned in the subsequent literature, and is particularly absent in recent works that have actually proved the optimization of crucial *structural* parameters in invertebrate and vertebrate nervous systems (e.g., see Refs. 28–30 as well as Allman's discussion[20]). However, the great challenge seems to be *functional* rather than structural. It is the quest for a neurodynamic optimization principle that matters. In other words, do nervous systems contain any neuronal (distributed) variable or dynamic core of such variables whose optimization may correspond with behavioral success in the "fitness" occasions that the organism encounters in its relationship with the environment? It seems paradoxical that, since neuroscientific explanations are situated between the ones of biology and economy, there would not exist any neuroscientific optimization principle in between the two towering optimization principles of those disciplines—namely, evolutionary maximization of *fitness* on the one side, and rational maximization of *utility* on the other. Clearly, both optimizations should be interconnected through the operation of our own brain.[31] The quest for a neurodynamic optimization principle, which we must relate to Cajal's insights one hundred years ago,[d] if successful, would boost our present understanding of consciousness and would help to fill the almost intractable breach separating the camps between the natural and the social sciences. Perhaps this theoretical aspect of *Textura*, ignored today, will receive widespread attention and development in the decades to come.

THE FIGURE OF CAJAL

This homage to Cajal on the centennial of the *Textura* would be incomplete without a closer approach to the author himself. Who was Cajal? On the scientific side, it is easier to answer: neuroscientist, microbiologist, theoretician, and even philosopher. But very little has been said here about him as a person. Alberto Portera's closing contribution tries to fill the gap by responding to the personal aspect of the question, "Who was Cajal?" "He was an extraordinary man...but also an extraordinary child" is the response. Curiously Portera's text has been crafted using Cajal's own words. While reading this recollection of excerpts taken from Cajal's autobiographical memories one can vividly imagine the personal collisions, the social circumstances, and the rugged landscapes among which his amazing character was forged.

Cajal was a native of a small village of Aragón (that medieval Spanish kingdom which, with Castille, formed the heart of modern Spain). How and why did a native from a remote village in an almost isolated, mountainous region find his way into world science? Some clues are given in Portera's text, but most readers may be un-

---

[d]Let us also remember Sigmund Freud's pioneering concept of neuronal energy in the dynamics of brain states.[32]

aware of the fascinating history of medieval science in the kingdom of Aragón (a history yet to be properly elaborated) as well as the three religious cultures—the Moorish, the Jewish, and the Christian—that brought forth persons of great stature. During the 11th century in particular, an amazing pool of scientific, philosophical, and mathematical talents was concentrated in Zaragoza, the capital of Aragón, as well as in other cities in that kingdom. The Moorish king al-Mutamin, himself a renowned mathematician, astronomer, and poet, amassed the largest scientific library of that time in his own palace of Aljafería. A multicultural school of translators had already been founded by his father al-Muqtadir in nearby Tarazona (which pre-dated the famous school of translators in Toledo), and scholars and scientists were also found in Huesca, Calatayud, Tudela, and Daroca, among other places.

Some of those past splendors are still kept alive in the background of Aragonese folk culture: as a quixotic ambition for knowledge. Avempace, al-Mutamin, Moshe Safaradi, Miguel Servet, Baltasar Gracián, Jordán de Asso, Félix de Azara, and Francisco de Goya are some of the individuals who in science, in culture, and in the arts have antedated the greatness of Santiago Ramón y Cajal. The resilience and focus of these Aragonese is proverbial. But it is perhaps Cajal who best exemplifies the highest peak of creativity and tenacity ever produced by the old nation of Aragón.

And so this celebration on the first centennial of the *Textura* is an affectionate tribute to Cajal's scientific and personal excellence as well as a view into the future of the ideas about which he was uncannily prescient.

ACKNOWLEDGMENTS

The Cajal and Consciousness conference was organized by the Government of Aragón (DGA) and the University of Zaragoza (UZ), with the co-operation of Consejo Social UZ, Heraldo de Aragón, and Instituto Ramón y Cajal (CSIC, Madrid). It was sponsored by DGA, IBERCAJA, CAI, and Fundación Airtel. I gratefully acknowledge the unstinting collaboration of my colleagues on the editorial committee: Constantino Sotelo, Alberto Portera, Alberto Ferrús, Juan Pérez Mercader, Antonio García Bellido, Ricard Guerrero, Carlos Belmonte, Enric Trillas, and Santiago Ramón y Cajal Junquera. I also salute the special collaboration of Santiago Ramón y Cajal Agüeras, Agustín Urdangarín, Morris Villarroel, Juan Santaolalla, Luis Joaquín Boya, Francisco Serón, Cristina Tejero, Antonio Valero, Stuart Hameroff, Floyd E. Bloom, and Michael Arbib. The friendly help extended by by Chon Durán (di&co) and Lynn Margulis, and by Barbara Goldman, Philip Zeigler, Justine Cullinan and their colleagues at the New York Academy of Sciences, in bringing these proceedings through the press is highly appreciated as well.

REFERENCES

1. RAMÓN Y CAJAL, S. 1899–1904. Textura del sistema nervioso del hombre y de los vertebrados. N. Moya. Madrid.
2. RAMÓN Y CAJAL, S. 1909–1911. Histologie du sistème nerveux de l'homme et les vertébrées. Maloine. Paris. [Translated by L. Azoulay.]
3. RAMÓN Y CAJAL, S. 1995. Histology of the Nervous System of Man and Vertebrates. Oxford University Press. New York. [Translated by L. & N. Swanson.]

4. RAMÓN Y CAJAL, S. 1999. Texture of the Nervous System of Man and the Vertebrates. Springer. Berlin/New York. [Translated by P. & T. Pasik.]
5. DEFELIPE, J. & E.G. JONES. 1988. Cajal on the Cerebral Cortex. Oxford University Press. New York.
6. LÓPEZ PIÑERO, J.M. 1985. Ramón y Cajal. Salvat. Barcelona.
7. DURÁN, G. & F. ALONSO. 1983. Cajal: Vida y obra. (2 vols.) Editorial científico-médica. Barcelona.
8. RAMÓN Y CAJAL, S. 1889. Dolores del parto considerablemente atenuados por la sugestión hipnótica. Gaceta Médica Catalana, 31 August 1889.
9. WHITEHEAD, A.N. 1929. Science and the Modern World. The Free Press (Macmillan). New York.
10. ORTEGA Y GASSET, J. 1930. La barbarie del "especialismo." *In* La rebelión de las masas. Obras Completas, Vol. IV. Ed. Revista de Occidente (1983) Madrid; 1932. The barbarism of specialization. *In* The Revolt of the Masses. Allen & Unwin. London.
11. DUPRÉ, J. 1993. The Disorder of Things. Harvard University Press. Cambridge,MA.
12. ROSENBERG, A. 1994. Instrumental Biology, or the Disunity of Science. University of Chicago Press. Chicago, IL.
13. MARIJUÁN, P.C. 1996. Foundations of Information Science: From Computers and Quantum Physics to Cells, Nervous Systems, and Societies. BioSystems **38**: 87–96.
14. TEGMARK, M. 2000. The importance of quantum coherence in brain processes. Phys. Rev. E **61**: 4194.
15. SEIFE, C. 2000. Cold numbers unmake the quantum mind. Science **287**: 791.
16. HORRIDGE, A. 1968. The origins of the nervous system. *In* Structure and Function of Neural Tissue. G. Bourne, Ed. Academic Press. New York.
17. FOX, R.F. 1988. Energy and the Evolution of Life. W.H. Freeman. New York.
18. NADER, K., G.E. SCHAFE & J.E. LE DOUX. 2000. Fear memories require protein synthesis in the amygdala for reconsolidation after retrieval. Nature **406**: 722–726.
19. DAMASIO, A.R. 1999. The Feeling of What Happens. Hartcourt Brace. New York.
20. ALLMAN, J.M. 1999. Evolving Brains. Scientific American Library. New York.
21. REED, E.S. 1996. Encountering the World. Oxford University Press. New York.
22. CONRAD, M. 1996. Cross-scale information processing in evolution, development and intelligence. BioSystems **38**: 97–109.
23. COLLINS, K.P. 1991. On the Automation of Knowledge within Central Nervous Systems. Unpublished manuscript.
24. CRICK, F.C.H. 1994. The Astonishing Hypothesis. Scribner. New York.
25. DEUTSCH, D. 1997. The Fabric of Reality. Allen Lane. London.
26. ARBIB, M. A., P. ÉRDI & J. SZENTÁGOTHA. 1998. Neural Organization: Structure, Function, and Dynamics. Bradford Books: The MIT Press. Cambridge, MA.
27. EDELMAN, G.M. & G. TONONI. 2000. A Universe of Consciousness: How Matter Becomes Imagination. Basic Books. New York.
28. CHERNIAK, C. 1994. Component Placement Optimization in the Brain. J. Neurosci. **14** (4): 2418–2427.
29. GRIFFIN, L.D. 1994. The Intrinsic Geometry of the Cerebral Cortex. J. Theor. Biol. **166**: 261–273.
30. VAN ESSEN, D. 1997. A tension-based theory of morphogenesis and compact wiring in the central nervous system. Nature **385**: 313–318.
31. PRINCE, A. & P. SMOLENSKY. 1997. Optimality: from neural networks to universal grammar. Science **275**: 1604–1610.
32. GERMINE, M. 1998. The Concept of Energy in Freud's "Project for a Scientific Psychology." Ann. N. Y. Acad. Sci. **843**: 80–90.

Progress in the Neural Sciences in the Century after Cajal (and the Mysteries That Remain)

THOMAS D. ALBRIGHT,[a] THOMAS M. JESSELL,[b] ERIC R. KANDEL,[b] AND MICHAEL I. POSNER[c]

[a]*Howard Hughes Medical Institute, The Salk Institute for Biological Studies, San Diego, California 92186, USA*

[b]*Howard Hughes Medical Institute and Center for Neurobiology and Behavior, Department of Biochemistry and Molecular Biophysics, College of Physicians & Surgeons of Columbia University, New York, New York 10032, USA*

[c]*Sackler Institute, Department of Psychiatry, Weill Medical College of Cornell University, New York, New York 10021, USA*

ABSTRACT: One hundred years after Santiago Ramón y Cajal provided critical evidence for the "neuron doctrine," his cellular view of the brain remains the basis of modern neural science. This article begins with a review of how the early work of Ramón y Cajal, Charles Sherrington, and John Eccles and their contemporaries laid the groundwork for our current understanding of the information processing of neural systems and for understanding the task faced by studies of how the brain develops. The visual system is examined in some detail as a model for experimental investigation into the structure, operational mechanisms, and functions of large neural systems. Discussion of the phenomena of visual awareness and consciousness, links between the visual system and other brain systems, and disorders that disrupt voluntary control of cognition and emotion lead to a broader consideration of the problem of consciousness.

KEYWORDS: Neuron; Brain; Nervous system; Vision; Consciousness

THE "NEURON DOCTRINE": BIRTH OF MODERN NEUROSCIENCE

Modern neural science, as we now know it, began at the turn of the century, when Santiago Ramón y Cajal provided the critical evidence for the "neuron doctrine," the idea that neurons serve as the functional signaling units of the nervous system and that neurons connect to one another in precise ways.[1–3] Ramón y Cajal's neuron doctrine represented a major shift in emphasis to a cellular view of the brain. Most nineteenth-century anatomists—Joseph von Gerlach, Otto Deiters, and Camillo Golgi, among them—were perplexed by the complex shape of neurons and by the seemingly endless extensions and interdigitations of their axons and dendrites.[4] As a result, these anatomists believed that the elements of the nervous system *did not* conform to the cell theory of Schleiden and Schwann, the theory that the cell was the functional unit of all eukaryotic tissues.

Address for correspondence: Dr. Eric Kandel, 1051 Riverside Drive, New York, New York 10032. erk5@columbia.edu

The confusion that prevailed amongst nineteenth-century anatomists took two forms. First, most were unclear as to whether the axon and the many dendrites of a neuron were in fact extensions that originated from a single cell. For a long time they failed to appreciate that the cell body of the neuron, which housed the nucleus, almost invariably gave rise to two types of extensions: to dendrites that serve as input elements for neurons and that receive information from other cells, and to an axon which serves as the output element of the neuron and conveys information to other cells, often over long distances. Appreciation of the full extent of the neuron and its processes came ultimately with the histological studies of Ramón y Cajal and from the studies of Ross Harrison, who observed directly the outgrowth of axons and dendrites from neurons grown in isolation in tissue culture.

A second confusion arose because anatomists could not visualize and resolve the cell membrane and therefore they were uncertain whether neurons were delimited by membranes throughout their extent. As a result many believed that the cytoplasm of two apposite cells was continuous at their points of contact and formed a syncytium or reticular net. Indeed, the neurofibrils of one cell were thought to extend into the cytoplasm of the neighboring cell, serving as a path for current flow from one cell to another. This confusion was solved intuitively and indirectly by Ramón y Cajal in the 1890s and definitively in the 1950s with the application of electron microscopy to the brain by Sanford Palay and George Palade.

Ramón y Cajal was able to address these two questions using two methodological strategies. First, he turned to studying the brain in newborn animals, where the density of neurons is low and the expansion of the dendritic tree is still modest. In addition, he used a specialized silver staining method developed by Camillo Golgi that labels only an occasional neuron, but labels these neurons in their entirety, thus permitting the visualization of their cell body, their entire dendritic tree, and their axon. With these methodological improvements, Ramón y Cajal observed that neurons, in fact, are discrete cells, bounded by membranes, and inferred that nerve cells communicate with one another only at specialized points of appositions, contacts that Charles Sherrington was later to call synapses.[5]

As Ramón y Cajal continued to examine neurons in different parts of the brain, he showed an uncanny ability to infer from static images remarkable functional insights into the dynamic properties of neurons. One of his most profound insights, gained in this way, was the principle of dynamic polarization. According to this principle, electrical signaling within neurons is unidirectional: The signals propagate from the receiving pole of the neuron the dendrites and the cell body to the axon, and then, along the axon to the output pole of the neuron the presynaptic axon terminal.

The principle of dynamic polarization proved enormously influential because it provided the first functionally coherent view of the various compartments of neurons. In addition, by identifying the directionality of information flow in the nervous system, dynamic polarization provided a logic and set of rules for mapping the individual components of pathways in the brain that constitute a coherent neural circuit (FIG. 1). Thus, in contrast to the chaotic view of the brain that emerged from the work of Golgi, Gerlach, and Deiters, who conceived of the brain as a diffuse nerve net in which every imaginable type of interaction appeared possible, Ramón y Cajal focused his experimental analysis on the brain's most important function: the processing of information.

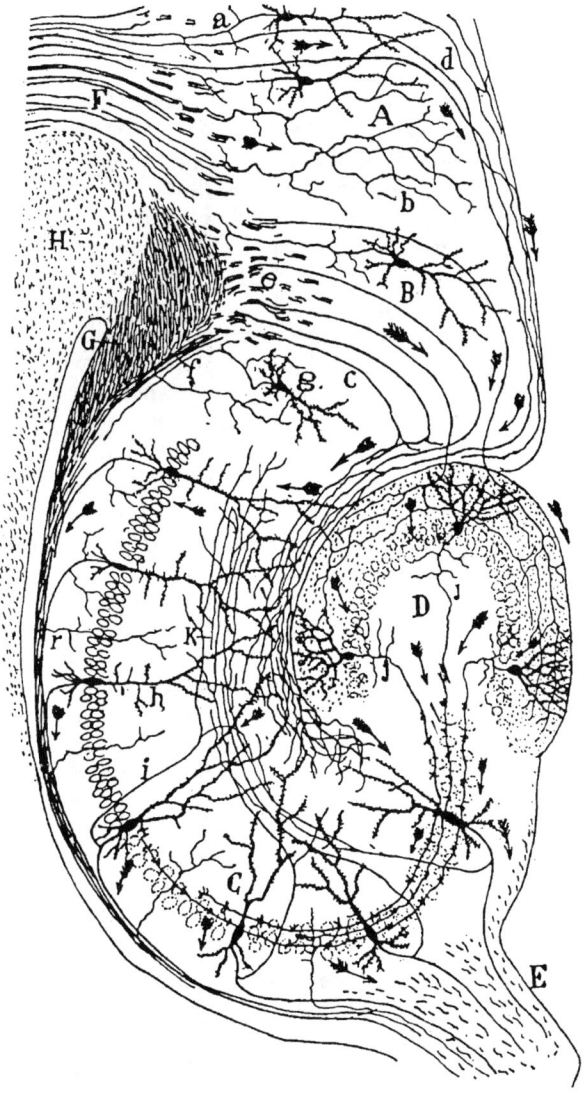

FIGURE 1. Ramón y Cajal's illustration of neural circuitry of the hippocampus. This drawing is based on sections of the rodent hippocampus, processed with a Golgi and Weigert stain. The drawing depicts the flow of information from the entorhinal cortex to the dentate granule cells (by means of the perforant pathway) and from the granule cells to the CA3 region (by means of the mossy fiber pathway), and from there to the CA1 region of the hippocampus (by means of the Schaeffer collateral pathway). (Based on Ramón y Cajal.[3])

Sherrington incorporated Ramón y Cajal's notions of the neuron doctrine, of dynamic polarization, and of the synapse into his book *The Integrative Action of the Nervous System*[6] (1906). This monograph extended thinking about the function of nerve cells to the level of behavior. Sherrington pointed out that the key function of the nervous system was integration; the nervous system was uniquely capable of weighing the consequences of different types of information and then deciding on an appropriate course of action based upon that evaluation. Sherrington illustrated the integrative capability of the nervous system in three ways. First, he pointed out that reflex actions serve as prototypic examples of behavioral integration; they represent coordinated, purposeful behavior in response to a specific input. For example in the flexion withdrawal and cross-extension reflex, a stimulated limb will flex and withdraw rapidly in response to a painful stimulus while, as part of a postural adjustment, the opposite limb will extend.[7] Second, since each spinal reflex—no matter how complex—used the motor neuron in the spinal cord for its output, Sherrington developed the idea that the motor neuron was the final common pathway for the integrative actions of the nervous system.[6] Finally, Sherrington discovered—what Ramón y Cajal could not infer—that not all synaptic actions were excitatory; some could be inhibitory.[8] Since motor neurons receive a convergence of both excitatory and inhibitory synaptic input, Sherrington argued that motor neurons represent an example—the prototypical example—of a cellular substrate for the integrative action of the brain. Each motor neuron must weigh the relative influence of two types of inputs, inhibitory and excitatory, before deciding whether or not to activate a final common pathway leading to behavior. Each neuron therefore recapitulates, in elementary form, the integrative action of the brain.

In the 1950s and 1960s, Sherrington's last and most influential student, John C. Eccles, used intracellular recordings from neurons to reveal the ionic mechanisms through which motor neurons generate the inhibitory and excitatory actions that permit them to serve as the final common pathway for neural integration.[9] In addition, Eccles, Karl Frank, and Michael Fuortes found that motor neurons had a specialized region, the initial segment of the axon, which served as a crucial integrative or decision-making component of the neuron.[10,11] This component summed the total excitatory and inhibitory input and discharged an action potential if, and only if, excitation of the motor neuron exceeded inhibition by a certain critical minimum.

The findings of Sherrington and Eccles implied that each neuron solves the competition between excitation and inhibition by using, at its initial segment, a winner-takes-all strategy. As a result, an elementary aspect of the integrative action of the brain could now be studied at the level of individual cells by determining how the summation of excitation and inhibition leads to an integrated, all-or-none, output at the initial segment. Indeed, it soon became evident that studies of the motor neuron had predictive value for all neurons in the brain. Thus, the initial task in understanding the integrative action of the brain could be reduced to understanding signal integration at the level of individual nerve cells.

The ability to extend the analysis of neuronal signaling to other regions of the brain was, in fact, already being advanced by two of Sherrington's contemporaries, Edgar Adrian and John Langley. Adrian developed methods of single-unit analysis within the central nervous system, making it possible to study signaling in any part of the nervous system at the level of single cells.[12] In the course of this work, Adrian found that virtually all neurons use a conserved mechanism for signaling within the cell: the action potential. In all cases, the action potential proved to be a large, all-or-none, regenerative electrical event that propagated without fail from the initial segment of the axon to the presynaptic terminal. Thus, Adrian showed that what made one cell a sensory cell carrying information of vision and another cell a motor cell carrying information about movement was not the nature of the action potential that each cell generated. What determined function was the neural circuit to which that cell belonged.

Sherrington's other contemporary, John Langley,[13] provided some of the initial evidence (later extended by Otto Loewi, Henry Dale, and Wilhelm Feldberg) that, at most synapses, signaling between neurons—synaptic transmission—was chemical in nature. Thus, the work of Ramón y Cajal, Sherrington, Adrian, and Langley set the stage for the delineation, in the second half of the twentieth century, of the mechanisms of neuronal signaling.

In his pioneering approach to the brain's processing of information, Ramón y Cajal had also introduced the principle of *connection specificity*: the idea that a given neuron will not connect randomly to another but that during development a given neuron will form specific connections only with some neurons and not with others. The precision of connections that characterizes the nervous system posed several deep questions: How are the intricate neural circuits that are embedded within the mature nervous system assembled during development? How does one reconcile the properties of a specifically and precisely wired brain with the known capability of animals and humans to acquire new knowledge in the form of learning? And how is knowledge, once learned, retained in the form of memory?

One solution to this problem was proposed by Ramón y Cajal in his 1894 Croonian Lecture to the Royal Society in which he suggested the development and reinforcement (plasticity) of connections in the part of the brain in use. Later on, experimental findings in the marine snail *Aplysia* have showed that memory is stored as a plastic change in synaptic strength,[14,15] and not as the self-reexciting loops of neurons postulated by the physiologist Alexander Forbes and other alternative solutions also proposed during the intervening decades. These experimental findings have reinforced the early ideas on neuronal connectivity of Ramón y Cajal, which have now become one of the major themes of the molecular study of memory storage and of the modern cognitive psychological studies of memory: Even though the anatomical connections between neurons develop according to a definite plan, the strength and effectiveness are not entirely predetermined and can be altered by experience.[16] Thus synaptic plasticity becomes a fundamental property in the information processing of neural systems.

FROM INDIVIDUAL NEURONS TO NEURAL SYSTEMS

The individual neurons that make up the brain work together in specialized groups, or systems, each of which serves a distinct function. Systems neuroscience is the study of these neural systems, which include those involved in vision, memory, and language. Neural systems possess a number of common properties, not the least of which is that they all process higher-order information about an organism's environment and biological needs. In humans, this information often gains access to consciousness. Systems neuroscience thus places great emphasis on uncovering the neural structures and events associated with the steps in an information-processing hierarchy. How is information encoded (sensation)? How is it interpreted to confer meaning (perception)? How is it stored or modified (learning and memory)? How is it used to predict the future state of the environment and the consequences of action (decision making/emotion)? How is it used to guide behavior (motor control) and to communicate (language)? The twentieth century saw remarkable progress in understanding these processes. This ascendance of modern systems neuroscience is attributable, in part, to the convergence of five key subdisciplines, each of which contributed major technical or conceptual advances.

Neuropsychology: Localization of the Biological Source of Mental Function

The first question one might ask about an information-processing device concerns its gross structure and the relationship between structural elements and their functions. The simplest approach to this question and the approach that has best withstood the test of time is to observe the behavioral or psychological consequences of localized lesions of brain tissue. The modern discipline of neuropsychology was founded on this approach and draws both from human clinical case studies often provided during the early decades of the twentieth century by brain injuries sustained in battle and from experimental studies of the effects of targeted destruction of brain tissue in animals. Through these means the functions of specific brain regions, such as those involved in sensation, perception, memory, and language, have been inferred.

Neuroanatomy: Patterns of Connectivity Identify Information-Processing Stages

The discipline of neuroanatomy, which blossomed at the turn of the century following the adoption of the neuron doctrine and which has benefited from many subsequent technical advances, has revealed much about the fine structure of the brain's components and the manner in which they are connected to one another. As we have seen, one of the earliest and most influential technical developments was the discovery by Camillo Golgi of a method for selective staining of individual neurons, which permitted their visualization by light microscopy. By such methods, it became possible to use differences in the morphology of cells in different brain regions as markers for functional diversity. This procedure, known as cytoarchitectonics, was promoted vigorously in the early decades of the twentieth century by the anatomists Korbinian Brodmann, and Oscar and Cecile Vogt. Brodmann's cytoarchitectonic map of the human cerebral cortex, which was published in 1909 and charted the positions of some 50 distinct cortical zones, has served as a guidebook for generations of scientists and clinicians, and as a catalyst for innumerable studies of cortical functional organization.

Arguably the most important outcome of the means to label neurons, however, was the ability to trace connections between different brain regions. To this end, cell-labeling techniques have undergone enormous refinement over the past three decades. Small quantities of fluorescent or radioactive substances, for example, can now be injected with precision into one brain region and subsequently detected in other regions, which provides evidence for connectivity. The products of anatomical tract tracing are wiring diagrams of major brain systems, which are continuously evolving in their precision and completeness, and have been indispensable to the analysis of information flow through the brain and for understanding the hierarchy of processing stages.

Neurophysiology: Uncovering Cellular Representations of the World

Adoption of the neuron doctrine and recognition of the electrical nature of nervous tissue paved the way to an understanding of the information represented by neurons via their electrical properties. Techniques for amplification and recording of small electrical potentials were developed in the 1920s by Edgar Adrian. This new technology enabled neurobiologists to relate a neuronal signal directly to a specific event, such as the presentation of a sensory stimulus, and became a cornerstone of systems neuroscience. By the 1930s, electrophysiological methods were sufficiently refined to enable recordings to be made from individual neurons. Sensory processing and motor control emerged as natural targets for study. The great successes of single-neuron electrophysiology are most evident from the work of Vernon Mountcastle in the somatosensory system, and David Hubel and Torsten Wiesel in the visual cortex, whose investigations, beginning in the late 1950s, profoundly shaped our understanding of the relationship between neuronal and sensory events.

Psychophysics: The Objective Study of Behavior

Historically, quantitation of behavior has been the province of experimental psychology, which emerged in the nineteenth century from deep-rooted philosophical traditions to become a distinct scientific discipline and a key component of modern systems neuroscience. Among the most notable steps in this emergence was the development by the German physicist and philosopher, Gustav Fechner, of a systematic scientific methodology for assessing the relationship between behavior and internal states. Fechner's *Elements of Psychophysics*, published in 1860, founded an "exact science of the functional relationship...between body and mind," based on the assumption that the relationship between brain and perception could be measured experimentally as the relationship between a stimulus and the sensation it gives rise to.[17] In practice, Fechner's psychophysics is applied by varying a sensory stimulus along some physical dimension such as the intensity or wavelength of light and obtaining reports from an observer regarding the sensations experienced. In this manner, one can identify the function that relates the physical dimension of the stimulus to an internal sensory dimension, and from that relationship infer the rules by which the sensory information is processed.

Throughout the twentieth century, the tools of psychophysics have been extremely useful in identifying the information-processing strategies of sensory, perceptual, and motor systems of the brain. Beginning with the work of Mountcastle in the 1960s,[18] psychophysics has frequently been paired directly with electrophysiological methods to extraordinary effect in identifying the neuronal events that give rise to specific sensory and perceptual processes.

Computation: Divining the Mechanisms of Information Processing

Large neural systems such as those involved in vision, combine and analyze incoming signals to "interpret" their causes and generate appropriate outputs. The logical steps in these neuronal mechanisms have become accessible to quantitative and theoretical treatment. The goal has been to extract generic computational principles that can account for existing data and have predictive value. Some of the earliest work along these lines was directed at sensory and motor processing and was founded on engineering techniques and principles designed for the study of simple linear systems. One of the most successful examples of this approach is Georg von Bekesy's investigation[19] of the cochlea and its relation to the frequency encoding of sound. von Bekesy began by investigating the patterns of vibration of the various components of the inner ear, and the relationship of these patterns to the characteristics of sound waves. From these observations he concluded that this system analyzes sound by a linear frequency decomposition, that is, the mechanical properties of the cochlea allow specific frequency components of sound to be independently isolated and detected by the sensory epithelium. Considerable gains have also been made using similar theoretical approaches to understand early stages of visual processing and the control of movements of the eyes.

Many levels of processing in neural systems deviate from linear forms of computation. The search for alternative computational principles, which was fueled in part by the rise of cognitive science in the 1980s and an unprecedented richness of physiological and anatomical data, has led to a number of novel and sophisticated theoretical approaches, such as those embodied by neural networks.[20] These networks operate on the biologically plausible principle that information can be represented in a distributed fashion across a large population of "units," or modeled neurons. Moreover, this information may be combined in many different ways to yield complex cellular representations, simply by changing the strength of "synaptic" connections between modeled neurons.

Collectively these five areas of neuroscience—neuropsychology, neuroanatomy, neurophysiology, psychophysics, and computation—constitute an experimental arsenal, which has already revealed in outline the structure, operational mechanisms, and functions of large neural systems, such as those involved in vision, memory, and language. Although the range of successes is broad, and many general principles of system organization and function have been discovered, the visual system has emerged as the model for experimental investigation and is consequently the area in which we have the greatest understanding. It will be the main focus of the rest of this review.

FUNDAMENTAL THEMES IN THE STUDY OF THE VISUAL SYSTEM

The complete legacy of twentieth century research on the visual system has led to a number of general principles of visual system organization and function. Some of the most important ones would be, for instance: (**i**) the visual system is hierarchically organized; (**ii**) the visual system is organized in parallel processing streams; (**iii**) many visual processing stages are topographically organized; (**iv**) the visual cortex is organized in vertical columns; and (**v**) the visual system is modifiable by experience during early postnatal development. But despite unprecedented progress, our understanding of visual system organization and function is far from complete. On the contrary, developments and discoveries of the past century have raised many new and often unanticipated questions regarding the visual system and other large brain systems. Here we focus on a few of the bigger issues at stake, with some predictions about where this field of research may be headed in the new millennium.

How Do Sensory Representations Lead to Perception?

The physiological studies of Hubel and Wiesel and many others over the past 50 years have revealed much about how basic features of the visual image, such as oriented lines and patches of color, are detected and represented by cortical neurons. But how do these cellular representations account for our perceptual experience of the world? The underlying assumption has been that perception of complex scenes would result from the collective activities of neurons whose properties we so far have considered and which were characterized under reduced stimulus conditions. It is, however, increasingly apparent that this assumption is flawed because it posits that individual neuronal representations of sensory features are independent of one another, and the field of sensory physiology is consequently at a turning point in its evolution.

In the search for an alternative approach to carry us into a new millennium, it is useful to return to the principles of Gestalt theory and to develop an operational distinction between candidate neuronal substrates for sensation and for perception. Accordingly, candidate neuronal substrates for sensation which have been the primary subjects of study over the past 50 years encode the physical properties of the proximal stimulus (the visual image), such as orientation or direction of motion. Perceptual representations, on the other hand, reflect the world (the visual scene) that likely gave rise to the sensory stimulus. Contextual manipulations make it possible to dissociate local sensory properties from perception, and thereby offer a means to identify neuronal responses that are correlated with perception rather than the proximal sensory stimulus. Francis Crick and Christof Koch[21] have recently equated perceptual representations of the sort defined here with "neural correlates of consciousness," owing to their belief that perceptual awareness is a legitimate operational definition of consciousness. We take this issue up below in the section on vision and consciousness.

There are many ways in which this research strategy for studying candidate neuronal substrates for perception can be applied. These fall into two complementary categories. First, one can investigate whether neuronal responses to identical receptive field stimuli co-vary with the different percepts determined by different contexts that those stimuli elicit. The set of stimuli illustrated in FIGURE 2 are of this class, and a valid experimental goal would be to identify neuronal responses that vary with the percept elicited, even though the receptive field stimulus (the gray rectangle in FIGURE 2) remains physically unchanged. Second, one can investigate the neuronal responses to different receptive field stimuli "sensory synonyms" that elicit the same percept, owing to context. Both of these situations, which are prevalent in normal experience, afford opportunities to experimentally decouple sensation and perception (FIG. 2).

The first of these two approaches to whether neuronal responses co-vary with different contexts was used by Thomas Albright, Gene Stoner, and colleagues to understand the role of cortical visual area MT in motion perception (for review see Albright and Stoner[22]). Moving objects in a typical visual scene commonly generate a complex array of moving visual image features. One objective of the visual system is to integrate these moving features to recover the coherent motions of the objects that gave rise to them. That integration process is heavily and necessarily context-

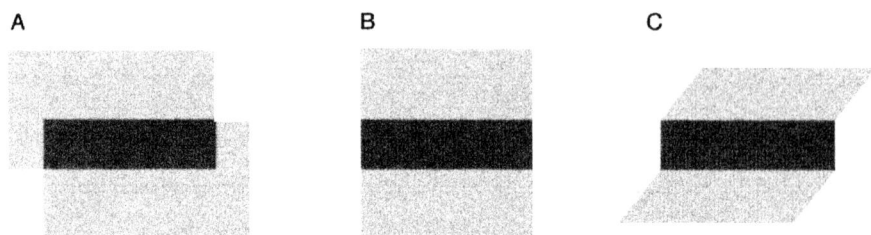

FIGURE 2. The influence of local sensory context on visual perception. Each of the three images displayed here contains a horizontal dark gray rectangle. Although the rectangles are physically identical, the surrounding features (the contexts) differ in the three images. As a result, the rectangle is attributed perceptually to different environmental causes in the three instances: In the image shown in (**A**), the rectangle appears to result from the overlap of two surfaces, one of which is transparent (e.g., a piece of tinted glass). In the image shown in (**B**), the rectangle appears to result from a variation in surface reflectance (e.g., a stripe painted across a large flat canvas). In the image shown in (**C**), the rectangle appears to result from partial shading of a three-dimensional surface (i.e., variation in the angle of the surface with respect to the source of illumination). These markedly different perceptual interpretations argue for the existence of different neuronal representations of the rectangle in each of the three instances. These representations can only be identified in neurophysiological experiments if the appropriate contextual cues are used for visual stimulation. See the text for details. (Courtesy of Albright and colleagues.)

dependent, such that, for example, the object motions that are perceived from two identical collections of image motions can vary greatly as a function of the context in which the motions appear.

Physiologists have only begun to employ the second approach. Several studies, for example, have recently explored a phenomenon termed "form-cue invariance," in which a percept of motion or shape is invariant across different "form cues," such as luminance, chrominance, or texture, that enable the stimulus to be seen. In one such study, Albright[23] discovered a population of motion-sensitive neurons in area MT that appear to encode the direction of motion of a stimulus independently of the fact that the form cue—an aspect of the retinal stimulus that is, in principle, irrelevant to motion detection—is varied. To paraphrase from Horace Barlow's "neuron doctrine for perceptual psychology,"[24] the main function of such cells appears not to be the encoding of specific characteristics of retinal illumination, "but to continue responding invariantly to the same external patterns," that is, to the meaningful attributes of the input.

From the outset, the physiological approach to the operations of the visual system has seen itself as being in the service of perceptual psychology. If the "exploration of psychological territory" is to continue, however, physiologists must advance beyond the acontextual approach that has been the standard of twentieth century research in this field. New experimental approaches in which contextual influences are exploited as tools for the study of neural substrates of perception are thus likely to be an important feature of future research in this area.

Binding It All Together

The representational strategy that the visual system has adopted is one in which the properties of the incoming signal are distributed across many neurons, such that each neuron only conveys a small piece of the larger picture. At the level of the retina, for example, the information represented by single cells is limited to a small circular region of space. At the level of primary visual cortex, cells integrate information from earlier stages in order to convey information about contour orientation, but they remain highly specialized. At still higher levels, visual information is further combined and abstracted to yield even more complex properties and greater specialization of function, as evidenced by the multiplicity of extrastriate visual areas.

In view of this strategy, one cannot help but wonder how all of the specialized representations are bound together to render a neuronal signal that conforms to the complex patterns that we perceive. How is it, for example, that the cells representing the edges, the varying orientations, the colors and textures, and the different distances associated with the tree outside my corner window, are linked together to produce my percept of that tree? How are other properties of the same visual image, such as the attributes of a different but nearby tree, "segmented" and bound together as a separate entity from the first? Even more puzzling is the fact that only some of these complex patterns enter my awareness at any point in time. How are those patterns selected, and how are objects that we are simultaneously aware of linked together? What role does visual attention play in this process? Is there a distinguishing feature of the collections of neurons that happen to represent objects or collections of objects that we have become conscious of? Is there, as contemplated by Sherrington[25] a half-century ago, one "pontifical cell" that represents the final outcome of this integration process? The representational problem addressed by these questions has become known as the "binding problem." In a more general form, the problem has preoccupied philosophers and cognitive scientists for decades, and it now stands among the most formidable challenges in modern neuroscience.

At its most basic level, the binding problem is simply that of representing conjunctions of attributes. There are, in principle, two mechanistic strategies that could accomplish this task, one based on neural space and the other based on time. On the one hand, attributes that must be conjoined such as the color and the direction of motion of an object could be represented in that form by selective convergence of information onto single neurons, yielding a neuron, for example, that selectively encodes rightward moving red objects. The appeal of such a strategy is that it follows naturally from what is already known of the hierarchical properties of the visual system. The neuronal representation of an oriented contour is, after all, nothing more than a product of selective convergence of information from the previous stage. Moreover, long-standing evidence indicates that neurons well up in the hierarchy encode very complex conjunctions of visual attributes, such as those associated with faces.[26] The problem with this form of binding, however, is one of generality: the variety of unique perceivable conjunctions of visual attributes vastly exceeds the number of available neurons. So while this may be a strategy that the visual system has adopted for early levels of integration and for highly specialized and vital functions like facial recognition, it is simply untenable as a general mechanism for binding.

The alternative strategy is one in which visual attributes are bound in time, rather than by static spatial convergence. The obvious advantage of a dynamic binding mechanism is that, unlike the static design, it places no serious combinatorial limits on the pieces of information that can be conjoined. A form of this mechanism was suggested as early as 1949 by the psychologist Donald Hebb,[27] who hypothesized the existence of "cell assemblies." Each such assembly was conceived as a collection of neurons that are dynamically associated with one another as needed to link the features they independently represent. A key feature of this concept is the ability of each cell to hold membership in multiple overlapping assemblies such that, for example, a cell that represents upward motion may be assembled with a cell representing the color red on one occasion, but assembled with a cell representing the color green on a different occasion. This view of binding was subsequently elaborated upon by Horace Barlow,[24] who noted it to be a particularly efficient form of representation because perceptions commonly "overlap with one another, sharing parts which continue unchanged from one moment to another."

The trick, of course, is identifying a dynamic binding code that can be used to transiently link cells into an assembly. One idea, which was implicit in Hebb's original proposal, developed significantly in the early 1980s by the theorist Christof von der Marlsberg,[28] and which has subsequently drawn a great deal of attention (see, for example, reviews in October 1999 issue of *Neuron*), is that temporal synchrony of neuronal firing patterns may underlie binding. As suggested in 1989 by Charles Gray, Wolf Singer, and colleagues, "synchrony of oscillatory responses in spatially separate regions of the cortex may be used to establish a transient relationship between common but spatially distributed features of a pattern."[29] This solution is in effect a dynamic switchboard that binds collections of complex features "on demand" via synchronized firing of the neurons that represent the individual features. Gray and Singer presented provocative data in support of this hypothesis. They found that the temporal spiking patterns of pairs of simultaneously recorded neurons in visual cortex were likely to be correlated if the separate visual stimuli that elicited those patterns appeared (to human observers) to be part of a common object. Other studies, however, have failed to find support for this synchrony hypothesis (e.g., Lamme and Spekreijse[30]; for review see Shadlen and Movshon[31]) and the matter remains unsettled.

If we accept the concept of dynamic cell assemblies, and the related proposal for temporal binding by synchronous firing (if only for the sake of argument), we face many critical questions. How, for example, are the transient patterns of synchrony "read out"? Does synchronous firing lead to transient synaptic facilitation of converging inputs onto a multipurpose pontifical cell (or, perhaps more appropriately, given the democratic and ephemeral nature of the hypothesized convergence, a "presidential cell")? Or is the perceptual binding simply implicit in the activity of the synchronized neurons, which constitute flexible cell assemblies for specific percepts? What elicits synchrony to begin with? Is there a top-down supervisory module that identifies attributes that experience tells us are likely to be parts of the same object? Or is the process bottom-up, using a variety of "image segmentation cues" to parse out attributes that belong to the same versus different objects? And what happens when, as is often the case, there are multiple objects perceived simultaneously? Is spike timing sufficiently precise to allow multiple synchrony events to occur simultaneously?

While we await the answers to these and other questions, it nevertheless appears likely that visual integration rests upon a combination of static and dynamic binding mechanisms. Indeed, except for a few clever hypotheses and controversial details, our understanding of these processes has advanced little beyond the view advocated by Barlow in the early 1970s (as a counterpoint to Sherrington's pontifical cell metaphor), according to which a series of "cardinal cells" reside at the top of static convergence hierarchies, but "among the many cardinals only a few speak at once" in the form of dynamic cell assemblies.[24] But research now moves rapidly on these fronts and, with vast improvements in technology for monitoring the firing patterns of many neurons simultaneously, the existence and operations of cell assemblies and their role in binding should come into sharper focus in the coming years.

Vision and Consciousness

Interestingly, the binding problem and its proposed solution by a dynamic code have also been coupled with the phenomena of visual awareness and consciousness. In the case of visual awareness, the argument is quite natural (if not tautological), as there are good reasons to believe that the perceptual binding of visual attributes is tantamount to their reaching the perceiver's awareness. Indeed, Singer and colleagues have argued that "appropriate synchronization among cortical neurons may be one of the necessary conditions for the...awareness of sensory stimuli."[32] Developing the concept of neuronal "metarepresentations," Singer[33] has furthermore suggested that this code may underlie all of the complex patterns that enter our awareness at any time. The extension of this line of argument to consciousness depends, of course, on how one defines the term. Although there is a long history of confusion about what consciousness actually means, and a plethora of colloquial uses of the term, Francis Crick and Christof Koch[21] have recently attempted to facilitate scientific progress by arguing for a specific and limited definition that is relevant to vision. (We consider the issue more broadly later in this article). Roughly speaking, that definition can be equated with perceptual awareness; it is "enriched" by visual attention, and may fill a window of time, which Gerald Edelman[34] has termed "the remembered present" (see also William James[35]). If we accept that operational and not-unreasonable definition, then dynamic representations of the sort proposed by Singer and others may be relevant to consciousness. But this is slick and unstable terrain, newly trodden by neuroscience and lacking the guideposts of established experimental paradigms (deflecting, to paraphrase Bertrand Russell, nearly all but fools and Nobel laureates). It is, nonetheless, one of the most compelling issues facing the future of neuroscience, and is certain to be a focal point of research in the next century.

How Do Cellular Representations Change with Visual Experience?

A central tenet of modern neuroscience is that stages in brain development correspond to specific stages in the development of perceptual abilities. These stages are known as critical periods, and they are characterized by an extraordinary degree of neuronal and perceptual plasticity. Only recently has it been recognized that the plasticity of the visual system is not restricted to these critical periods early in development, but is modifiable throughout the adult life of the organism. The forms of this adult plasticity are many and varied, but all can be viewed as recalibration of incoming signals to compensate for changes in the environment, the fidelity of signal detection (such as that associated with normal aging or trauma to the sensory periphery), or behavioral goals.

One of the most striking and revealing forms of adult neuronal plasticity is that associated with perceptual learning, which is an improvement with practice in the ability to discriminate sensory attributes. In humans, these learning phenomena are ubiquitous in everyday life and generally self-evident, and they have been a subject of scientific investigation for decades (for review see Karni and Bertini[36]). Consider, for example, the copy editor who over time becomes particularly sensitive to graceless word pairings, or the assembly line worker who can instantly recognize the miswired transistor. Until recently, however, little effort had been made to investigate their neuronal bases. Indeed, the critical period concept had become so widespread and deeply rooted that there seemed little ground for believing that visual representations might be modifiable throughout life.

Thus, it was well before the modern neuroscience community was prepared to embrace the concept of plastic representations in mature animals, that Michael Merzenich began to address the degree to which sensory maps could change in response to a variety of manipulations (for review see Buonomano and Merzenich[37]). This work began to have a broad impact in the mid-1980s with the demonstration of marked and systematic reorganization of somatosensory cortex in response to a change in the peripheral sensory field (e.g., selective deafferentation). Even more exciting and provocative was the subsequent demonstration that cortical maps reorganize, in response to selective use of components of a sensory modality, in a manner that mirrors perceptual learning.

Following in the footsteps of Merzenich, Charles Gilbert has recently begun to investigate the relationship between adult visual perceptual learning and the receptive field properties of cortical neurons. In one set of experiments, Gilbert and colleagues have found that increases in perceptual sensitivity fail to generalize to spatial locations or stimulus configurations beyond those in the set of training stimuli.[38] This high degree of spatial specificity suggests that the underlying neuronal changes may occur at a very early stage of processing where the spatial resolving power of cortical neurons is greatest. Other behavioral observations support this conclusion (e.g., Karni and Sagi[39]). Using a complementary approach, Gilbert and others have demonstrated plasticity of cortical representations more directly.[40,41] In this case, the receptive field properties of V1 neurons were found to change following localized interruption of retinal input (caused by small retinal lesions). Similar to previous findings from the somatosensory system, these changes took the form of shifts in the spatial profile of receptive fields, such that cells normally responding to light in the area covered by the retinal lesion become sensitive to stimulation of adjacent regions of visual space. These changes began to occur in a matter of minutes following deafferentation. Although in this case, unlike perceptual learning, the plasticity was not induced by repeated exposure to a sensory stimulus, but was rather a response to a marked loss of stimulation, both can be viewed as forms of renormalization and the underlying cellular mechanisms may be similar.

This is among the most exciting areas of systems neuroscience today, bridging as it does the topics of sensory processing and learning. Early contributions to this field have been particularly inspiring and influential because the prevailing wisdom held that sensory representations were largely immutable following critical periods of developmental reorganization. As we have seen, recent observations prove that this is not the case. On the contrary, representational changes occur throughout life as part of a normalization process to compensate for damage or deterioration of the sensory periphery or to meet novel behavioral and perceptual requirements. But these findings naturally raise many new questions that will occupy neuroscientists for years to come. Little is yet known, for example, of the specific neuronal events that give rise to plasticity of the adult visual system, although such processes are sure to include changes in synaptic efficacy, changes in neuronal cell structure, and possibly neurogenesis. Future research is also likely to address the following questions: How are these experience-dependent changes in visual processing mediated? Evidence indicates that higher cortical areas, such as regions of the frontal cortex, contain neurons that represent attributes of memorized stimuli. What role, if any, do these mnemonic representations play in the formation of experience-dependent changes in visual cortex? What are the control signals that initiate such changes? Does representational plasticity occur at all stages of visual processing? Does it occur in the retina? Do such changes constitute the neuronal repository of long-term visual memories?

BEYOND VISION: EXPLORING LINKS WITH OTHER BRAIN SYSTEMS

It is a pedagogical convenience to treat the visual system as we have done here as functionally independent and separable from other brain systems. The fact of the matter is that vision is but one cog in the wheel and is in many ways integrated with other major systems, including those responsible for memory, emotion, and motor control. Although we know less much less, in some cases, about these other systems, it is now clear that the areas of interface between vision and those systems that serve storage, evaluation, and action are among the most important targets for future research in systems neuroscience. Here we consider one of these areas of interface: that associated with motor control.

Visual Guidance of Behavior: From Retina to Muscle

A major function of the visual system is to provide sensory input to guide actions, such as moving through the environment. Visual and motor control systems have in common the fact that they both represent space. But the relevant frames of reference—retinal space, in the case of vision, and ultimately muscle space, in the case of action—are radically different. How then does light falling on a particular location on my retina lead to a reaching arm movement (or an eye movement, or a leg movement, etc.) to the source of the light? The problem becomes even more puzzling if we consider that exactly the same arm movement will be executed regardless of what direction I am looking, implying that vastly different retinal signals can lead to the same motor output. In principle, there are a number of different means by which this coordinate transformation could be accomplished.

Perhaps in large part because of the compelling subjective sense that space is stable regardless of the orientations of our sense organs and our muscles, it has often been proposed that the brain contains a unified representation of space. This unified map might represent space in a three-dimensional "world-centered" frame of reference, as opposed to the more specific coordinates of the sensory (retina) and effector (muscle) organs. According to this view, we have an internal neuronal map of the spatial locations of all of the items on my desk in front of us. That map remains coherent and unchanged regardless of which way we are looking or, for that matter, which way the entire body is oriented. The advantage of such a system is that it provides a generic source of spatial information that can be used to guide all movements, which is independent of the state of the sense organs or muscles. The disadvantage is that, because of its independence from sense organs and muscles, a generic reference frame is extremely difficult to compute.

Numerous studies conducted over the past few decades have evaluated the hypothesis that space is transformed from sensation to action via a unified reference frame. Neuropsychologists have examined the effects of damage to brain regions that lie between early visual processing and motor control, specifically the parietal and premotor areas of the cerebral cortex. The typical consequence of such damage is "neglect," in which subjects ignore stimuli that appear in certain regions of visual space (FIG. 3) (for review see Mesulam[42]). (Neglect is distinguished from blindness by the fact a patient with unilateral neglect syndrome can clearly see a neglected stimulus if his or her attention is drawn to it.) If there were a single unified map of space, one would expect that neglect would be manifested in the same part of the spatial map always to the right side of the observer, for example. On the contrary, results indicate that neglect can be present in any of a number of different spatial reference frames (retinal coordinates, body part coordinates, object-based coordinates, world-based coordinates), suggesting that there are multiple spatial maps, which may serve specialized functions (for review see Colby and Goldberg[43])(FIG. 3).

Neurophysiological data also support the hypothesis that there are multiple types of spatial maps used to transform information from sensory to motor coordinates. This issue has been explored extensively by Richard Andersen and colleagues, who recorded from neurons in the parietal cortex in search of a representation of visual space in head-centered coordinates (which would, in principle, be useful for directing movements of the eyes). Andersen discovered instead that these neurons possess "gain fields," by which the amplitude of the response to a visual stimulus is modulated systematically by the direction of gaze.[44] Because these neuronal responses take eye position into account, it is in principle possible to deduce the spatial location of the visual stimulus from the activity of a population of such neurons, regardless of where the eyes are looking (for review see Andersen et al.[45]). This information can then be used to guide movements to the stimulus.

Recent physiological experiments by two groups, Carl Olson and Sonya Gettner and Michael Graziano and Charles Gross, provide fascinating evidence for more explicit but highly specialized spatial maps that could mediate visual-motor control. Olson and Gettner[46] recorded from individual neurons in premotor cortex of monkeys and found that the neurons responded if an eye movement was made to a particular part of an object, regardless of the spatial location of the object. These neurons thus appear to represent space in an object-based coordinate frame. Graziano and Gross studied single neurons in the premotor cortex that possess both visual and tactile receptive fields. The visual receptive field of each neuron was found to be linked to the spatial location of the tactile receptive field, such that, for exam-

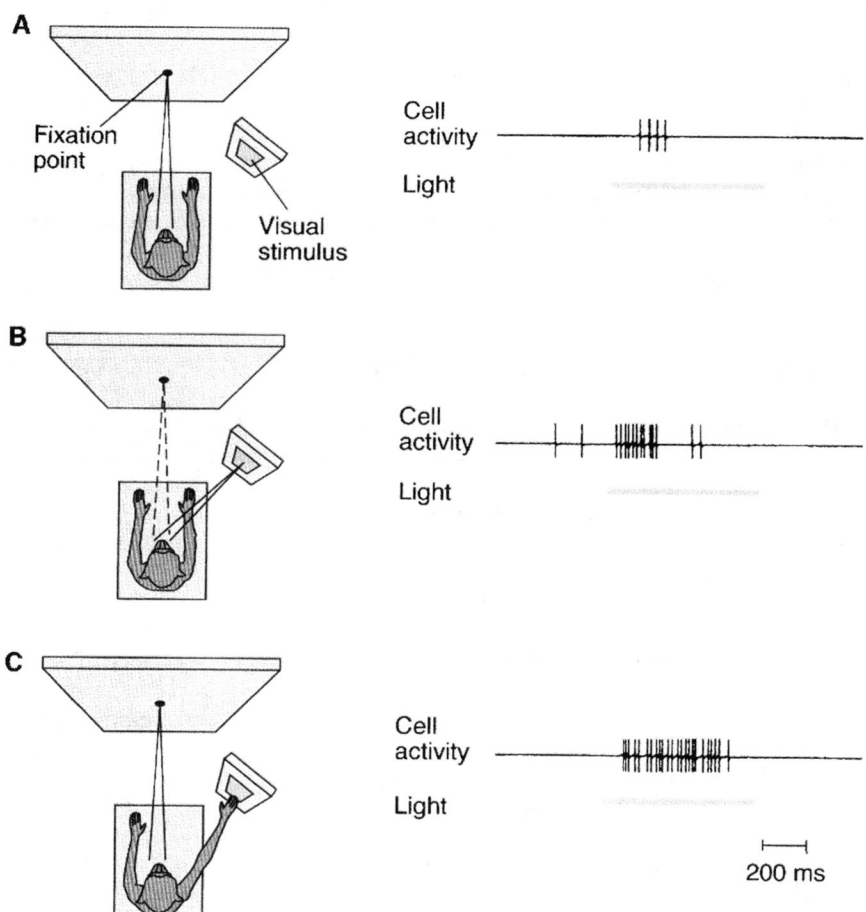

FIGURE 3. The influence of attention on the response of cortical neurons. Neurons in the posterior parietal cortex of a monkey respond more effectively to a stimulus when the animal is attentive to the stimulus. (**A**) A spot of light elicits only a few action potentials in a cell when the animal's gaze is fixed away from the stimulus. (**B**) The same cell's activity is enhanced when the animal takes visual notice of the stimulus through a saccadic eye movement. (**C**) The cell's activity is enhanced further when the monkey touches the spot, even without eye movement. (From Wurtz and Goldberg,[84] as illustrated in Kandel et al.[86])

ple, a neuron that was activated by tactile stimulation of the arm was also activated by a visual stimulus in the vicinity of the arm.[47] Remarkably, if the arm moved to a new location, the visual receptive field moved along with it. The visual receptive fields of these neurons thus appear to have been transformed from a retinal frame of reference to a reference frame centered on the position of the arm. Graziano and Gross propose that this arm-centered reference frame may be well suited for orchestrating movements of the arm to stimuli that are near the arm. More generally, they speculate that visual-motor transformations of many types may rely upon specialized body part–centered maps of space, rather than upon a single unified spatial map. Although both of these physiological findings suggest promising new approaches to the study of sensorimotor coordinate transformations, they leave many questions of a mechanistic nature unanswered. Perhaps the most nagging question raised by the Graziano and Gross study concerns the apparently profound spatial mobility of the visual receptive field, which dances across retinal space with every movement of the arm. How are retinal signals dynamically rerouted, as it were, to continuously update the visual receptive field of the premotor neuron, using information about arm position as a guide? This and other related questions will be an important focus of research in years to come.

CONSCIOUSNESS: A CHALLENGE FOR THE NEXT CENTURY

Perhaps the greatest unresolved problem in visual perception, in memory, and, indeed, in all of biology, resides in the analysis of consciousness. This is a particularly difficult problem, in part because there is no widespread agreement on exactly what constitutes a successful solution. There is agreement nevertheless that a successful solution will require, at a minimum, insight into two major issues that lie at the heart of the study of consciousness: (1) awareness of the sensory world and (2) volition, the voluntary control of thoughts and feelings.

In this section we consider awareness by focusing on two of its components: attentional orienting to sensory signals in the presence and in the absence of stimuli (imagery). We shall then go on to consider volition by focusing on the self-regulation of thoughts, feelings, and actions. These two problems are at once relevant to consciousness, yet tractable, and therefore serve to illustrate how consciousness can be dissected biologically.

As with other problems in biology there are both reductionist and holistic approaches to these components of consciousness. A reductionist approach would view these aspects of consciousness from a genetic, synaptic, and cellular level. However, in the case of consciousness it is hard to imagine any solution that would not also require an understanding of the large neural networks that underlie cognition, actions, and emotion. In our view, the appropriate direction in seeking a solution to the problems of consciousness lies in successfully linking understanding at all of these levels, from genes to behavior. In this section we try to illustrate this integrative approach in relation to orienting to sensory stimuli, and self-regulation. Finally, we examine how far these scientific approaches will take us in understanding the most subjective aspects of consciousness.

Rigorous top-down approaches to consciousness have been limited by the lack of good methods for resolving the activity of populations of cells. The use of neuroimaging methods during the last decade has made it possible to observe the activity of large numbers of neurons in human subjects while they are studied for their awareness of the sensory world and for their voluntary control of thoughts and feelings.[48,49] Cognitive studies using these imaging methods, such as positron emission tomography (PET) and functional magnetic resonance imaging (fMRI), are based upon changes in blood flow and blood oxygenation that occur in localized regions of the brain when neurons increase their activity.[50,51] These methods have now been applied with some success to the study of attentional orienting, visual imagery, and regulation of cognitive and emotional states. In each of these domains, the individual functional components have proven to be surprisingly well localized; however, each of the major functions of consciousness such as attentional orienting to sensory stimuli and volition involves not one but several functional components. As a result each function of consciousness appears to involve several networks and these are distributed across a variety of brain areas. Fortunately the enormous complexity of the problems has been made somewhat more tractable by use of appropriate animal models. In the best case, as with studies of the visual system, it has proven possible to relate neural activity studied at the cellular level in nonhuman primates to the activity of large neural networks studied in the same brain areas but now in human subjects using brain imaging.[52] While the results are not definitive, they show that specific aspects of consciousness can even now be analyzed on the cellular level with methods currently available to neuroscience.

Awareness

All Visual Areas, Including Primary Visual Cortex (V1), Can Be Biased by a Shift of Attention

To obtain an idea of how brain areas become involved in selection of a stimulus, consider the task of looking for a file on your computer desktop. If the desk is cluttered with files, you will have to search for the one you want. Such a search may be accompanied by eye movements, but, if the objects are close, the search may involve covert shifts of attention without eye movements. Such visual search tasks involve the coordinated action of the two large-scale brain networks. One network, the ventral visual pathway, which we discussed in the previous section, is concerned with objects and with form recognition, required for obtaining the identity of each file. The second network, located in the posterior parietal cortex of the dorsal visual pathway, is related to the act of shifting attention to the locations where the file might be found. Early studies of the dorsal pathway were conducted by Michael Goldberg and Robert Wurtz.[53] They found that cells in the posterior parietal cortex of alert monkeys responded differentially to identical stimuli depending on whether or not the monkey was attending to the stimulus (FIG. 3). When the monkey attended, the firing of the cell was much more intense than when the monkey ignored the stimulus. These results provided the first data on the cellular level that neurons in the parietal cortex are correlated with attention to the location of visual objects. With the advent of neuroimaging, it became possible to see the distributed network of brain areas involved in attention in human subjects. This network includes the frontal eye fields, the superior colliculus, and posterior parietal lobe, all of which are also involved in eye movements[54] (FIG. 3).

Studies conducted by Robert Desimone and colleagues have addressed the role of the ventral visual pathway (particularly areas V4 and IT) in attentional control. A typical paradigm involves first establishing the stimulus selectively for a cortical neuron. Suppose, for example, that the neuron under study responded well to a red bar of light and poorly to a green bar when these stimuli were individually placed in the neuronal receptive field. At this point, both stimuli—the red and green bars—would be placed in the receptive field of the cell at the same time. If the animal was instructed to attend to the "good" stimulus (red bar), then the neuron responded well. If, however, the animal was instructed to attend to the "poor" stimulus (green bar), then the response was correspondingly poor despite the fact that the retinal stimulus was the same in both cases. Desimone and colleagues interpreted these results as evidence that the receptive field shrinks to conform to the attended stimulus, thereby excluding the unattended stimulus and implementing a filtering mechanisms of the sort proposed by Broadbent (see Desimone and Duncan[55] for review).

The exact visual area that will be biased in the manner revealed by these physiological studies appears to depend upon the task required of the subject.[55–57] Imaging studies have shown that if people are asked to attend to target motion, activity is increased in a brain area in the dorsal visual pathway sensitive to movement (area MT). Quite different visual areas become active for attention to other stimulus dimensions such as color or orientation.[58] When attention is shifted to a new location, the neural activity of cells in the ventral, object recognition network is increased even before any target is presented at that location.[56]

There Is a Fundamental Distinction between Focal and Ambient Attention

Of course there is a sense in which, without even trying to attend, you are conscious of all the objects on your desktop. However, when careful tests are made that involve making changes in a complex visual scene, these tests reveal that when attention is focused on one object, other objects within the scene—even large and important ones—can be altered without the subject's being aware that a change has taken place.[59] Thus, while attention can be summoned efficiently to a novel event, there is surprisingly little awareness of changes that occur at loci that are not attended. It is therefore useful to distinguish between focal attention, which allows reporting of details of the scene, and ambient attention, which forms our general awareness of the scene around us. While both are aspects of consciousness, their underlying neurobiological mechanisms may be quite different. It seems likely that ambient attention may depend primarily upon posterior brain areas. By contrast, focal attention, which is often switched between objects based on instructions, may depend on more anterior areas related to voluntary control of action.

There May Be Only a Small Number of Networks Concerned with Attention, and These Can Be Distinguished on the Cellular and Even on the Molecular Level

It seems likely that the neuronal computation that occurs in most cortical areas can be influenced by attention. Indeed, there are a surprisingly large number of sites in the brain where attentional influences can be demonstrated. However, the source of those effects is thought to emanate from a small number of networks that perform different functions.

For example, a novel visual stimulus serves both to alert the organism and to orient attention to the location of the stimulus. This distinction can be demonstrated by using separate cues for alerting and orienting. An alerting cue provides the monkey with information about when a target will occur, but not about where that target will be located. An orienting cue provides the monkey with specific information about where the target will be located and thus allows the subject to move attention to the cued location. Two separate brain networks, both located in the parietal lobe, but using distinctly different chemical transmitter systems, are involved in changing the level of alertness and in switching attention toward the stimulus. Thus, the influence of alerting cues is reduced by drugs that block norepinephrine activity, but these drugs do not influence orienting. By contrast, drugs that block cholinergic activity influence orienting to the cue, but do not diminish the alerting effect.[60] These pharmacological studies illustrate how one can separate a simple act of attention to a novel event into two distinct components, and pinpoint both the anatomical systems and the modulatory synaptic mechanisms involved.

Findings in patients confirm the importance of neural systems for alerting and orienting to our normal awareness of the world around us. Strokes that interfere with the blood supply to the posterior parietal cortex on the right side produce an inability to orient attention to the left side, the side opposite the lesion. Patients that suffer from these right-sided lesions will show striking deficits in body image and in their perception of spatial relations. Although their somatic sensations are intact, these patients may ignore (neglect) the spatial aspects of all sensory input from the left side of their body as well as of external space, and they will ignore the left half of any visual object with which they are confronted. For example, patients with neglect syndrome will exhibit a severe disturbance in their ability to copy drawn figures. This deficit can be so severe that the patient may draw a flower with only petals on the right side of the plant. When asked to copy a clock, the patient may ignore the digits on the left and try to fill in all the digits on the right, or draw them down the side running off the clock face. These patients also may ignore the left half of the body and fail to dress, undress, and wash the affected side.

Less dramatic but similar difficulties in orienting accompany loss of parietal neurons due to degenerative disorder such as Alzheimer's dementia.[61] In these cases, stimuli going directly to the lesioned area, which would normally produce orienting of attention, may no longer do so and consequently the person may be completely unaware of these stimuli.

Many researchers agree with Francis Crick's view that sensory awareness probably is the most tractable area for a rigorous understanding of consciousness at a mechanistic level. As a result, much research has recently been focussed on the study of orienting to sensory stimuli. The discovery that attention can influence activity within primary visual cortex (area 17) has allowed investigators to explore attentional effects within a visual area whose other cellular and physiological features and anatomical characteristics are extremely well characterized.[57] The work in area 17 therefore provides an opportunity to specify exactly what cellular structures and functions can be modified by the act of attending.

Volition

Areas of the Frontal Midline Appear to be Important in Voluntary Control of Cognition and Emotion

Normal people have a strong subjective feeling of their intentions. They have a clear sense that they have voluntary control of their own behavior. These subjective feelings of intentions and voluntary control can be freely verbalized. Indeed, asking people about their goals or intentions is probably the single most predictive indicator of their behavior during problem solving.[62] The importance of intention is also illustrated in patients with frontal lesions[63] or in patients suffering from with mental disorders,[64] who show disruption in either their voluntary control over behavior or their subjective feelings of control. What are the neural mechanisms of voluntary control?

Norman and Shallice[65] have argued that an executive attention system is necessary for situations in which routine or automatic processes are inadequate. These nonroutine, nonautomatic executive functions include selection among conflicting inputs, resolution of conflict among responses, and monitoring and correcting errors.

The Dorsal Anterior Cingulate Cortex Is Essential for Executive Control

Suppose you are asked how many objects you see between the brackets: [two, two, two]. You may at first want to say two, even though the correct answer is three. This is because there is a conflict in your mind between the meaning of the word as read and the specified task of saying how many words are present. This is one form of the Stroop effect. The most frequent form of Stroop effect occurs when a subject has to name the color of ink in which a word is written when the color of the word conflicts with the word name (e.g., when the word red is written in blue ink). These conflicting tasks involve focal attention to the critical element of the task when that element must be selected in competition with a more dominant element. Imaging studies of the Stroop effect produced by conflict between elements tend to find very strong activity in the dorsal anterior cingulate gyrus (FIG. 4B) often in concert with areas of the basal ganglia and lateral frontal cortex.[66] For this reason dorsal anterior cingulate gyrus has been thought to be involved in some aspect of focal or executive attention[67] (FIG. 4).

As is the case with humans, rhesus monkeys trained to associate digits with a quantity, show conflict between deciding which of two displays has the greatest number of objects when there is an incompatible relation between the two (e.g., when the larger number of objects is made up of the smaller digit). The monkeys made many more errors on incompatible trials than do humans, despite many hundreds of trials at the task.[68] It is as though the monkeys have somewhat less capacity for avoiding interference, despite very extensive training.

In humans, activity in the anterior cingulate gyrus generally is related to the degree of practice or automation of the task. Perhaps the best example is a task where subjects are required to ascribe a use for each noun in a list (e.g., hammer → pound). There is a conflict between saying the word name aloud and the required task of generating the use of the word. There was strong activation of anterior cingulate when the list was first presented, but with practice on a single list, activity in the cingulate disappears and instead there is activity in the anterior insula, a portion of cortex that lies buried beneath Broca's area.[69] Both the anterior insula and Broca's area are closely related to the automatic task of reading the word aloud. Imaging studies have identified two different pathways for producing the use of a word. One pathway is involved when conscious thought is needed to generate a word. This pathway involves the cingulate in conjunction with left lateral areas of the cortex and the right cerebellum. Another, more automatic, pathway is involved when the words are well practiced so that the feeling of conscious search disappears. Now the activity in the cingulate (as well as in the lateral cortex and cerebellum) disappears, and instead one finds activity in Broca's area and in the anterior insula, the structures that are usually involved in the automatic tasks of reading words out loud.

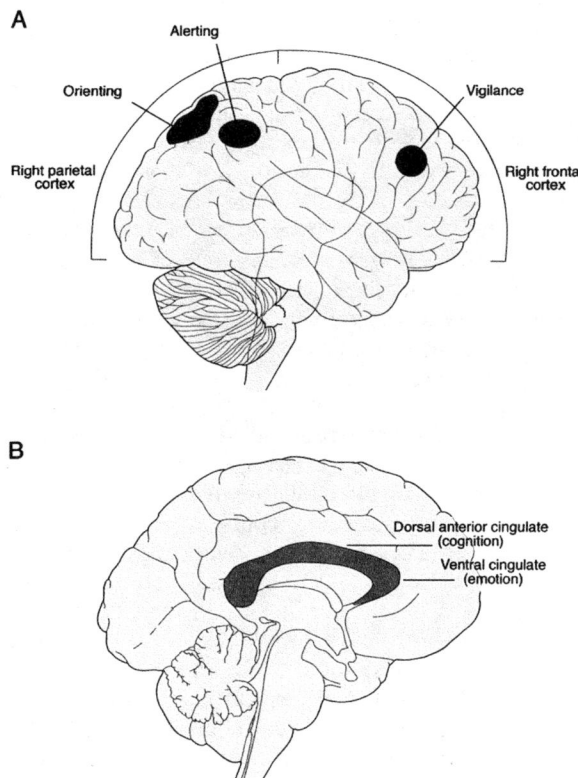

FIGURE 4. Localization of alerting and emotional function. (**A**) The localization of alerting and orienting functions in the parietal lobe. A diagram of the lateral surface of the human brain indicating the relation of alerting and orienting mechanisms in the right parietal lobe to the vigilance area in the right frontal cortex. (Courtesy of M. Posner.) (**B**) The localization of cortical regions involved in cognitive and emotional states. A diagram of the medial part of the human brain indicating the dorsal anterior cingulate which appears to be involved in the monitoring and/or regulation of cognitive activity and of the more ventral portions of the cingulate that appears to be related to the regulation of emotion. (Adapted from Bush *et al.*[66])

The Ventral and Dorsal Anterior Cingulate Are Concerned with Emotion and Cognition, Respectively

We often think of sensory orienting and memory retrieval as related to focal attention. However, another source of information that frequently engages our attention is emotion. When emotional words are presented in the same conflict tasks described above, a more ventral area of the anterior cingulate becomes active (see FIGURE 4B). In some neuroimaging experiments, the cognitive and emotional areas of the cingulate seem to be mutually inhibitory.[70] Thus, when strong emotions are involved in the task, the dorsal area is less active than at rest, and cognitive conflict tasks tend to reduce activity in the more ventral area of the cingulate.

If the dorsal area of the cingulate is involved in selecting dimensions of a stimulus when there is conflict among competing dimensions, a reasonable idea might be that the dorsal area serves a similar selecting function for emotional conflict. Indeed, we have already discussed the idea that orienting of attention in infancy serves as one means by which caregivers seek to distract their infants from the expression of distress. The control of distress is an important concern of early childhood, and caregivers have the task of first regulating emotions in their infant and later teaching the child to regulate its own emotions. Perhaps areas of the brain that regulate emotion in infancy have acquired the ability to perform the same functions in response to cognitive challenges. If this idea is correct, children who are well-advanced in emotional regulation should be at a specific advantage in regulating cognitive conflict.

We know that children differ in their ability to regulate their emotions. This can be elicited from caregivers when they are asked specific questions about the child's ability to control distress, orient attention and be sensitive to pleasures. The dimension of individual variation in regulation has been called effortful control. Studies of 6- to 7-year olds have found that effortful control can be defined in terms of scales measuring attentional focusing, inhibitory control, low-intensity pleasure, and perceptual sensitivity.[71] Effortful control is consistently negatively related to a negative affect in keeping with the notion that attentional skill may help attenuate negative affect. Effortful control also is correlated with the performance of 2- to 4-year-old children in Stroop tasks that require them to handle conflict.[72] Effortful control is related both to empathy and to the acquisition of conscience, of a sense of moral behavior. Kochanska has found that individual differences in effortful control have important implications both for the inhibition of antisocial behavior and for the acquisition of prosocial behavior.[73] Children who can effectively employ attention to regulate behavior are better able to inhibit prepotent responses (e.g., striking out, stealing) and are better at taking into consideration the effect of their actions on others.

Empathy and a sense of moral behavior or conscience are at the heart of children's socialization. The link between the attentional network of the frontal lobe and conscience might make it possible to at least imagine how aspects of morality might be studied on the neuronal level discussed below in relation to disorders.

Disorders that Recruit the Cingulate Cortex Suggest a Connection between Cognition and Emotion

Attention deficit disorder is defined by a set of cognitive and emotional symptoms. This disorder is usually diagnosed in children, but often remains present into adulthood. Neuroimaging of adults who suffer from attention deficit disorder has been carried out under circumstances that require them to do a numerical version of the Stroop effect. Here they are asked to respond to the number of items present. When that number is sometimes in conflict with the quantity indicated by the word (e.g., three copies of the word two), adults with attention deficit disorder performed on conflict trials only slightly less efficiently than normal subjects. But unlike the normal controls, adults with attention deficits show no activation of the anterior cingulate. Instead, they showed greater activity on incompatible trials in the anterior insula.[74] As was suggested in the study of word association discussed above, the insula represents a more automatic pathway than the anterior cingulate, thus allowing for less effortful control over the task.

Another disorder that produces a disruption of voluntary control as well as other emotional and cognitive problems is schizophrenia. Benes[75] has reported subtle abnormalities of the anterior cingulate in postmortem analyses of schizophrenic brains. She argues that the problem with the anterior cingulate, in the brains of schizophrenics, may be a shift in dopamine regulation from pyramidal to nonpyramidal cells. She has also argued that these changes in the cingulate are related to circuitry involving the amygdala and hippocampus. The schizophrenia studies provide a lead at the cellular level of the possible disregulation of the anterior cingulate in a second abnormality noted for its attentional deficits.

Both schizophrenia and attention deficit disorder have a genetic basis. Studies of families with attention deficit disorder have shown that some of them possess a particular allele of the dopamine 4 receptor.[76,77] These studies provide some potential cellular and genetic links between attentional abnormalities found in various pathologies.

Further Aspects in the Study of Consciousness

We have outlined that the problem of consciousness can be considered to consist of two subproblems: awareness and volition. Studies of orienting and of imagery are concerned with the first, and self-regulation with the second. As future research penetrates the organization of attention networks in the frontal cortex, the two functions could prove to be linked. Studies of complex scenes show that presentation of a stimulus does not lead automatically to awareness of even the most central aspects of the scene.[59] Even though subjects report that they are aware of a whole scene, they only become aware of a change when their attention is drawn to a change in the scene. We have suggested that posterior brain areas involved in orienting to sensory stimuli may be closely related to ambient awareness and that focal attention might be more associated with the anterior cingulate and other frontal areas related to voluntary control. Perhaps only as we understand the neural basis of the distinction between focal attention to limited aspects of the external world and a more general ambient awareness of the general scene will we be able to understand the parts of the brain related to consciousness of sensory events.[78]

The exact functions that the anterior cingulate plays in higher-level attention are not yet clear. We have learned that even very simple acts of attention such as orienting to sensory stimuli involve a network of brain areas that carry out specific functions. During conflict tasks activation of the anterior cingulate is usually accompanied by activity in lateral frontal cortical areas and in the basal ganglia. It is an important goal to find out what each of these areas contribute.

The functions of attention also relate to issues other than those usually discussed under the term *consciousness*. Recently, the contribution of biology to understanding the acquisition of high-level skills such as those learned in schools has been extensively debated.[79] In some areas, such as the neural networks involved in reading and arithmetic, progress has been extensive.[80,81] Both skills required attention networks related to those discussed in this section. A better understanding of these mechanisms might help in realizing the goal of a neuroscience-based approach to aspects of education.

CODA: FUTURE BREAKTHROUGHS

What is the future for neural science in the next millennium? We have seen remarkable and rapid progress in understanding neuronal and synaptic signaling. These advances now invite a structural approach to visualize the static and dynamic structures of ion channels, receptors, and the molecular machinery for signal transduction postsynaptically and for vesicle transport, fusion, and exocytosis presynaptically. We also have made some progress in the analysis of the elementary synaptic mechanisms that contribute to memory storage. These studies have revealed that the different memory systems of brain seem to use similar synaptic mechanisms for the storage of both declarative and nondeclarative knowledge. Similarly, we now have achieved an understanding, at least in broad outline, of the development of the nervous system. Specific inducers, morphogens, attractants, and repellants of process outgrowth and synapse organizing molecules have now been defined, providing a molecular reality to concepts that previously were shrouded in mystery.

Progress in these several areas has in turn made possible a molecular-based neurology, a neurology that will, one hopes, finally be able to address the degenerative diseases of the brain that have for so long eluded our best scientific efforts. In time, advance in these areas may also yield insight into and perhaps solutions for some of the most debilitating diseases confronting medical science—the psychiatric and neurological illnesses of schizophrenia, depression, and Alzheimer's disease. Implicit in this prediction is the expectation that in the future molecular biology will be able to contribute to the system problems of cognitive neural science much as it has recently contributed to signaling, plasticity, and development.

The advances in the cellular understanding of the organization of the somatosensory and visual system by Mountcastle, Hubel, and Wiesel and their followers have helped turn our interest to perception and in the broader sense to cognitive psychology. In turn, contact between cognitive psychology and neural science has given us a new approach to the classical problems of mental function including attention and consciousness. In both early sensory processes and higher cognitive perceptual and motor systems, we find evidence for the localization of components within a broadly distributed network carrying out complex functions. Indeed, one of the early insights into consciousness is that it shares the properties of other cognitive systems in that, like vision and action, it can be dissected into components: attention, imagery, and volition. Each component consists of a set of subcomponents that can be localized within a larger, distributed neural system.

Having pointed to that similarity, we must nevertheless acknowledge that of all fields in neural science, in fact of all the fields in all of science, the problems of perception, action, memory, attention, and consciousness provide us with the greatest evidence for our lack of understanding as well as the greatest challenge.

Even if one agreed that the scientific agenda outlined here may be adequate to handle the issues of awareness and volition, there is another aspect of consciousness that needs to be confronted and that is the nature of subjectivity . The subjective aspect of consciousness is seen by philosophers of mind such as Searle[82,83] and Nagel[84] as its defining characteristic and the aspect that poses the greatest scientific challenge. Searle and Nagel argue that each of us experiences a world of private and unique experiences and that these seem much more real to us than the experiences of others. We experience our own ideas, moods, and sensations, our successes and disappointments, joys and pains directly, whereas we can only appreciate other people's ideas, moods, and sensations. Are the purple you see and the jasmine you smell identical to the purple that we see and the jasmine that we smell? The fact that conscious experience is uniquely personal and intensely subjective raises the question of whether it is ever possible to determine objectively some common characteristics of experience. We cannot, the argument goes, use those same senses to arrive at an objective understanding of experience.

Clearly we should be prepared for the possibility that there are aspects of consciousness that will not be solved by the approaches discussed in this review. Some might believe that all that is scientific about the study of life is illuminated at all levels from the molecular to the behavioral by what we know about DNA. But others might believe that there are issues about what it means to be a living being that are really not explained by the most detailed account of DNA. Many issues of awareness and voluntary control are likely to be explained at all levels, from genes to behavior. This might constitute a theory of consciousness in much the same way as DNA serves as the basis for any scientific analysis of what constitutes life. Nonetheless, it is hard to imagine at present how the progress discussed above, even if it continues and intensifies, will solve all the issues of the subjective nature of our experience. We leave it to the readers of the *Annals* in the next millennium to determine how much insight about human consciousness will result from the type of work we have discussed here.

ACKNOWLEDGMENTS

This article originally appeared as part of the review entitled "Neural Science: A Century of Progress and the Mysteries that Remain," *Cell* Vol. 100/*Neuron* Vol. 25, Millennial Review Supplement, February 2000, and is edited with the permission of Cell Press.

REFERENCES

1. RAMÓN Y CAJAL, S. 1894. The Croonian Lecture: la fine structure des centres
2. RAMÓN Y CAJAL, S. 1906. The structure and connexions of neurons. *In* Nobel Lectures: Physiology or Medicine (1901–1921). :220–253. Elsevier. Amsterdam (1967).
3. RAMÓN Y CAJAL, S. 1911. Histologie du Systeme Nerveux de l'Homme et des Vertebretes, Vols. 1 and 2. A. Maloine. Paris. [Reprinted in 1955 by Consejo Superior de Investigaciones Cientificas, Inst. Ramón y Cajal. Madrid.]
4. SHEPHERD, G.M. 1991. Foundations of the Neuron Doctrine. Oxford University Press. New York.
5. SHERRINGTON, C.S. 1897. The Central Nervous System, Vol. III. *In* A Textbook of Physiology, 7th ed. M. Foster, Ed. MacMillan. London.
6. SHERRINGTON, C.S. 1906. The Integrative Action of the Nervous System, 2nd ed. Yale University Press. New Haven, CT.
7. SHERRINGTON, C.S. 1910. Flexor-reflex of the limb, crossed extension reflex, and reflex stepping and standing (cat and dog). J. Physiol. **40:** 28–116.
8. SHERRINGTON, C.S. 1932. Inhibition as a Coordinative Factor. Nobel Lecture. PA Norstedt. Stockholm.

9. ECCLES, J.C. 1953. The Neurophysiological Basis of Mind. The Principles of Neurophysiology. Clarendon Press. Oxford.
10. FUORTES, M.G.F., K. FRANK & M.C. BECKER. 1957. Steps in the production of motoneuron spikes. J. Gen. Physiol. **40:** 735–752.
11. ECCLES, J.C. 1964. The Physiology of Synapses. Academic Press. New York.
12. ADRIAN, E.D. 1957. The analysis of the nervous system. Sherrington Memorial Lecture. Proc. R. Soc. Med. **50:** 993–998.
13. LANGLEY, J.N. 1897. On the regeneration of pre-ganglionic and post-ganglionic visceral nerve fibers. J. Physiol. **22:** 215–230.
14. KANDEL, E.R. & W.A. SPENCER. 1968. Cellular neurophysiological approaches in the study of learning. Physiol. Rev. **48:** 65–134.
15. CASTELLUCCI, V., H. PINSKER, I. KUPFERMANN & E. KANDEL. 1970. Neuronal mechanisms of habituation and dishabituation of the gill-withdrawal reflex in *Aplysia*. Science **167:** 1745–1748.
16. SQUIRE, L. & E.R. KANDEL. 1999. Memory: From Mind to Molecules. Scientific American Books. New York.
17. FECHNER, G. 1860. Elements of Psychophysics, Vol. 1. H.E. Adler, Trans. [1966]. Holt, Rinehart and Winston. New York.
18. MOUNTCASTLE, V.B., W.H. TALBOT, H. SAKATA & J. HYVARINEN. 1969. Cortical neuronal mechanisms in flutter-vibration studied in unanesthetized monkeys. J. Neurophysiol. **32:** 452–484.
19. VON BEKESY, G. 1960. Experiments in Hearing, E.G. Wever, Ed. and Trans. McGraw-Hill. New York.
20. RUMELHART, D.E., J.L. MCCLELLAND & P.R. GROUP. 1987. Parallel Distributed Processing. MIT Press. Cambridge, MA.
21. ALBRIGHT, T.D. & G.R. STONER. 1995. Visual motion perception. Proc. Natl. Acad. Sci. USA **92:** 2433–2440.
22. ALBRIGHT, T.D. 1992. Form-cue invariant motion processing in primate visual cortex. Science **255:** 1141–143.
23. BARLOW, H.B. 1972. Single units and sensation: a neuron doctrine for perceptual psychology? Perception **1:** 371–394.
24. SHERRINGTON, C.S. 1941. Man on His Nature. Macmillan. New York.
25. GROSS, C.G., D.B. BENDER & C.E. ROCHA-MIRANDA. 1969. Visual receptive fields of neurons in inferotemporal cortex of the monkey. Science **166:** 1303–1306.
26. HEBB, D.O. 1949. The Organization of Behavior: A Neuropsychological Theory. Wiley. New York.
27. VON DER MALSBURG, C. 1981. The correlation theory of brain function. MPI Biophysical Chemistry, Internal Report 81-2. Reprinted *in* Models of Neural Networks II. 1994. E. Domany, J.L. van Hemmen & K. Schulten, Eds. Springer. Berlin.
28. GRAY, C.M., P. KONIG, A.K. ENGEL & W. SINGER. 1989. Synchronization of oscillatory responses in visual cortex: a plausible mechanism for scene segmentation. Proceeding of Conference on Synergetics of the Brain.
29. LAMME, V.A. & H. SPEKREIJSE. 1998. Neuronal synchrony does not represent texture segregation. Nature **396:** 362–366.
30. SHADLEN, M.N. & J.A. MOVSHON. 1999. Synchrony unbound: a critical evaluation of the temporal binding hypothesis. Neuron **24:** 67–77.
31. ENGEL, A.K., P. FRIES, P. KONIG, M. BRECHT & W. SINGER. 1999. Temporal binding, binocular rivalry, and consciousness. Conscious. Cogn. **8:** 128–151.
32. SINGER, W. 1998. Consciousness and the structure of neuronal representations. Philos. Trans. R. Soc. Lond. B. Biol. Sci. **353:** 1829–1840.
33. EDELMAN, G.M. 1983. Cell adhesion molecules. Science **219:** 450–457.
34. JAMES, W. 1890. Principles of Psychology. Henry Holt. New York.
35. KARNI, A. & G. BERTINI. 1997. Learning perceptual skills: behavioral probes into adult cortical plasticity. Curr. Opin. Neurobiol. **7:** 530–535.
36. BUONOMANO, D.V. & M.M. MERZENICH. 1998. Cortical plasticity: from synapses to maps. Annu. Rev. Neurosci. **21:** 149–186.

37. CRIST, R.E., M.K. KAPADIA, G. WESTHEIMER & C.D. GILBERT. 1997. Perceptual learning of spatial localization: specificity for orientation, position, and context. J. Neurophysiol. **78:** 2889–2894.
38. KARNI, A. & D. SAGI. 1993. The time course of learning a visual skill. Nature **365:** 250–252.
39. GILBERT, C.D. & T.N. WIESEL. 1992. Receptive field dynamics in adult primary visual cortex. Nature **356:** 150–152.
40. CHINO, Y.M., J.H. KAAS, E.L.D. SMITH, A.L. LANGSTON & H. CHENG. 1992. Rapid reorganization of cortical maps in adult cats following restricted deafferentation in retina. Vision Res. **32:** 789–796.
41. MESULAM, M.M. 1999. Spatial attention and neglect: parietal, frontal and cingulate contributions to the mental representation and attentional targeting of salient extrapersonal events. Philos. Trans. R. Soc. Lond. B. Biol. Sci. **354:** 1325–1346.
42. COLBY, C.L. & M.E. GOLDBERG. 1999. Space and attention in parietal cortex. Annu. Rev. Neurosci. **22:** 319–349.
43. ANDERSEN, R.A., G.K. ESSICK & R.M. SIEGEL. 1985. Encoding of spatial location by posterior parietal neurons. Science **230:** 456–458.
44. ANDERSEN, R.A., L.H. SNYDER, C.S. LI & B. STRICANNE. 1993. Coordinate transformations in the representation of spatial information. Curr. Opin. Neurobiol. **3:** 171–176.
45. OLSON, C.R. & S.N. GETTNER. 1995. Object-centered direction selectivity in macaque supplementary eye field. Science **269:** 985–988.
46. GRAZIANO, M.S.A., G.S. YAP & C.G. GROSS. 1994. Coding of visual space by premotor neurons. Science **266:** 1054–1057.
47. POSNER, M.I. & M.E. RAICHLE. 1994. Images of Mind. Scientific American Books. New York.
48. POSNER, M.I. & M.E. RAICHLE, Eds. 1998. The neuroimaging of human brain function. Proc. Natl. Acad. Sci. USA **95:** 763–929.
49. RAICHLE, M.E. 1998. Behind the scenes of functional brain imaging: a historical and physiological perspective. Proc. Natl. Acad. Sci. USA **95:** 765–772.
50. ROSEN, B.R., R.L. BUCKNER & A.M. DALE. 1998. Event-related functional MRI: past, present, and future. Proc. Natl. Acad. Sci. USA **95:** 773–780.
51. TOOTELL, R.B.H., K. NOUCHINE, W.V. HADJIKHANI, A.K. LIU, J.D. MENDOLA, M.I. SERENO & A.M. DALE. 1998. Functional analysis of primary-visual cortex in humans. Proc. Natl. Acad. Sci. USA **95:** 811–817.
52. GOLDBERG, M.E & R.H. WURTZ. 1972. Activity of superior colliculus in behaving monkey. II. Effect of attention on neuronal responses. J. Neurophysiol. **35:** 560–574.
53. CORBETTA, M. 1998. Frontoparietal cortical networks for directing attention and the eye to visual locations: identical, independent, or overlapping neural systems? Proc. Natl. Acad. Sci. USA **95:** 831–838.
54. DESIMONE, R. & J. DUNCAN. 1995. Neural mechanisms of selective visual attention. Annu. Rev. Neurosci. **18:** 193–222.
55. KASTNER, S., M.A. PINSK, P. DE WEERD, R. DESIMONE & L.G. UNGERLEIDER. 1999. Increased activity in human visual cortex during directed attention in the absence of visual stimulation. Neuron **22:** 751–761.
56. POSNER, M.I. & C.D. GILBERT. 1999. Attention and primary visual cortex. Proc. Natl. Acad. Sci. USA **96:** 2585–2587.
57. CORBETTA, M., F.M. MIEZIN, S. DOBMEYER, G.L. SHULMAN & S.E. PETERSEN. 1991. Selective and divided attention during visual discriminations of shape, color, and speed: functional anatomy by positron emission tomography. J. Neurosci. **11:** 2383–2402.
58. RENSINK, R.A., J.K. O'REGAN & J.J. CLARK. 1997. To see or not to see: the need for attention to perceive changes in scenes. Psychol. Sci. **8:** 368–373.
59. MARROCCO, R.T. & M.C. DAVIDSON. 1998. Neurochemistry of attention. In The Attentive Brain. R. Parasuraman, Ed. MIT Press. Cambridge, MA.
60. PARASURAMAN, R. & P.M. GREENWOOD. 1998. Selective attention in aging and dementia. In The Attentive Brain. R. Parasuraman, Ed. MIT Press. Cambridge, MA.
61. NEWELL, A. & H.A. SIMON. 1972. Human Problem Solving. Prentice-Hall. Englewood Cliffs, NJ.

62. DUNCAN, J. 1986. Disorganization of behavior after frontal lobe damage. J. Cogn. Neuropsychol. **3:** 271–290.
63. FRITH, C. & R.J. DOLAN. 1998. Images of psychopathology. Curr. Opin. Neurobiol. **8:** 259–262.
64. NORMAN, D.A. & T. SHALLICE. 1986. Attention to action: willed and automatic control of behavior. *In* Consciousness and Self-Regulation. R.J. Davidson, G.E. Schwartz & D. Shapiro, Eds. :1–18. Plenum Press. New York.
65. BUSH, G., P.J. WHALEN, B.R. ROSEN, M.A. JENIKE, S.C. MCINEREY & S.L. RAUCH. 1998. The counting Stroop: an interference task specialized for functional neuroimaging validation study with functional MRI. Hum. Brain Mapping **6:** 270–282.
66. CARTER, C.S., M.M. BOTVINICK & J.D. COHEN. 1999. The contribution of the anterior cingulate to executive processes in cognition. Rev. Neurosci. **10:** 49–57.
67. WASHBURN, D.A. 1994. Stroop-like effects for monkeys and humans: processing speed or strength of association? Psychol. Sci. **5:** 375–379.
68. RAICHLE, M.E., J.A. FIEZ, T.O. VIDEEN, A.M.K. MCCLEOD, J.V. PARDO, P.T. FOX & S.E. PETERSEN. 1994. Practice-related changes in the human brain: functional anatomy during non-motor learning. Cerebral Cortex **4:** 8–26.
69. DREVETS, W.C. & M.E. RAICHLE. 1998. Reciprocal suppression of regional blood flow during emotional versus higher cognitive processes: implications for interactions between emotion and cognition. Cogn. Emotion **12:** 353–385.
70. ROTHBART, M.K., S.A. AHADI & D.W. EVANS. 2000. Temperament and personality: origins and outcomes. J. Personality Soc. Psychol. In press.
71. POSNER, M.I. & M.K. ROTHBART. 1998. Attention, self-regulation and consciousness. Philos. Trans. R. Soc. Lond. B. Biol. Sci. **353:** 1915–1927.
72. KOCHANSKA, G. 1995. Children's temperament, mothers' discipline, and security of attachment: multiple pathways to emerging internalization. Child Dev. **66:** 597–615.
73. BUSH, G., J.A. FRAZIER, S.L. RAUCH, L.J. SEIDMAN, P.J. WHALEN, B.R. ROSEN & J. BIEDERMAN. 1999. Anterior cingulate cortex dysfunction in attention-deficit/hyperactivity disorder revealed by fMRI and the counting Stroop. Biol. Psychiatry **45:** 1542–1552.
74. BENES, F.M. 1998. Model generation and testing to probe neural circuitry in the cingulate cortex of postmortem schizophrenic brains. Schiz. Bulletin **24:** 219–230.
75. LAHOSTE, G.J., J.M. SWANSON, S.B. WIGAL, C. GLABE, T. WIGAL, N. KING & J.L. KENNEDY. 1996. Dopamine D4 receptor gene polymorphism is associated with attention deficit hyperactivity disorder. Mol. Psychiatry **1:** 121–124.
76. SMALLEY, S.L., J.N. BAILEY, C.G. PALMER, D.P. CANTWELL, J.J. MCGOUGH, M.A. DEL'HOMME, J.R. ASARNOW, J.A. WOODWARD, C. RAMSEY & S.F. NELSON. 1998. Evidence that the D4 receptor is a susceptibility gene in attention deficit hyperactivity disorder. Mol. Psychiatry **3:** 427–430.
77. IWASAKI, S. 1993. Spatial attention and two modes of visual consciousnes. Cognition **49:** 211–233.
78. BRUER, J.T. 1999. The Myth of the First Three Years: A New Understanding of Early Brain Development and Lifelong Learning. Free Press. New York.
79. DEHAENE, S. 1997. The Number Sense. Oxford University Press. New York.
80. POSNER, M.I., Y.G. ABDULLAEV, B.D. MCCANDLISS & S.E. SERENO. 1999. Neuroanatomy, circuitry and plasticity of word reading. NeuroReport **10:** R12–R23.
81. SEARLE, J.R. 1993. The problem of consciousness. *In* Experimental and Theoretical Studies of Consciousness **174:** 61–80. Wiley Interscience/CIBA Foundation. New York.
82. SEARLE, J.R. 1998. How to study consciousness scientifically. *In* Towards an Understanding of Integrative Brain Function, K. Fuxe, S. Grillner, T. Hokfelt, L. Olson & L.F. Agnati, Eds. : 379–387. Elsevier. Amsterdam.
83. WURTZ, R.H. & M.E. GOLDBERG, Eds. 1989. The Neurobiology of Saccadic Eye Movements: Reviews of Oculomotor Research, Vol. 3. Elsevier. A msterdam.
84. NAGEL, T. 1993. What is the mind-brain problem? Experimental and Theoretical Studies of Consciousness **174:** 1–13. Wiley Interscience/CIBA Foundation. New York.
85. KANDEL, E.R., J.H. SCHWARTZ & T. JESSELL. 2000. Principles of Neural Science, 4th ed. McGraw-Hill. New York.

Consciousness, Reduction, and Emergence
Some Remarks

MURRAY GELL-MANN

Santa Fe Institute, Santa Fe, New Mexico 87501, USA

ABSTRACT: Consciousness is often seen as requiring a special kind of explanation. But the various aspects of self-awareness can presumably emerge when certain levels of complexity are reached in an organism: it is not necessary to assume additional mechanisms or hidden causes. Looking at the most fundamental level, that of elementary particle physics, three principles appear—the conformability of nature to herself, the applicability of the criterion of simplicity, and the utility of certain parts of mathematics in describing physical reality—which are in themselves emergent properties of the fundamental laws of physics. At successive levels, it is the availability of similar mathematical descriptions from related problems that makes the next step appear with simplicity and elegance. Thus, once the concept of emergence is properly established, a huge burden is lifted from the inquiring mind. The whole explanatory loop may be closed by looking at the ability of the human mind to figure out the laws of nature. All the other sciences emerge in principle from fundamental physics plus historical accidents, even though "reduction" is obviously inadequate as a strategy. While bridges or staircases are under construction connecting the various sciences, each science needs to be studied at its own level as well. Although the idea of "vital forces" in biology alien to physics and chemistry has largely disappeared, consciousness remains the last refuge of obscurantists. Finally, it is argued that appeals to the alleged weirdness of quantum mechanics are based on a misunderstanding and are unlikely to have any place in a discussion of consciousness.

KEYWORDS: Consciousness; Reductionism; Emergence; Laws of nature; Self-similarity; Quantum interpretations; Decohering histories; Quantum non-locality

I am delighted to be here at this conference dedicated to the memory of Ramón y Cajal. I must apologize, however, for my ignorance of the field to which he made such notable contributions. The main thing I know about nerves is that at this moment, having to speak to a distinguished gathering that includes so many experts on the subject, I am rather nervous.

In any discussion of the human mind and brain, the concept of reduction is bound to come up. Now "reduction" is a bad word in some circles. Indeed, my own institute is supposed to stand for opposition to "reductionism."[1] If reduction is properly de-

Address for correspondence: Santa Fe Institute, 1399 Hyde Park Road, Santa Fe, New Mexico 87501. Voice: 505-984-8800; fax: 505-982-0565
mgm@santafe.edu

scribed, however, there is nothing wrong with it except that it needs to be supplemented by other approaches, in particular by the concept of emergence.

The most basic of the sciences (except perhaps for mathematics, if we call that a science) is fundamental physics, which deals with the elementary particles and their interactions and with the cosmos. There are two fundamental laws of physics, but those do not by themselves determine the history of the universe. One of them is the unified quantum theory of all the elementary particles, the basic building blocks of all matter, and all their interactions, which give the fundamental forces of nature. The other is the theory of the condition of the universe near the beginning of its expansion some ten to thirteen billion years ago. Both are probably simple.

Those laws are probabilistic, however, and they do not therefore determine by themselves the history of the universe. Instead, they co-determine it along with an inconceivably long sequence of accidents or chance events, the outcomes of which cannot be predicted in advance except for their probabilities. (We can take as an example the direction of emission of an alpha particle emitted by a radioactive nucleus. All directions are equally probable.)

Everything about the universe is attributable in principle to some combination of a contribution from the fundamental laws and a contribution from historical accidents. Since the laws are believed to be simple, we should attribute most of the complexity in the history of the universe to the results of accidents.

FROM SIMPLICITY (FUNDAMENTAL PHYSICS) TO COMPLEXITY (BIOLOGY, FOR EXAMPLE)

Now the laws of chemistry follow from physics plus the special circumstances (such as temperature) that permit atoms and molecules to exist. (In the deep interior of the sun, for example, they don't exist and there is no chemistry.) Those special circumstances are often dependent on the accidents of history of the universe. Some Swedish prizes have been awarded (one recently to my Caltech colleague Rudy Marcus, for example) for deriving some simple chemical results from basic physics. However, for most purposes it is not *practical* to go all the way back to the quantum mechanics of electrons and nuclei interacting through electromagnetic forces. Instead, chemists employ concepts at the level of chemistry, such as bonds and reaction rates. Certainly, no one seriously proposes to geologists that they explain plate tectonics directly in terms of quarks, gluons, electrons, and photons.

Just as chemistry and geology emerge from fundamental physics plus special circumstances, so biology on Earth emerges from physics and chemistry and geology plus the special circumstances attending the origin of life and the accidents occurring in biological evolution ever since. No serious scientist today believes that life depends on special "vital forces" alien to physics and chemistry. But reduction has to include the special circumstances as well as the more fundamental sciences. Even so, we must recognize that as a strategy reduction by itself is wholly inadequate. Bridges or staircases can be built to connect biology with chemistry and physics, but, in addition, treating biological phenomena at the level of biology is just as important as not dealing with earthquakes in terms of quarks. We see how using this concept of emergence frees us from silly, sterile controversies over the merits of "reductionism."[2]

While "vital forces" have fortunately disappeared, consciousness remains as the last refuge of obscurantists in science. There are still some scientists who resist the obvious conclusion that mental processes in animals, including humans, simply emerge from biology plus accidents, that the mind is just the activity of the brain and of chemicals distributed throughout the body, that psychology emerges from neurobiology. Again reduction here depends on incidental features as well as the more fundamental science. Biology doesn't predict exactly what we think. Chance plays some role, and so do thought processes and motivations that are deeply buried and not easily accessible to conscious awareness. But again emergence is the key.

Somehow consciousness strikes some people as requiring a special kind of explanation. I don't see any reason why that should be so. The various aspects of self-awareness can presumably emerge when certain levels of complexity are reached in an organism on Earth or in some complex adaptive system that has evolved on a planet orbiting a distant star, or even, very likely, in a suitable man-made machine.

Claude Shannon was once asked by a student, "Do you believe that machines can be made to think?" He answered, "You bet. I'm a machine and so are you." I'm sure that he would have given a similar reply to a question about the C-word.

CHARACTERIZING CONSCIOUSNESS

What are some aspects of self-awareness? We may list a few, and mention in some cases that they do or may show up to some degree in other animals as well as human beings.

Of course when these aspects are studied one should fold in subjective reports along with observation of one's self and others from the outside. Evidence is evidence. But pay no attention to philosophers who tell you that this creates the need for some special forms of translation other than the correlation of the subjective with the objective. Try and think whether it would make any difference whatsoever if their tortured questions remain forever unanswered while the correlation is becoming better and better understood. Suppose we learn more and more about how light with various mixtures of frequencies, in the presence of various backgrounds of color and of light and shadow, is processed in the eye and the brain and correlate that information with subjective reports of redness. Do we really have to worry in addition about why red light feels red?

As a first example of an aspect of consciousness, take the sense of self. When you look into a mirror, you know that you are seeing yourself, not someone else. Narcissus, in the myth, did not realize that and fell in love with his image, treating it as another person. Note that Narcissus was not being narcissistic!

Now do an experiment with a great ape. Make a mark on one of his hands. He will wipe it off, or try to. Then make a mark on his forehead and let him look in a mirror. If he is a gorilla, he will not attempt to wipe it off, presumably not knowing that he is seeing himself in the mirror. However, a chimpanzee (or, presumably, a bonobo or pygmy chimp) will try to wipe the mark off his forehead, and will succeed if the mark is not indelible.

A related property of the mind, somewhat more advanced, is knowing that others of the same species have the same sorts of needs, reactions, thoughts, and so on as one's self.

One aspect of human consciousness that is especially prominent is that of mechanisms of attention. Those mechanisms are beginning to receive the *attention* they deserve from scientific investigators, who are also considering situations where attention is attenuated in various ways.

What happens to the mechanisms of attention when we are anaesthetized with something like sodium pentothal, so that we have no awareness of elapsed time when we wake up?

In the presence of very serious cognitive deficits and/or memory deterioration, can we say that certain features of conscious awareness decline? Do some of them move toward the levels in other primates? What about conscious awareness in babies or even fetuses? When and at what rates do the various features come in?

Some people study different degrees of burial of thoughts beneath conscious awareness. One may distinguish material that is not immediately available, but can be brought up after a short while; material that requires a long time or a great effort, even something like psychotherapy, to recover; and material that is unavailable to conscious memory but nevertheless influences behavior, as in the case of split brains or of transactions at a very low level in the nervous system.

Human beings have the ability to discuss not only absent things, but even things that are only imagined and don't necessarily exist. Putting such imagined entities alongside real ones throws light on the real ones, as in Gibbsian ensembles in physics, and as in fiction, drama, poetry, and the visual arts, as well as myth. Is that ability just a matter of intelligence or should we classify it as relating somehow to consciousness?

Finally, we may look at the ability of the human mind to figure out the laws of nature, at least in a sequence of approximations. Here we close the loop. The laws of nature, together with local circumstances dependent on historical accidents, allow the evolution of relatively intelligent, somewhat self-aware organisms. They are complex adaptive systems that, after many thousands of years of cultural evolution, succeed in achieving a considerable degree of understanding of the world around them, using the methods of science, and discovering the laws of nature.[3]

SELF-SIMILARITY IN THE PHYSICAL DESCRIPTION OF NATURE

Let me take the most fundamental level, that of elementary particle physics, which, as we discussed, is associated with one of the two basic laws, the other one being the state of the universe near the beginning of its expansion. What does it mean about us that we can give such a good description of the fundamental building blocks of all matter and their interactions? Actually, the standard model, successful though it is, is clearly not the last word. It cries out for unification of all the forces, including gravitation, and for the unified description of all the types of elementary particle. Today, theorists may even be studying the correct unified theory, in the form of what used to be called superstring theory and is now understood to be a wider system sometimes called M-theory.[4] The change of name is part of a process of learning the structure of the theory. It is a process of discovery, not invention, which should end in the elucidation of the full content of the theory—a unique, self-consistent system—and then in predictions that can be compared with observation to test the correctness of the theory.

It has already scored one great triumph. More than twenty years ago, John Schwarz and Joël Scherk showed that it predicts Einstein's general-relativistic theory of gravitation.[5] Moreover it predicts it within the context of quantum mechanics and without encountering any of the preposterous infinite corrections that plagued previous attempts to reconcile general relativity and quantum mechanics.

Some people have used the term "theory of everything" to describe the unified quantum theory of all the particles and forces.[6,7] But that term is a misnomer, as we have seen, since in order to describe "everything" we require in addition not only the initial condition of the universe (which might be determined by the unified theory), but also the results of all the accidents.

Let us suppose that M-theory really is the correct unified theory of the elementary particles and the forces of nature, or at least that we human theoreticians are capable of finding the correct theory, whatever it is. We can then throw some light on the old question of why simplicity and elegance have proved such valuable criteria in choosing scientific theories, especially in fundamental physics.

Take the case of Yang–Mills theories. These authors found, some forty-five years ago, an abstract generalization of Maxwell's equations for electromagnetism.[8] Some of us showed later that it was just one of a class of such generalizations. There was no known application at the time, but these theories looked very simple and beautiful. Of course they did, because we already had the relevant mathematical form as a result of the process of generalization.

Seventeen years later, after we proposed quarks and gluons as the fundamental constituents of strongly interacting objects such as the neutron and proton,[9] one of the Yang–Mills theories turned out to give the correct theory—quantum chromodynamics—of those quarks and gluons. Another Yang–Mills theory, with symmetry breaking added in, gives the theory of the weak and electromagnetic interactions treated together.

We can also go back much earlier, to the seventeenth century and Newton's discovery of the nonrelativistic theory of gravitation, with its force inversely proportional to the square of the distance. Naturally, gravitation was the first force to be described with some accuracy because it is not only long-range but also of only one sign, so that it always adds up and never cancels. Electricity, the other long-range force, was next. When Coulomb found its nonrelativistic law, the simplicity and elegance of it could be easily described, since the distance-dependence was the same as in Newton's law of gravitation.

For magnetism, the law for single magnetic poles, insofar as they can be separated in space from their opposites, was found to be the same. Then came the observation that electric charges in motion are responsible for magnetism. That kind of research culminated in Maxwell's electromagnetic synthesis, which showed the possibility of electromagnetic waves and the identification of light with such waves within a certain band of frequencies.

Seventy years ago, that description of electromagnetism was united with quantum mechanics to produce the enormously successful quantum electrodynamics. A quarter of a century later, the elaborations and generalizations of the work of Yang and Mills helped to formulate the standard model, which describes the strong, electromagnetic, and weak forces so well.

But, at each step, it is the availability of similar mathematics from related problems in science that makes the next step appear simple and elegant. We can describe that situation by saying that the unified quantum theory of elementary particles possesses the property that its solutions have a certain degree of self-similarity from one scale to the next. Thus, as we peel the onion of fundamental microscopic physics, we are going from layer to layer with some similarity between neighboring layers.

The underlying theory is universal and intrinsic, and so is the approximate similarity. It is not a function of the human mind, although the particular mathematical notation we use is somewhat arbitrary and even variable. (We know that what is essentially the same mathematics can often be expressed in very different ways.) On another planet orbiting some other star, intelligent organisms with seven tentacles, thirteen sense organs, and brains shaped like pretzels would eventually arrive at the same universal law, in whatever form or forms appealed to them.

EMERGENCE AND THE LAWS OF PHYSICS

We see that three principles—the conformability of nature to herself, the applicability of the criterion of simplicity, and the utility of certain parts of mathematics in describing physical reality—are thus consequences of the underlying law of the elementary particles and their interactions. Those three principles need not be assumed as separate metaphysical postulates. Instead, they are emergent properties of the fundamental laws of physics.

In my opinion, a great deal of confusion can be avoided, in many different contexts, by making use of the notion of emergence. Some people may ask questions like these: "Doesn't life on Earth somehow involve more than physics and chemistry plus the results of chance events in the history of the planet and the course of biological evolution? Doesn't mind, including consciousness or self-awareness, somehow involve more than neurobiology and the accidents of primate evolution? Doesn't there have to be something more?" But these questioners are not taking sufficiently into account the possibility of emergence. Life can perfectly well emerge from the laws of physics plus accidents, and mind from neurobiology. It is not necessary to assume additional mechanisms or hidden causes. Once emergence is considered, a huge burden is lifted from the inquiring mind. We don't need something more in order to get something more.

Although the "reduction" of one level of organization to a previous one—plus specific circumstances arising from historical accidents—is possible in principle, it is not by itself an adequate strategy for understanding the world. At each level, as emphasized earlier, new regularities emerge that should be studied for themselves. New phenomena appear that should be appreciated and valued at their own level.

It in no way diminishes the importance of the chemical bond to know that it arises from quantum mechanics, electromagnetism, and the prevalence of temperatures and pressures that allow atoms and molecules to exist. Similarly, it does not diminish the significance of life on earth to know that it emerged from physics and chemistry and the special historical circumstances permitting the chemical reactions to proceed that produced the ancestral life form and thus initiated biological evolution. Finally, it does not detract from the achievements of the human race—including the triumphs of the human intellect and the glorious works of art that have been produced for tens of thousand of years—to know that our intelligence and self-awareness, greater than those of the other animals, have emerged from the laws of biology plus the specific accidents of hominid evolution.

When we human beings experience awe in the face of the splendors of nature, when we show love for one another, and when we care for our more distant relatives —the other organisms with which we share the biosphere—we are exhibiting aspects of the human condition that are no less wonderful for being emergent phenomena.

ON THE INTERPRETATIONS OF QUANTUM MECHANICS

I should, in closing, say a few words about quantum mechanics. My colleague James Hartle and I are part of a small group of theoreticians in several countries constructing what I call the modern interpretation of quantum mechanics, and since quantum mechanics has been mentioned here, I thought I should discuss briefly our work on demystifying it. The conventional Copenhagen interpretation is not wrong, but it is special, and far too special to give a reasonable picture of how quantum mechanics really works. That interpretation is altogether unsuitable for quantum cosmology because it involves an observer, preferably a physicist, outside the system in question, making repeated measurements on multiple copies of the system. All of that is hard to do with the universe. Also, while the observer does have some importance, the importance assigned to it in the usual description is manifestly absurd. How did the universe manage for billions of years without complex adaptive systems, let alone conscious observers? Didn't it follow the same quantum-mechanical laws as it does now? The absence of what we call observers made no difference at all.

The basis of our method is to study histories of the universe.[10,11] A fine-grained history would follow every particle at every instant of time, recording its position or its momentum and other properties. But fine-grained histories cannot be assigned probabilities because they interfere with one another, and thus we must make use of coarse-grained histories for which the interference terms cancel out. In these coarse-grained histories a great many things are omitted, for example, all times except a set of discrete ones with a short interval in between. Even at those times many variables are neglected, so that we concentrate, for example, on hydrodynamic variables, averages over small volumes of space of conserved or nearly conserved quantities such as energy or momentum density. The time interval and the volumes are such that the interference terms between coarse-grained histories cancel out. One integrates over all the unimportant little soft photons and motions of tiny dust grains and so forth that interact with the quantities that are followed. That integration makes the coarse-grained histories decohere.

Of course, within such a coarse-grained history, an experiment can still exhibit interference patterns, but the coarse-grained histories themselves do not interfere with one another and they possess well-defined probabilities. At each of the instants of time considered, the histories thus split into branches with various probabilities. Except for those probabilities, it is impossible to predict which outcome will take place until the time comes. Thus the coarse-grained histories form a branching tree with probabilities at all the branchings. The theory places the history actually experienced alongside a gigantic array of possible alternative histories that don't happen, at least in our universe.

The great Argentine author Jorge Luis Borges wrote a story about someone who constructed a model of these alternative histories of the universe in the form of a garden of forking paths, "El jardín de senderos que se bifurcan."[12]

The useful histories are subjected to the condition that they are quasiclassical: the variables that are followed obey approximately deterministic laws interrupted by frequent small fluctuations and occasional major branchings.

A measurement situation for a quantum variable—or a classical one for that matter—exists when the variable at a given time is in strong correlation with the coarse-grained quasiclassical histories of the universe. It makes no difference whether a human being or a chinchilla or cockroach comes along to see what happens. For example, a spontaneous nuclear fission in a uranium impurity in a sheet of mica leaves a classical track independent of whether any living thing comes along to look at it.

The mysterious collapse of the wave function is now reduced to the ordinary collapse of probabilities that we experience at the race track when a race is won by one of the horses, and the probabilities for the horses in that race become one, zero, zero, zero, etc.

The notion of Schrödinger's cat becomes a triviality. It is interesting, of course, that a quantum fluctuation can be amplified so as to kill or not kill a cat, or, for that matter, to annihilate or not annihilate a large city. But the cat, especially the live cat, is in interaction with all sorts of variables, and when many of them are integrated over, the dead cat and the live cat situations decohere. There is then no sense in a formula that contains dead-cat amplitude plus live-cat amplitude over the square root of two. The probabilities involved are now ordinary classical ones, and the resulting situation is similar to the one in which we ship a cat by air. When the box is opened at the destination the poor creature may be alive or dead with a certain probability for each.

NONLOCALITY AND QUANTUM WEIRDNESS

Finally, let us deal with the claim that quantum mechanics is nonlocal. My late friend John Bell was an excellent physicist, and what he wrote about quantum mechanics was not wrong, but he didn't much like quantum mechanics and was not above giving it a bad name by a choice of words. The word "nonlocal" is used here in a very special way. The meaning is that *if the behavior were to be interpreted classically*, it would have to involve nonlocality or negative probabilities or both. But since the behavior in question is not classical, there is no actual nonlocality.

Take the famous EPRB experiment in which a meson at rest decays into two photons moving in opposite directions, unimpeded. They are correlated, of course, by their common origin, and that could happen just as well classically. If we measure the circular polarization of one, that tells us the circular polarization of the other. No information is passed from one to the other. It is simply the correlation that is used, as in a classical analogue.

Now the peculiarity of quantum mechanics is that the entanglement of the two photons is deeper than could occur classically, so that besides the correlation of circular polarization measurements there is also a correlation of, say, linear polarization measurements. If we measure the linear polarization of one photon, we learn the linear polarization of the other. But we must understand that the two measurements, one of circular and one of linear polarization, take place on different, decoherent branches of history and have nothing to do with each other. They are alternatives. There is no nonlocality (except by the curious definition) and no action at a distance.

The same is true of the example of Lucien Hardy. The different measurement situations are completely separate alternatives, occurring on different branches of history, and the results are not to be lumped together.

Quantum mechanics is not weird and not mysterious. It is just quantum-mechanical, and, as far as we can tell, it is completely correct.

Finally, my colleague James Hartle has shown that our method can be applied to a theory (say M-theory) in which gravitation is quantized.[13] The use of histories gets rid of any problems that may arise from possible difficulties in foliating spacetime into time slices when the gravitational curvature is subject to quantum variation. If there ever were such problems, they are now cured and no monkeying with quantum mechanics is required.

Invoking quantized gravitation in a discussion of consciousness leads us back to our discussion of redness, but I am afraid it is only the redness of herrings that is involved.

REFERENCES

1. GELL-MANN, M. 1987. The concept of the institute. *In* Emerging Syntheses in Science. D. Pines, Ed. Addison-Wesley. Reading, MA.
2. GELL-MANN, M. 1994. The Quark and the Jaguar. W.H. Freeman. New York.
3. GELL-MANN, M. 1994. Complex adaptive systems. *In* Complexity: Metaphors, Models, and Reality: Vol. XIX, Santa Fe Institue Series in the Sciences of Complexity. :17–45. Addison-Wesley. Reading, MA.
4. WITTEN, E. 1995. String theory dynamics in various dimensions. Nucl. Phys. **B443**: 85–128.
5. SCHERK, J. & J.H. SCHWARZ. 1975. Dual model approach to a renormalizable theory of gravitation. Caltech preprint CALT-58-488 [5 pages]. Honorable Mention in the 1975 Gravitation Essay Contest, Gravity Research Foundation.
6. GREEN, M.B. & J.H. SCHWARZ. 1985. Infinite cancellations in SO(32) superstring theory. Phys. Lett. **151B**: 21–25.
7. WEINBERG, S. 1992. Dreams of a Final Theory. Pantheon. New York.
8. YANG, C.N. & R.L. MILLS. 1954. Conservation of isotopic spin and gauge invariance. Phys. Rev. **96**: 191–195.
9. GELL-MANN, M. 1972. Quarks: developments in the quark theory of hadrons. Acta Phys. Austriaca **9**: 733–761.
10. GELL-MANN, M. & J.B. HARTLE. 1989. Quantum mechanics in the light of quantum cosmology. *In* Proceedings of the 3rd International Symposium on the Foundations of Quantum Mechanics. :321–343. Tokyo, Japan.
11. GELL-MANN, M. & J.B. HARTLE. 1991. Alternative decohering histories in quantum mechanics. *In* Proceedings of the 25th International Conference on High Energy Physics (1990), Vol. 2. :1303–1310. South East Asia Theoretical Physics Association & Physical Society of Japan. Teaneck, NJ.
12. BORGES, J.L. 1941–1942. El jardín de senderos que se bifurcan. Sur. Buenos Aires.
13. HARTLE, J.B. 1991. The quantum mechanics of cosmology. *In* Quantum Cosmology and Baby Universes: Proceedings of the 1989 Jerusalem Winter School for Theoretical Physics. S. Coleman, J.B. Hartle, T. Piran & S. Weinberg, Eds. World Scientific. Singapore.

The Epistemic Paradox of Mind and Matter

HAROLD J. MOROWITZ

*Krasnow Institute for Advanced Study at George Mason University,
Fairfax, Virginia 22030, USA*

> ABSTRACT: The attempt to posit independent mind and matter results in an unavoidable circularity. We propose to accept this circularity and then explore the steps from the various "constructs" of matter to those biological structures associated with mind. This enables us to explore the hierarchical levels of emergence that take us from the periodic table of the elements to consciousness as it develops in the evolutionary radiation. The possibility of undiscovered principles of the same epistemological status as the Pauli exclusion principle is discussed.
>
> KEYWORDS: Mind and matter; Complexity; Biological information processing; Pauli exclusion principle; Nervous system evolution; Epistemology

MIND AND MATTER: A FUNDAMENTAL PARADOX

This essay deals with certain epistemological difficulties inherent in the designated title of this section: mind and matter. Since I come from an institute charged with studying the intersection of neurobiology, cognitive psychology and computational neuroscience, I am continually mindful of these problems in the philosophy of science. I am also mindful of the somewhat whimsical view of philosophies expressed by Ramón y Cajal in his autobiographical work, *Recollections of My Life,* in which he noted, "In the spirit of frivolous curiosity I read, without always understanding them, the works of Berkeley, Hume, Fichte, Kant, and Balmes. By good luck those of Hegel, Krause, and Sanz del Rio were not in the university library."[1] In the same vein, Cajal has a character in one of his short stories describe Hegel as "the prodigious sophist, who paralyzed with the toxin of idea the positive philosophical analysis initiated by Kant."[2] Well, if I focus on Kant rather than Hegel, I will be in the Cajal tradition. And so I proceed.

We start with the philosophy of science of mid- to late-twentieth century associated with the neo-Kantians Karl Popper[3] and Henry Margenau.[4] One begins with observations, sense data, phenomena. These are in the domain of the conscious and require the mind of the observer. Pure phenomenology is rejected following Kant, as the mind brings certain structures to the observation. From these sensory experiences and their relations, one constructs objects and higher-order abstractions such as atoms. These are the basis of the *Ding an Sich* as described by Kant.[5] They are not directly knowable and have come to include quarks and super strings.

Next, if we wish to study cognition and consciousness, we forget that the elementary particles are in the domain of the mind and proceed to characterize a series of

---

Address for correspondence: Dr. Harold Morowitz, The Krasnow Institute, Mail Stop 2AI, George Mason University, Fairfax, Virginia 22030.

emergences from atoms to conscious minds. Our epistemology and our science then have a certain inevitable circularity,[6] starting with the mind of the observer as the irreducible minimum and then trying to explain the conscious mind in terms of the constructs that have been erected. I find nothing objectionable about this circularity, but it is important to recognize it and to realize that it is not very fashionable in contemporary science.

COSMIC GROWTH OF COMPLEXITY

Let us then trace the series of emergences from elementary particles to human consciousness, which is our present focus, and ask when we see those emergences which have a noetic feature and how these can make more meaningful the epistemological circle. The earliest hint I can find of this is in the Pauli exclusion principle, which first is applicable in our universe when the electrons and post-fusion nuclei of nucleosynthesis cool down enough for atoms to form from a dense plasma. Given quantum mechanics alone, we would expect a sea of nuclei and lowest-energy-state electrons. That is not the case. Instead we find all the complexities of atomic chemistry, chemical binding, crystal formation, and phase phenomena. The exclusion principle is a non-dynamical law dealing with symmetry of quantum states in systems of two or more electrons. It overrides energy minimization and so leads to shell structure of atoms. For example, calculations have shown[7] that on the basis of energy minimization, atoms of lithium would have three 1S electrons. Instead, the neutral lithium atom has two 1S electrons and one 2S electron. It is as if the third electron had some non-Coulombic awareness of the state of the other two electrons. Because of this principle, matter is information-laden. It is not the point mass of mechanics or the continuum of hydrodynamics. It has informational aspects because of the Pauli principle. Thus the periodic table of the elements emerges, and we are currently using the results to study the emergence of cellular metabolism.[8,9]

As a result of quantum mechanics and the Pauli principle, a further feature emerges: the covalent bond. This is the core of organic chemistry and all of the molecular structure, generated by intermediary metabolism and reified in the structure of macromolecules. The covalent bond connects quantum mechanics with cellular metabolism.

Because of the Pauli principle, there is a deep common root to mind and matter. Might some other non-dynamical principle like this be lurking in higher hierarchical levels, as, for example, the emergence of life or of mind? I stress that these would need to be no more mystical or vital than is the Pauli principle.

Somehow in the discussion of physics and consciousness, I find very little discussion of the Pauli principle. It would, I believe, be wise to give this more consideration in order to focus on the notion of mind and matter.

FOUNDATIONS OF BIOLOGICAL INFORMATION PROCESSING

The first biological emergence where there is a hint of *mind* is in the swimming of motile bacteria uphill in a food gradient and downhill in a gradient of toxic substance. This is not well understood. It requires a cell to sense concentration and to interpret the time derivative as the spatial gradient. By randomly changing direction with a frequency that responds to the gradient, the cell can statistically swim in the appropriate direction. The cognitive feel about this is that the cell can let its profits run and cut its losses.

Single-celled eukaryotes (protoctista) have behavioral repertoires in seeking food, mating, and avoiding predation, which also have a cognitive feel to them (see Margulis, this volume). Jennings[10] has presented an elegant description of the behavior of the protozoan *Stentor*, which is again suggestive of a kind of consciousness.

Current studies of consciousness tend to be anthropomorphic and to focus on human brains and conscious minds. Damasio has recently expressed this[11] in an article entitled "How the Brain Creates the Mind." He notes:

> Nothing indicates that we have reached the edge of an abyss that would separate, in principle, the mental from the neural.

> Therefore, I contend that the biological processes now presumed to correspond to mind processes in fact are mind processes and will be seen to be so when understood in sufficient detail. I am not denying the existence of the mind or saying that once we know what we need to know about biology the mind ceases to exist. I simply believe the private personal mind, precious and unique, indeed is biological and will one day be described in terms both biological and mental.

Damasio was reiterating the viewpoint of Ramón y Cajal,[1] who wrote:

> Nevertheless, in spite of the weakness of our methods of analysis, the problem attracted us irresistibly. We saw that an exact knowledge of the structure of the brain was of supreme interest for the building up of a rational psychology. To know the brain, we said, is equivalent to ascertaining the material course of thought and will, to discovering the intimate history of life in its perpetual duel with external forces; a history summarized, and in its way engraved in the defensive neuronal coordination of the reflex of instinct, and of the association of ideas.

I think it fair to say that this view has been part of the mainstream of the neurosciences since the late eighteen hundreds. By referring to the intimate history of life, Ramon y Cajal was placing the problem of emergence of mind in the evolutionary context, where all problems of biology are rooted. In so doing, he was in advance of his time. The problem is not to imagine mind as something that appeared suddenly with *Homo sapiens*; the problem is to trace mind from the protist to humans.

Although the earliest examples are fascinating, consciousness is mainly the property of multicellular animals. We argue that a study of the evolution of the brain and the evolution of consciousness is a pathway to understanding mind.

The key to multicellularity is that a single fertilized egg formed by the fusion of two gametes can give rise, by way of morphogenic processing, to a variety of specialized cells. Thus, switches must be available to turn on and off genetic sequences to distinguish the cell morphology and biochemistry. A hair cell is vastly different from a liver cell, which is vastly different from a nerve cell; yet they are all clonal progeny of a single fertilized ovum. The number of cell types appears to increase substantially along the evolutionary pathway.[12]

The present-day descendants of the earliest animals are probably the placozoa and the porifera (sponges). Communication between cells in the protists and early animals is largely chemical. There are two methods of communication: (1) the cell releases into the environment molecules that freely diffuse and may adsorb on the surface of a second cell or be transported across the membrane to a receptor site; (2)

gap junctions may exist between neighboring cells, which permits intercellular transport of matter. Thus, signaling between cells is limited by diffusion as well as being concentration-limited by dilution.

A nerve cell, on the other hand, receives a chemical signal at a given locus on the surface and converts it into an electrical signal, the action potential. In the electrical form the signal moves rapidly along the axon and triggers chemical release at contacts with other cells. The axon may be thousands of cell diameters in length, so that a cell-to-cell signal may be sent rapidly over large distances.

Now an animal may be sessile (such as sponges) or very small (such as dicyemids), but a large and responsive animal will require the rapid signaling between remote parts. The emergence of the neuron as a cell type was a critical stage in cell evolution. It may have taken a billion years from the first multicellular animal to animals with nervous systems.

THE EVOLUTION OF NERVOUS SYSTEMS

Returning to the most primitive animals, we find the sponges and lacazoa. They lack nerve cells. The most primitive nervous system is in the Cnidaria or coelenterates. Their axons lack a myelin sheath, and the nerves are capable of signal transmission in both directions. The nerve cells form a loose network throughout the organisms. It appears that nerve cells were derived from epithelial cells. In present-day animal embryos, epithelium and nerves derive from the same tissue layer. The necessity for excitable cell membranes seems clear and can be traced back to the behavior of bacteria and protists.

In trying to track the oldest and simplest neural system, we find the following description by Professor Andrew N. Spencer: "It was probably in the ancestral cnidarian that the earliest evolutionary experiments in neuro-neuronal and neuro-effector communication were carried out."[13]

By studying present-day cnidarians, we hope we are examining those synaptic mechanisms that were selected for perhaps as far back as the Pre-Cambrian Era, and that have been conserved with only minimal modification. Of course, we cannot be certain that physiological evolution proceeded at the same rate as morphological changes; nevertheless, the close resemblance of extant forms to fossilized imprints of cnidarians from this era (for example, the Edicara fauna of Australia) hint of slow rates of evolution.

How the first neurons arose remains speculative. It is known that in many hydras epithelial cells can conduct action potentials. Some sponge cells exhibit similar phenomena. This suggests an evolutionary pathway.

In any case, the neuron is an emergent structure that arose 700 or more million years ago. Once evolved, it rapidly acquired many of the features seen in more advanced neural systems. The existence of neural nets permitted the selection of fit behaviors from all possible behaviors. To some, this would be an emergent step on the way to the mind.

Of course, a neuron does not exist alone, but is part of a network of neurons that is nested within a complex organism generated by morphogenesis. Recent studies on homeotic genes in mice and *Drosophila* indicate a higher order of organization mapping from chromosomes to features of developmental patterns across the taxa. Mappings both from genes to nervous systems and from sensory organs to addresses within the brain do indeed suggest higher-order principles at which we may seek emergences that lead to consciousness. Clearly, we are at the beginning of a new level of understanding.

The evolution of mind and brain then goes from jellyfish and hydra to flatworms to the most primitive chordates (such as amphioxus) to the earliest fish to true bony fish to amphibians to reptiles to mammals. We know very little about the behavior of most animals. Donald Griffin has gathered much of the available information in *Animal Minds*,[14] and John Allman has reviewed the anatomy and physiology of the developing brain.[15] Both works agree that minds and brains developed as a buffer against the perils of an ever-shifting environment. That is, mind (or consciousness) has an enormous fitness value and, once discovered, will be selected for along the evolutionary pathway.

The approach of this essay is to emphasize an evolutionary strategy for the study of consciousness. It consists of a parallel analysis of behavior, neuroanatomy, and neurophysiology. The study should start with coelenterates and playhelminthes and at first focus on the earliest organisms in order to seek the most fundamental underlying phenomena. The evolution of consciousness will be a major aid in seeking the nature of the phenomenon of consciousness.

ACKNOWLEDGMENT

I would like to thank Pedro C. Marijuán for discussing this manuscript.

REFERENCES

1. CAJAL, RAMÓN Y, S. 1989. Recollections of My Life. MIT Press. Cambridge, MA.
2. OTIS, LAURA. 1999. Membranes, Metaphors of Invasion in Nineteenth-Century Literature, Science, and Politics. :68. The Johns Hopkins University Press. Baltimore, MD.
3. POPPER, KARL. 1968. The Logic of Scientific Discovery. Harper and Row. New York.
4. MARGENAU, HENRY. 1950. The Nature of Physical Reality. Ox Bow Press [reprint, 1977]. Woodbridge, CT.
5. KANT, IMMANUEL. 1787. Critique of Pure Reason [translation, 1929]. MacMillan and Co. New York.
6. MOROWITZ, HAROLD. 1981. *In* The Mind's I. D. R. Hofstadter and D.C. Dennett, Eds. Bantam Books. New York.
7. EYRING, H., J. WALTER & G. F. KIMBALL. 1944. Quantum Chemistry. John Wiley and Sons. New York.
8. MOROWITZ, HAROLD. 1999. Complexity **4(6):** 4–6, 39–53.
9. MOROWITZ, HAROLD, J. KOSTELNIK, J. YANG & G. CODY. 2000. Proc. Natl. Acad. Sci. USA **97:** 7704–7708.
10. JENNINGS, H.S. 1906/1967. Behavior of Lower Organisms [reprint]. Indiana University Press. Bloomington, IN.
11. DAMASIO, A. 1999. Scientific American **281-6:** 112–117.
12. VALENTINE, J., A.G. COLLINS & C.P. MEYER. 1994. Paleobiology **20:** 137–142.
13. SPENCER, A. 1989. *In* Evolution of the First Nervous Systems. Peter Andersen, Ed. Plenum Press. New York.
14. GRIFFIN, D. 1992. Animal Minds. University of Chicago Press. Chicago, IL.
15. ALLMAN, J. 1999. Evolving Brains. Scientific American Library. W.H. Freeman. New York.

The Conscious Cell

LYNN MARGULIS

*Department of Geosciences, University of Massachusetts,
Amherst, Massachusetts 01003-5820, USA*

ABSTRACT: The evolutionary antecedent of the nervous system is "microbial consciousness." In my description of the origin of the eukaryotic cell via bacterial cell merger, the components fused via symbiogenesis are already "conscious" entities. I have reconstructed an aspect of the origin of the neurotubule system by a hypothesis that can be directly tested. The idea is that the system of microtubules that became neurotubules has as its origin once-independent eubacteria of a very specific kind. Nothing, I claim, has ever been lost without a trace in evolution. The remains of the evolutionary process, the sequence that occurred that produced Cajal's neuron and other cells, live today. By study of obscure protists that we take to be extant decendants of steps in the evolution of cells, we reconstruct the past directly from living organisms. Even remnants of "microbial mind" can be inferred from behaviors of thriving microorganisms. All of the eukaryotes, not just lichens or an animal's neurons, are products of symbiogenesis among formerly free-living bacteria, some highly motile. Eukaryotes have evolved by the inheritance of acquired genomes; they have gained all their new features by ingesting and not digesting whole bacterial cells with complete genomes.

KEYWORDS: *Borrelia*; Karyomastigonts; *Mixotricha*; Nuclear origins; *Spirosymplokos*; Evolutionary novelties; Minimal cell; Symbiosis

Almost one hundred years ago, Ramón y Cajal in his *Historia de Vacaciones* wrote[1]:

> It is certain that science, internally rebellious, seemingly against fate, has invented the microscope with the aim of surprising such small enemies. Yet this already represents an intellectual gain by the microbe. This microscope, this toy—still imperfect because of limitations of its resolving power—from it escape millions of infinitesimal lives; ultramicroscopical bacteria have their bacteria, the impalpable dust of myriad lives dispersed in the air, the water and on the land, the imperceptible intracellular colonies, a kind of symbiotic federation that only now begin to dawn as if they were risky conjectures in the minds of some audacious wise men. One day perhaps it will be legal to track the morphology and customs of such diminutive and ultramicroscopic beings that border on the void even though they are so much larger than molecular constructions. And thus, in all, science can never deplete the domains of life. The invisible, infinitely more important than the visible, infinitely delicate and still unknown, will surround us always. Each age will have its inaccessible enemies because the steed of progress gallops, spurred only by the heel of death.[1]

What is the "statue interior," the "statue inside" that François Jacob[2] alludes to in his autobiography, *The Statue Within*? What is "the invisible infinitely more important than the visible"? (FIG. 1). This is what I plan to discuss in this paper.

Address for correspondence: Morrill Science Center, University of Massachusetts, Amherst, Massachusetts 01003-5820.

FIGURE 1. *Top:* statue of Ramón y Cajal (by sculptor Mariano Benlliure, 1924). *Bottom:* close-up of three Nobel prize winners—Murray Gell-Mann, François Jacob, and Gerald Edelman [left to right]—at the base of the statue.

Illustrious predecessors to my commentary, as well as to the nervous system, abound. The illustrious predecessor to the nervous system is "microbial consciousness." When I describe the origin of the eukaryotic cell via bacterial cell merger, I emphasize that the components that fused in symbiogenesis are already "conscious" entities. I speak within the evolutionary context developed for us by one of my illustrious predecessor scientists: Professor Harold J. Morowitz.[3] I present an aspect of the origin of the neurotubule system by a hypothesis that can be directly tested. The idea is that the system of microtubules that became neurotubules has as its origin once-independent eubacteria of a very specific kind. In our films I show live beings that help us comprehend how evolution has proceeded since the beginning.[4] Nothing, I claim, has ever been lost without a trace in evolution. The remains of the evolutionary process, the sequence that occurred that produced Cajal's neuron and other cells, persist today. By study of what thrives now we can reconstruct the past directly from living organisms, even "microbial mind."[5]

SYMBIOSIS AND THE EVOLUTION OF EUKARYOTIC CELLS

The protein synthetic system, the cytoplasm of your favorite cell, the neuron, as the cytoplasm of all eukaryotic cells, we claim is archaebacterial in origin. We postulate that the protein synthetic system of eukaryotic cells mainly derives from a type of archaebacterium called *Thermoplasma*.

The undulipodium, that is, the microtubular system in its [9(2)+2] array, the shaft called the axoneme, evolved from motile eubacteria close to the genus *Spirocheta*. The simplified equation, by hypothesis, is *Thermoplasma* (archaebacteria) + *Spirocheta* (eubacteria) = the first protist. This motile, nucleated cell, the first protist, resembled mastigotes like extant *Mastigamoeba* or *Trichomonas*. The first merger occurred in the absence of oxygen, prior to acquisition of mitochondria. The earliest microbes, both bacteria and protists, were already greatly sensitive to their environment. The earliest protists bore, in their cells, the karyomastigont. The organelle system, the karyomastigont, is found in many extant protists. The karyomastigont comprises a nucleus and a nucleus connector or rhizoplast that links the nucleus to centrioles and axonemes. The karyomastigont, in our opinion,[6] preceded the unattached nucleus. The nucleus as a double membrane-bounded sphere in the cytoplasm originated when it was severed from the karyomastigont. This scheme posits that spirochete plus thermoplasma generated basal new eukaryotes: protists with karyomastigonts. When the karyomastigont was cut, the nucleus, an organelle that from the beginning represented DNA from two different sources (archaebacterial and eubacterial), was released. From protists evolved the cells of all animals, plants and those of all other familiar eukaryotic organisms.[6,7]

The timeline has been given to us by the geochronologists: four eons. The origin of life is still a big question mark. The units by which we represent the ancient history are tens of millions of years (FIG. 2).

The fossil record of the marine animals begins with the "Cambrian explosion" 541 millions years ago. The Mesozoic age of reptiles began 225 mya. The age of mammals, the Cenozoic, occupies the last portion, 65–0 mya. People are not even visible on this scale. We count in thousands of millions of years. The entire "Precambrian," the long period prior to any animal or plant, is the age of bacteria and protoctists. The eukaryote fossil record begins about 2,000 million years ago. The first hard-shelled marine animals appeared at 541 million years ago. This dates the evolution of hard parts. Brains appear later, but consciousness, awareness of the surrounding environment, starts with the beginning of life itself, which is the point of this paper.

The origin of life is represented in FIGURE 2 as a question mark. The earliest cells generated the two great groups of bacteria: the one to which *Thermoplasma* belongs (archaebacteria) and the one to which the spirochetes belong (eubacteria). The process of symbiogenesis in the evolution of nucleated cells began about 2,000 mya. The emergent property of the symbiont fusion was the origin of all larger forms of life. We concentrate here on only one of the many, many evolutionary transitions in the origin of ourselves: we mammals who talk too much.

Let us review the very earliest life forms from the point of view of their chemistry. This simplified diagram is based completely on the analysis that Morowitz made some 25 years ago: the minimal cell (FIG. 3).[3] The minimal cell must be surrounded by a membrane of its own making. In today's world, on Earth at least, the cell makes its own genetic material, DNA. Of course it synthesizes messenger RNA coded off that DNA, as well as transfer RNAs, and the rest of ribosomal RNAs to make the ribosomal system that synthesizes more proteins that make more DNA. All cells require sources of carbon, nitrogen, oxygen, hydrogen, phosphorus, and sulfur. A source of energy too is required by all life. Life's energy system is always visible light or chemical (inorganic or organic chemical) only. No other known sources of energy for cells exist besides photo- and chemical. All of life's chemical transformation occurs in a watery matrix. The minimal system, at least on Earth today, dia-

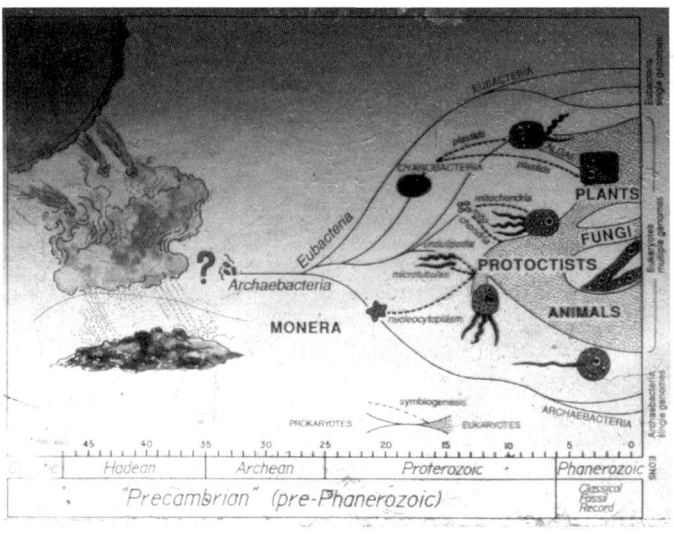

FIGURE 2. History of life on geological time scale (by Kathryn Delisle).

grammed in FIGURE 3, suggests that any organelle that began as a free-living microbe at first contained FIGURE 3's entire complement of features.

In cells of green hydra, for example, the green animal's gastrodermal cell is clearly a product of symbiogenesis: the cnidarian animal and the alga. But three genomes occur in the *Chlorella,* the green algal cell: nucleocytoplasm, chloroplast, mitochondrion. At least two coexist in the hydra cell: nucleocytoplasm and mitochondrion. Thus the single digestive system cell of the animal is a composite of at least five genomes. The point is that all eukaryotic cells, including the neuron, all are products of more than a single genome with more than one single ancestor. All are complex, all are heterogenomic with multiple ancestors. All eukaryotes, all nucleated organisms, are composed of cells that are products of symbiogenetic mergers.

Symbiosis has nothing to do with "co-operation" or "mutual benefit." Leave that kind of talk for the sports announcers, bankers, and other money people. Symbiosis simply refers to the long-term physical association between members of different species. (Or different strains—since bacteria lack species.)[21]

Symbiogenesis, on the other hand, is an evolutionary term. Symbiosis refers to partner physiology and ecology. Symbiogenesis is the evolutionary consequence of symbiosis. Because of long-term symbiosis in some cases new forms appear. That green hydra cell appeared as the outcome of symbiogenesis when green algae were ingested but not digested. The algae were maintained by the animal long enough to become a normal component of all green hydra animal digestive epithelia. New forms emerge: like the green hydra, they may be entire new organisms. Many different features (i.e., new organs, new tissues) emerge via symbiogenesis. "Symbiogenesis" is an evolutionary term, whereas "symbiosis" is an ecological or physiological concept.

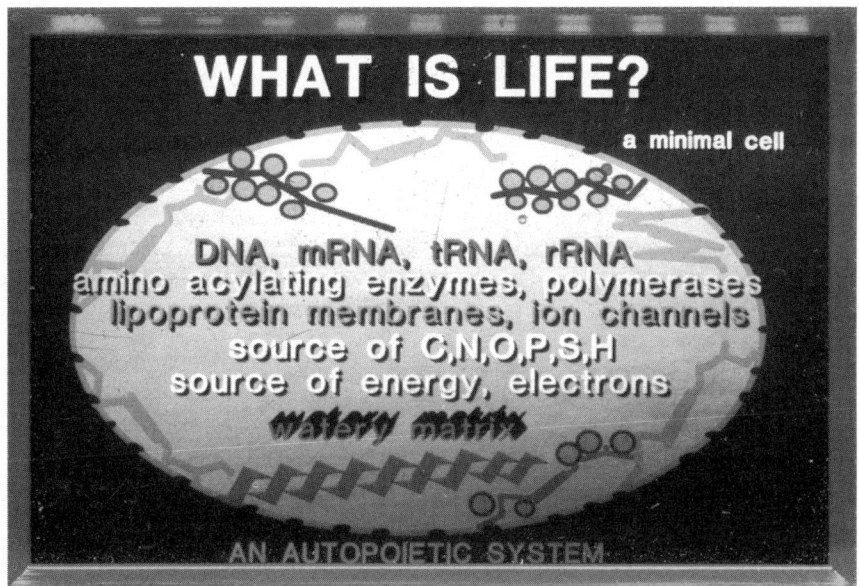

FIGURE 3. Minimal cell.

ANTECEDENTS OF SYMBIOGENESIS

The idea of symbiogenesis developed first in Russia and was well known to the Russian botanists. Actually, I have six illustrious predecessors in this talk: Ramón y Cajal, François Jacob, Harold Morowitz, and three Russian botanists.[8]

Andrey Sergeevich Famintsyn (1835–1918) broke open plant cells in his attempt to grow chloroplasts, the green organelles inside. Konstantin Sergeevich Merezhkovsky (1855–1921) studied green hydras and many other symbioses. He framed the concept of "symbiogenesis." He said very clearly that Darwinism could never generate novelty; he denied that biological novelty is generated randomly or by natural selection. Symbiogenesis, which included the acquisition of microbes and the inheritance of acquired microbes, he claimed, generates inherited variation. Merezhkovsky was not a fan of Papa Carlos Darwin.

Now Boris Mikhaylovich Kozo-Polyansky (1890–1957), who was never translated into English, or any other Western language, wrote a book in 1924 called *A New Principle of Biology: Essay on the Theory of Symbiogenesis*. He united the Darwinian idea of natural selection with the genesis of novelty by symbiogenesis. Kozo-Polyansky accepted Merezhkovsky's idea that new life forms evolve by symbiotic merger. The novel life forms are then selected for by natural selection. Although his book *A New Principle of Biology* was never translated, Kozo-Polyansky's ideas were paraphrased by Arman Takhtajian, who still today is our greatest living botanist. Whereas these two Russian scientists (Famintsyn, Merezhkovsky) were anti-Darwin, Kozo-Polyansky admired Darwin. He suggested that natural selection selects the novel properties of organisms that symbiogenesis generates.

These Russians were contemporaries of Ramón y Cajal, but I have no idea whether Ramón y Cajal was aware of their work when he wrote the above statement about symbiotic federations. I do not know whether Cajal read Russian literature. It would be interesting to know whether Cajal knew anything about Russian work directly or through interpretations by German scientists. The biologist Merezhkovsky's brother, Dimitri, wrote the novel *The Romance of Leonardo Da Vinci*. Konstantin and Dimitri were from a well-known literary family.

Ivan Wallin, the fourth symbiogeneticist, was an intellectually isolated American. A son of Swedish immigrants, he was a professor of anatomy in Colorado. He never read Russian, of course, nor was it likely that he read German, French, or Spanish either. Like almost all the people in the United States, he was monolingual. He wrote a fantastic book called *Symbionticism and the Origin of Species* (1927).[9] His ideas could not be more explicit: symbionticism (a concept virtually identical to Merezhkovsky's symbiogenesis) and the origin of species. Wallin claimed that innovation in evolution, including the origin of mitochondria and chloroplasts, was by "acquisition of microsymbiotic complexes." By this he meant that the acquisition of bacteria, the integration of bacteria, generates novelty in evolution. His extremely clear views were roundly rejected. One of my colleagues at the Marine Biological Laboratory of Woods Hole, Massachusetts, was going to throw out his copy of Wallin's book. He said to me "you would be interested in this kind of stuff," implying "this nonsense." Wallin's book is remarkable. If you try to find it on the Internet, you'll see that to buy a copy today is very expensive.

Now where did these Russians get the symbiogenesis idea? The reindeer culture in Siberia depends on lichens. In some remote places of Lapland and Siberia the ecosystem completely depends on lichens as a food source. There is nothing else to eat. So these Russian botanists analyzed the lichens.

A fungal colony growing on a petri plate for three weeks is shown in FIGURE 4b Also seen are colonies of the green alga *Trebouxia* growing on a plate for about three weeks as well. Yet in nature, the two types of organisms live together and form the brightly colored lichen in FIGURE 4a.

Only together do the fungus and the alga compose the British-soldier lichen called *Cladonia cristatella*. These Russian botanists understood that there was no single ancestor to the lichen. It makes no sense to ask "what is the ancestor of the lichen?" Lichens are composites. Do you know that you are Schwendenerist? A Schwendenerist is one who believes that lichens are not plants, that lichens are products of symbiogenetic association between algae and fungi. Without both components no red pigment is made. No lichenic acids are synthesized. No tissue differentiates. No sexuality appears. The two different components are absolutely necessary to produce the lichen. The Russians understood that symbiogenesis was an emergent property of the living together of alga and fungus.

We assert that consciousness appears at the left in FIGURE 2, there at the origin. We claim that all the large organisms are products of symbiogenesis, just as lichens are. There is no single ancestor to any large organism: there are at least two and usually more than two. In this paper we only discuss that very first step, the origin of protists, members of the great group called Protoctista. There are estimated to be 250,000 species of Protoctista alive today. Protists, single or few-celled, are the smaller members of the Kingdom Protoctista.[10] Let us examine ideas of the origin of the protists from the bacteria.

FIGURE 4a. Lichen *Cladonia cristatella* holobiont (both fungal and algal components).

FIGURE 4b. Bionts: three algal colonies (*Trebouxia*) on a petri plate (*top*); fungal colony (*Cladonia*) on plate (*bottom*).

EVOLUTIONARY ORIGINS OF THE PROTOCTISTA: THE KARYOMASTIGONT ORGANELLE SYSTEM

The arrow in FIGURE 5 points to the karyomastigont of a highly motile organism that, I suggest, already had 24-nanometer tubules when it became a symbiont. Such microtubules are homologous to the neurotubules of the neurons. These squiggly organisms, today if they are free-living and small, belong to the genus *Spirocheta*. By hypothesis they associated with *Thermoplasma*-type archaebacteria, seen in FIGURE

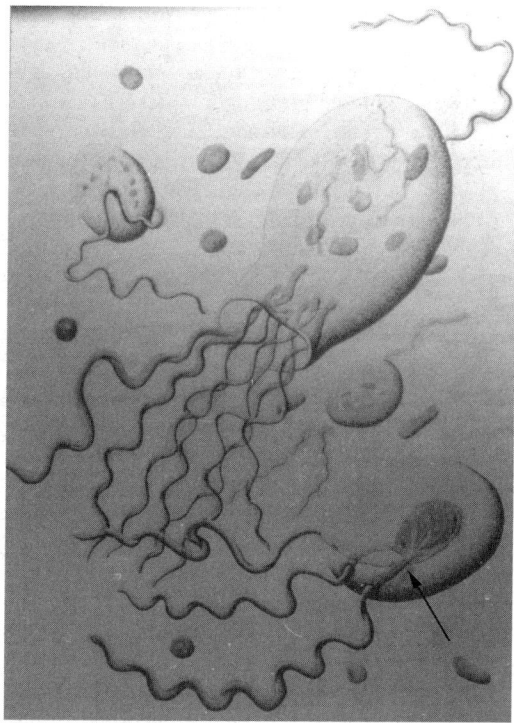

FIGURE 5. Spirochetes become undulipodia (illustration by Christie Lyons).

5 as well. Together archaebacterium + eubacterium produced the first protoctist. Evolution of intracellular "anima" begins here. The idea is that this type of motile organism, which already has proteins involved in motility, associated with the *Thermoplasma*-like organism resistant to acid and heat. Together they formed an emergent structure: the *Spirocheta* became the motile organelle, the undulipodium. The fused DNA of the archaebacterium and the eubacterium became the nucleus. Free-living organisms to begin with, by the end of the process the spirochetes had become organelles. The holdfast structures of the spirochetes became the kinetosomes. The entire structure, made of tubules, fibers, the holdfast organelles (the former *Spirocheta*), and the nucleus is called karyomastigont. The karyomastigont is the early organelle system of all nucleated organisms from which the mitotic apparatus evolved. The release of the nucleus occurred over and over again in evolutionary time as new protoctists evolved.

I remind you that these are exactly the same microtubules about which Drs. Penrose and Hameroff write in their papers in this volume. The generic term for microtubules organized with nine-fold symmetry that grow from a base is "undulipodium." The sense organs of animals—auditory, visual, tactile, and gustatory—are composed of undulipodiated cells. The nine-fold symmetrical body with triplets at the base of all undulipodia, when there is no shaft, is called the centriole. When the shaft exists as in a sperm tail or cilium, or eukaryotic flagellum (undulipodium), the centriole's name changes to kinetosome. For historical reasons, the centriole–kinetosome structure has many names. The identity of centrioles and kinetosomes was not understood until after 1963, when glutaraldehyde fixation came into widespread use. Henneguy, the great histologist from the Sorbonne, and Lenhossek, the Hungarian, who wrote in German, in 1899, over one hundred years ago, developed the Henneguy–Lenhossek theory.[11] It is absolutely correct. The theory claims identity of the kinetosome and the centriole. The centriole, from the previous mitotic division, moves to the edge of the cell in animal epithelium and produces the kinetosomes. The centriole reproduces to produce the kinetosomes of ciliated epithelium. André Lwoff (1904–1989) speaks to us from wherever he is today. He stated that the centriole goes to the edge of the cell, reproduces, and grows the shafts. The Henneguy–Lenhossek theory says that the centriole of the previous mitosis gives rise to the kinetosomes and their cilia of the epithelium. This entirely correct theory, one hundred years old, explains why the microtubules and other proteins of the two structures (centrioles, kinetosomes) are virtually identical.

Let us examine the evolutionary origin of the centriole–kinetosome structure. First, to reduce confusion, a generic term was required. The word undulipodium comes from the German biologist Max Hartmann (1925)[12] via Shmagina[13] and other Russian scientists. Many aliases exist for the undulipodium even today.

The cilium, the sperm tail, and even sperm tails of ginkgo trees display the same nine-fold structure. They are undulipodia. So do the kinocilia of the auditory epithelium. Many sensory hairs, including those of rod and cone cells of the retina, as I will show you, are homologous. Eukaryotic flagella, kinocilia, euflagella, cilia, all of these terms are subsumed by the name "undulipodia." The hypothesis is that the undulipodium, and the entire structure of the centriole–kinetosome in which it is embedded, the kinetid, comes from the eubacteria attachment structures of once free-living microbes of the spirochete sort. In short, the idea that the centrioles that develop into kinetosomes are remnant spirochete attachment sites is my extension of the Henneguy–Lenhossek theory.

The large, complicated scheme is shown in its entirety in FIGURE 2.[6,7] Photosynthesis began in bacteria and oxygen respiration also began in bacteria. Motility of many kinds evolved in bacteria as did fermentation and other basic metabolic systems including protein synthesis. Many other features first evolved in bacteria, but the ones shown here are those that ended up in nucleated organisms. In this paper I limit my discussion to the first fusion: that of motile eubacteria of the spirochete type with a thermoplasmic archaebacterium in the first merger that produced the first protists. These earliest protists bore karyomastigonts, structures in which the centrioles are connected directly to the nucleus.

Ironically, the only organisms that evolved their traits by random accumulation of mutations are the bacteria. The eukaryotes gain new features by ingesting and not digesting whole bacterial cells with complete genomes. All of the eukaryotes, not just lichens, are products of symbiogenesis. Eukaryotes evolve by the inheritance of acquired genomes.

Those of you who work with nerve cells know very well about the importance of intracellular motility: movement inside cells. You may not know that no intracellular motility, except Brownian movement, of course, which is not active protein-based motility, exists in prokaryotic cells. Bacteria lack intracellular motility. All other organisms, nucleated organisms, bear a cytoskeleton in their cells. Many different proteins underlie the phenomenon of cell motility.

Centrioles and their shafts, that is, the centriole–kinetosome and its axoneme extension are composed of many proteins (i.e., tubulin, dynein, cenexin, pericentrin). The number of proteins involved is not a single one like the "flagellin" of flagellated bacteria. At least 600 and maybe a thousand proteins are within the centriole–kinetosome's axoneme (i.e., the undulipodium). We can no longer use the word "flagellum" for two fundamentally different structures.

EUKARYOSIS: A SPIROCHETE AND THERMOPLASMA MERGER

"Eukaryosis" is a term coined by Professor John Corliss. This term refers to a process, the origin of the earliest eukaryotes.

Some spirochetes and an example of *Thermoplasma acidofilum*, the archaebacterium, are diagrammed in FIGURE 6. Thermoplasmas resemble amoebae, but they are not amoebae at all. They are prokaryotes. The fusion that occurred between spirochetes and thermoplasmas, I think, led to the earliest protists. In my video we see five different thermoplasma archaebacteria. Fluorescent-labeled DNA associated with the centriole–kinetosomes, the work of John Hall,[14,15] is also seen in the video. Kinetosome DNA is underneath the nuclear membrane, but Hall's DNA images are relevant to the remnant spirochete, in my opinion.

We have seen in the laboratory spirochetes that are not polarized, that is, they cannot tell their head from their rear end. In the video we see small spirochetes; these motile bacteria range in size by a factor of more than a hundred. Viewed under a strobe light, we see that the movement of these organisms is stopped by the flashing light. We also see typical group-moderated movement of free-swimming spirochetes that once were independent. They separate when water is added. We saw a new light-sensitive spirochete: *Spirosymplokos deltaeiberi*. (It is either light- or heat-sensitive).[16] It swam to the edge of the field of the microscope; it did not like darkness. It swam away and returned. Why? Because it feeds on exudate from light-requiring cyanobacteria. In nature *Spirosymplokos* follows cyanobacteria.

We also saw a bloom of *Spirosymplokos deltaeiberi* in mixed culture. We were never able to put them into pure culture. They do the following: they pull in, that is, they retract and form resistant bodies. These structures are called "cryptic forms" when they occur in *Borrelia burgdorferi*, the Lyme disease spirochete.[17] Some spirochetes (probably *Hollandina*) have cytoplasmic tubules in 2 + 2 arrays. We have not found [9(2)+2] spirochetes, but we have seen 2+2 so far. These spirochetes have cytoplasmic spherical structures from which emerge cytoplasmic tubules. In some cases the tubules have diameters as large as 24 nanometers, that is, the size of neurotubules. Each cell length has one of these CTACs (cytoplasmic tubule–associated centers) that look like microtubule-organizing centers (MTOCs). They can be compared directly. Tubules extend outward.[20]

We studied a *bona fide* microtubule-organizing center in a fungal nucleus (*Taphrina*). We think that the prokaryotic precursors of the microtubule-organizing centers evolved in spirochetes. The work was done by André Hollande, who believed that all cells must divide by mitosis. He called the prokaryotic spirochetal structures "microtubules," but they are, of course, only cytoplasmic tubules until their composition is determined to be related to tubulin.

When the head of normal animal sperm, with the mitochondrion and the nucleus attached are demembranated and the mitochondria and the nucleus removed, the tails by themselves continue to swim. In the presence of ATP, calcium removal and the proper hydrogen-ion concentrations, the tails continue to beat and swim for 45 minutes. Why? Because, in my view, these sperm tails are a legacy of the former bacteria from which they evolved. These [9(2)+2] tails of sea urchin sperm will continue swimming for many minutes until they die from lack of nutrients and disconnection from the nucleus and the rest of the sperm cell.

If you had sectioned those tails with the electron microscope you would have seen nine pairs of microtubules with two in the center. That is, the classical [9(2)+2] undulipodial cross-section would be obvious (see Margulis[7] for discussion).

The great Spanish–Swedish paleontologist (1936–1998) Gonzalo Vidal found fossils, at least 1,800 million years old, of eukaryotes. These unidentified eukaryotic microfossils are called acritarchs.[18] Thus the process of which I speak, the origin of eukaryotes, must have occurred almost 2,000 million years ago.

The spirochete moves around, feeding on exudate from larger organisms. When a protist is entirely beset by spirochetes, the spirochetes will swim near and attach in a bundle to many other organisms. When enough of them are present, their swimming will actually move the larger organism to which they are attached. Our model of the hypothetical evolutionary sequence can be seen in FIGURE 6.

Undulipodia are compared to free-living organisms in spirochete culture. The protist, a trichomonad, bears the standard undulipodium. When it alights, it moves and takes with it spirochetes attached to its posterior end. Very commonly spirochetes attach to other organisms.

The protist *Mixotricha paradoxa* is a single cell composed of five different genomes. Two very different kinds of spirochetes coat its surface. The major one, the small *Treponema*, occurs at the quantity of 250,000 spirochetes per protist (FIG. 7). Electron microscopy shows that in addition to dividing *Treponema* spirochetes on the protist's surface there is another dividing surface eubacterium. The pattern of the spirochete, the eubacterium and the protist's surface occurs along nearly the whole outer edge of *Mixotricha*. Inside a centriole lumen in *Mixotricha*-like protists unidentified 32-nm-diameter granules are seen. The Catalan spirochete *Spirosymplokos deltaeiberi* has similar-appearing, similar-sized granules in it. One hypothesis is that these granules will have in common the same chemical composition.

When first discovered in the 1930s *Mixotricha* was reported to be a ciliate. Now we know that *Mixotricha*'s surface is covered not with undulipodia (cilia) but with symbiotic spirochetes that confer motility on the protist. The *Mixotricha* protist is almost 1 millimeter in size. The single cell is 750 or 800 micrometers. The "anchor bacterium" and the spirochetes adhere to a raised portion of the protist. Half a million of "anchor bacteria," half a million of the *Treponema* spirochetes, cover each protist cell just prior to its division in two.

A large still unidentified (probably a new genus)[a] kind of spirochete is also attached to the *Mixotricha* surface. At least two or three kinds of epibionts and two

---

[a]The new genus, *Canaleparolina,* is described and illustrated in FIGURE 7.

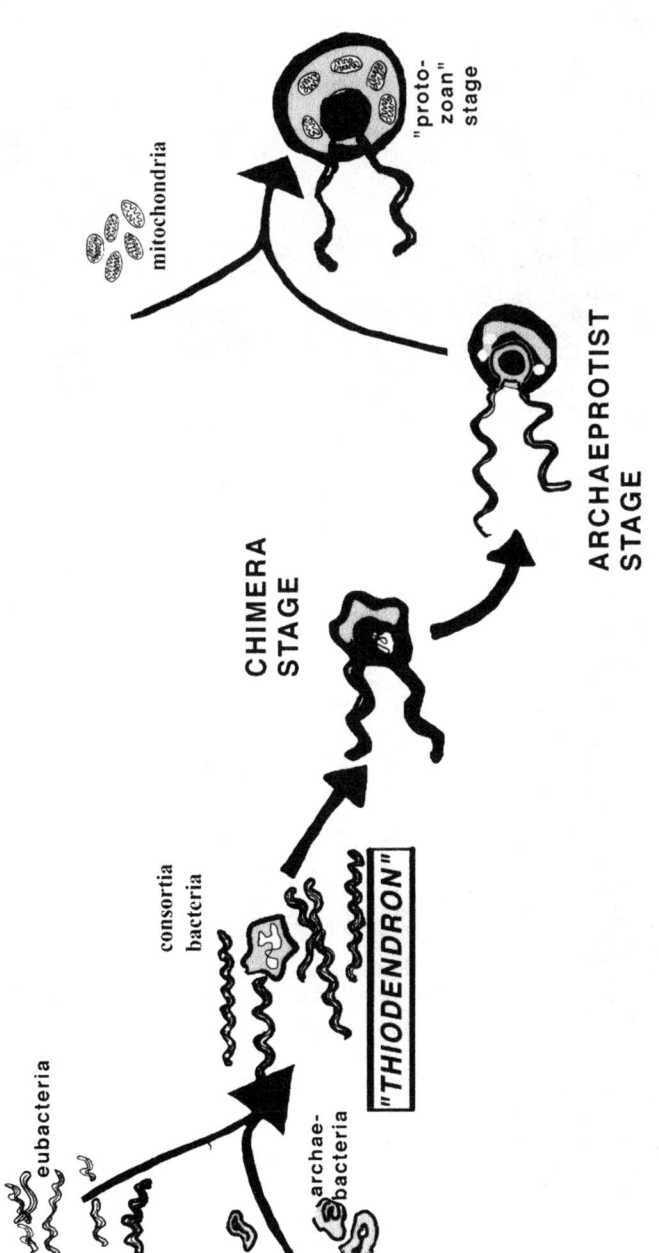

FIGURE 6. History of the karyomastigont.

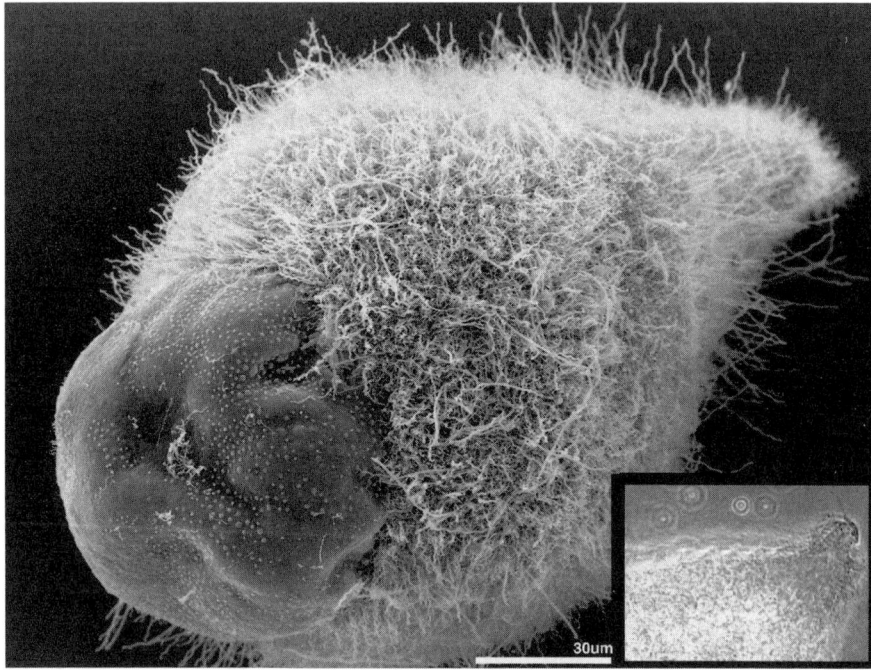

FIGURE 7. An individual cell of *Mixotricha paradoxa*, composed of the unusually large (hypertrophied) trichomonad with its four anterior undulipodia connected to the nucleus (i.e., the karyomastigont organellar system), at least three types of regularly associated surface bacteria, and a fourth spherical endosymbiotic bacterium. Four of the five types of components, the giant trichomonad covered by more than a million bacterial cells that together behave as an individual protist during coordinated forward-directed swimming [*inset*] are seen in these images. The live individual swims forward as visualized by phase-contrast microscopy [*inset*]; the scanning electron micrograph reveals two different types of epibiotic spirochetes: the long *Canaleparolina* cells extend from the surface, whereas the smaller treponemes cover it like short curly living hairs. Both kinds of spirochetes and the undulipodia probably serve as *Mixotricha*'s "sense organs" as it moves through the lumen of the gut of *Mastotermes darwiniensis*, the termite. Scanning electron micrograph courtesy of Dean C. Soulia.

kinds of internal endobionts exist. This stained *Mixotricha* cell looks like André Lwoff's preparation of cilia on the surface of a ciliate cell. It is not. It is a silver preparation similar to that Ramón y Cajal used. This silver preparation of the surface of *Mixotricha* is reminiscent of the surface of ciliates because, by hypothesis, they have the same origin from adhering eubacterial epibionts. Further discussion of *Mixotricha* can be found in Margulis.[7]

A generalized view of the karyomastigont is shown in FIGURE 6. The parts of the karyomastigont include the nucleus, nucleus connector (rhizoplast), centriole–kinetosomes, axoneme, and membranes. The nucleus resides by the Golgi membranes. The isolated karyomastigont here includes four undulipodia, four centrioles, nucleus, microtubules of the axon style, and the Golgi (or parabasal body). This corresponds to the early attachment organellar system, the structure in the earliest eukaryotes. All the early eukaryotic organisms do not tolerate oxygen. Their descendants today live in anoxic muds or in the anoxic hindguts of insects and other animals. These swimming protists still function today without any mitochondria and live in the absence of any oxygen. Some of their relatives have karyomastigonts with nuclei and others bear structures that are the karyomastigonts, but without the nuclei. Organelle systems that are the same as karyomastigonts but without nuclei are called "akaryomastigonts." When they contain nuclei, the term is karyomastigont. Some obscure protists that we study bear as many as 1,000 nuclei, all as karyomastigonts, per cell.[19] This evolutionary series of protists is called Family Calonymphidae of the Archaeprotists (protists without mitochondria). In the calonymphids, in certain genera the nuclei are released. They have been freed. We hypothesize that a comparable liberation of nuclei occurred also in the origin of plant, animal, fungal, and many other protist cells.

ACKNOWLEDGMENTS

We thank the NASA Space Science program (Michael A. Meyer) and the University of Massachusetts for support of our research. I am grateful to Dr. Michael Dolan, Professor Ricardo Guerrero, Dr. Mónica Solé, and Andrew Wier for aid on this manuscript.

REFERENCES

1. RAMON Y CAJAL, S. 1924. Historia de Vacaciones [Vacation Stories: Pseudo-Scientific Tales].: 182. Austral. Madrid. [Extract cited translated by Prof. R. Guerrero.]
2. JACOB, F. 1988. The Statue Within: An Autobiography. Basic Books. New York.
3. MOROWITZ, H.J. 1992. Beginnings of Cellular Life. Yale University Press. New Haven, CT.
4. WIER, A.M. & L. MARGULIS. 2000. Microcosmos videos. Jones and Bartlett. Sudbury, MA.
5. MARGULIS, L. 2000. Microbial minds. *In* Forces of Change. D. Botkin *et al.*, Eds.: 128–129. Smithsonian Institution. Washington, DC.
6. MARGULIS, L., R. GUERRERO, & M. DOLAN. 2000. The chimeric eukaryote: origin of the nucleus from the karyomastigont in amitochondriate protists. Proc. Natl. Acad. Sci. USA **97:** 6954–6959.
7. MARGULIS, L. 1993. Symbiosis in Cell Evolution, 2nd ed. W.H. Freeman. New York.
8. KHAKHINA, L.N. 1992. Concepts of Symbiogenesis: A Historical and Critical Study of the Research of Russian Botanists. Yale University Press. New Haven, CT.
9. WALLIN, I.E. 1927. Symbionticism and the Origin of Species. Williams & Wilkins. Baltimore, MD.
10. MARGULIS, L., J.O. CORLISS, M. MELKONIAN & D.J. CHAPMAN, Eds. 1990. Handbook of Protoctista. Jones and Bartlett. Boston, MA.
11. MARGULIS, L. & M. DOLAN. 1999. Did centrioles and kinetosomes evolve from bacterial symbionts? Report of the Henneguy–Lenhossek theory meeting. Symbiosis **26:** 199–204.
12. HARTMANN, M. 1925. Allgemeine Biologie. G. Fischer. Jena.
13. SHMAGINA, A.P. 1948. Ciliary Movement [in Russian]. MEDGIZ. Moscow.
14. HALL, J.L., Z. RAMANIS & D.L. LUCK. 1989. Basal body/centriolar DNA: molecular genetic studies in *Chlamydomonas*. Cell **59:** 121G–132.
15. HALL, J.L. & D.J.L. LUCK. 1995. Basal body-associated DNA: *in situ* studies in *Chlamydomonas reinhardtii*. Proc. Natl. Acad. Sci. USA **92:** 5129–5133.

16. MARGULIS, L., J.B. ASHEN, M. SOLÉ & R. GUERRERO. 1993. Composite, large spirochetes from microbial mats: spirochete structure review. Proc. Natl. Acad. Sci. USA **90:** 6966–6970.
17. BRORSON, O. & S.H. BRORSON. 1999. An *in vitro* study of the susceptibility of mobile and cryptic forms of *Borrelia burgdorferi* to Metronizadole. APMIS **107:** 566–576.
18. VIDAL, G. 1984. The oldest eukaryotic cells. Sci. Am. **250:** 48–57.
19. DOLAN, M.F., A.M. WIER & L. MARGULIS. 2000. Budding and asymmetric reproduction of a trichomonad with as many as 1000 nuclei in karyomastigonts: *Metacoronympha* from *Incisitermes*. Acta Protozoologica **39:** 275–280.
20. WIER, A.M., J. ASHEN & L. MARGULIS. 2000. *Canaleparolina darwiniensis*, gen. nov., sp. nov., and other pillotinaceae spirochetes from insects. Int. Microbiol. **3:** 215–222.
21. SONEA, S. & L.G. MATHIEU. 2000. Prokaryotology: A Coherent View. Les Presses de l'Université de Montréal. Montréal, Quebec, Canada.

Complexity and Tinkering

FRANÇOIS JACOB

Institut Pasteur, Département de Biologie Moléculaire, 75724 Paris Cedex 15, France

ABSTRACT: All recent results in the fields of development and evolution point to a role of regulatory circuits as a major cause of evolutionary changes.

KEYWORDS: Duplication; Evolutionary novelties; Molecular recognition; Reshuffling; Tinkering

It is a great pleasure and a great honor to be included in this symposium in the memory of Ramón y Cajal. Every medical student has been immersed in Cajal's ideas, and it is rare to find a book which, a hundred years after it was written, is still read by students.[1] Cajal was as much an artist as a scientist. He was also some kind of a poet: when writing about neurons he called them "the mysterious butterflies of the soul."

It is difficult to recall that it is now fifty years since the first sequence of a protein was described by Sanger: it was the sequence of insulin.[2,3] At that time it was considered that every organism had its own molecules: that the molecules that composed a mouse were different from those that composed a chicken or a cow—and that it was because a cow was made of cow's molecules that a cow was a cow.

Very soon after the first description of insulin by Sanger, it turned out that several insulins looked very much alike and that they differed only by one or two or three amino acids. Then it turned out that the cytochromes and hemoglobins were also very similar. But the big conceptual change came after an experiment by Alan Wilson and MarieClaire King in 1975.[4] They compared the proteins of humans and of chimpanzees and found that 99% of the proteins were alike. So it became very difficult to still think that every organism had its own proteins and that the properties and performances of an organism resulted from the particular structure of its particular proteins.

For a long time it was thought that evolution worked like an engineer. Yet this is not a good comparison because an engineer works on first principles; he uses special machines and special material for whatever he wants to make. Since organisms derive from organisms, evolution makes new from old. The best comparison would then be that it acts like a tinkerer, like a *bricoleur*.[5,6] But this is still not a good comparison because obviously a *bricoleur* knows what he wants to do, while evolution does not know what it is going to produce. It works on what is available. And what is available at any time are the genes of the organisms.

The first way of getting novelties is by gene duplication. Rounds of duplication have produced protein families which contain several copies of the same gene. The

Address for correspondence: Institut Pasteur, 25 rue du Dr. Roux, 75724 Paris Cedex 15, France.

second way of getting new proteins is by reshuffling, either of genes or of pieces of genes. Proteins are made of domains which can fold independently of other parts.

The important structure of a domain is generally a molecular-recognition site. Molecular recognition has been considered for a long time to operate only in the active site of enzyme—to recognize the substrates—or in antibody–antigen reaction. Today, it has been acknowledged that molecular recognition acts at almost every stage of cellular activity, as in protein–protein interactions, the recognition of DNA by proteins for the regulation of gene activity, and in cell–cell interactions.

Duplication, reshuffling, and a third mode of producing new proteins—recruitment. Recruitment has been demonstrated, for instance, in crystallins, which are the proteins of the lens. It was found that in most cases these proteins are known for having another function. For instance, the alpha cristallin is a small heat-shock protein. Many crystallins of birds, reptiles and others have an enzymatic activity such as arginosuccinate lyase and lactate dehydrogenase.

Recently, it has been possible to compare the complete genome of a unicellular eukaryotic organism, *Saccharomyces cerevisiae*, with the complete genome of one of the simplest multicellular organisms—*C. elegans*, a small nematode—which has 959 cells.[7] The open reading frames of the two organisms, and therefore the expected proteins, have been compared. A number of similarities have been found: almost identical proteins are used for performing most of the functions of the cell such as DNA replication and protein synthesis.

Divergencies are also found. They are extremely interesting because one can begin to see how, going from unicellularity to multicellularity, things occur: there are a number of extracellular signaling systems, such as the adhesion molecules, the EGF molecule, and some hormone receptors, in particular the nuclear hormone receptor.

Since similar proteins are found in chimpanzees and in humans, it is obviously not the protein structures that are important, but the way these proteins are distributed. It seemed clear already in 1975 that what distinguishes a fly from a dog or a worm from a whale, is not the nature of the components but the way these components are distributed[4]—when and where they are produced during embryonic life. In other words, regulatory novelties appear to be much more important than structural novelties.

It seems that many instances of evolution can be ascribed to the tinkering of regulatory circuits. Several examples of different species using similar regulatory genes have been described in insects. For instance, it was shown by Sean Carroll and his group in Madison that butterflies have regulatory genes very similar to those of *Drosophila*.[8,9] In all likelihood the differences observed between these organisms come from differences in the way these genes are geared in the regulatory circuits. It appears that the evolutionary *bricolage* has been amazingly parsimonious in choosing the basic building blocks, but enormously creative in deploying these gene products in a variety of forms.

The most complex outcome of evolutionary *bricolage* is the human brain. Yet we know little about how it is built and how the combined developmental and physiological processes within the brain work together to produce the emergence of consciousness. In my view, this is the most fascinating story that can be told on Earth.[5] And it is here where Cajal excelled: by starting to tell us the first chapter of that very story.

REFERENCES

1. RAMÓN Y CAJAL, S. 1909–1911. Histologie du système nerveux de l'homme et les vertébrés. (2 vols.) Maloine, Paris. [French translation of: Textura del sistema nervioso del hombre y de los vertebrados. 1899-1904. Imprenta N. Moya. Madrid.]
2. SANGER, F. 1949. Some chemical investigations on the structure of insulin. Cold Spring Harbor Symposia Quant. Biol. **14:** 153–160.
3. SANGER, F. 1952. The arrangement of amino acids in proteins. Adv. Protein. **7:** 1–67.
4. KING, M.C. & A.C. WILSON. 1975. Evolution at two levels in humans and chimpanzees. Science **188:** 107–116.
5. JACOB, F. 1977. Evolution and tinkering. Science **196:** 1161–1166
6. JACOB, F. 1981. Le Jeu des Possibles. Librairie Arthème Fayard, Paris. [English translation: The Possible and the Actual. 1982. Pantheon, New York].
7. CHERVITZ, S.A. et al. 1998. Comparison of the complete protein sets of worm and yeast: orthology and divergence. Science **282:** 2022–2028.
8. CARROLL, S.B. et al. 1994. Pattern formation and eyespot determination in butterfly wings. Science **265:** 109–114.
9. CARROLL, S.B., S.D. WEATHERBEE & J.A. LANGELAND. 1995. Homeotic genes and the regulation and evolution of insect wing number. Nature **375:** 58–61.

Consciousness, the Brain, and Spacetime Geometry

STUART HAMEROFF

Departments of Anesthesiology and Psychology, and the Center for Consciousness Studies, University of Arizona, Tucson, Arizona, and Starlab NV/SA, Brussels, Belgium

ABSTRACT: What is consciousness? Conventional approaches see it as an emergent property of complex interactions among individual neurons; however these approaches fail to address enigmatic features of consciousness. Accordingly, some philosophers have contended that "qualia," or an experiential medium from which consciousness is derived, exists as a fundamental component of reality. Whitehead, for example, described the universe as being composed of "occasions of experience." To examine this possibility scientifically, the very nature of physical reality must be re-examined. We must come to terms with the physics of spacetime—as described by Einstein's general theory of relativity, and its relation to the fundamental theory of matter—as described by quantum theory. Roger Penrose has proposed a new physics of objective reduction: "OR," which appeals to a form of quantum gravity to provide a useful description of fundamental processes at the quantum/classical borderline.[1,2] Within the OR scheme, we consider that consciousness occurs if an appropriately organized system is able to develop and maintain quantum coherent superposition until a specific "objective" criterion (a threshold related to quantum gravity) is reached; the coherent system then self-reduces (objective reduction: OR). We contend that this type of objective self-collapse introduces non-computability, an essential feature of consciousness which distinguishes our minds from classical computers. Each OR is taken as an instantaneous event—the climax of a self-organizing process in fundamental spacetime—and a candidate for a conscious Whitehead "occasion of experience." How could an OR process occur in the brain, be coupled to neural activities, and account for other features of consciousness? We nominate a quantum computational OR process with the requisite characteristics to be occurring in cytoskeletal microtubules within the brain's neurons [3–5].

In this model, quantum-superposed states develop in microtubule subunit proteins ("tubulins") within certain brain neurons, remain coherent, and recruit more superposed tubulins until a mass–time–energy threshold (related to quantum gravity) is reached. At that point, self-collapse, or objective reduction (OR), abruptly occurs. We equate the pre-reduction, coherent superposition ("quantum computing") phase with pre-conscious processes, and each instantaneous (and non-computable) OR, or self-collapse, with a discrete conscious event. Sequences of OR events give rise to a "stream" of consciousness. Micro-

---

Portions of this paper are reprinted by permission from "Conscious events as orchestrated space-time selections" by Stuart Hameroff and Roger Penrose, Journal of Consciousness Studies **2**: 36–53 (1996).

Address for correspondence: Department of Anesthesiology, The University of Arizona Health Sciences Center, Tucson, Arizona 85724.

HYPERLINK "mailto:hameroff@u.arizona.edu" hameroff@arizona.edu
Web: HYPERLINK "http://www.consciousness.arizona.edu/hameroff"

tubule-associated proteins can "tune" the quantum oscillations of the coherent superposed states; the OR is thus self-organized, or "orchestrated" ("Orch OR"). Each Orch OR event selects (non-computably) microtubule subunit states which regulate synaptic/neural functions using classical signaling.

The quantum gravity threshold for self-collapse is relevant to consciousness, according to our arguments, because macroscopic superposed quantum states each have their own spacetime geometries.[1,2] These geometries are also superposed, and in some way "separated," but when sufficiently separated, the superposition of spacetime geometries becomes significantly unstable and reduces to a single universe state. Quantum gravity determines the limits of the instability; we contend that the actual choice of state made by Nature is noncomputable. Thus each Orch OR event is a self-selection of spacetime geometry, coupled to the brain through microtubules and other biomolecules.

If conscious experience is intimately connected with the very physics underlying spacetime structure, then Orch OR in microtubules indeed provides us with a completely new and uniquely promising perspective on the difficult problems of consciousness.

KEYWORDS: Brain; Cajal; Consciousness; Cytoskeleton; Decoherence; Dendrites; Gap junctions; General relativity; London forces; Microtubules; Microtubule-associated proteins (MAPs); Orch OR; Objective reduction; Protein conformation; Quantum computation; Quantum theory; Spacetime geometry; Tubulin; van der Waals forces

INTRODUCTION: CAJAL AND CONSCIOUSNESS

A century ago Santiago Ramón-y-Cajal showed the brain to be a large group of individual neuronal cells that communicate by synapses, an idea that eclipsed the previous view of the brain (put forth by Camillo Golgi) as a threaded-together reticulum, or "syncytium."[6] Cajal's discoveries led to the "neuron doctrine" and eventually to widespread analogies between the brain and computers, with neurons and synapses playing the roles of discrete information "bits." Cajal also discovered dendritic spines as key sites for adjustable synaptic plasticity; similarly, computer models of brain function use adjustably weighted connections to learn and remember. Cajal's work laid the foundation for the modern view of brain/mind as computer.

If Cajal were alive today, he would find that two types of neuronal circuits are generally believed to organize higher cognition and consciousness in cerebral cortex. One type of circuit involves sensory relays from thalamus to appropriate sensory cortex (visual input → visual cortex, auditory input → auditory cortex, etc.).[7-9] These thalamo-cortical projections release mostly small amino acid neurotransmitters such as glutamate at their cortical dendrite targets, for example, pyramidal cells. Other cortical projections arise from basal forebrain and midbrain, release acetylcholine and monoamines, and are more global in their cortical distribution. Woolf[10] has suggested that these global basal forebrain projections select (focus attention) and modulate sensory representations broadcast to cortical dendrites by thalamic projections, somewhat like plucking the strings of a harp.

Electrophysiological recordings reveal coherent firing of these cortical projection systems, with frequencies varying from slow EEG (2–12 Hz) to rapid "gamma oscillations" in the 30- to 70-Hz range and upward. Coherent gamma frequency oscillations (collectively known as "coherent 40 Hz") are suggested to mediate temporal

TABLE 1. Enigmatic features of consciousness and their explanations by conventional approaches and Orch OR

Enigmatic Feature of Consciousness	Conventional Approaches	Orch OR
Nature of human experience, "qualia"	"Emergence": qualia emerge at unspecified critical level of complexity of inter-neuronal interactions	Pan-protopsychism: qualia are fundamental properties of spacetime geometry accessed by Orch OR events (Whitehead's "occasions of experience")
Unitary binding, e.g., in vision, "self"	Temporal correlation, e.g., coherent 40-Hz synchrony	Unity of quantum state reduction; coherent 40-Hz-synchrony
Preconscious to conscious transition	"Emergence": consciousness emerges at unspecified critical level of complexity	Preconscious processes are quantum superpositions of possibilities (choices, perceptions) which collapse, reduce to definite classical states
Nonalgorithmic processes, non-computability (Penrose)	Not applicable	OR influenced by non-computable "Platonic" factors intrinsic to fundamental spacetime geometry
Non-deterministic "free will"	?	Experience of noncomputable influence on deterministic process
Subjective time flow; apparent time anomalies (e.g., Libet [81])	?	Time asymmetry of quantum-state collapse; atemporality of OR intervals; temporal nonlocality

binding of conscious experience and to act as the neural correlate of consciousness.[11–14]

Cajal might ask: "How are these oscillations synchronized?" Possible mechanisms include pacemaker cells broadcasting coherently (i.e., via chemical synapses) to cortex, interneurons, global network oscillations, and electrical coupling by gap junctions. Synchronization among neuronal populations dispersed widely throughout the brain occurs with zero phase lag, suggestive of electrical coupling provided by gap junctions.[15]

The role of gap junctions would be of particular interest to Cajal. In addition to chemical synapses, neurons may be electrically coupled, either by field effects or more specifically by electrotonic gap junctions, window-like portholes between adjacent neural processes (axon-dendrite, dendrite-dendrite, dendrite-glia, etc.). Gap junctions separate connected processes by only 4 nanometers and couple them electrically; neurons connected by gap junctions "behave like one giant neuron."[16]

Gap junctions are generally considered more primitive than chemical synapses, essential for embryological development, but fading into the background in mature brains. However, brain gap junctions remain active throughout adult life, and are being appreciated as more and more prevalent (though far fewer than chemical synapses). In recent years, increasing evidence points to gap junction–connected networks of cortical interneurons mediating coherent 40 Hz.[17–19] Some interneurons connect to cortical dendrites by "dual synapses": both GABAergic (inhibitory) chemical and gap junction electrical synapses.[19] It is ironic that gap junctions connect together neurons and glia, at least transiently, into a sort of reticular syncytium—Golgi's idea overthrown by Cajal's demonstration of discrete neurons and chemical synapses. Gap junction assemblies of transiently woven-together neurons have been termed "hyper-neurons" and suggested as a neural correlate of consciousness.[20]

Cajal might also wonder how computer-like neuronal oscillations produce conscious experience. Why do we feel love, hear a flute, see the redness of a rose? Philosophers call the raw components that compose conscious experience *qualia*.[21] They are one of several enigmatic features of consciousness (TABLE 1).

Proponents of computer-like neuronal oscillations account for these activities through the phenomenon of "emergence," which implies that a specific novel property occurs ("emerges") at some level in a hierarchical system, dependent on activities at both lower and higher levels of organization.[22] The brain is commonly viewed as a hierarchical system, comprising layers of organization with bottom-up, as well as top-down feedback. In the modern view Cajal's neuronal interactions are seen as the bottom level, with consciousness emerging as a novel property at an upper level of the hierarchy, for example, coherent 40-Hz oscillations. Novel properties can indeed emerge from complex interactions among simple components in a variety of systems (e.g., wetness from interactions of water molecules, music or hurricanes from vibrations of air molecules). The extrapolation is that consciousness emerges as a novel property of complex interactions among relatively simple neurons.

But Cajal might wonder why other emergent phenomena were not conscious. What critical threshold or level of complexity produced consciousness? Were neurons and synapses really that simple? Other than emergence from computer-like neuronal oscillations, what other explanations for enigmatic features of consciousness could be hidden in the brain?

SELF-SELECTION IN AN EXPERIENTIAL MEDIUM?

The problem of incorporating the phenomenon of consciousness into a scientific world-view involves finding scientific explanations of qualia, or the subjective experience of mental states.[21] On this, conventional science is still at sea. Why do we have an inner life, and what exactly is it?

As an alternative to emergence, one set of philosophical positions addressing the problem of qualia views consciousness as a fundamental component of physical reality. For example an extreme view—"panpsychism"—is that consciousness is a quality of all matter, atoms and their subatomic components having elements of consciousness.[23,24] "Mentalists" such as Leibniz [25] and Whitehead [26,27] contended that systems ordinarily considered to be physical are constructed in some sense from mental entities. Bertrand Russell[28] described "neutral monism" in which a common underlying entity, neither physical nor mental, gave rise to both. In monistic idealism, matter and mind arise from consciousness—the fundamental constituent of reality.[29] Wheeler[30] has suggested that information is fundamental to the physics of the universe. From this, Chalmers[21] proposes a double-aspect theory in which information has both physical and experiential aspects—"pan-protopsychism."

Among these positions, the philosophy of Alfred North Whitehead[26,27] may be most directly applicable. Whitehead described the ultimate concrete entities in the cosmos as being actual "occasions of experience," each bearing a quality akin to "feeling." Whitehead construes "experience" broadly—in a manner consistent with panpsychism—so that even "temporal events in the career of an electron have a kind of 'protomentality'." Whitehead's view may be considered to differ from panpsychism, however, in that his discrete "occasions of experience" can be taken to be related to "quantum events."[31] In the standard descriptions of quantum mechanics, randomness occurs in the events described as quantum state reductions—these being events that appear to take place when a quantum-level process gets magnified to a macroscopic scale.

Quantum-state reduction ("collapse of the wave function"), denoted here by the letter R,[1,2] is the random procedure that is adopted by physicists in their descriptions of the quantum measurement process. It is still a highly controversial matter whether R is to be taken as a "real" physical process or whether it is some kind of illusion and not to be regarded as a fundamental ingredient of the behavior of Nature. Our position is to take R to be indeed real—or, rather to regard it as a close approximation to an objectively real process, OR (objective reduction), which is to be a non-computable process instead of merely a random one.[1,2] In almost all physical situations, OR would come about in situations in which the random effects of the environment dominate, so OR would be virtually indistinguishable from the random R procedure that is normally adopted by quantum theorists. However, when the quantum system under consideration remains coherent and well isolated from its environment, then it becomes possible for its state to collapse spontaneously, in accordance with the OR scheme we adopt, and to behave in non-computable rather than random ways. Moreover, this OR scheme intimately involves the geometry of the physical universe at its deepest levels.

Our viewpoint is to regard experiential phenomena as also inseparable from the physical universe, and in fact to be deeply connected with the very laws that govern the physical universe. The connection is so deep, however, that we perceive only glimmerings of it in our present-day physics. One of these glimmerings, we contend, is a necessary non-computability in conscious thought processes, and we argue that this non-computability must also be inherent in the phenomenon of quantum state self-reduction—the "objective reduction" (OR) referred to above. This is the main thread of argument in *Shadows of the Mind*.[2] The argument that conscious thought, whatever other attributes it may also have, is non-computable (as follows most powerfully from certain deductions from Gödel's incompleteness theorem) grabs hold of one tiny but extremely valuable point. This means that at least some conscious states cannot be derived from previous states by an algorithmic process—a property that distinguishes human and other animal minds from computers. Non-computability *per se* does not directly address the nature of conscious experience, but it is a clue to the kind of physical activity that lies behind it. This points to OR, an underlying physical action of a completely different character from that which seems to underlie non-conscious activity. Following this clue with sensitivity and patience should ultimately lead to real progress towards understanding mental phenomena in their inward as well as outward manifestations.

In the OR description, consciousness occurs if an organized quantum system is able to isolate and sustain coherent superposition until its quantum gravity threshold for spacetime separation is met; it then self-reduces (non-computably). For consciousness to occur, self-reduction is essential, as opposed to "decoherence," reduction being triggered by the system's random environment. (In the latter case, the reduction would itself be effectively random and would lack useful non-computability, being unsuitable for direct involvement in consciousness.) We take the self-reduction to be an instantaneous event—the climax of a self-organizing process fundamental to the structure of spacetime—and apparently consistent with a Whitehead "occasion of experience."

As OR could, in principle, occur ubiquitously within many types of inanimate media, it may seem to imply a form of "panpsychism" (in which individual electrons, for example, possess an experiential quality). However, according to the principles of OR (as expounded in Penrose[1,2,32]), a single superposed electron would spontaneously reduce its state (assuming it could maintain isolation) only once in a period much longer than the present age of the universe. Only large collections of particles acting coherently in a single macroscopic quantum state could possibly sustain isolation and support coherent superposition in a time frame brief enough to be relevant to our consciousness. Thus only very special circumstances could support consciousness:

(1) High degree of coherence of a quantum state—a collective mass of particles in superposition for a time period long enough to reach threshold, and brief enough to be useful in thought processes.

(2) Ability for the OR process to be at least transiently isolated from a "noisy" environment until the spontaneous state reduction takes place. This isolation is required so that reduction is not simply random. Mass movement in the environment which entangles with the quantum state would effect a random (not non-computable) reduction.

(3) Cascades of ORs to give a "stream" of consciousness, and huge numbers of OR events taking place during the course of a lifetime.

By reaching quantum gravity threshold, each OR event has a fundamental bearing on spacetime geometry. One could say that a cascade of OR events charts an actual course of physical spacetime geometry selections. It may seem surprising that quantum gravity effects could plausibly have relevance at the physical scales relevant to brain processes, for quantum gravity is normally viewed as having only absurdly tiny influences at ordinary dimensions. However, we shall show later that this is not the case, and the scales determined by basic quantum gravity principles are indeed those that are relevant for conscious brain processes. We must ask how such an OR process could actually occur in the brain. How could it be coupled to neural activities at a high rate of information exchange; how could it account for preconscious to conscious transitions, have spatial and temporal binding, and both simultaneity and time flow?

Roger Penrose and I have nominated an OR process with the requisite characteristics occurring in cytoskeletal microtubules within the brain's neurons. In our model, microtubule-associated proteins "tune" the quantum oscillations leading to OR; we thus term the process "orchestrated objective reduction" (Orch OR).

SPACETIME: QUANTUM THEORY AND EINSTEIN'S GRAVITY

Quantum theory describes the extraordinary behavior of the matter and energy which compose our universe at a fundamental level. At the root of quantum theory is the wave/particle duality of atoms, molecules and their constituent particles. A quantum system such as an atom or subatomic particle which remains isolated from its environment behaves as a "wave of possibilities" and exists in a coherent complex-number-valued "superposition" of many possible states. The behavior of such wave-like, quantum-level objects can be satisfactorily described in terms of a state vector which evolves deterministically according to the Schrödinger equation (unitary evolution), denoted by U.

Somehow, quantum microlevel superpositions lead to unsuperposed stable structures in our macro-world. In a transition known as wave-function collapse, or reduction (R), the quantum wave of alternative possibilities reduces to a single macroscopic reality, an "eigenstate" of some appropriate operator. (This would be just one of many possible alternative eigenstates relevant to the quantum operator.) This process is invoked in the description of a macroscopic measurement, when effects are magnified from the small, quantum scale to the large, classical scale.

According to conventional quantum theory (as part of the standard "Copenhagen interpretation"), each choice of eigenstate is entirely random, weighted according to a probability value that can be calculated from the previous state according to the precise procedures of quantum formalism. This probabilistic ingredient was a feature with which Einstein, among others, expressed displeasure: "You believe in a God who plays dice and I in complete law and order"(from a letter to Max Born). Penrose[1,2] has contended that, at a deeper level of description, the choices may more accurately arise as a result of some presently unknown "non-computational" mathematical/physical (i.e., "Platonic realm") theory—that is they cannot be deduced algorithmically. Penrose argues that such non-computability is essential to consciousness, because (at least some) conscious mental activity is unattainable by computers.

It can be argued that present-day physics has no clear explanation for the cause and occurrence of wave-function collapse R. Experimental and theoretical evidence through the 1930s led quantum physicists (such as Schrödinger, Heisenberg, Dirac, von Neumann, and others) to postulate that quantum-coherent superpositions persist indefinitely in time, and would, in principle be maintained from the micro to macro levels. Or perhaps they would persist until conscious observation collapses, or reduces, the wave function (subjective reduction, or "SR"). Accordingly, even macroscopic objects, if unobserved, could remain superposed. To illustrate the apparent absurdity of this notion, Erwin Schrödinger[33] described his now-famous "cat in a box" being simultaneously both dead and alive until the box was opened and the cat observed.

As a counter to this unsettling prospect, various new physical schemes for collapse according to objective criteria (objective reduction, or "OR") have recently been proposed. According to such a scheme, the growth and persistence of superposed states could reach a critical threshold, at which collapse, or OR, rapidly occurs.[34,35] Some such schemes are based specifically on gravitational effects mediating OR.[1,2,36–41] TABLE 2 categorizes types of reduction.

TABLE 2. Descriptions of wave-function collapse

Context	Cause of collapse (reduction)	Description	Acronym
Quantum coherent superposition	No collapse	Evolution of the wave-function function (Schrödinger equation)	U
Conventional quantum theory (Copenhagen interpretation)	Environmental decoherence, measurement, conscious observation	Reduction, subjective reduction	R, SR
New physics (Penrose, 1994)	Self-collapse induced by quantum gravity	Objective reduction	OR
Consciousness	Self-collapse by OR quantum gravity in microtubules orchestrated by MAPs, etc.	Orchestrated objective reduction	Orch OR

The physical phenomenon of gravity, described to a high degree of accuracy by Isaac Newton's mathematics in 1687, has played a key role in scientific understanding. However, in 1915, Einstein created a major revolution in our scientific worldview. According to Einstein's theory, gravity plays a unique role in physics for several reasons.[1] Most particularly, these are:

(1) Gravity is the only physical quality that influences causal relationships between spacetime events.

(2) Gravitational force has no local reality, as it can be eliminated by a change in spacetime coordinates; instead, gravitational tidal effects provide a curvature for the very spacetime in which all other particles and forces are contained.

It follows from this that gravity cannot be regarded as some kind of "emergent phenomenon," secondary to other physical effects, but is a "fundamental component" of physical reality.

There are strong arguments [42,43] to suggest that the appropriate union of general relativity (Einstein's theory of gravity) with quantum mechanics—a union often referred to as "quantum gravity"—will lead to a significant change in both quantum theory and general relativity, and, when the correct theory is found, will yield a profoundly new understanding of physical reality. And although gravitational forces between objects are exceedingly weak (feebler than, for example, electrical forces by some 40 orders of magnitude), there are significant reasons for believing that gravity has a fundamental influence on the behavior of quantum systems as they evolve from the micro to the macro levels. The appropriate union of quantum gravity with biology, or at least with advanced biological nervous systems, may yield a profoundly new understanding of consciousness.

CURVED SPACETIME SUPERPOSITIONS AND OBJECTIVE REDUCTION (OR)

According to modern, accepted physical pictures, reality is rooted in three-dimensional space and a one-dimensional time, combined together into a four-dimensional spacetime. This spacetime is slightly curved, in accordance with Einstein's general theory of relativity, in a way that encodes the gravitational fields of all distributions of mass density. Each mass density effects a spacetime curvature, albeit tiny.

This is the standard picture according to classical physics. On the other hand, when quantum systems have been considered by physicists, this mass-induced tiny curvature in the structure of spacetime has been almost invariably ignored, gravitational effects having been assumed to be totally insignificant for normal problems in which quantum theory is important. Surprising as it may seem, however, such tiny differences in spacetime structure can have large effects, for they entail subtle but fundamental influences on the very rules of quantum mechanics.

Superposed quantum states for which the respective mass distributions differ significantly from one another will have spacetime geometries that correspondingly differ. Thus, according to standard quantum theory, the superposed state would have to involve a quantum superposition of these differing spacetimes. In the absence of a coherent theory of quantum gravity there is no accepted way of handling such a superposition. Indeed the basic principles of Einstein's general relativity begin to come into profound conflict with those of quantum mechanics.[4] Nevertheless, various tentative procedures have been put forward in attempts to describe such a superposition. Of particular relevance to our present proposals are the suggestions of certain authors[2, 32, 36–41, 43–45] that it is at this point that an objective quantum state reduction (OR) ought to occur, and that the rate or timescale of this process can be calculated from basic quantum gravity considerations. These particular proposals differ in certain detailed respects, and for definiteness we shall follow the specific suggestions made in Penrose.[2,32] Accordingly, the quantum superposition of significantly differing spacetimes is unstable, with a lifetime given by that timescale. Such a superposed state will decay—or "reduce"—into a single universe state, which is one or the other of the spacetime geometries involved in that superposition.

Whereas such an OR action is not a generally recognized part of the normal quantum-mechanical procedures, there is no plausible or clear-cut alternative that standard quantum theory has to offer. This OR procedure avoids the need for "multiple universes."[46,47] There is no agreement among quantum gravity experts about how else to address this problem. For the purposes of the present article, it will be assumed that a gravitationally induced OR action is indeed the correct resolution of this fundamental conundrum.

FIGURE 1 (adapted from Penrose[2] [p. 338]) schematically illustrates the way in which spacetime structure can be affected when two macroscopically different mass distributions take part in a quantum superposition. Each mass distribution gives rise to a separate spacetime, the two differing slightly in their curvatures. So long as the two distributions remain in quantum superposition, we must consider that the two spacetimes remain in superposition. Since, according to the principles of general relativity, there is no natural way to identify the points of one spacetime with corresponding points of the other, we have to consider the two as separated from one another in some sense, resulting in a kind of "blister" where the spacetime bifurcates.

A bifurcating spacetime is depicted in the lowest of the three diagrams, this being the union ("glued together version") of the two alternative spacetime histories that are depicted at the top of FIGURE 1. The initial part of each spacetime is at the lower end of each individual spacetime diagram. The bottom spacetime diagram (the bifur-

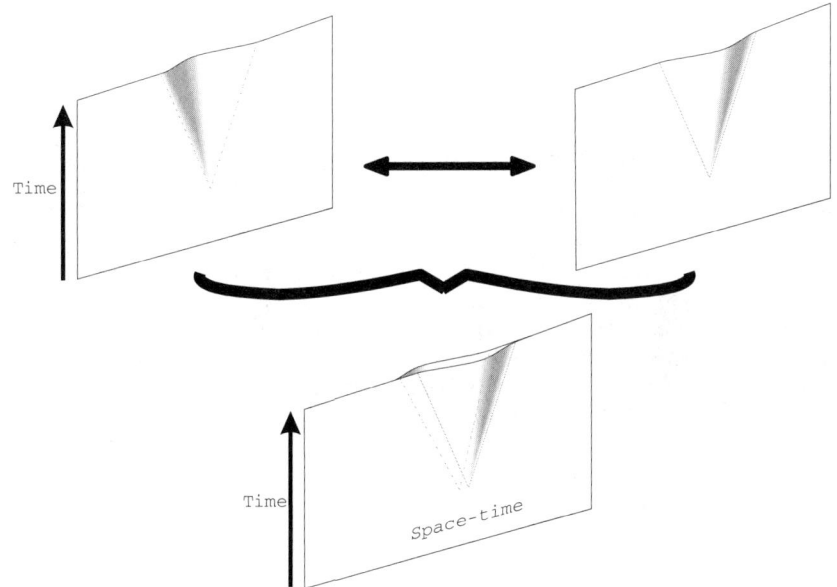

FIGURE 1. Quantum coherent superposition represented as a separation of spacetime. In the *lowest* of the three diagrams, a bifurcating spacetime is depicted as the union ("glued together version") of the two alternative spacetime histories that are depicted at the top of the figure. The bifurcating spacetime diagram illustrates two alternative mass distributions actually in quantum superposition, whereas the *top* two diagrams illustrate the two individual alternatives which take part in the superposition.

cating one) illustrates two alternative mass distributions actually in quantum superposition, whereas the top two illustrate the two individual alternatives, which take part in the superposition. The combined spacetime describes a superposition in which the alternative locations of a mass move gradually away from each other as we proceed in the upward direction in the diagram. Quantum mechanically (so long as OR has not taken place), we must think of the "physical reality" of this situation as being illustrated as an actual superposition of these two slightly differing spacetime manifolds, as indicated in the bottom diagram. As soon as OR has occurred, one of the two individual spacetimes takes over, as depicted as one of the two sheets of the bifurcation. For clarity only, the bifurcating parts of these two sheets are illustrated as being one convex and the other concave. Of course there is additional artistic license involved in drawing the spacetime sheets as two-dimensional, whereas the actual spacetime constituents are four-dimensional. Moreover, there is no significance to be attached to the imagined "three-dimensional space" within which the spacetime sheets seem to be residing. There is no "actual" higher dimensional space there, the "intrinsic geometry" of the bifurcating spacetime being all that has physical significance. When the "separation" of the two spacetime sheets reaches a critical amount, one of the two sheets "dies"—in accordance with the OR criterion—the other being the one that persists in physical reality. The quantum state thus reduces (OR), by choosing between either the "concave" or "convex" spacetime of FIGURE 1.

It should be made clear that this measure of separation is only very schematically illustrated as the "distance" between the two sheets in the lower diagram in FIGURE 1. As remarked above, there is no physically existing "ambient higher dimensional space" inside which the two sheets reside. The degree of separation between the spacetime sheets is a more abstract mathematical thing; it would be more appropriately described in terms of a symplectic measure on the space of four-dimensional metrics,[43] but the details (and difficulties) of this will not be important for us here. It may be noted, however, that this separation is a spacetime separation, not just a spatial one. Thus the time of separation contributes as does the spatial displacement. Roughly speaking, it is the product of the temporal separation T with the spatial separation S that measures the overall degree of separation, and OR takes place when this overall separation reaches the critical amount. [This critical amount would be of the order of unity, in absolute units, for which the Planck-Dirac constant $\hbar$ (Planck's constant over 2π), the gravitational constant G, and the velocity of light c, all take the value unity (cf. Penrose[2)].] Thus for small S, the lifetime T of the superposed state will be large; on the other hand, if S is large, then T will be small. To calculate S, we compute (in the Newtonian limit of weak gravitational fields) the gravitational self-energy E of the difference between the mass distributions of the two superposed states. (That is, one mass distribution counts positively and the other, negatively; see Penrose.[2,32]) The quantity S is then given by:

$$E = S$$

Thus, restoring standard units

$$T = \hbar\, E^{-1}$$

Schematically, since S represents three dimensions of displacement rather than the one dimension involved in T, we can imagine that this displacement is shared equally among each of these three dimensions of space—and this is what has been depicted in FIGURE 1. However, it should be emphasized that this is for pictorial purposes only, the appropriate rule being the one given above. These two equations relate the mass distribution, time of coherence, and spacetime separation for a given OR event. If, as some philosophers contend, experience is contained in spacetime as self-organizing processes in that experiential medium, OR events are candidates for consciousness. But where in the brain, and how, could coherent superposition and OR occur? Quantum computation uses quantum superposition—perhaps a particular type of quantum computation occurs in the brain.

Proposals for quantum computation rely on superposed states implementing multiple computations simultaneously, in parallel, according to quantum linear superposition.[48–51] Rather than "bits" of 1 or 0 as in classical computers, quantum computers utilize "qubits" of superposition of both 1 *and* 0. The qubits interact and compute by quantum entanglement, effecting near-infinite massive parallelism and significant advantages over classical computers. A number of technological systems aimed at realizing these proposals have been suggested and are being evaluated as possible substrates for quantum computers.[52,53] A process of quantum computation/superposition in the brain with reduction by Penrose OR would be an ideal candidate for consciousness.

MICROTUBULES

Are there quantum computation and qubits in the brain? A number of sites and various types of quantum interactions have been proposed. We strongly favor proteins as qubits, and in particular microtubules, as assemblies of entangled qubit proteins, but various organelles and biomolecular structures including clathrins, myelin (glial cells), presynaptic vesicular grids,[54] and neural membrane proteins[55] might also participate.

Proteins perform a myriad of cell functions through changes in their shape, or conformation. Conformational dynamics of proteins are regulated by quantum mechanical dipole couplings called van der Waals London forces.[56] The influential London forces seem to act in non-polar regions within proteins called hydrophobic pockets, where general anesthetic gases also exert their effects.[57] Proteins involved in anesthetic effects in erasing consciousness include receptors for acetylcholine, serotonin, GABA and glycine, as well as microtubules and other proteins. Anesthetics bind in hydrophobic pockets within these proteins by their own London forces, apparently preventing normally occurring London forces necessary for consciousness and protein conformational dynamics.[58] As London forces are quantum mechanical, the involved electrons in the absence of anesthetic (conscious state) may be expected to be in quantum superposition, indicating the protein may also be in quantum superposition of possible alternative conformational states. Quantum interactions have also been implicated in the problem of protein folding. Roitberg *et al.*[59] showed

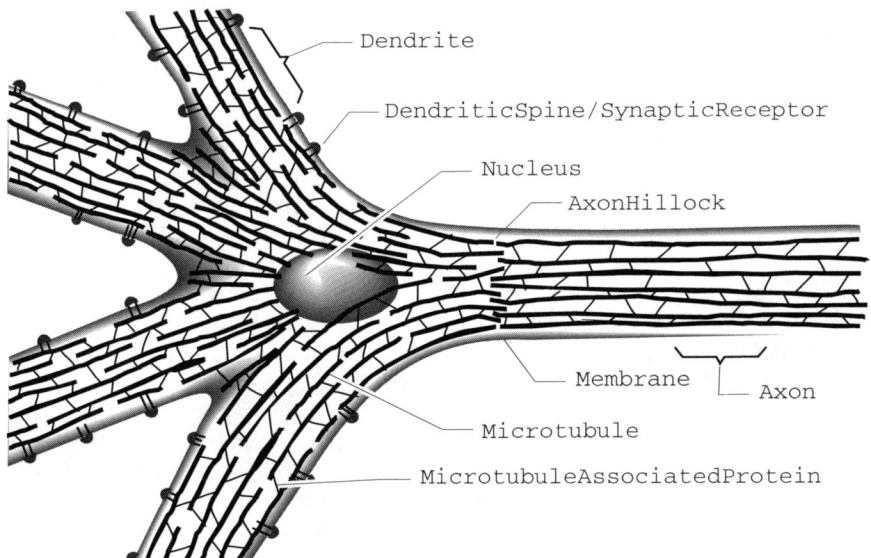

FIGURE 2. Schematic diagram of central region of neuron (distal axon and dendrites not shown), showing parallel arrayed microtubules interconnected by MAPs. Microtubules in axons are lengthy and continuous, whereas in dendrites they are interrupted and of mixed polarity. Linking proteins connect microtubules to membrane proteins including receptors on dendritic spines.

functional protein vibrations, which depend on quantum effects centered in two hydrophobic phenylalanine residues, and Tejada et al.[60] have evidence to suggest quantum coherent states exist in the protein ferritin. If proteins are qubits, organized geometric assemblies of qubit proteins such as microtubules could serve as quantum computers.

Properties of brain structures suitable for quantum coherent superposition, OR and relevant to consciousness might include: (1) high prevalence; (2) functional importance (for example regulating neural connectivity and synaptic function); (3) periodic, crystal-like lattice dipole structure with long range order; (4) ability to be transiently isolated from external interaction/observation; (5) functionally coupled to quantum-level events; (6) hollow, cylindrical (possible waveguide); and (7) suitable for information processing. Membranes, membrane proteins, synapses, DNA and other types of structures have some, but not all, of these characteristics. Cytoskeletal microtubules appear to qualify in all respects.

Interiors of living cells, including the brain's neurons, are spatially and dynamically organized by self-assembling protein networks: the cytoskeleton. Within neurons, the cytoskeleton establishes neuronal form, and maintains and regulates synaptic connections. Its major components are microtubules, hollow cylindrical polymers of individual proteins known as tubulin. Microtubules (MTs) are interconnected by linking proteins (microtubule-associated proteins: MAPs) to other microtubules and cell structures to form cytoskeletal lattice networks (FIG. 2).

MTs are hollow cylinders 25 nanometers (nm) in diameter whose lengths vary and may be quite long within some nerve axons. MT cylinder walls comprise 13 longitudinal protofilaments which are each a series of subunit proteins known as tubulin (FIG. 3). Each tubulin subunit is a polar, 8-nm dimer which consists of two slightly different 4-nm monomers (alpha and beta tubulin). Tubulin dimers are dipoles, with surplus negative charges localized toward alpha monomers,[61] and within MTs are arranged in a hexagonal lattice which is slightly twisted, resulting in helical pathways that repeat every 3, 5, 8, 13 and other numbers of rows (Fibonacci series).

Tubulin is a peanut-shaped dimer which can undergo conformational changes, including a 30-degree hinge-like bending at monomer interfaces.[62] Three-dimensional structural analysis of tubulin by electron crystallography[63] shows large hydrophobic, non-polar pockets in which quantum interactions (van der Waals London forces: instantaneous couplings of electron pairs) can govern protein movement. Cooperative dynamics due to ferroelectric, spin glass, and Fröhlich coherence effects have been proposed in microtubule lattices to serve information processing roles.[64-66]

While microtubules have traditionally been considered as purely structural components, recent evidence demonstrates mechanical signaling and communication functions.[67-70] Microtubules interact with membrane structures and activities by linking proteins (e.g., fodrin, ankyrin) and "second messenger" chemical signals. In neurons, microtubules self-assemble to extend axons and dendrites and form synaptic connections; microtubules then help maintain and regulate synaptic strengths responsible for learning and cognitive functions. Within dendritic spines, dynamics of actin gelation regulate spine shape, thus adjusting synaptic efficacy, a critical factor in cognition.[71-73] (For a more complete description of the role of microtubules and other cytoskeletal structures in cognitive functions, see Refs. 4 and 74–76).

How might information processing occur in the cytoskeleton? Collective Fröhlich excitations of tubulin subunits within microtubules have been suggested to support

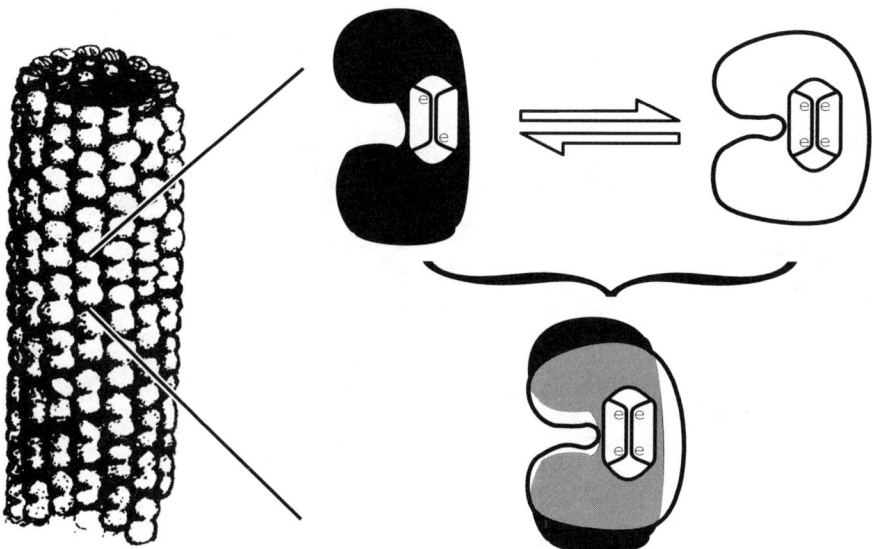

FIGURE 3. *Left:* Microtubule (MT) structure: a hollow tube 25 nanometers in diameter, consisting of 13 columns of tubulin dimers arranged in a skewed hexagonal lattice.[2] *Right top:* Each tubulin molecule may switch between two (or more) conformations, coupled to London forces in a hydrophobic pocket. *Right bottom:* Each tubulin can also exist in quantum superposition of both conformational states.[4]

computation and information processing via classical "cellular automata" behavior, coherently pumped by metabolic processes.[64–66] Molecular-level information processing can account for regulation of intra-neuronal activities including synaptic function, learning, and memory. However, to address the enigmatic features of consciousness, a form of quantum computation with objective reduction requires quantum superposition at the level of tubulin proteins.

QUANTUM COMPUTATION IN MICROTUBULES? THE PENROSE–HAMEROFF ORCH OR MODEL

In Refs. 4 and 5 and in summary form,[3] we present a model (Orch OR) whose key points are summarized here:

(1) Conformational states of individual tubulin proteins in brain microtubules are sensitive to internal quantum events (e.g., London forces in hydrophobic pockets) and able to cooperatively interact with other tubulins in classical "automata" computation, which regulates and interacts with chemical synapses, axon hillock, and other neural membrane activities (e.g., see FIGURE 4).

(2) Quantum superposition of London forces leads to quantum coherent superposition of tubulin conformation supporting quantum computation in micro-

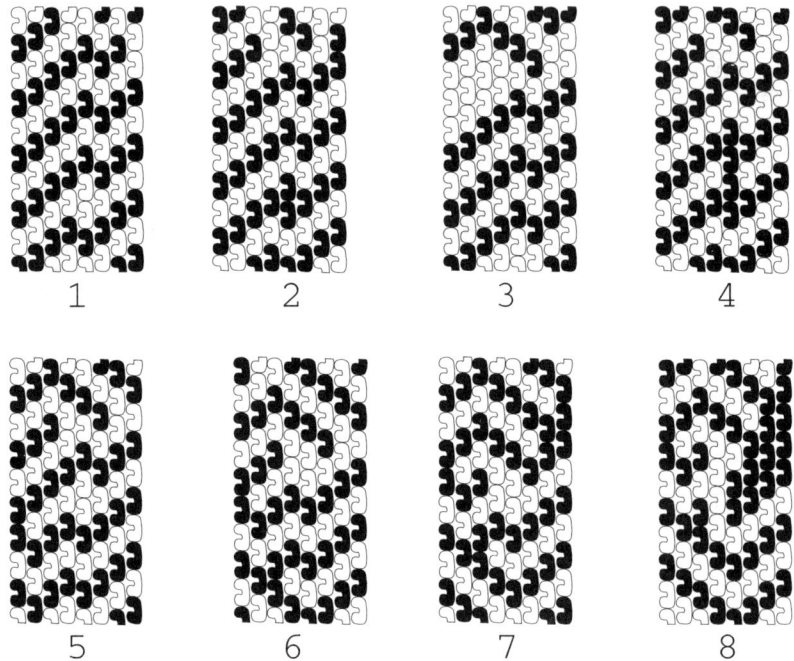

FIGURE 4. Microtubule automaton simulation.[65] Black and white tubulins correspond to states shown in FIGURE 3. Eight-nanosecond time steps of a segment of one microtubule are shown in "classical computing" mode in which patterns move, evolve, interact, and lead to emergence of new patterns.

tubules. In this phase, quantum computation among tubulins evolves linearly according to the Schrödinger equation (quantum microtubule automata).

(3) Quantum states in microtubules avoid random environmental decoherence by mechanisms that include actin gelation, coherent pumping, ordered water, a condensed charge phase surrounding MT, and topological quantum error correction. Enhanced surface area in actin gelation ("gel") leads to ordering of water, and isolates microtubules during the quantum phase; actin depolymerization leads to a liquid (solution: "sol") state for classical communication (see the section DECOHERENCE AND BIOLOGICAL FEASIBILITY OF QUANTUM STATES IN THE BRAIN).

(4) The proposed quantum superposition/computation phase in neural microtubules corresponds to pre-conscious (implicit) processing, which continues until the threshold for Penrose objective reduction is reached. Objective reduction (OR)—a discrete event—then occurs (FIGS. 5–7), and post-OR tubulin states (chosen non-computably) proceed by classical microtubule automata to regulate synapses and other neural membrane activities. Transitions from pre-conscious possibilities into unitary choices or experiences may be seen as quantum computations in which quantum superpositions of

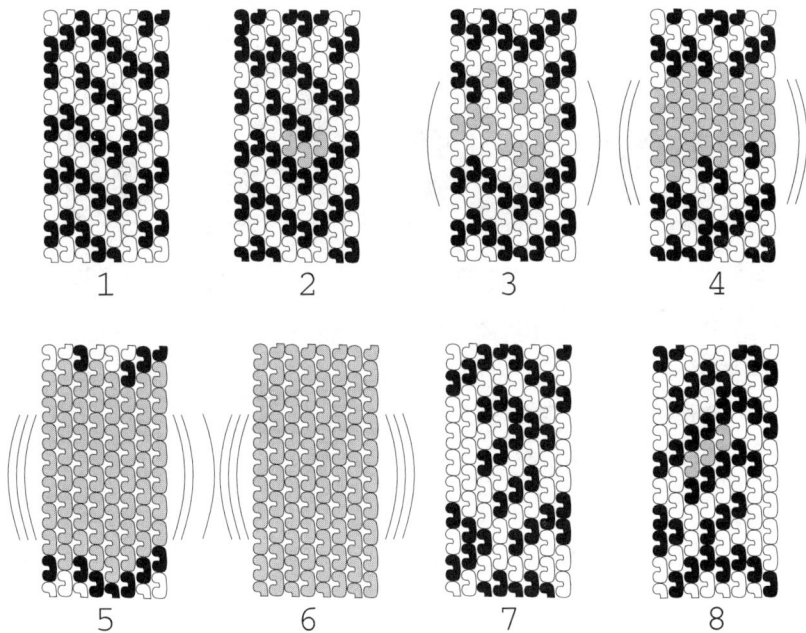

FIGURE 5. Microtubule automaton sequence simulation in which classical computing (step 1) leads to emergence of quantum coherent superposition (steps 2–6) in certain (gray) tubulins due to pattern resonance. Step 6 (in coherence with other microtubule tubulins) meets critical threshold related to quantum gravity for self-collapse (Orch OR). Consciousness (Orch OR) occurs in the step 6 to 7 transition. Step 7 represents the eigenstate of mass distribution of the collapse, which evolves by classical computing automata to regulate neural function. Quantum coherence begins to re-emerge in step 8.

multiple states abruptly collapse (reduce) to definite states at each "conscious moment."

(5) Orch OR events are proposed to be conscious (to have qualia, experience) because proto-conscious qualia are fundamental, embedded at the Planck scale. Each Orch OR event selects a particular configuration of fundamental geometry and a particular set of experiential qualia.

(6) Microtubule quantum states link to those in other neurons and glia by tunneling through gap junctions (or quantum coherent photons traversing membranes[77,78]). Gap junction interneurons mediate coherent 40-Hz oscillations, and enable macroscopic quantum states in networks of gap junction–connected cells ("hyper-neurons" [20]) throughout large brain volumes (FIG. 8).

(7) Probabilities and possibilities for pre-conscious quantum superpositions are influenced by biological feedback including attachments of microtubule-associated proteins (MAPs), which tune and "orchestrate" quantum oscillations and provide input/output during classical ("sol") phase. We thus term the self-tuning OR process in microtubules "orchestrated" objective reduction or Orch OR.

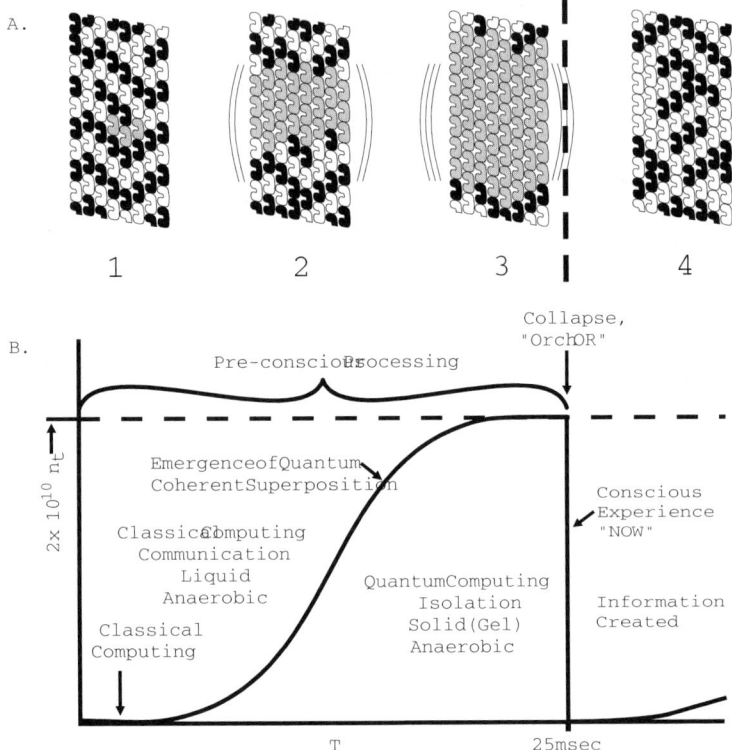

FIGURE 6. An Orch OR event. (**A**) Microtubule simulation in which classical computing (step 1) leads to emergence of quantum coherent superposition (and quantum computing [steps 2 and 3]) in certain (gray) tubulins. Step 3 (in coherence with other microtubule tubulins) meets critical threshold related to quantum gravity for self-collapse (Orch OR). A conscious event (Orch OR) occurs in the step 3 to 4 transition. Tubulin states in step 4 are noncomputably chosen in the collapse and evolve by classical computing to regulate neural function. (**B**) Schematic graph of proposed quantum coherence (number of tubulins) emerging versus time in microtubules. Area under curve connects superposed mass energy E with collapse time T in accordance with $E = \hbar/T$. E may be expressed as N_t, the number of tubulins whose mass separation (and separation of underlying space time) for time T will self-collapse. For $T = 25$ msec (e.g., 40-Hz oscillations), $N_t = 2 \times 10^{10}$ tubulins.

(8) Orch OR events may be of variable intensity and duration of pre-conscious processing. Calculating from $E = \hbar/T$ for a pre-conscious processing time of, e.g., $T = 25$ msec (40 Hz), E is roughly the superposition/separation of 2×10^{10} tubulins. For $T = 100$ msec (alpha EEG) E would involve 5×10^9 tubulins. For $T = 500$ msec as a typical pre-conscious processing time for low-intensity stimuli[81]), E is equivalent to 10^9 tubulins. Thus 2×10^{10} tubulins maintained in isolated quantum coherent superposition for 25 msec (or 5×10^9 tubulins for 100 msec, or 10^9 tubulins for 500 msec, etc.) will self-collapse (Orch OR) and elicit a conscious event. Faster, larger superpositions

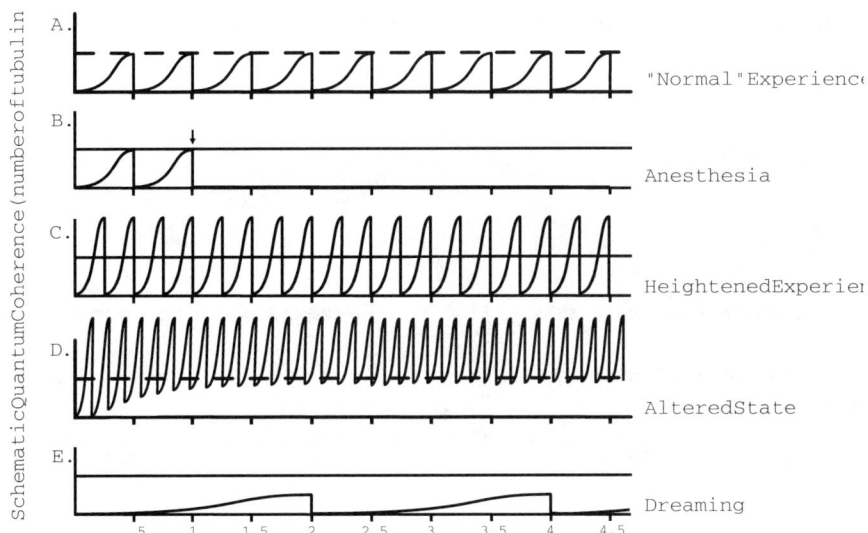

FIGURE 7. Quantum superposition/entanglement in microtubules for five states related to consciousness. Area under each curve is equivalent in all cases. (**A**) Normal 40-Hz experience: as in FIGURE 6. (**B**) Anesthesia: anesthetics bind in hydrophobic pockets and prevent electron delocalizability and coherent superposition. (**C**) Heightened experience: increased sensory experience input (for example) increases rate of emergence of quantum superposition. Orch OR threshold is reached faster, at higher intensity of experience, and more frequently. (**D**) Altered state: even greater rate of emergence of quantum superposition due to sensory input and other factors promoting quantum state (e.g., meditation, psychedelic drug, etc.). Predisposition to quantum state results in baseline shift and collapse so that conscious experience merges with normally subconscious quantum computing mode. (**E**) Dreaming: prolonged subthreshold quantum superposition time.

may also occur, but without electrophysiological consequences. For example, sequences of thousands of $T = 10^{-6}$ sec (microsecond) OR events, each involving $\sim 10^{15}$ tubulins, may lead to climactic 25-msec OR events which do influence neurophysiology

(9) Each brain neuron is estimated to contain about 10^7 tubulins.[82] If, say, 10 percent of each neuron's tubulins became coherent, then Orch OR of tubulins within roughly 20,000 (gap junction–connected) neurons would be required for a 25-msec conscious event, 5,000 neurons for a 100-msec event, or 1,000 neurons for a 500-msec event, etc. Microsecond events would involve roughly one billion neurons, 1% of brain capacity.

(10) Each instantaneous Orch OR event binds superposed information encoded in microtubules whose net displacement reaches threshold at a particular moment: a variety of different modes of information is thus bound into a "now" event. As quantum state reductions are irreversible in time, cascades of Orch OR events present a forward flow of time and "stream of consciousness."

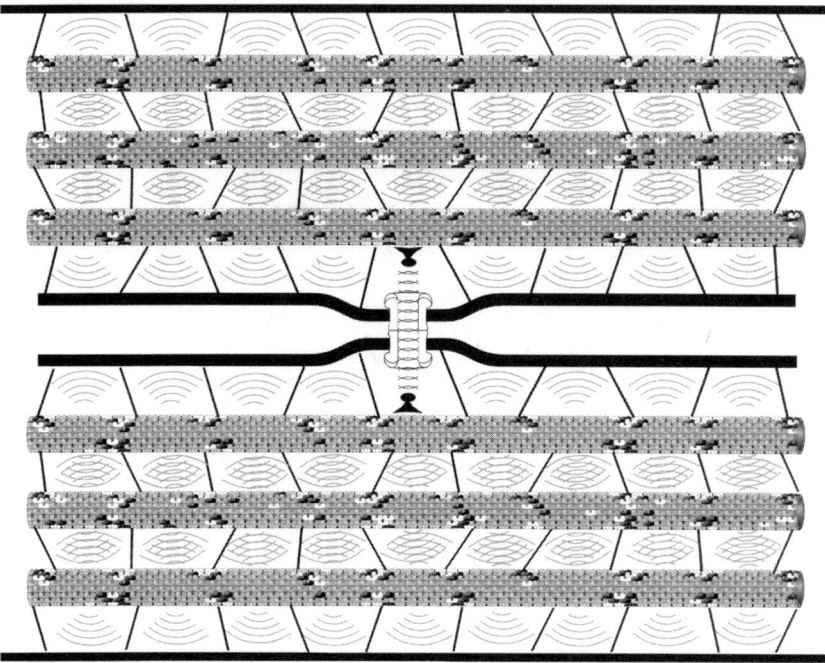

FIGURE 8. Schematic representation of a gap junction connecting two dendrites in which microtubules are in quantum superposition/quantum computation "tuned" by interconnecting MAP proteins, as suggested in the Penrose–Hameroff Orch OR model. On either side of the gap junction, dendritic lamellar bodies[79,80] containing mitochondria may act as tunneling diodes to convey the quantum state between the dendrites.

DECOHERENCE AND BIOLOGICAL FEASIBILITY OF QUANTUM STATES IN THE BRAIN

The Orch OR model and other quantum approaches have significant explanatory potential for enigmatic features of consciousness (TABLE 1). However, technological quantum devices often require extreme cold to avoid thermal decoherence by environmental interactions which would otherwise disrupt quantum coherent superposition. As brain environment is considered "warm, wet, and noisy," survival of superposition over times relevant to neurophysiology (e.g., 25 msec for 40 Hz) may seem unlikely. Is the brain truly "warm, wet, and noisy"?

Yes, the brain is *warm*, but lasers maintain quantum coherence at warm temperatures by incoherent pumping. In the Orch OR model biochemical energy and heat may collectively pump tubulin dipoles and surrounding water[83,84] to produce coherence and avoid decoherence. In any case technological quantum devices are operating at ever-increasing temperatures, including room-temperature magnetic quantum cellular automata.[85]

Is the brain *wet*? The brain is 60 percent water, but interiors of neurons and all of our cells exist in alternating phases of (1) liquid (solution, "sol") and (2) solid (gelatinous, "gel"). The solid, gel phase is caused by polymerization of the cytoskeletal protein actin. The particular character of actin gel depends on the specific type of actin cross-linking. Of the various types of gels, some are viscoelastic, but others (e.g., those induced by the actin cross-linker avidin) are solid and can be deformed by an applied force without any response.[86] Cycles of actin gelation/solution can be quite rapid, occurring for example at 40 Hz. In neurons cycles of actin gelation/solution correlate with release of neurotransmitter vesicles from presynaptic axon terminals.[87,88] In dendritic spines, whose synaptic efficacy mediates learning, rapid actin gelation and motility mediate synaptic function, and are sensitive to anesthetics.[71–73]

Even in the "sol," or liquid phase of cytoplasm, water within cells is not truly liquid and random. Water molecules form various transient forms, and water within cells is to a large extent "ordered," and plays the role of an active component rather than inert background solvent. Cytoskeleton including actin gel binds water, and neutron diffraction studies indicate several layers of ordered water on such surfaces, with several additional layers of partially ordered water.[89–91] Within a dense actin gel water may be completely ordered.

Quantum field theorists have historically proposed that ordering of cytoplasmic water leads to biological quantum states through spontaneous symmetry breaking and generation of bosons. Specifically it has been suggested that water in the hollow microtubule core and on MT surfaces is ordered by microtubule dynamics leading to spontaneous symmetry breaking and generation of evanescent photons, "super-radiance" and "self-induced transparency" of photons in microtubule cores.[78]

Charged surfaces (cytoskeleton, membranes) also attract soluble ions of the opposite charge, leading to plasma-like layers (Debye layer) which can have quantum properties, and/or quantum isolation properties. At precisely physiological pH there exists a plasma sleeve around microtubules that could serve to isolate MT quantum processes from thermal decoherence.[92]

Is the brain *noisy*? Intracellular noise, presumably from thermal energy of water, would be obviated by coherent pumping and ordered water. Apparent electrical noise as manifest in electrophysiological recordings may be something other than noise. Electrophysiological recordings of single cell events detect fluctuations in baseline voltage over various time scales, but eliminate them by signal averaging. The assumption is that background fluctuations are meaningless noise. However, this background "noise" has been found to correlate over wide regions of brain, suggesting it isn't noise at all, but some ongoing activity of unknown etiology that could indicate underlying order or coherence.[93,94] The brain may not be as inhospitable to quantum states as generally believed.

Recently physicist Max Tegmark [95] attempted to "refute" the possibility of quantum computation in brain microtubules (MT) on the basis of calculated decoherence times of 10^{-13} sec by ions in the brain's milieu. Tegmark determines the time to decoherence τ due to the long range electromagnetic effects of an environmental ion to be:

$$\tau \cong \frac{4\pi\varepsilon_0 a^3 \sqrt{mkT}}{Nq_e^2 s}$$

where τ is the decoherence time, ε_0 is the tissue dielectric permittivity (estimated at 10 to 100), a is the distance from the microtubule quantum state to the nearest decohering ion, m is the mass of the decohering ion, k is Boltzmann's constant, T is brain temperature (37 degrees centigrade), N is the number of elementary charges in the superpositioned tubulin mass (18), q is the charge of an electron, and s is the maximal "separation" between the positions of the tubulin mass in the alternative geometries of the quantum superposition. Several problems appear to invalidate Tegmark's approach.

A full reply to Tegmark is available,[96] of which key points are summarized here:

Tegmark's formula for decoherence has the (root of) temperature in the numerator. Consider the limiting cases for Tegmark's formula: as temperature goes to absolute zero, decoherence times go to zero, and as the temperature becomes impossibly high, decoherence times become long. As this is the opposite of what actually occurs, the formula itself is highly suspect.

The quantum microtubule model which Tegmark attacks is not the Orch OR model, nor any other previously published model, but one of his own invention. Tegmark imagines a soliton traveling along a microtubule, with the soliton separated from itself (s in Tegmark's formula) by 24 nanometers ($\sim 10^{-8}$ m). This is apparently a quantum version of a purely classical soliton model put forth by Sataric et al., in 1993.[97] In the Orch OR model the separations s is at the level of atomic nuclei within each tubulin, hence s is in femtometers, 10^{-15} m. This discrepancy accounts for an erroneous 10^{-7} reduction in Tegmark's calculated decoherence time.

Tegmark also mistakenly considers microtubules as lines of charge, rather than lines of dipoles, thus neglecting permittivity, another false 10^{-2} to 10^{-1} reduction in his calculated decoherence time. Thus correctly applying Tegmark's (albeit disputed) formula to Orch OR (appropriately altering separation s and permittivity ε_0) changes the calculated decoherence time τ from Tegmark's 10^{-13} sec to a range of 10^{-5} to 10^{-4} sec.

The target for decoherence time in the Orch OR model is the time scale for recognized neural events in the range of 10^{-2} to 10^{-1} sec (e.g., coherent 40 Hz, alpha EEG, evoked potentials, etc). There are two possible ways in the framework of the Orch OR model to sufficiently avoid decoherence. In the more direct approach, decoherence must be avoided (coherence must be sustained) for tens to hundreds of milliseconds so that threshold is reached for Penrose objective reduction as described by $E = \hbar/T$ in neurophysiologically relevant time.

In a second approach the critical time for avoidance of decoherence is given by a "collective" coherent pumping mechanism, the manner in which lasers manifest quantum coherence at warm temperatures. If the microtubule system including water molecules ordered at cytoskeletal surfaces is indeed coherently pumped by biochemical energy, along the lines of the mechanism proposed by Fröhlich, then this cohering mechanism will repeatedly refresh the environment and avoid decoherence. Coherent oscillations in the nanosecond time scale would be expected, so the target for avoiding decoherence would be 10^{-9} sec.

This type of collective effect has been suggested to protect quantum states from thermal decoherence in high-temperature superconductors.[98]

The target for sustained coherence in Orch OR is thus either 10^{-9} sec, or 10^{-2} to 10^{-1} sec, depending on whether or not Fröhlich-like coherent pumping[83,84] is required. Tegmark's equation correctly applied to the Orch OR model would predict decoherence time τ of 10^{-5} to 10^{-4} sec. This is long enough for the Orch OR model with Fröhlich oscillations, and long enough for microsecond Orch OR events, a sequence of which would lead to neurophysiological events.

The other critical parameter in Tegmark's equation is a^3, in which a is the distance from the quantum state to the nearest decohering ion (in quantum computing terminology: the "decoherence-free zone"). Tegmark uses a of 24 nanometers, though he calculates it from the center of the microtubule, meaning roughly 12 nanometers from the microtubule surface.

As previously described, several strategies may have evolved to isolate and sustain quantum states in microtubules, which would modify a. In addition to coherent pumping these include ordered water at cytoskeletal surfaces, ionic "double layers," gelation/encasement, and quantum error correction codes.

When encased in actin gelation, the water-ordering surfaces of microtubules are within a few nanometers of actin surfaces, which also order water. Thus a bundle of microtubules transiently encased in actin gelation may be isolated through the entire bundle, with a thus equal to about half the width of the bundle, hundreds of nanometers. As a^3 appears in the numerator of Tegmark's equation, an increase in a of one order of magnitude (i.e., from Tegmark's 24 nm to several hundred nm of a microtubule-actin bundle) increases decoherence time three orders of magnitude. Applied to the previously corrected values of 10^{-5} to 10^{-4} sec, this results in a microtubule bundle decoherence time of 10^{-2} to 10^{-1} sec, precisely that required for Orch OR.

Based on quantum technology, the particular structural geometry of microtubules may serve to avoid decoherence in several ways. In high-temperature superconductors, stable quantum states are promoted by two-dimensional (as opposed to either one-dimensional or three-dimensional) lattice structures, which provide a "delicate balance between order and fluctuations."[99] Microtubules are two-dimensional lattice structures wrapped into cylinders.

Technological quantum computing is, in general, feasible because of the use of quantum error correction codes which may be facilitated by topologies—for instance, toroidal surfaces[100, 101] in which global, topological degrees of freedom are protected from local errors and decoherence. Topological quantum computation and error correction have been suggested in microtubules.[102] The microtubule lattice features a series of helical winding patterns which repeat on longitudinal protofilaments at 3, 5, 8, 13, 21 and higher numbers of subunit dimers (tubulins). The repeat intervals of these particular winding patterns match the Fibonacci series and define attachment sites of microtubule-associated proteins (MAPs). These same global patterns are found in simulations of self-localized phonon excitations in microtubules,[103] suggesting that topological global states in microtubules may be resistant to local decoherence.[102] Penrose[104] suggested that the Fibonacci patterns on microtubules may be optimal for error correction.

Another possible feature promoting quantum coherence would be involvement of nuclear spin in protein conformational regulation. Nuclear spin coherence is quite stable, lasting for seconds. Superposition separation in Orch OR occurs at the level of atomic nuclei, where nuclear spins may couple London forces to protein conformation.[105] A new method for magnetic resonance imaging (MRI) of the brain is based on detection of nuclear spin quantum coherence. It turns out that quantum dipole couplings of water and protein nuclear spins separated by distances ranging from 10 microns to 1 millimeter yield detectable MRI signals correlating with conscious activity.[106,107] The quantum coherence is induced by the MRI magnet and excitation, and so is basically an induced artifact. However, the fact that the brain can support detectable quantum coherence of any kind over such distances is surprising to most observers, and supports the possibility of endogenous, intrinsic quantum coherence.

Conditions for Orch OR require spread, or entanglement of the quantum state, among microtubules in, say, 2×10^{10} tubulins, or roughly 20,000 neurons distributed throughout the brain for a 40-Hz, 25-msec event.

Assuming that isolation is achieved in microtubule bundles within neurons, how could the quantum state traverse cell membranes and/or synapses? It has been proposed that quantum optical phonons generated by microtubule dynamics result in 50-micron coherent zones.[78] We suggest another possibility—that gap junctions may enable the spread via quantum tunneling. Gap junctions separate cytoplasm within connected neuronal and/or glial processes by only 4 nm, within range for quantum tunneling. Specific mitochondria-containing organelles (dendritic lamellar bodies) are found on opposite sides of gap junctions between dendrites, attached to microtubules by connecting proteins[79,80] (FIG. 8). (Dendritic-dendritic processing has been cited as a possible primary site of consciousness.[108,109]) Perhaps tunneling between pairs of dendritic lamellar bodies permits spread of microtubule quantum states throughout "hyper-neurons,"[20] (e.g., 20,000 Cajal neurons momentarily unified by gap junctions)

How would quantum hyper-neurons interact in terms of chemical synapses? Woolf[110,111] argues that acetylcholine binding to dendritic receptors results in MAP2 decoupling from microtubules, and suggests that the isolation facilitates microtubule quantum states. A possible scenario is then: synaptic event → MAP2–MT decoupling → actin gelation → quantum isolation → quantum coherent superposition → Orch OR.

CONCLUSION: PERCEPTION/VOLITION, EVOLUTION, AND SUBJECTIVE EXPERIENCE

The Orch OR model has significant explanatory potential for the enigmatic features of consciousness (TABLE 1). A main tenet in Orch OR is that pre-conscious processing is equivalent to the quantum superposition phase of quantum computation. Potential possibilities interact in the pre-conscious, quantum superposition phase and then abruptly self-collapse: a moment of conscious awareness, a slight quake/rearrangement in spacetime geometry. As quantum state reductions are irreversible, cascades of such Orch OR events present a forward flow of subjective time and "stream of consciousness" which charts a course through fundamental spacetime geometry.

Perception/Volition

The Orch OR scheme is applicable to cognitive activities. Functions like face recognition and volitional choice may require a series of conscious events arriving at

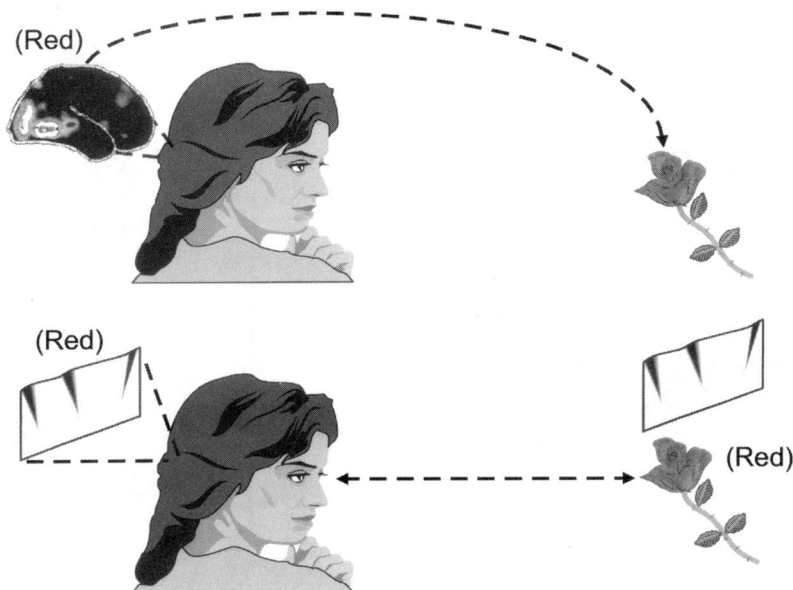

FIGURE 9. Are mental qualia like the redness of a rose pattern in fundamental spacetime geometry?

intermediate solutions, but for the purposes of illustration we shall consider single events.

Imagine you briefly see a familiar woman's face. Is she Amy, Betty, or Carol? Possibilities may superpose in a quantum computation. For example during pre-conscious processing, quantum computation occurs with information (Amy, Betty, Carol) in the form of "qubits" of superposed states of microtubule tubulin subunits within groups of neurons. As threshold for objective reduction is reached, an instantaneous conscious event occurs. The superposed tubulin qubits reduce to definite states, becoming bits. Now, you recognize that she is Carol! (an immense number of possibilities could be superposed in a human brain's 10^{19} tubulins).

In a volitional act possible choices may be superposed. Suppose for example you are selecting dinner from a menu. During pre-conscious processing, shrimp, sushi, and pasta are superposed in a quantum computation. As threshold for objective reduction is reached, the quantum state reduces to a single classical state. A choice is made. You'll have sushi! In both perception and volition, non-computable influences may be exerted which reflect Platonic influences encoded in fundamental spacetime geometry.[1,2]

Evolution

Where in the course of evolution may consciousness have evolved? The Orch OR model implies that an organism able to sustain quantum coherence among, for example, 10^9 tubulins for 500 msec would be capable of having a conscious experi-

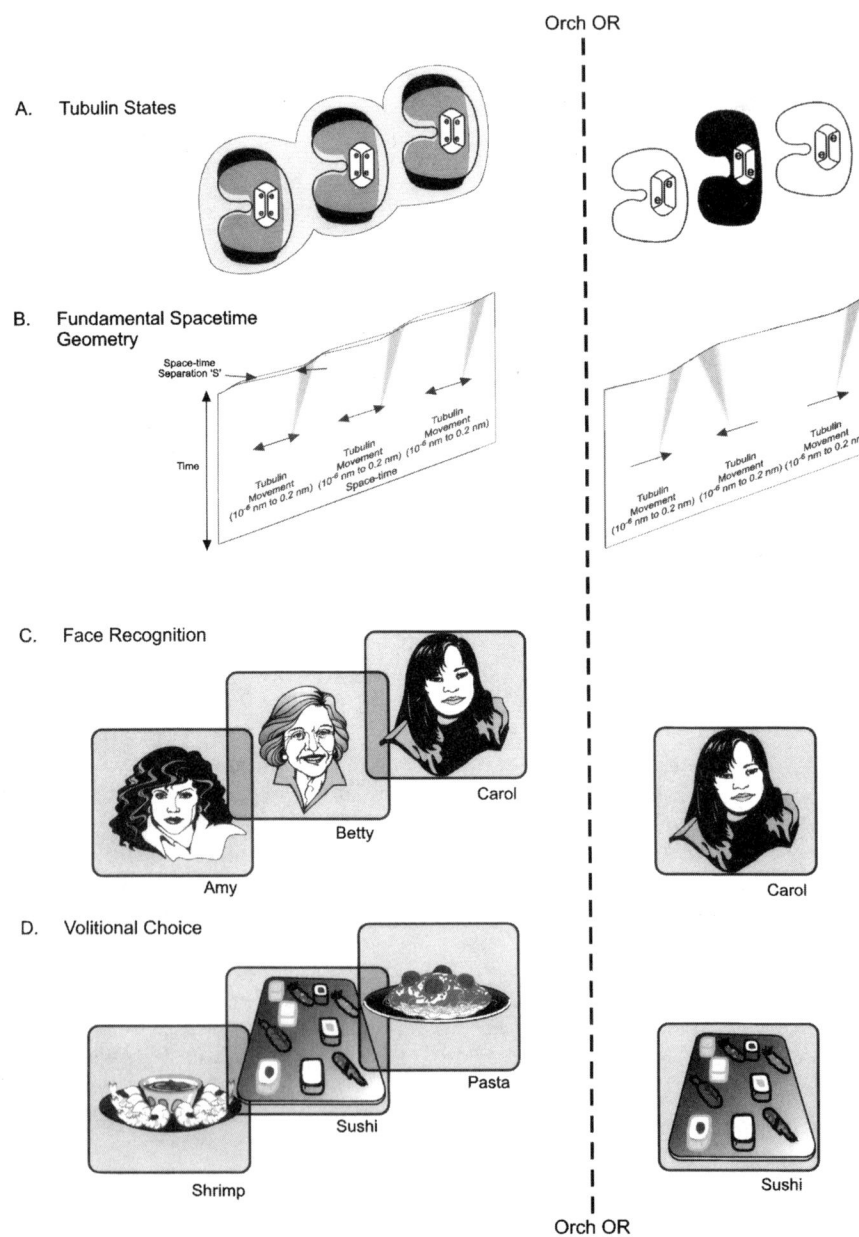

FIGURE 10. *See following page for caption.*

ence. More tubulins coherent for a briefer period, or fewer for a longer period ($E = \hbar/T$) will also have conscious events.

Human brains may be capable of, for example, 2×10^{10} tubulin, 25-msec experiences, but what about simpler organisms? The place of consciousness in evolution is unknown, but the actual course of evolution itself may offer a clue. Fossil records indicate that animal species as we know them today including conscious humans all arose from a burst of evolutionary activity some 540 million years ago (the "Cambrian explosion"). MT-based cilia and organelles were apparently common in primitive vision and sensory systems, and organisms present at the beginning of the Cambrian explosion included small worms and urchins whose modern descendants of similar form and size include the well-studied nematode *C. elegans*, and the spiny urchin *Echinosphaerum*. *C. elegans* has 307 neurons (about 3×10^9 tubulins) and *Echinosphaerum* has 3×10^9 tubulins in each of its spiny axonemes.[112] Quantum coherent assemblies of this number of tubulins would reach threshold for objective reduction in about 133 msec, a not unreasonable duration for isolation and avoidance of decoherence by actin gelation and ordered water. Perhaps the onset of rudimentary consciousness by Orch OR in these simple organisms precipitated the Cambrian explosion?[113]

Subjective Experience

In our approach experiential "qualia" derive from pan-protopsychism—qualia are patterns in fundamental spacetime geometry accessed and selected by the Orch OR process. Our view also suggests that consciousness is a sequence of discrete events. It may be interesting to compare our considerations with subjective viewpoints that have been expressed with regard to the nature of the progression of conscious experience. For example, support for consciousness consisting of sequences of individual, discrete events is found in Buddhism: trained meditators describe distinct "flickerings" in their experience of reality.[114] Buddhist texts portray consciousness as "momentary collections of mental phenomena," and as "distinct, unconnected and impermanent moments which perish as soon as they arise." Each conscious moment successively becomes, exists, and disappears—its existence is instantaneous, with no duration in time, as a point has no length. Our normal perceptions, of course, are seemingly continuous, presumably as we perceive "movies" as continuous despite their actual makeup's being a series of frames. Some Buddhist writings even quan-

---

FIGURE 10. An Orch OR event. (**A**) (*left*) Three tubulins in quantum superposition prior to 25-msec Orch OR. After reduction (*right*), particular classical states are selected. (**B**) Fundamental spacetime geometry view. Prior to Orch OR (*left*), spacetime corresponding with three superposed tubulins is separated as Planck scale bubbles: curvatures in opposite directions. The Planck-scale spacetime separations, S, are very tiny in ordinary terms, but relatively large mass movements (e.g., hundreds of tubulin conformations, each moving from 10^{-6} to 0.2 nm) indeed have precisely such very tiny effects on the spacetime curvature. A critical degree of separation causes Orch OR and an abrupt selection of single curvatures (and a particular geometry of experience). (**C**) Cognitive facial recognition: A familiar face induces superposition (*left*) of three possible solutions (Amy, Betty, Carol) which "collapse" to the correct answer Carol (*right*). (**D**) Cognitive volition: Three possible dinner selections (shrimp, sushi, pasta) are considered in superposition (*left*), and collapse via Orch OR to choice of sushi (*right*).

tify the frequency of conscious moments. For example the Sarvaastivaadins[115] described 6,480,000 "moments" in 24 hours (an average of one "moment" per 13.3 msec), and some forms of Chinese Buddhism describe one "thought" per 20 msec. These accounts, including variations in frequency, are consistent with our proposed Orch OR events. For example a 13.3-msec pre-conscious interval would correspond with an Orch OR involving 4×10^{10} coherent tubulins, and a 20-msec interval with 2.5×10^{10} coherent tubulins. Thus Buddhist "moments of experience," Whitehead "occasions of experience," and our proposed Orch OR events seem to correspond tolerably well with one another.

Consciousness has an important place in the universe. Orch OR in microtubules is a model depicting consciousness as sequences of non-computable self-selections in fundamental spacetime geometry. If experiential qualia are qualities of spacetime, then Orch OR indeed begins to address the nature of conscious experience in a serious way.

ACKNOWLEDGMENTS

I am grateful to Roger Penrose, collaborator and coauthor on "Consciousness events as orchestrated space-time selections," which was published in the *Journal of Consciousness Studies* **2**: 36–53 (1996), from which portions of the present paper are reprinted. Thanks are also extended to Dave Cantrell for artwork, to Carol Ebbecke, Marjan Macphee, Patti Bergin, and Scott Morgan for technical support, to Justine Cullinan and the *Annals* for editorial assistance, and to Nancy Woolf, Scott Hagan, Jack Tuszynski, and Mitchell Porter for useful discussions. I am also most grateful to Pedro Marijuán and the other organizers of the Cajal conference and to Cajal himself for illuminating the brain.

REFERENCES

1. PENROSE, R. 1989. The Emperor's New Mind. Oxford University Press. Oxford, UK.
2. PENROSE, R. 1994. Shadows of the Mind. Oxford University Press. Oxford, U.K.
3. PENROSE, R. & S.R. HAMEROFF. 1995. What gaps? Reply to Grush and Churchland. J. Consc. Studies **2(2)**: 99–112.
4. HAMEROFF, S.R. & R. PENROSE. 1996. Orchestrated reduction of quantum coherence in brain microtubules: a model for consciousness. *In* Toward a Science of Consciousness—The First Tucson Discussions and Debates. S.R. Hameroff, A. Kaszniak & A.C. Scott, Eds. : 507–540. MIT Press. Cambridge, MA.
5. HAMEROFF, S. & R. PENROSE. 1996. Conscious events as orchestrated space-time selections. J. Consc. Studies **3(1)**: 36–53.
6. CAJAL, S.R. 1997. Texture of the Nervous System of Man and the Verterbrates: An Annotated and Edited Translation of the Original Spanish Text [translated from the original 1899 text by Pedro Pasik and Tauba Pasik]. Springer-Verlag. Wien/New York.
7. JASPER, H. & I. KOMAYA. 1968. Amino acids released from the cortical surface in cats following stimulation of the mesial thalamus and midbrain reticular formation. Electroencephalogr. Clin. Neurophysiol. **24(3)**: 292
8. BAARS, B. 1988. A Cognitive Theory of Consciousness. Cambridge University Press. Cambridge, UK.
9. TONONI, G. & G. EDELMAN. 1998. Consciousness and complexity. Science **282**: 1846–1852.

10. WOOLF, N.J. 1996. Global and serial neurons form a hierarchically arranged interface proposed to underlie memory and cognition. Neuroscience **74(3)**: 625–651.
11. SINGER, W., C. GRAY, A. ENGEL, P. KONIG, A. ARTOLA & S. BROCHER. 1990. Formation of cortical cell assemblies. Cold Spring Harbor Symp. Quant. Biol. **55**: 939-952.
12. CRICK, F. & C. KOCH, C. 1990. Towards a neurobiological theory of consciousness. Sem. Neurosci. **2**: 263–275.
13. JOLIOT, M., U. RIBARY & R. LLINAS. 1994. Human oscillatory brain activity near 40 Hz coexists with cognitive temporal binding. Proc. Natl. Acad. Sci. USA **91**: 11748–11751.
14. GRAY, J.A. 1998. Creeping up on the hard question of consciousness. *In* Toward a Science of Consciousness II—The Second Tucson Discussions and Debates. S. Hameroff, A. Kaszniak & A Scott, Eds. :279–291. MIT Press. Cambridge, MA.
15. JOHN, E.R. 1988. Resonating fields in the brain: the hyperneuron. *In* Springer Series on Brain Dynamics. Erol Basar, Ed. :64–84. Springer- Verlag. Berlin.
16. KANDEL, E.R., S.A. SIEGELBAUM & J.H. SCHWARTZ. 1991. Synaptic transmission. *In* Principles of Neural Science, 3rd ed. E.R. Kandel, J.H. Schwartz & T.M. Jessell, Eds. :121–134. Elsevier. New York.
17. GALARRETA, M. & S. HESTRIN. 1999. A network of fast-spiking cells in the neocortex connected by electrical synapses. Nature **402**: 72–75.
18. FUKUDA, T. & T. KOSAKA. 2000. Gap junctions linking the dendritic network of GABAergic interneurons in the hippocampus. J. Neurosci. **20(4)**: 1519–1528
19. TAMAS, G., E.H. BUHL, A. LORINCZ & P. SOMOGYI. 2000. Proximally targeted GABAergic synapses and gap junctions synchronize cortical interneurons. Nature Neurosci. **3(4)**: 336–371.
20. JOHN, E.R., Y. TANG, A.B. BRILL, R. YOUNG R. & K. ONO. 1986. Double-labeled metabolic maps of memory. Science.**233**:1167–1175.
21. CHALMERS, D.J. 1996. The Conscious Mind: In Search of a Fundamental Theory. Oxford University Press. New York.
22. SCOTT, A. 1995. Stairway to the Mind. Springer-Verlag (Copernicus). New York.
23. SPINOZA, B. 1677/1914. Ethica in Opera quotque reperta sunt, 3rd ed. J. van Vloten and J.P.N. Land, Eds. Den Haag, Netherlands .
24. RENSCH, B. 1960. Evolution Above the Species Level. Columbia Uiversity Press. New York..
25. LEIBNIZ, G.W. 1768. Opera Omnia (6 vols.). Louis Dutens. Fratres de Tournes. Geneva.
26. WHITEHEAD, A.N. 1929. Science and the Modern World. Macmillan. New York.
27. WHITEHEAD, A.N. 1933. Process and Reality. Macmillan. New York.
28. RUSSELL, B. 1954. The Analysis of Matter. Dover Publications. New York.
29. GOSWAMI, A. 1993. The Self-Aware Universe: How Consciousness Creates the Material World. Tarcher/Putnam. New York.
30. WHEELER, J.A. 1990. Information, physics, quantum: the search for links. *In* Complexity, Entropy, and the Physics of Information. W. Zurek, Ed. Addison-Wesley. Reading, MA.
31. SHIMONY, A. 1993. Search for a Naturalistic World View. Vol. II: Natural Science and Metaphysics. Cambridge University Press. Cambridge, UK.
32. PENROSE, R. 1996. On gravity's role in quantum state reduction: general relativity and gravitation. **28 (5)**:581–600.
33. SCHRÖDINGER, E. 1935. Die gegenwarten situation in der quantenmechanik. Naturwissenschaften **23**: 807–812, 823–828, 844–849. [Translation by J.T. Trimmer (1980) in Proc. Amer. Phil. Soc. **124**: 323–338.] *In* Quantum Theory and Measurement. J.A. Wheeler & W.H. Zurek, Eds. Princeton University Press. Princeton, NJ (1983).
34. PEARLE, P. 1989. Combining stochastic dynamical state vector reduction with spontaneous localization. Phys. Rev. D. **13**: 857–868
35. GHIRARDI, G.C., A. RIMINI & T. WEBER. 1986. Unified dynamics for microscopic and macroscopic systems. Phys. Rev. D. **34**: 470.
36. KAROLYHAZY F. 1966. Gravitation and quantum mechanics of macroscopic bodies. Nuo. Cim. A **42**: 390–402.
37. KAROLHAZY, F., A. FRENKEL& B. LUKACS. 1986. On the possible role of gravity on the reduction of the wave function. *In* Quantum Concepts in Space and Time. R. Penrose & C.J. Isham, Eds. Oxford University Press. Oxford, UK.

38. DIOSI, L. 1989. Models for universal reduction of macroscopic quantum fluctuations. Phys. Rev. A. **40:** 1165–1174.
39. GHIRARDI, G.C., R. GRASSI & A. RIMINI. 1990. Continuous-spontaneous reduction model involving gravity. Phys. Rev. A. **42:** 1057–1064.
40. PEARLE, P. & E. SQUIRES. 1994. Bound-state excitation, nucleon decay experiments and models of wave-function collapse. Phys. Rev. Lett. **73 (1):** 1–5.
41. PERCIVAL, I.C. 1995. Quantum space-time fluctuations and primary state diffusion, Proc. R. Soc. London A **451:** 503–513.
42. PENROSE, R. 1987. Newton, quantum theory and reality. In 300 Years of Gravity. S.W. Hawking & W. Israel, Eds. Cambridge University Press. Cambridge, UK.
43. PENROSE, R. 1993. Gravity and quantum mechanics. In General Relativity and Gravitation. Proceedings of the Thirteenth International Conference on General Relativity and Gravitation held at Cordoba, Argentina 28 June–4 July 1992. Part 1: Plenary Lectures. R.J. Gleiser, C.N. Kozameh & O.M. Moreschi, Eds. Institute of Physics Publications. Bristol, UK.
44. KAROLYHAZY, F. 1974. Gravitation and quantum mechanics of macroscopic bodies. Magyar Fizikai Polyoirat **12:** 24.
45. KIBBLE, T.W.B. 1981. Is a semi-classical theory of gravity viable? In Quantum Gravity 2: A Second Oxford Symposium. C.J. Isham, R. Penrose & D.W. Sciama, Eds. Oxford University Press. Oxford, UK.
46. EVERETT, H. 1957. Relative state formulation of quantum mechanics. In Quantum Theory and Measurement. J.A. Wheeler & W.H. Zurek, Eds. Princeton University Press, Princeton, New Jersey (1983); originally in Rev. Mod. Phys. **29:** 454–462.
47. WHEELER, J.A.. 1957. Assessment of Everett's "relative state" formulation of quantum theory. Revs. Mod. Phys. **29:** 463–465.
48. BENIOFF, P. 1982. Quantum mechanical Hamiltonian models of Turing machines. J. Stat. Phys. **29:** 515–546.
49. FEYNMAN, R.P. 1986. Quantum mechanical computers. Foundations of Physics **16 (6):** 507–531.
50. DEUTSCH, D. 1985. Quantum theory, the Church-Turing principle and the universal quantum computer. Proc. R. Soc. London **A400:** 97–117.
51. DEUTSCH, D. & R. JOSZA. 1992. Rapid solution of problems by quantum computation. Proc. R. Soc. London **A439:** 553–556.
52. BENNETT, C.H. & D.P. DIVINCENZO. 2000. Quantum information and computation [review article]. Nature **404:** 247–255.
53. MILBURN, G.J. 1998. The Feynman Processor: Quantum Entanglement and the Computing Revolution 1998. Frontiers of Science–Perseus Books. New York.
54. BECK, F. & J.C. ECCLES. 1992. Quantum aspects of brain activity and the role of consciousness. Proc. Natl. Acad. Sci. USA **89 (23):** 11357–11361.
55. MARSHALL, I.N. 1989. Consciousness and Bose-Einstein condensates. New Ideas in Psychology **7:** 73–83.
56. VOET, D. & J.G. VOET. 1995. Biochemistry, 2nd ed. Wiley. New York.
57. FRANKS N.P. & W.R. LIEB. 1982. Molecular mechanisms of general anaesthesia. Nature **300:** 487–493
58. HAMEROFF, S. 1998. Anesthesia, consciousness and hydrophobic pockets: a unitary quantum hypothesis of anesthetic action. Toxicology Lett. **100/101:** 31–39.
59. ROITBERG, A., R.B. GERBER, R. ELBER & M.A. RATNER. 1995. Anharmonic wave functions of proteins: quantum self-consistent field calculations of BPTI. Science **268 (5315):** 1319–1322.
60. TEJADA, J., A. GARG, S. GIDER, D.D. AWSCHALOM, D.P. DIVINCENZO & D. LOSS. 1996. Does macroscopic quantum coherence occur in ferritin? Science **272:** 424–426.
61. DEBRABANDER, M. 1982. A model for the microtubule organizing activity of the centrosomes and kinetochores in mammalian cells. Cell Biol. Intern. Rep. **6:** 901–915.
62. MELKI, R., M.F. CARLIER, D. PANTALONI & S.N. TIMASHEFF. 1989. Cold depolymerization of microtubules to double rings: geometric stabilization of assemblies. Biochemistry **28:** 9143–9152.
63. NOGALES, E., S.G. WOLF, & K.H. DOWNING. 1998. Structure of the alpha beta tubulin dimer by electron crystallography. Nature **391:** 199–203.

64. HAMEROFF, S. & R.C. WATT. 1982. Information processing in microtubules. J. Theoret. Biol. **98:** 549–561.
65. TUSZYNSKI, J., S. HAMEROFF, M.V. SATARIC, B. TRPISOVA & M.L.A. NIP. 1995. Ferroelectric behavior in microtubule dipole lattices: implications for information processing, signaling and assembly/disassembly. J. Theor. Biol. **174:** 371–380.
66. RASMUSSEN, S., H. KARAMPURWALA, R. VAIDYANATH, K.S. JENSEN & S. HAMEROFF. 1990. Computational connectionism within neurons: a model of cytoskeletal automata subserving neural networks. Physica D **42:** 428–449.
67. GLANZ, J. 1997. Force carrying web pervades living cell. Science **276:** 678–679.
68. MANIOTIS, A.J., K. BOJANOWSKI & D.E. INGBER. 1997. Mechanical continuity and reversible chromosome disassembly within intact genomes removed from living cells. J. Cell. Biochem. **65:** 114–130.
69. MANIOTIS, A.J., C.S. CHEN & D.I. INGBER. 1997. Demonstration of mechanical connections between integrins, cytoskeletal filaments, and nucleoplasm that stabilize nuclear structure. Proc. Natl. Acad. Sci. USA **94:** 849–854.
70. VERNON, G.G. & D.M. WOOLLEY. 1995. The propagation of a zone of activation along groups of flagellar doublet microtubules. Exp. Cell Res. **220 (2):** 482–494.
71. FISCHER, M., S. KAECH, D. KNUTTI & M. MATUS. 1998. Rapid actin-based plasticity in dendritic spines. Neuron **20:** 847–854.
72. KAECH, S., M. FISCHER, T. DOLI & A. MATUS. 1997. Isoform specificity in the relationship of actin to dendritic spines. J. Neurosci. **17 (24):** 9565–9572.
73. KAECH, S, H. BRINKHAUS & A. MATUS. 1999. Volatile anesthetics block actin-based motility in dendritic spines. Proc. Natl. Acad. Sci. USA. **96:** 10433–10437.
74. DAYHOFF, J., S. HAMEROFF, R. LAHOZ-BELTRA & C.E. SWENBERG. 1994. Cytoskeletal involvement in neuronal learning: a review. Eur. Biophys. J. **23:** 79–83.
75. HAMEROFF, S. 1987. Ultimate Computing: Biomolecular Consciousness and Nanotechnology. Elsevier–North Holland. Amsterdam.
76. HAMEROFF, S.R. 1994. Quantum coherence in microtubules: a neural basis for emergent consciousness. J. Consci. Stud. **1(1):** 91–118.
77. JIBU, M. & K. YASUE. 1995. Quantum brain dynamics: an introduction. John Benjamins. Amsterdam.
78. JIBU, M., S. HAGAN, S.R. HAMEROFF, K.M. PRIBRAM & K. YASUE. 1994. Quantum optical coherence in cytoskeletal microtubules: implications for brain function. BioSystems **32**: 195–209.
79. DE ZEEUW, C.I., S.K. KOEKKOEK, D.R. WYLIE & J.I. SIMPSON. 1997. Association between dendritic lamellar bodies and complex spike synchrony in the olivocerebellar system. J. Neurophysiol. **77 (4):** 1747–1758.
80. DE ZEEUW, C.I., C.C. HOOGENRAAD, E. GOEDKNEGT, E. HERTZBERG, A. NEUBAUER, F. GROSVELD & N. GALJART. 1997. CLIP-115, a novel brain-specific cytoplasmic linker protein, mediates the localization of dendritic lamellar bodies. Neuron **19 (6):** 1187–1199
81. LIBET, B., E.W. WRIGHT, JR., B. FEINSTEIN & D.K. PEARL. 1979. Subjective referral of the timing for a conscious sensory experience. Brain **102:** 193–224.
82. YU, W. & P.W. BAAS. 1994. Changes in microtubule number and length during axon differentiation. J. Neurosci. **14 (5):** 2818–2829.
83. FROHLICH, H. 1968. Long-range coherence and energy storage in biological systems. Int. J. Quantum Chem. **2:** 641–649.
84. FRÖHLICH, H. 1970. Long range coherence and the actions of enzymes. Nature **228:** 1093.
85. COWBURN, R.P. & M.E. WELLAND. 2000. Room temperature magnetic quantum cellular automata. Science **287:** 1466–1468.
86. WACHSSTOCK, D.H., W.H. SCHWARZ & T.D. POLLARD. 1994. Cross-linker dynamics determine the mechanical properties of actin gels. Biophys. J. **66 (3 Pt 1):** 801—809.
87. MIYAMOTO, S. 1995. Changes in mobility of synaptic vesicles with assembly and disassembly of actin network. Biochim. Biophys. Acta **1244:** 85–91.
88. MUALLEM, S., K. KWIATKOWSKA, X. XU & H.L. YIN. 1995. Actin filament disassembly is a sufficient final trigger for exocytosis in nonexcitable cells. J. Cell Biol. **128:** 589–598.
89. CLEGG, J.S. 1984. Properties and metabolism of the aqueous cytoplasm. Am. J. Physiol. **246:** R133–R151.

90. PAUSER, S., A. ZSCHUNKE, A. KHUEN & K. KELLER. 1995. Estimation of water content and water mobility in the nucleus and cytoplasm of *Xenopus laevis* oocytes by NMR microscopy. Magnetic Res. Imaging. **13 (2):** 269–276.
91. CAMERON, I.L., K.R. COOK, D. EDWARDS, G.D. FULLERTON, G. SCHATEN, A.M. ZIMMERMAN & S. ZIMMERMAN. 1987. Cell cycle changes in water properties in sea urchin eggs. J. Cell Physiol. **133 (1):** 14–24.
92. SACKET, D. 1995. Subcellular biochemistry: proteins, structure, function and engineering **24:** 255.
93. ARIELI, A., A. STERKIN, A. GRINVALD & A. AERTSEN. 1996. Dynamics of ongoing activity: explanation of the large variability in evoked cortical responses. Science **273:** 1868–1874.
94. FERSTER D. 1996. Is neural noise just a nuisance? Science **272:** 1812.
95. TEGMARK, M. 2000. The importance of quantum decoherence in brain processes. Phys. Rev. E **61:** 4194
96. HAGAN, S., S.R. HAMEROFF & J.A. TUSZYNSKI. 2000. Quantum computation in brain microtubules? Decoherence and feasibility. Submitted for publication. http://xxx.lanl.gov/abs/quant-ph/0005025
97. SATARIC, M.V., R.B. ZAKULA & J.A. TUSZYNSKI. 1993. Kinklike excitations as an energy transfer mechanism in microtubules. Phys. Rev. E **48:** 589–597.
98. PATEL, A. 2000. Quantum algorithms and the genetic code. http://xxx.lanl.gov/abs/quant-ph/0002037 v2 (February 15, 2000).
99. ANDERSON, P.W. 1997. Fault-tolerant quantum computation by anyons. <http://lanl.gov/abs/quant-ph/9707021>
100. KITAEV, A.Y. 1997. Fault-tolerant quantum computation by anyons. http://xxx.lanl.gov/abs/quant-ph/9707021
101. FREEDMAN, M.H., A. KITAEV, M.J. LARSEN & Z. WANG. 2001. Topological quantum computation. <http://xxx.lanl.gov/abs/quant-ph/0101025>
102. PORTER, M.J. 2001. Personal communication; c.f. www.u.arizona.edu/~mjporter<http://www.u.arizona.edu/~mjporter>
103. SAMSONOVICH, A., A. SCOTT & S. HAMEROFF. 1992. Acousto-conformational transitions in cytoskeletal microtubules: implications for intracellular information processing. Nanobiology **1:** 457–468.
104. PENROSE, R. 1997. Personal communication.
105. CONRAD, M. 1994. Amplification of superpositional effects through electronic-conformational interactions. Chaos, Solitons and Fractals **4:** 423–438.
106. RIZI, R.R., S. AHN, D.C. ALSOP, *et al.* 2000. Intermolecular zero-quantum coherence imaging of the human brain. Magn. Res. Med. **43:** 627–632.
107. RICHTER, W., M. RICHTER, W.S. WARREN, *et al.* 2000. Functional magnetic resonance imaging with intermolecular multiple-quantum coherences. Magn. Res. Imaging **18:** 489–494.
108. ECCLES, J.C. 1992. Evolution of consciousness. Proc. Natl. Acad. Sci. USA **89(16):** 7320–7324.
109. PRIBRAM, K.H. 1991. Brain and Perception. Lawrence Erlbaum. Hillside, NJ.
110. WOOLF, N.J. 1997. A possible role for cholinergic neurons of the basal forebrain and pontomesencephalon in consciousness. Consciousness & Cognition **6(4): 574–596.**
111. WOOLF, N.J., M.D. ZINNERMAN & G.V. JOHNSON. 1999. Hippocampal microtubule-associated protein-2 alterations with contextual memory. Brain Res. 821(1):241–249.
112. DUSTIN, P. 1985. Microtubules, 2nd ed.. Springer-Verlag. Heidelberg.
113. HAMEROFF, S. 1998. Did consciousness cause the Cambrian evolutionary explosion? *In* Toward a Science of Consciousness II. The Second Tucson Discussions and Debates. S. Hameroff, A. Kaszniak & A Scott, Eds. :421–437. MIT Press. Cambridge, MA.
114. TART, C.T. 1995. Personal communication and information gathered from "Buddha-1 newsnet".
115. VON ROSPATT, A. 1995. The Buddhist Doctrine of Momentariness: A Survey of the Origins and Early Phase of This Doctrine up to Vasubandhu. Franz Steiner Verlag. Stuttgart.

Consciousness, the Brain, and Spacetime Geometry: An Addendum

Some New Developments on the Orch OR Model for Consciousness

ROGER PENROSE

Mathematical Institute, Oxford, UK, and
Gresham College, London, UK

Center for Gravitational Physics and Geometry, Pennsylvania State University, State College, Pennsylvania, USA

ABSTRACT: Brain action is both physically controlled and beyond computational simulation. Accordingly, there is a strong case for examining brain organization in a way that specifically seeks out structures in the brain that might plausibly support such putative non-computational action at the ill-understood borderline between quantum and classical physics. Thus, we must seek out structures in the brain where the actual physics that operates at this level could plausibly have important influence on brain action. This is the basis of the Orch-OR model that Stuart Hameroff and I have been proposing, and which he describes in the foregoing article. The case is strongly put forward that the neuronal microtubules play a key role in the required quantum/classical borderline activities which might have an essential relevance to the phenomenon of consciousness. The exploration of such deeper level of neuronal structure and function is very much a continuation of the line of work so wonderfully initiated by Cajal.

KEYWORDS: Consciousness; Non-computability; Orch-OR model; Microtubules; Quantum-classical borderline; Measurement problem; Quantum non-locality; Binding problem

ABOUT CAJAL'S INFLUENCE

This addendum provides my own personal input to the accompanying article by my colleague Stuart Hameroff. I thoroughly endorse what he says, since my own particular perspective on the problem of consciousness does not differ substantially from his, although my choice of emphasis might be a little different in places. Rather than making any attempt to sort out any such differences, I feel that it is more appropriate, in my expressions of respect for the great Spanish neurophysiologist Santiago Ramón-y-Cajal, that I simply provide an addendum to Hameroff's article in which I point to some interesting new developments that have a bearing on the "Orch OR" model for conscious brain activity that Hameroff and I have been developing.

Before doing so, however, I wish to offer some expression of appreciation of Cajal's work, although my own comments can come from only a very limited perspective. I first became acquainted with some of Cajal's achievements in the late 1950s, when I was a research Fellow at St. John's College Cambridge. Even at that time, I had taken some interest in the structure and operation of the brain, despite the fact that my training had been entirely in mathematics and mathematical physics. I had obtained a copy of D.A. Sholl's *The Organization of the Cerebral Cortex*[1] and had read something of Cajal's remarkable achievements. Later, I remember being particularly struck by Cajal's very careful and accurate drawings of neurons and related structures. For many years, however, I laid this interest largely aside, and it is only comparatively recently—some 30 years later—that I became concerned again about the structure of the brain and the mysterious question of what it is in the brain's action that can actually evoke conscious experience.

Having this background in mathematics and basic physics, I had come to this problem of consciousness from a different point of view from that of most people concerned with this issue. There is a fundamental question of how it is that any physical structure whatsoever can give rise to the puzzling phenomenon of awareness. Since the advent of modern electronic computers, the feeling has grown up in much of the scientific community that whatever it is in the organization of the brain that indeed evokes awareness, it should, at least, be possible to imitate that organization—and subsequent behavior—by some action of an electronic computer. But is this so? There are well-known arguments from mathematical logic which appear to imply that conscious understanding allows us to achieve something that no specific computational procedure is able to achieve. These arguments depend upon reasoning that emerges from, and is directly connected with, Gödel's famous incompleteness theorem of mathematical logic. The issues remain very controversial, and although I believe that the case is a very strong one, I do not wish to re-open the arguments here. (See my book *Shadows of the Mind*[2] and the *Psyche* commentaries[3] for a full discussion of these matters.) In fact, it is possible to give arguments that do not in any way involve Gödel's theorem, to support the view that consciousness is actually not a feature of of computational activity of any kind (cf. Ref. 4).

A belief that there is something fundamentally outside computational activity in conscious processes, coupled with the scientific attitude that it is the brain's physical action that is responsible for its consciousness, leads us to search for something within physics itself that is not governed by computational laws. Non-computational activity—as opposed to action that is computationally or randomly determined—is certainly a *mathematical* possibility (although this fact is not very well appreciated outside the mathematical community). See my "toy model universes" described in Refs. 2 and 5, and see Ref. 6 for an illustration of such theoretical possibilities. Although it is known that such non-computational (and non-random) action is indeed *mathematically* possible, it does not at all follow that any such action can be realized physically. It is an intriguing but certainly unconventional supposition that there might be actual physical processes in the universe that lie fundamentally beyond computation in this way. Moreover, one should certainly also question whether such exotic physical processes, even if they exist, could have any important relevance to real physical brain action.

On the other hand, if we take the view, as I do, that brain action is both physically controlled and beyond computational simulation, then we do have reason to believe in the fundamental role for such putative exotic physics in conscious brain action. Accordingly, there is, I believe, a strong case for examining brain organization in a way that specifically seeks out structures that might plausibly support such putative non-computational action. I believe that the only plausible place in which there might be non-computational physical behavior is at the ill-understood borderline between quantum and classical physics. Thus, we must seek out structures in the brain where the actual physics that operates at this level could plausibly have important influence on brain action. This is the basis of the Orch-OR model that Stuart Hameroff and I have been proposing, and which he describes in the previous article (see pp. 74–104). The case is strongly put forward that the neuronal microtubules play a key role in the required quantum/classical borderline activities.

In this view we need to look more deeply into the structure of neurons than is normally done in connection with the usual computational models. Neurons are far more than just "switches" or the biological equivalent of transistors. Their intricate internal structure must play a vital additional role that cannot be subsumed into the present-day computer analogy. The exploration of such deeper structure is very much a continuation of the line of work so wonderfully initiated by Cajal, and I regard this exploration as something that is completely at one with the spirit of what Cajal was trying to do. We have learned a lot about which parts of the brain are responsible for different kinds of mental function, particularly with the advent of modern imaging techniques. But the issue of what it is that can be responsible for conscious mentality needs a great deal more, and different kinds of investigation will certainly be required. Indeed, there may well be fundamental surprises awaiting us in the future.

THE QUANTUM MEASUREMENT PROBLEM

Why must we explore the quantum/classical borderline if we are to find actions that are fundamentally non-computable and which might have an essential relevance to the phenomenon of consciousness? The reasons are partly negative, in that we see scope for non-computability neither at the classical level of macroscopic objects nor at the quantum level of particles, atoms, or molecules, where Schrödinger's equation provides a deterministic and computable evolution of the quantum state. It appears to be a common view amongst computational neuroanatomists that classical physics is sufficient for the description of brain activity, quantum mechanics being essentially irrelevant. On the other hand many quantum physicists would be of the opinion that it is quantum mechanics that is ultimately responsible for all the actions of the physical universe, including the action of the brain. In neither view, so it would seem, would there be room for actions that lie fundamentally outside computational behavior.

My own position is that neither of these extreme positions is appropriate, since neither has the breadth to accommodate consciousness as a physical phenomenon. Independently of this, there is the fundamental incompleteness of present-day quantum mechanics itself. This is not the place to enter into a discussion of this highly controversial issue.[a] Suffice it to say that the description of the evolution of a quantum state, as described by the Schrödinger equation, does not provide us with a realistic picture of the evolution of macroscopic systems. One needs, in addition, a

---

[a] See, for example, Bohm and Hiley,[7] d'Espagnat[8] (pp. 270–271), and Home.[9]

procedure that is described as the "collapse of the wavefunction," and which accompanies the process of quantum measurement. There are numerous different philosophical standpoints with regard to this (real or apparent) phenomenon and there is no real agreement between protagonists. (A particular standpoint, that of Gell–Mann and Hartle,[10,11] is that mentioned by Professor Gell-Mann in his paper in this volume (see p. 41).[b] It is my own particular standpoint (shared by Einstein) that quantum mechanics is an incomplete theory, and that new developments will be needed before it can be made fully consistent. I have presented[2,12,13] a particular scheme within which the difficulties of the measurement problem can find resolution, but this requires a mild departure from the standard procedures. It is motivated from general principles that come from Einstein's general theory of gravity and that are subtly in conflict with the procedures of standard quantum theory. I have suggested specific experiments (most particularly the FELIX space-borne experiment, which is a technically feasible, but difficult (see Refs. 13 and 14). The Orch OR scheme would depend upon a positive result from experiments of this nature, and would be refuted if such experiments fail to exhibit an effect of the type that the experiments are designed to detect. A positive result of such experiments would lead to a resolution of the measurement paradox.

QUANTUM MEASUREMENT AND NON-LOCALITY

Quite apart from the measurement issue, there are examples of quantum phenomena that have the appearance of paradox; yet they are now firmly established in numerous experiments. These are effects known as EPR (Einstein–Podolsky–Rosen) phenomena, which illustrate the fundamental non-locality of quantum mechanics. Some people object to the term "non-local" in this context, and the technically more appropriate term is quantum entanglement, a notion introduced by Schrödinger. One of the most familiar EPR experiments is that performed by Aspect and his colleagues[15] in Paris in 1982. In the Aspect experiment, pairs of photons are emitted from a source and detected at two places some 12 meters apart. The polarizations of the two photons are measured at these distant detectors, where the choice as to which of two measurements to use is not made until the photons are in full flight. The upshot of all this is that the results of the experiments cannot be explained if the photons are taken to be separate independent objects. The experiment confirms the quantum-mechanical expectation that the photon pairs have to be considered as single entities right up until the measurements are made. One says that the photon pairs constitute *entangled states* and cannot be regarded as pairs of independent entities. There is the *appearance* that the "information" of the photon's polarization travels instantaneously from one photon to the other, upon measurement, is in seeming conflict with the requirements of relativity. In some more modern EPR experiments, the 12 meter separation of Aspect's experiment has been increased to some 10 kilometers.

A point worth making is that which was forcefully put by John Bell.[16] He pointed to a seemingly analogous "everyday" situation referred to as *Bertlmann's socks*.

---

[b]For discussions of the adequacy of this point of view, see in particular Ref. 7 (p. 331), Ref. 8 (p. 270), and Ref. 9 (p. 86).

Bell's colleague Bertlmann had the eccentric habit of always wearing socks of different colors. Thus, if one were to catch sight of one of his socks and saw that it was green, one could be instantly assured that the color of the other sock was *not* green. Thus one might take the position that the information traveled from one foot to the other *instantaneously* in apparent conflict with the requirements of relativity. But it is clear that in this case there is no puzzle. There is no superluminary propagation of actual information here.

In fact, in the Aspect-type experiment, it is still not possible to propagate actual information faster than light by such means. Nevertheless, there is a fundamental distinction between the two cases, and the very reason that Bell introduced his parable of Bertlmann's socks was to point out this fundamental distinction. In neither case is actual information propagated from one place to the other, but in the EPR situations there is no way to describe the correlations between measurements that can be made in the two places by regarding the quantities measured to be separate independent entities. Quantum entanglement effects have no analogue in classical physics. We may regard quantum-entangled objects as being "connected" in a way that is weaker than being in direct communication with one another, but stronger than their being fully independent of each other when they are separated.[c] This characteristic property of EPR effects that is exhibited in these experiments is a violation of what are known as Bell inequalities.[18] Whenever the correlations between these widely separated measurements actually violate the Bell inequalities, then we know that no explanation of the "Bertleman-sock" type is possible.

QUANTUM NON-LOCALITY IN PERCEPTION?

An interesting family of suggestions was recently put to me by my colleague Andrew Duggins, who cited various experiments which might demonstrate violations of Bell inequalities in perception, thereby indicating the relevance of quantum entanglements in the forming of a conscious picture, in accordance with the Orch OR proposal. Indeed, one of the most serious issues confronting theories of perception is that referred to as the *binding problem*. It is known that quite separate regions of the brain are responsible for different aspects of a (say) visual perception. In particular, the perception of color and the perception of motion occur in two quite different regions, and there is not much in the way of direct neural connection between the two. Yet, on perceiving a scene in which motion and color are both present simultaneously, one still perceives a consistent overall picture with both motion and color. Specifically, in certain experiments performed by Zeki and his colleagues, random patterns of squares are shown on a screen, where they move up and down in

---

[c]In relation to the discussion that took place following Gell-Mann's lecture at this conference, it should be pointed out that the essential difference between EPR effects and "Bertlmann sock" effects (violation of Bell inequalities) only manifests itself when there are non-orthogonal alternative measurements being performed on each separated component of system. This feature was not exhibited in Gell-Mann's particular example. (There is a curiously misleading comment on page 172 of Gell-Mann's intriguing book *The Quark and the Jaguar*,[17] where it is asserted that the EPR situation "is like that of Bertlmann's socks," for Bell had specifically introduced the comparison in order to emphasize the difference.)

a period of about half a second. They also change color—say, from red to green and back—with the same period of half a second. The phase relation between the two changes is then allowed to be varied, and subjects are then asked what they consciously perceive. Apparently, the color change and the motion change are always perceived as occurring together, but with a certain probability as to which way around, depending on the phase difference. In a preliminary study Duggins informed me that there was some evidence that perhaps supported Bell-inequality violation, but clearly a lot more detailed work would be needed before any kind of definitive conclusion of this kind could be made.

REFERENCES

1. SHOLL, D.A. 1956. The Organization of the Cerebral Cortex. Methuen & Co. Ltd. London.
2. PENROSE, R. 1994. Shadows of the Mind. Oxford University Press. Oxford, UK.
3. PENROSE, R. 1996. Beyond the doubting of a shadow. Psyche **2(1):** 89–129. @ www: http://psyche.cs.monash.edu.au/psyche-index-v2_1.html
4. PENROSE, R. 1997. On understanding understanding. Int. Stud. Philos. Sci. **11:** 7–20.
5. PENROSE, R. 1989. The Emperor's New Mind. Oxford University Press. Oxford, UK.
6. PENROSE, R. 1997. The Large, the Small and the Human Mind. Cambridge University Press. Cambridge, England.
7. BOHM, D. & B. HILEY. 1994. The Undivided Universe. Routledge. London.
8. D'ESPAGNAT, B. 1995. Veiled Reality: An Analysis of Present-Day Quantum Mechanical Concepts. Addison-Wesley. Reading, MA.
9. HOME, D. 1997. Conceptual Foundations of Quantum Physics: An Overview from Modern Perspectives. Plenum. New York and London.
10. GELL-MANN, M. & J.B. HARTLE. 1990. *In* Complexity, Entropy, and the Physics of Information. SFI Studies in the Science of Complexity, Vol. VIII. W. Zurek, Ed. Addison Wesley. Reading, MA.
11. GELL-MANN, M. & J.B. HARTLE. 1993. Phys. Rev. D **47:** 3345.
12. PENROSE, R. 1996. On gravity's role in quantum state reduction: general relativity and gravitation. **28 (5):** 581–600.
13. PENROSE, R. 2000. Wavefunction collapse as a real gravitational effect. *In* Mathematical Physics 2000. A. FoKas, T.W.B. Kibble, A. Grigouriou & B. Zegarlinski, Eds. In press.
14. PENROSE, R. 1999. The Large, the Small and the Human Mind [new paperback edition]. Cambridge University Press. Cambridge, England.
15. ASPECT, A., P. GRANGIER & G. ROGER. 1982. Experimental realization of Einstein-Podolsky-Rosen-Bohm Gedankenexperiment: a new violation of Bell's inequalities. Phys. Rev. Lett **48:** 91–94.
16. BELL, J.S. 1966. Speakable and Unspeakable in Quantum Mechanics. Cambridge University Press. Cambridge, England [reprint 1987].
17. GELL-MANN, M. 1994. The Quark and the Jaguar: Adventures in the Simple and the Complex W.H. Freeman. New York.
18. CLAUSER, J.F., A.H. HORNE, A. SHIMONY & R.A. HOLT. 1969. Proposed experiment to test local hidden-variable theories. *In* Quantum Theory and Measurement. J.A. Wheeler & W.H. Zurek, Eds. Princeton University Press. Princeton, NJ [reprinted in 1983; originally in Phys. Rev. Lett. **23:** 880–884].

Consciousness: The Remembered Present

GERALD EDELMAN

The Neurosciences Institute, San Diego, California 92121

> *Something definite happens when to a certain brain-state a certain 'sciousness' corresponds.*
> —WILLIAM JAMES

ABSTRACT: This chapter summarizes a theory of consciousness based on brain structure and dynamics. The theory centers around the notion of reentry—ongoing recursive signaling across multiple reciprocally connected brain regions present mainly in the thalamocortical system. It recognized the fundamental beginnings provided by the complementary efforts of Ramón y Cajal and William James.

KEYWORDS: Primary consciousness; Higher-order consciousness; Reentrant connections; Perceptual categorization; Memory; Consciousness, primary and higher-order

It is an honor to participate in the centennial celebration of the work of a very great scientist, work beautifully captured in his monumental book, *Textura del sistema nervioso del hombre y de los vertebrados.*[1] In thinking about this conference, I had a fantasy: What would have transpired if the greatest experimental psychologist of Cajal's time, William James, had met Cajal, the greatest neuroanatomist? In writing his *Principles of Psychology,*[2] published less than ten years before Cajal's *Textura,* James realized that he was not in a position to say much about the brain. Cajal would have filled in much that James could not deal with. Given his situation, James had to fall back on the position that consciousness was a property of the whole brain. We now know, of course, that only certain parts of the brain are critical, mainly the thalamocortical system and the mesencephalic reticular system.

Whatever the case, it is notable that Cajal, like James, had a kind of scientific modesty. Cajal stated:

> In fact, in the present state of science, it is not possible to formulate a definitive theory about the architectonic and functional plan of the cerebrum. We still lack many precise histological data concerning the association or intellectual areas of Flechsig, as well as the anatomico-physiological determination of the cortical connections of numerous thalamic, mesencephalic, and pontine nuclei....In places where we were bereft of exact anatomico-physiological facts, we have resorted to the teachings of psychology in order to fill certain gaps; since, as Vogt correctly notes, at the present time the phenomena of consciousness are better known than cerebral architecture, and the science of the mind can more effectively aid the science of the cerebrum than the science of the cerebrum can aid that of the mind. It is idle to say that we do not seek to give to our conjectures the slightest dogmatic character; in science, hypotheses vary with the inexorable progression of facts that could not be anticipated, and ours would be very fortunate if, on being compared with future contributions, it were capable of maintaining some of the principles on which it is based.[3]

Both of these great men exhibited a central characteristic of profound scientific efforts—imagination tempered by modest skepticism, a combination that fueled their remarkable creative syntheses, which still serve us today.

As James pointed out in his famous essay "Does Consciousness Exist?,"[4] consciousness is not a thing, but is rather a process. It is individual and personal (or subjective), it is continuous but continually changing, it has intentionality but does not exhaust all properties of the objects to which it refers. Perhaps most striking of all its properties is its unitary nature—a conscious scene is all of a piece and cannot be decomposed into its individual parts by the person who experiences that scene. At the same time, the number of conscious states that can be experienced by that person is enormous. So, in understanding consciousness, we have to deal with unity and, at the same time, with endless variety. This combination of properties has been extensively analyzed in a recent book, *A Universe of Consciousness*.[5] Here, I review some hypotheses on the neural mechanisms underlying consciousness by reprinting a chapter from a previous book, *Bright Air, Brilliant Fire: On the Matter of the Mind*.[6] This chapter encapsulates a pivotal feature of my lecture at the Cajal conference. Although no references are given in this reprinted chapter, I append to it a list of suggested readings in the hope that they may be useful for those readers who wish to pursue the subject further.

Before turning to this material, it may be important to emphasize that consciousness is the basis for everything we consider valuable as human beings. If the scheme I have outlined is true, every act of perception is to some degree an act of creation, and every act of memory is to some degree an act of imagination. Our dreams lay ahead of us. And one of these conscious dreams, reflecting Cajal's remarkable prescience, is finally to understand this most important property of the human brain.

≥●

Most people, asked what it is about the mind that is truly distinctive and strange, would probably hark back to Descartes' lonely music of the self and say, "Consciousness." We are now at that point in our excursion when we may profitably ask whether we can do better than postulate a thinking substance that is beyond the reach of a science of extended things.

What is daunting about consciousness is that it does not seem to be a matter of behavior. It just *is*—winking on with the light, multiple and simultaneous in its modes and objects, ineluctably ours. It is a process and one that is hard to score. We know what it is for ourselves, but can only judge its existence in others by inductive inference. As James put it, it is something the meaning of which "we know as long as no one asks us to define it."

Indeed, it is initially best defined by considering some of its properties (of course the temptation is to indulge in a circular definition, made in terms of "awareness"). Consider what I call its "Jamesian" properties (after James, who discussed them): It is personal (possessed by individuals or selves); it is changing, yet continuous; it deals with objects independent of itself; and it is selective in time, that is, it does not exhaust all aspects of the objects with which it deals.

Consciousness shows intentionality; it is of or about things or events. It is also to some extent bound up with volition. Some psychologists suggest that consciousness is marked by the presence of mental images and by their use to regulate behavior. But it is *not* a simple copy of experience (a "mirror of reality"), nor is it necessary for a good deal of behavior. Some kinds of learning, conceptual processes, and even some forms of inference proceed without it.

I have made a distinction, which I believe is a fundamental one, between primary consciousness and higher-order consciousness. Primary consciousness is the state of being mentally aware of things in the world—of having mental images in the present. But it is not accompanied by any sense of a person with a past and future. It is what one may presume to be possessed by some nonlinguistic and nonsemantic animals (which ones they may be, I discuss later on). In contrast, higher-order consciousness involves the recognition by a thinking subject of his or her own acts or affections. It embodies a model of the personal, and of the past and the future as well as the present. It exhibits direct awareness—the noninferential or immediate awareness of mental episodes without the involvement of sense organs or receptors. It is what we as humans have in addition to primary consciousness. We are conscious of being conscious.

There are other resonances in the term "consciousness"—these are revealed, for example, in the criteria used by clinicians to assess whether a traumatized patient is "conscious" or not—criteria concerned with alertness, orientation, self-awareness, and motivational control. Physicians talk of consciousness as being "clouded," in which state perceptual acuity and memory capacity are diminished. In extreme cases of disease, the Jamesian properties, the "flights and perchings of consciousness," become random, automatized, or show perseveration, with no evidence of the existence of introspection or any attention to novelty. And in the last extreme—nothing, nothing to report.

There is no end of hypotheses about consciousness, particularly by philosophers. But most of these are not what we might call principled scientific theories, based on observables and related to the functions of the brain and body. Several theories of consciousness based on functionalism and on the machine model of the mind have recently been proposed. These generally come in two flavors: one in which consciousness is assumed to be efficacious, and another in which it is considered an epiphenomenon. In the first, consciousness is likened to the executive in a computer systems program, and in the second, to a fascinating, but more or less useless byproduct of computation.

In none of these notions, however, is there a direct appeal to biology or to the nature of embodiment. Such an appeal would obviously be essential to any theory of consciousness that is based on evolution. A theory of this kind must propose explicit neural models that explain how consciousness arises. It must of necessity explain how consciousness emerges during evolution and development. It must connect consciousness to other mental matters such as concept formation, memory, and language. And it must describe stringent tests for the models it proposes in terms of neurobiological facts. These tests should be undertaken, preferably with real experiments, or at least with what are called *gedankenexperiments*—thought experiments. In the latter, any properties postulated must be completely consistent with presently known scientific observations from whatever field of inquiry and, above all, with those from brain science.

Given the present state of affairs, this is a tall order because analyses of consciousness in biology are a bit like analyses of early cosmological events: Right from the beginning, certain manipulations and observations are just not possible. Under these circumstances, one must be careful to spell out the assumptions underlying any proposed theory. I will spell out three that are part of the underpinnings of my theory of consciousness. Two of these assumptions are straightforward, but the third is a bit tricky. I call them the physics assumption, the evolutionary assumption, and the qualia assumption (the tricky one). I have to make these assumptions clear beforehand to avoid certain pitfalls, for example, into the Cartesian position, into panpsychism, or into the cognitivist-objectivist quagmire.

The physics assumption is that the laws of physics are not violated, that spirits and ghosts are out; I assume that the description of the world by modern physics is an adequate, but not completely sufficient basis for a theory of consciousness. Modern quantum field theory provides a description of a set of formal properties of matter and energy at all scales. It does not, however, include a theory of intentionality or a theory of names for macroscopic objects, nor does it need them. What I mean by physics being just adequate is that I allow no spooks—no quantum gravity, no action at a distance, no superphysics—to enter into this theory of consciousness.

The evolutionary assumption is also reasonably straightforward. It is that consciousness arose as a phenotypic property at some point in the evolution of species. Before then it did not exist. This assumption implies that the acquisition of consciousness either conferred evolutionary fitness directly on the individuals having it, or provided a basis for other traits that enhanced fitness. The evolutionary assumption implies that consciousness is *efficacious*—that it is *not* an epiphenomenon ("merely the redness of the melting metal," when pouring is what counts).

Now, however, with the third assumption, we come to more subtle issues. They are methodological ones, forced on us by the peculiar way in which consciousness is made manifest. To explain the difficulty, I must make a detour here to discuss phenomenal or felt properties, otherwise known as qualia.

Qualia constitute the collection of personal or subjective experiences, feelings, and sensations that accompany awareness. They are phenomenal states—"how things seem to us" as human beings. For example, the "redness" of a red object is a quale. Qualia are discriminable parts of a mental scene that nonetheless has an overall unity. They may range in intensity and clarity from "raw feels" to highly refined discriminanda. These sensations may be very precise when they accompany perceptual experiences; in the absence of perception, they may be more or less diffuse, but nonetheless discernible as "visual," "auditory," and so on. In general, in the normal waking state, qualia are accompanied by a sense of spatiotemporal continuity. Often, the phenomenal scene is accompanied by feelings or emotions, however faint. Yet the actual *sequence* of qualia is highly individual, resting on a series of occasions in one's own personal history or immediate experience.

Given the fact that qualia are experienced directly only by single individuals, our methodological difficulty becomes obvious. *We cannot construct a phenomenal psychology that can be shared in the same way as a physics can be shared.* What is directly experienced as qualia by one individual cannot be fully shared by another individual as an observer. An individual can report his or her experience to an observer, but that report must always be partial, imprecise, and relative to his or her own personal context. Not only are qualia fleeting, but interventions designed to probe them may change them in unforeseen ways. Furthermore, many conscious and nonconscious processes simultaneously affect each person's subjective experience. Individuals may have their own private theories of the totality of their individual conscious experiences, but these can never be scientific theories. This is because other observers do not have adequate experimental controls available to them.

The paradox is a poignant one: To do physics, I employ my conscious life, perceptions, and qualia. But in my intersubjective communication, I leave them out of my description, assured that fellow observers with their own individual conscious lives can carry out the prescribed manipulations and achieve comparable experimental results. When for some reason qualia do affect interpretations, the experimental design is modified to exclude such effects; the mind is removed from nature.

But in investigating consciousness, we cannot ignore qualia. The dilemma is that phenomenal experience is a first-person matter, and this seems, at first glance, to prevent the formulation of a completely objective or causal account. Is this a completely hopeless situation?

I think not. But what alternatives are open to us if we want to pursue a scientific analysis of consciousness? One alternative that definitely does not seem feasible is to ignore completely the reality of qualia, formulating a theory of consciousness that aims *by its descriptions alone* to convey to a hypothetical "qualia-free" observer what it is to feel warmth, see green, and so on. In other words, this is an attempt to propose a theory based on a kind of God's-eye view of consciousness. But no *scientific* theory of whatever kind can be presented without already assuming that observers have sensation as well as perception. To assume otherwise is to indulge the errors of theories that attempt syntactical formulations mapped onto objectivist interpretations—theories that ignore embodiment as a source of meaning. There is no qualia-free scientific observer.

If we exclude such an avenue, what other recourse is there? I believe there is one, based on the fact that human beings are in a privileged position. While we may not be the only conscious animals, we are, with the possible exception of the chimpanzee, the only self-conscious animals. We are the only animals capable of language, able to model the world free of the present, able to report on, study, and correlate our phenomenal states with the findings of physics and biology.

This suggests an approach to the problem of qualia. As a basis for a theory of consciousness, it is sensible to *assume* that, just as in ourselves, qualia exist in other conscious human beings, whether they are considered as scientific observers or as subjects. (It does not matter whether these qualia are exactly the same in all observers, only that they exist.) We can then take human beings to be the best canonical referent for the study of consciousness. This is justified by the fact that human subjective reports (including those about qualia), actions, and brain structures and function can all be correlated. After building a theory based on the assumption that qualia exist in human beings, we can then look anew at some of the properties of qualia based on these correlations. It is our ability to report and correlate while individually experiencing qualia that opens up the possibility of a scientific investigation of consciousness.

This qualia assumption distinguishes between higher-order consciousness and primary consciousness. Higher-order consciousness is based on the occurrence of direct awareness in a human being who has language and a reportable subjective life. Primary consciousness may be composed of phenomenal experiences such as mental images, but it is bound to a time around the measurable present, lacks concepts of self, past, and future, and lies beyond direct descriptive individual report from its own standpoint. Accordingly, beings with primary consciousness alone cannot construct theories of consciousness—even wrong ones!

A research program built on the assumptions I have discussed obviously has a number of inherent difficulties. We must first build a model for primary consciousness, build on that a model for higher-order consciousness, and then proceed to check the connections of each of these models with human phenomenal experience. To be consistent with the evolutionary assumption, this procedure must explain how primary consciousness evolved, and then explain how it was followed by higher-order consciousness. The order of the experimental enterprise (which, according to the qualia assumption, must be based on correlations obtained mainly on human subjects) must therefore be exactly opposite that of the theoretical one, which must begin with the evolutionary precursors to humans.

I hope it is now clear why a biological theory based on our three assumptions cannot take a God's-eye view. To be scientists we cannot expect any theory of consciousness to render obvious to a hypothetical qualia-free animal what qualia are by any linguistic description. To maintain intersubjective communication and carry out scientific correlation, which is a human activity, we *must* assume qualia. Qualia cannot be derived as experiences from any theory. This does not mean, however, that different qualia cannot be theoretically discriminated in terms of modality, intensity, continuity, or their temporal and spatial properties. Nor does it mean that, after making the qualia assumption, we cannot consider the actual mechanisms by which qualia arise. Our cosmological comparison is not so far afield; we may ask modern physics to explain certain aspects of cosmology beginning at the earliest moment, consistent with the understanding given to us by modern physical theory. But we cannot ask a theory of physics to give a satisfactory answer to Gottfried Leibniz's question of why there is something rather than nothing.

As it will turn out after we consider models for primary and higher-order consciousness, qualia may be usefully viewed as forms of higher-order categorization, as relations reportable to the self and then somewhat less satisfactorily reportable to others with similar mental equipment. Such a terse statement hardly satisfies. But instead of expanding on it now, I will describe a model of primary consciousness, based on our three assumptions, that appears to be consistent with the facts of brain structure and function. The elements of this model include several systems already discussed, ones that give rise to value, to perceptual and conceptual categorization, and to memory. The dynamics of the model depend on a special kind of reentrant circuit. This is why I have explained these matters at length elsewhere. (I will keep qualia to one side for now, but I will return to them later when considering higher-order consciousness.)

PRIMARY CONSCIOUSNESS

The model I have proposed has a number of parts. (Would you believe a model of consciousness that had only one part?) Before describing their interactions, I want to say a few things about each part that might make an explanation of their interactions clearer. There are, grossly speaking, two kinds of nervous system organization that are important to understanding how consciousness evolved. These systems are very different in their structure, even though they are both made up of neurons. The first is the brain stem, together with the limbic (hedonic) system, the system concerned with appetite, sexual and consummatory behavior, and evolved defensive behavior patterns. It is a value system; it is extensively connected to many different body organs, the endocrine system, and the autonomic nervous system. Together, these systems regulate heart and respiratory rate, sweating, digestive functions, and the like, as well as bodily cycles related to sleep and sex. It will come as no surprise to learn that the circuits in this limbic–brain stem system are often arranged in loops, that they respond relatively slowly (in periods ranging from seconds to months), and that they do not consist of detailed maps. They have been selected during evolution to match the body, not to match large numbers of unanticipated signals from the outside world. These systems evolved early to take care of bodily functions; they are systems of the interior.

The second major nervous system organization is quite different. It is called the thalamocortical system. (The thalamus, a central brain structure, consists of many nuclei that connect sensory and other brain signals to the cortex.) The thalamocortical system consists of the thalamus and the cortex acting together, a system that evolved to receive signals from sensory receptor sheets and to give signals to voluntary muscles. It is very fast in its responses (taking from milliseconds to seconds), although its synaptic connections undergo some changes that last a lifetime. As we have seen, its main structure, the cerebral cortex, is arranged in a set of maps, which receive inputs from the outside world via the thalamus. Unlike the limbic–brain stem system, it does not contain loops so much as highly connected, layered local structures with massively reentrant connections. In many places these are topographically arranged. The cerebral cortex is a structure adapted to receive a dense and rapid series of signals from the world through many sensory modalities simultaneously—sight, touch, taste, smell, hearing, joint sense (feeling the position of your extremities). It evolved later than the limbic–brain stem system to permit increasingly sophisticated motor behavior and the categorization of world events. To handle time as well as space, the cortical appendages—the cerebellum, basal ganglia, and hippocampus—evolved along with the cortex to deal with succession both in actual motion and in memory.

The two systems, limbic–brain stem and thalamocortical, were linked during evolution. The later-evolving cortical system served learning behavior that was adaptive to increasingly complex environments. Because this behavior was clearly selected to serve the physiological needs and values mediated by the earlier limbic–brain stem system, the two systems had to be connected in such a way that their activities could be matched. Indeed, such matching is a critical part of learning. If the cortex is concerned with the categorization of the world and the limbic–brain stem system is concerned with value (or with setting its adjustments to evolutionarily selected physiological patterns), then learning may be seen as the means by which categorization occurs on a background of value to result in adaptive changes in behavior that satisfy value.

Learning certainly occurs in animals that show no evidence of conscious behavior. But in some animal species with cortical systems, the categorizations of separate causally unconnected parts of the world can be correlated and bound into a *scene*. By a scene I mean a spatiotemporally ordered set of categorizations of familiar and nonfamiliar events, *some with and some without necessary physical or causal connections to others in the same scene*. The advantage provided by the ability to construct a scene is that events that may have had significance to an animal's past learning can be related to new events, however causally unconnected those events are in the outside world. Even more importantly, this relationship can be established in terms of the demands of the value systems of the individual animal. By these means, the salience of an event is determined not only by its position and energy in the physical world, but also by the relative value it has been accorded in the past history of the individual animal as a result of learning.

It is the evolutionary development of the ability to create a scene that led to the emergence of primary consciousness. Obviously, for that emergence to have survived, it must have resulted in increased fitness. But before considering how, let's consider the model itself.

The appearance of primary consciousness, according to the model, depends on the evolution of three functions. Two of these evolutionary developments are necessary but not sufficient for consciousness. The first is the development of the cortical system in such a way that when conceptual functions appeared they could be linked strongly to the limbic system, extending already existing capacities to carry out learning. The second is the development of a new kind of memory based on this linkage. Unlike the system of perceptual categorization, this conceptual memory system is able to categorize responses in the different brain systems that carry out perceptual categorization and it does this according to the demands of limbic–brain stem value systems. This "value-category" memory allows conceptual responses to occur in terms of the mutual interactions of the thalamocortical and limbic–brain stem systems.

A third and critical evolutionary development provides a sufficient means for the appearance of primary consciousness. This is a special reentrant circuit that emerged during evolution as a new component of neuroanatomy. This circuit allows for continual reentrant signaling between the value-category memory and the ongoing global mappings that are concerned with perceptual categorization in real time. An animal without these new reentrant connections can carry out perceptual categorizations in various sensory modalities and can even develop a conceptual value-category memory. Such an animal cannot, however, link perceptual events into an ongoing scene. With the appearance of the new reentrant circuits in each modality, *a conceptual categorization of concurrent perceptions* can occur *before* these perceptual signals contribute lastingly to that memory. This interaction between a special kind of memory and perceptual categorization gives rise to primary consciousness. Given the appropriate reentrant circuits in the brain, this "bootstrapping process" takes place in all sensory modalities in parallel and simultaneously, thus allowing for the construction of a complex scene. The coherence of this scene is coordinated by the conceptual value-category memory, even if the individual perceptual categorization events that contribute to it are causally independent.

My use of the word "scene" is meant to convey the idea that responses to roughly contemporaneous events in the world are connected by a set of reentrant processes. As human beings possessing higher-order consciousness, we experience primary consciousness as a "picture" or a "mental image" of ongoing categorized events. But as we shall see when we examine higher-order consciousness, there is no actual image or sketch in the brain. The "image" is a *correlation* between different kinds of categorizations.

To summarize: The brain carries out a process of conceptual "self-categorization." Self-categories are built by matching past perceptual categories with signals from value systems, a process carried out by cortical systems capable of conceptual functions. This value-category system then interacts via reentrant connections with brain areas carrying out ongoing perceptual categorizations of world events and signals. Perceptual (phenomenal) experience arises from the correlation by a conceptual memory of a set of ongoing perceptual categorizations. Primary consciousness is a kind of "remembered present."

These notions are illustrated in FIGURE 1. While the diagram hardly conveys the complexity of the neural circuits involved, it does highlight several points. The first concerns what we may call self and nonself components. (By self in this context I mean a unique biological individual, not a socially constructed "human" self.) The self, or internal systems, arise from interactions between the limbic and the cortical systems. This differentiates them from outside-world systems that are strictly cortical.

The second point concerns the formation of value-category memory. This conceptual memory depends on constant interaction between self and world systems. The third point concerns the occurrence in real time and *in parallel* of perceptual categorizations for *each* sensory modality via the cortical system, including the organs of succession. The final and critical point heralds the appearance of primary consciousness: A correlative scene results from the function of reentrant connections between those cortical systems mediating conceptual value-category memory and those thalamocortical systems mediating ongoing perceptual categorizations across all the senses.

Notice that primary consciousness as I have characterized it has the necessary Jamesian properties: It is individual ("self" systems contribute to it), it is continuous and yet changing (as both world and internal signals evolve), and it is intentional (referring necessarily to internally given or outside-world signals derived alternately from things and events). If FIGURE 1 were to be reiterated in a series of time steps, it would serve to stress these Jamesian properties of primary consciousness and the kind of perceptual bootstrapping that primary consciousness represents. Jamesian properties stress the flow of consciousness, its "before" and "after." In the conscious process, current value-free perceptual categorization interacts with value-dominated memory. This occurs *before* perceptual events contribute further to the alteration of that memory. When such events do contribute to the alteration of that memory, they are, in general, no longer in the specious or remembered present, that is, they are no longer in primary consciousness.

What is the evolutionary value of such a system? Obviously, primary consciousness must be efficacious if this biological account is correct. Consciousness is not merely an epiphenomenon. According to the theory of neuronal group selection (TNGS), primary consciousness helps to abstract and organize complex changes in an environment involving multiple parallel signals. Even though some of these signals may have no direct causal connection to each other in the outside world, they may be significant indicators *to the animal* of danger or reward. This is because primary consciousness connects their features in terms of the saliency determined by the animal's past history and its values.

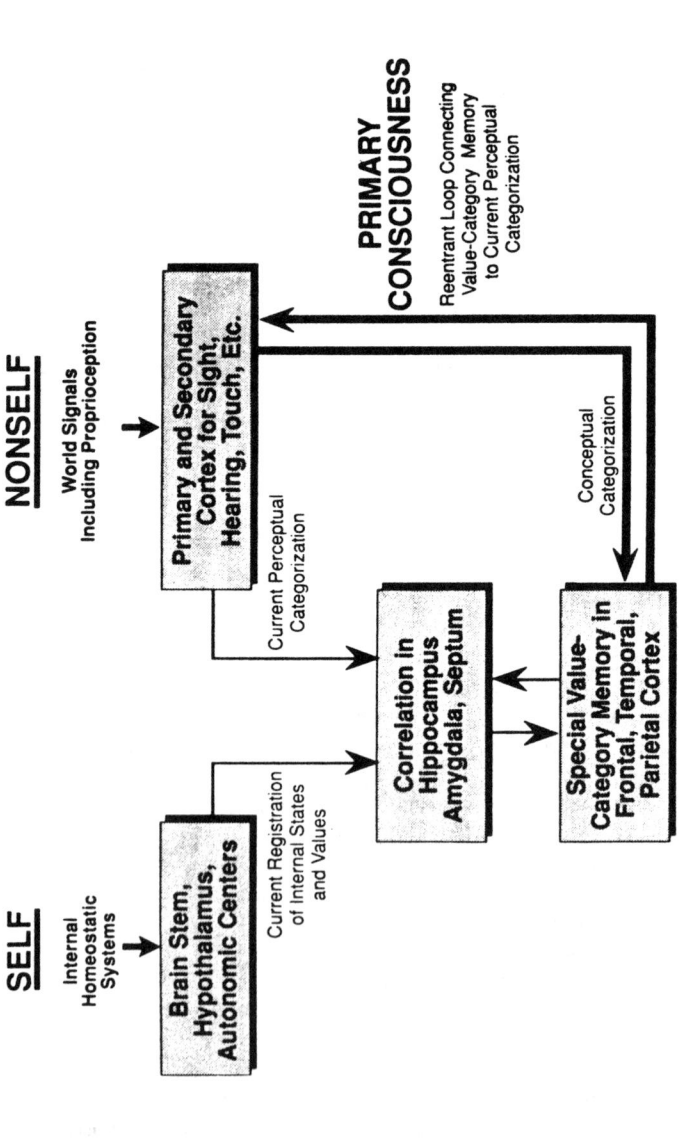

FIGURE 1. A model of primary consciousness. Past signals related to value (set by internal control systems) and categorized signals from the outside world are correlated and lead to memory in conceptual areas. This memory, which is capable of conceptual categorization, is linked by reentrant paths to *current* perceptual categorization of world signals (*heavy lines*). This results in primary consciousness. When it occurs through many modalities (sight, touch, and so forth), primary consciousness is of a "scene" made up of objects and events, some of which are not causally connected. An animal with primary consciousness can nonetheless connect these objects and events through memory via its previous value-laden experience.

Primary consciousness provides a means of relating an individual's present input to its acts and past rewards. By presenting a correlative scene, it provides an adaptive way of directing attention during the sequencing of complex learning tasks. It also provides an efficient means of correcting errors. These performances might conceivably be carried out without the construction of a scene. But it seems likely that an animal with primary consciousness would have the ability to generalize its learning abilities across many more cues more quickly than an animal without it. Consciousness, I repeat, is efficacious and likely to enhance evolutionary fitness.

Primary consciousness is required for the evolution of higher-order consciousness. But it is limited to a small memorial interval around a time chunk I call the present. It lacks an explicit *notion* or a concept of a personal self, and it does not afford the ability to model the past or the future as part of a correlated scene. An animal with primary consciousness sees the room the way a beam of light illuminates it. Only that which is in the beam is explicitly in the remembered present; all else is darkness. This does not mean that an animal with primary consciousness cannot have long-term memory or act on it. Obviously, it can, but it cannot, in general, be aware of that memory or plan an extended future for itself based on that memory.

Where are the actual brain loci mediating primary consciousness? I have written elsewhere about the possibility that certain circuits in the thalamus, between the cortex and the thalamus, and connecting one cortical region to another, may be the sites of the key reentrant circuits. I will not overload this discussion with the actual neuroanatomy (see FIGURE 1 for the names of the areas involved). Nevertheless, it may be useful to mention here that, as revealed by cognitive testing, certain brain lesions lead to the selective loss of the explicit *conscious* recognition of a signal within a given perceptual domain that is nonetheless implicitly recognized, as shown by psychological tests of the affected person.

A good example is provided by stroke patients who have prosopagnosia—the inability to recognize faces as such. Although they have no awareness of faces, some of these patients will, while denying that they recognize their spouse's face, perform on tests in such a way as to indicate strong discriminatory knowledge of that face. Another example is blindsight. Individuals with lesions in their primary visual cortex report blindness—no awareness of vision—but can locate objects in space when tested. I mention these examples to point out that they may be explained by assuming disruptions (within the appropriate perceptual domains) of the reentrant loops that I have postulated as important for primary consciousness (FIG.1). Let us defer the discussion of tests for consciousness.

With regard to the development of higher-order consciousness, a few words about some sticky matters are in order. The first is: Which animals have primary consciousness? I really cannot answer this except by relating it to the human referent that we agreed on. Going backward from the human referent, we may be reasonably sure (for reasons that will be made clear later) that chimpanzees have it. In all likelihood, most mammals and some birds may have it, although we can only test for its presence indirectly. Unfortunately, such tests are only neuroanatomical or behavioral (not by sign communication or report). If the brain systems required by the present model represent the *only* evolutionary path to primary consciousness, we can be fairly sure that animals without a cortex or its equivalent lack it. An amusing speculation is that cold-blooded animals with primitive cortices would face severe restrictions on primary consciousness because their value systems and value-category memory lack a stable enough biochemical milieu in which to make appropriate linkages to a system that could sustain such consciousness. So snakes are in (dubiously, depending on the temperature), but lobsters are out. If further study bears out this surmise, consciousness is about 300 million years old.

ACKNOWLEDGMENTS

Most of this paper constitutes Chapter 11 of *Bright Air, Brilliant Fire* by Gerald Edelman copyright © 1992 by Basic Books and reprinted by permission of Basic Books, a member of Perseus Books, L.L.C.

REFERENCES

1. RAMON Y CAJAL, S. 1899–1904. Textura del sistema nervioso del hombre y de los vertebrados. Imprenta N. Moya. Madrid.
2. JAMES, W. 1890/1950. The Principles of Psychology [reprint]. Dover. New York.
3. DEFELIPE, J. & E.G. JONES. 1988. Cajal on the Cerebral Cortex. Oxford University Press. New York.
4. JAMES, W. 1997. Does consciousness exist? *In* The Writings of William James. J.J. McDermott, Ed. :169–183. University of Chicago Press. Chicago, IL.
5. EDELMAN, G.M. & G. TONONI. 2000. A Universe of Consciousness: How Matter Becomes Imagination. Basic Books. New York.
6. EDELMAN, G.M. 1992. Bright Air, Brilliant Fire: On the Matter of the Mind. [chapt. 11 :111–123]. Basic Books. New York.

SUGGESTED READINGS

CHANGEUX, J.P. & A. DANCHIN. 1976. Selective stabilization of developing synapses as a mechanism for the specification of neuronal networks. Nature **64:** 705–712.
EDELMAN, G.M. & V. MOUNTCASTLE. 1978. The Mindful Brain: Cortical Organization and the Group-Selective Theory of Higher Brain Function. MIT Press. Cambridge, MA.
EDELMAN, G.M. 1987. Neural Darwinism: The Theory of Neuronal Group Selection. Basic Books. New York.
EDELMAN, G.M. 1989. The Remembered Present: A Biological Theory of Consciousness. Basic Books. New York.
GRAY, C.M. & W. SINGER. 1989. Stimulus-specific neuronal oscillations in orientation columns of cat visual cortex. Proc. Natl. Acad. Sci. USA (March): 1698–1702.
TONONI, G. & G.M. EDELMAN. 1998. Consciousness and complexity. Science **282:** 1846–1851.

Consciousness and the Binding Problem

WOLF SINGER

Max Planck Institute for Brain Research, Frankfurt/Main, Germany

ABSTRACT: It is proposed that phenomenal awareness, the ability to be aware of one's sensations and feelings, emerges from the capacity of evolved brains to analyze their own cognitive processes by iterating and reapplying on themselves the very same cortical operations that they use for the interpretation of signals from the outer world. Search for the neuronal substrate of awareness therefore converges with the search for the cognitive mechanisms through which brains analyze their environment. The hypothesis is put forward that the mammalian brain generates continuously highly dynamic states that, when modulated by input signals, rapidly converge towards points of transient stability that correspond to the respective input constellation. It is proposed that these states are characterized by the dynamic binding of feature-specific cells into functionally coherent cell assemblies which as a whole represent the constellation of features defining a particular perceptual object. Arguments are presented that favor the notion that the cognitive operations supporting awareness consist of an iteration of such dynamic binding processes which then lead to the formation of higher-order assemblies that correspond to the contents of conscious awareness. Experimental data are reviewed relating to the questions of how assemblies are formed and which signatures define the relations among the responses of distributed neurons. It is argued that assemblies self-organize through reciprocal interactions of neurons coupled by reentrant loops and that the signature of relatedness consists of the transient synchronization of the discharges of the respective neurons. Evidence is presented that these synchronization phenomena depend on the same state variables as awareness: Both require for their manifestation activated brain states characterized by desynchronized EEGs. It is concluded that phenomenal awareness is amenable to neurobiological reductionism; but it is also proposed that self-consciousness requires a different explanatory approach because it emerges from the dialogue between different brains and hence has the quality of a cultural construct.

Keywords: Consciousness; Binding problem; Cerebral cortex; Synchronization; Visual perception; Awareness; Theory of mind; Social reality

The term *consciousness* has a number of different connotations ranging from awareness of one's perceptions and sensations to self-awareness, the perception of oneself as an agent that is endowed with intentionality and free will. In this contribution I take the position that the first connotation of consciousness, phenomenal awareness, should in principle be tractable within neurobiological description systems because the problem can probably be reduced to the questions of how cognitive processes are

---

Address for correspondence: Max Planck Institute for Brain Research, Deutschordenstr. 46, 60528 Frankfurt am Main, Germany. Voice: ++49-(0)69-96769-218.
singer@mpih-frankfurt.mpg.de

organized. The latter connotations, by contrast, transcend purely neurobiological descriptions because they have a social, a cultural, and a historical dimension.

AWARENESS

Brains capable of processing signals at a conscious level appear to have the ability to express the outcome of their distributed computational operations in a common format. They can run protocols of their own performance, both past and present, representing not only sensory and motor processes, but also the state of value-assigning systems. Thus, brains that have consciousness possess a meta-level at which their own internal states are subject to cognitive operations; they have what one might call an "inner eye" function. They can compare protocols of their own performance with incoming signals and derive from the outcome of these "internal deliberations" decisions for future acts. This allows them to respond with more flexibility to changing conditions than is the case for brains that lack consciousness and are confined to reacting to stimuli without the option of further reflection and internal deliberation. The implementation of such a reflexive meta-level has obvious adaptive functions and this may have contributed to the evolution of brains capable of being conscious of their own performance.

In order to run protocols of processes occurring within the brain, additional cognitive structures are required that analyze these processes. Thus, implementation of monitoring functions requires second-order processing of the computational results provided by first-order processes. The most likely substrate for such operations are cortical areas that have been added in the course of evolution and that treat the output of lower-order cortical areas in the same way as these treat input from the sensory periphery.[1] The inner-eye function could thus be realized by a reflexive iteration of self-similar cortical processes. This interpretation is compatible with the neuroanatomical evidence that the phylogenetically more recent cortical areas are remote from primary sensory input and interact mainly either through the thalamus or directly through cortico-cortical connections with areas of lower order.

If these more recent monitoring structures have, in turn, access to the motor system—and available evidence indicates that this is the case—brains endowed with such monitoring functions would in addition have the possibility to signal to other organisms the result of the internal monitoring. Through mimickings, gestures, vocalizations and, in humans, language also, such brains could signal to others what their perceptions, intentions, value-assignments and plans of action are. Since such information increases dramatically the predictability of future actions of the respective other, it is likely to have an important function in the stabilization of labor-sharing societies, yet another adaptive function of consciousness that could have favored its evolution.

Two arguments, one based on evolution and the other on ontogeny, suggest that consciousness is a graded phenomenon whereby the gradations are correlated with the phylogenetic and ontogenetic differentiation of the cerebral cortex. The evolutionary argument is derived from the evidence that brains have evolved gradually, the most recent evolutionary changes being confined to an expansion of cerebral cortex and the apposition of new cortical areas. This suggests that consciousness evolved as a consequence of cortical expansion and therefore is probably not an all-or-none phenomenon. The ontogenetic argument is based on the observation that the various manifestations of consciousness, from rudimentary awareness of sensations to the fully expressed self-consciousness of the adult, go in parallel with the gradual maturation of cerebral structures, in particular of the phylogenetically more recent cortical areas.

If one accepts the scenario that the aspect of consciousness that we address as phenomenal awareness results from an iteration of the same cognitive operations that support primary sensory processing, the explanatory gap reduces itself to the question of how the brain accomplishes its cognitive functions. If this question is answered with respect to primary sensory processes, the discovered strategies should be generalizable to the higher-order processes that serve the reanalysis of some of the brains' own computational operations and assume the postulated inner-eye function.

SELF-CONSCIOUSNESS

Other aspects of consciousness such as self-awareness and the experience of individuality seem to require explanations that transcend purely neurobiological reductionism. It is my perception that the ontological status of these phenomena differs from that of the qualia of phenomenal awareness and that it is these aspects of consciousness that give rise to the hard problems in the philosophy of mind and provide the incentive for adopting dualistic positions. The most challenging phenomenon in this context is that we perceive ourselves as agents that are endowed with the freedom to decide, implying that the self is actually capable of controlling by will processes in the brain. We experience these aspects of consciousness as immaterial mental entities that are capable of influencing the neuronal processes required for the execution of actions and, hence, we perceive them as not derivable from the material processes in the brain.

I propose that these latter connotations of consciousness differ from phenomenal awareness because they cannot solely be accounted for by the performance of individual brains, but require for their development interactions among brains. These interacting brains need to be sufficiently differentiated to produce phenomenal awareness and to generate a theory of mind. In addition, they must be able to signal to one another and to comprehend that they are endowed with this capacity; they need to be able to enter dialogues of the kind that would say, for example, "I know that you know how I feel" or "I know that you know what my intentions are." My proposal is that the concept of the "self" with all its subjective mental attributes, emerges from such dialogues among human beings, above all from the early interactions between caregivers and babies. Being told repeatedly: "Do this, otherwise you will be punished" or "leave this, because it is dangerous" is inevitably experienced as evidence that one is free to choose among one's actions. The experience of individuality and responsibility, and as a consequence the intuition that one is endowed with free will would then have to be considered as a product of social interactions. The consequence is that the subjective attributes of consciousness would have the ontological status of social realities, of cultural constructs, and would, therefore, transcend pure neurobiological description systems that focus on individual brains.

The mechanisms that enable us to experience ourselves as endowed with mental capacities do, of course, reside in individual brains, but the contents of this experience are derived from social interactions. Why then should the experience of the self be so obviously different from other experiences that we derive from social interactions? Why do we experience the self as different from other social realities such as value systems or social rules. One explanation could be that the dialogue that leads to the experience of the self is already initiated during an early developmental stage, before episodic memory matures and begins to keep track of what the brain experiences. If so, there would be no conscious record of the processes that led to the experience of the self and the associated subjective connotations of consciousness. Because of this amnesia, these early experiences would lack causation, they would appear as timeless and detached from any real world context. Nevertheless, the contents of these early learning processes are bound to determine the way we act and experience ourselves. In consequence, the subjective connotations of consciousness, although they have been acquired by learning, would be perceived as having transcendental qualities that resist reductionistic explanations.

THE ORGANIZATION OF COGNITIVE PROCESSES

If the argument is valid that the internal monitoring functions are the result of an iteration of the same cognitive operations as the sensory processes which deal with signals conveyed by the sense organs, search for the neuronal substrate of phenomenal awareness converges with the search for the organization of cognitive processes in general. In the following paragraphs I shall, therefore, present hypotheses on the putative organization of cognitive operations in the mammalian brain.

Classical concepts of cognition are based on the assumption that the end result of a cognitive operation should be the generation of explicit neuronal representations of a particular content; in perception this content would be a distinct perceptual object that is characterized by a unique constellation of elementary features. Its neuronal representation is thought to consist of individual neurons that are tuned to particular constellations of input activity. Through their selective responses these neurons establish explicit representations of particular constellations of features. It is commonly held that the specificity of these neurons is brought about by selective convergence of input connections in hierarchically structured feed-forward architectures. This representational strategy allows for rapid processing and is ideally suited to the representation of frequently occurring stereotyped combinations of features; but this strategy is expensive in terms of the number of required neurons and not suited to cope with the virtually infinite diversity of possible constellations of features encountered in real-world objects. Such a representational strategy is also inappropriate for the encoding of syntactic structures and the hierarchical relations among elements of composite perceptual objects because it lacks systematicity (for review see Roelfsema et al.[2] Therefore, alternative concepts have been developed that emphasize more distributed dynamical processes that rely on self-organization. At the basis of these concepts is the assumption that neurons get associated into functionally coherent assemblies which as a whole stand for a particular content whereby each of the participating neurons is tuned to only a subset of the elementary features of composite perceptual objects. This processing strategy is more economical with respect to neuron numbers because a particular neuron can, at different times, participate in different assemblies just as a particular features can be part of many different perceptual objects. Moreover, this representational strategy is more flexible. It allows for the rapid *de novo* representation of constellations that have never been experienced before because there are virtually no limits to the dynamic association of neurons in ever-changing constellations, provided that the participating neurons are interconnected. The correlate of a particular percept would thus be a specific dynamic state of a large number of interacting but distributed neurons rather than the enhanced firing of a few highly specialized neurons at the top of a hierarchically organized feed-forward architecture.

The cognitive process required for the implementation of the inner-eye function has to cope with contents that are particularly unpredictable and rich in combinatorial complexity. The contents that need to be bound together are necessarily polymodal and change at the same pace as the contents of phenomenal awareness change. Thus, the cognitive processes supporting phenomenal awareness need to be especially flexible and able to deal with novelty, compositionality, and syntactic data structure; and this suggests that they, too, should be based on dynamic assembly formation rather than on explicit single-cell codes. If so, it follows that conditions favoring the formation of dynamically organized assemblies ought to be the same as those required for awareness to occur. As detailed below, brain states that are compatible with the manifestation of consciousness also favor the emergence of ordered spatio-temporal activity patterns that could serve as substrate for the formation of assemblies. By contrast, the response properties of individual neurons tend to differ only little in awake, sleeping, and anesthetized brains. It is unlikely, therefore, that the tuned responses of individual neurons are alone sufficient to support consciousness.

The following chapters will, therefore, focus on the question of whether there is any evidence for the existence of dynamically associated assemblies, and if so, what the electrophysiological manifestations of such assemblies might be. The hypothesis will be advanced that one signature of transiently stabilized assemblies is the synchronization of responses of participating neurons. Subsequently, data will be reviewed which suggest a correlation between perceptual processes and the occurrence of response synchronization, on the one hand, and between brain states favorable for the occurrence of awareness and the occurrence of synchronization, on the other.

THE SIGNATURE OF ASSEMBLIES

In assembly coding two important constraints need to be met. First, a selection mechanism is required that permits dynamic yet consistent association of neurons into distinct, functionally coherent assemblies. Second, responses of neurons that have been identified as groupable must get labeled so that they can be recognized by subsequent processing stages as belonging together. This is necessary in order to assure that responses, once they are bound together, are evaluated jointly as constituents of a coherent code and do not get confounded with responses of cells belonging to other, simultaneously formed assemblies that represent different contents. Numerous theoretical studies have addressed the question of how assemblies can self-organize on the basis of cooperative interactions within associative neuronal networks.[3–6] Here I shall focus on the second problem of assembly coding: the question how responses of cells that have been grouped into an assembly can be tagged as related. An unambiguous signature of relatedness is absolutely crucial for assembly codes because, unlike the case in explicit single-cell codes, the meaning of responses changes with the context in which they are interpreted. Hence, in assembly coding false conjunctions are deleterious. Tagging responses as related is equivalent to assuring that they ignite selectively and conjointly corresponding assemblies at subsequent processing stages. This, in turn, can only be achieved by jointly raising the saliency of the selected responses, and here there are three options. First, non-grouped responses can be inhibited; second, the amplitude of the selected responses can be enhanced; and third, the selected cells can be made to discharge in precise temporal synchrony. All three mechanisms enhance the relative impact of the grouped responses at the next-higher processing level. Selecting responses by modulating discharge rates is common in labeled line coding, where a particular cell always signals the same content. This condition is usually met at low levels of processing, as in afferent and efferent pathways close to the respective sensory or effector organs. However, this strategy may not always be suited for the distinction of assemblies because it introduces ambiguities[7] and reduces processing speed.[8] Ambiguities could arise because discharge rates of feature selective cells vary over a wide range as a function of the match between stimulus and receptive field properties, and these modulations of response amplitude would not be distinguishable from those signaling the relatedness of responses. Processing speed would be reduced because rate-coded assemblies can only be identified after a sufficient number of spikes have been integrated to distinguish high from low rates. Therefore, they need to be maintained for some time in order to be distinguishable. This costs processing time, especially if several different assemblies need to be configured within the same matrix of neurons. Different assemblies cannot coexist in time if they share common subsets of neurons because it would be impossible to distinguish which responses belong to which assembly. Therefore, assemblies have to be multiplexed and configured in sequence. The rate at which different contents can be encoded does thus depend on the duration over which assemblies have to be maintained to be distinguishable. If defined exclusively by rate codes, assemblies need to have a lifetime of at least 50 to 100 ms, which slows down processing speed.

Both the ambiguities resulting from stimulus-related rate fluctuations and the temporal constraints can be overcome if the selection and labeling of responses is achieved through precise synchronization of individual discharges.[7,9,10] Expressing the relatedness of responses by synchronization resolves the ambiguities resulting from stimulus-dependent rate fluctuations because synchronization can be modulated independently of rates. Response amplitudes could thus be reserved to signal how well particular features match the preferences of neurons, and synchronicity could be used in parallel to signal how these features are related. Defining assemblies by synchronization also accelerates the rate at which different assemblies can follow one another because the selected event is the individual spike or a brief burst of spikes; saliency is enhanced only for those discharges that are precisely synchronized and generate coincident synaptic potentials in target cells at the subsequent processing stage. The rate at which different assemblies can follow one another without getting confounded is then limited only by the duration of the interval over which synaptic potentials summate effectively (for a detailed discussion, see Singer[11]).

Another advantage of selecting responses by synchronization is that the timing of input events is preserved with high precision in the output activity of cells because synchronized input is transmitted with minimal latency jitter.[12–14] This, in turn, can be exploited to preserve the signature of relatedness across processing stages, thus reducing further the risk of getting false conjunctions. Finally, synchronization enhances processing speed also by accelerating synaptic transmission per se because synchronized EPSPs trigger action potentials with minimal delay.

PREREQUISITES FOR SELECTION BY SYNCHRONIZATION

At the level of cellular mechanisms two prerequisites need to be fulfilled in order to exploit synchrony as a signature of relatedness: First, neurons must be able to act as coincidence detectors, that is, they must be particularly sensitive to coincident synaptic inputs. Second, mechanisms must exist which permit rapid and context-dependent temporal coordination of distributed discharge patterns.

The question of whether neurons in the central nervous system are capable of performing coincidence detection with the required precision is controversial since both theoretical arguments and simulation studies led to opposite conclusions.[13–15] However, experimental evidence indicates clearly that neurons can evaluate temporal relations among incoming activity with sometimes surprising precision. In the auditory system coincidence detection is used to locate sound sources. Neurons in auditory nuclei of the brainstem evaluate the delays among incoming signals from the two ears with a precision in the submillisecond range (for review see Carr[16]). Another example is the oscillatory responses of retinal ganglion cells that can be synchronized over large distances with close to zero phase lag.[17] Because of the high frequency of these oscillations (up to 100 Hz), the neuronal mechanism responsible for synchronization must operate with time constants in the millisecond range. This time-modulated activity is reliably transmitted up to cortical neurons as indicated by cross-correlation analysis between retinal ganglion cells and cortical neurons.[18] The implication is that neurons along the transmission chain must have operated with integration time constants not longer than a half cycle of the oscillation, and hence no more than 5 ms. The ability of cortical networks to handle temporally structured activity with high precision can also be inferred from the abundant evidence on the oscillatory patterning and synchronization of neuronal responses in the neocortex (reviewed in Singer and Gray[10]). Such temporally coordinated discharge patterns can only emerge and stabilize if the temporal structure of activity is preserved during synaptic transmission and does not get dispersed and smeared too much by temporal integration. In the awake, performing brain the oscillatory patterning of cortical responses is typically in the gamma frequency range (30 to 60 Hz), and synchronization peaks often have a width at base in the range of 10 to 15 ms, indicating that temporal integration intervals should be on average no longer than 10 ms.

If synchronization is to play a role as signature of assemblies it must be possible to synchronize discharges rapidly because of the constraints set by processing speed.

Early simulation studies, which used harmonic oscillators rather than single spiking neurons, showed that it may indeed take a few cycles before synchronicity is established through phase locking.[19] However, later simulations with spiking neurons revealed that networks of appropriately coupled units can undergo sudden state changes whereby the synchronization of discharges and their oscillatory patterning occurs promptly and virtually simultaneously (for review see Singer et al.[8]).

Very rapid synchronization has been observed recently in the visual cortex of cats. When neurons were activated by the onset of an appropriately oriented grating stimulus, their initial responses were already better synchronized than expected from mere stimulus locking.[20] Comparison between actual response latencies and immediately preceding fluctuations of the local field potential revealed that the response latency shifted as a function of the polarity of the preceding field potential fluctuation. Because these fluctuations were not independent between the different recording sites, response latencies became synchronized. Thus, coordinated fluctuations of excitability act like a dynamic filter and cause a virtually instantaneous synchronization of the very first discharges of responses.[20] Since the spatio-temporal patterns of these fluctuations reflect the architecture of intracortical association connections, grouping by synchronization can be extremely fast and can still occur as a function of the pre-wired associational dispositions of the cortical network.

Evidence suggests that an oscillatory patterning of responses may be instrumental for the internal synchronization of neurons, in particular when interactions comprise substantial conduction delays or occur across polysynaptic pathways.[21] Experiments in slices support this conjecture, showing that subthreshold oscillatory modulation of the membrane potential is ideally suited to establish synchronization.[22] In cells with oscillating membrane potential, responses can become delayed considerably, whereby the maximally possible delay interval depends on oscillation frequency and can amount to nearly the duration of one cycle. With such a mechanism, responses to temporally dispersed EPSPs can become synchronized within less than an oscillation cycle in cells exhibiting coherent fluctuations of their membrane potential.

FUNCTIONAL CORRELATES OF RESPONSE SYNCHRONIZATION

Following the discovery of stimulus-related response synchronization among neurons in the cat visual cortex,[23,24] numerous experiments have been performed in search of a correlation between the occurrence of response synchronization and particular stimulus configurations. The prediction to be tested was that synchronization probability should reflect some of the Gestaltcriteria according to which the visual system groups related features during scene segmentation. Among the grouping criteria examined so far are continuity, vicinity, similarity, and colinearity in the orientation domain, and common fate in the motion domain (Refs. 9, 25–27 for the cat; Ref. 28 for the monkey). So far, the results of these investigations are compatible with the hypothesis that the probability of response synchronization reflects the Gestaltcriteria applied for perceptual grouping (FIG. 1). Stimulus-specific response synchronization has been found within and across different areas, and even between hemispheres (for review see Singer and Gray[10]) and, most importantly, none of these synchronization phenomena were detectable by correlating successively recorded responses. This indicates that synchronization was not due to stimulus locking, but to internal dynamic coordination of spike timing. Thus, the observed temporal coherence among responses exceeds that expected from mere co-variation of event-related rate changes.

Studies involving lesions[29,30] and developmental manipulations[31,32] indicate that the interactions responsible for these dynamic synchronization phenomena are mediated to a substantial extent by reciprocal cortico-cortical connections. The criteria for perceptual grouping should then be reflected in the architecture of these connections, and this postulate agrees with the evidence that cortico-cortical connections preferentially link neurons with related feature preferences (for review see Schmidt *et al.*[33]).

RESPONSE SYNCHRONIZATION AND BEHAVIORAL STATES

Most of the early experiments in search of synchronization phenomena have been performed in lightly anesthetized animals and it was important, therefore, to investigate whether response synchronization occurs also during states, where the EEG is actually desynchronized, as is characteristic for the awake, attentive brain. Evidence from cats and monkeys indicates that highly precise, internally generated synchrony is considerably more pronounced in the awake than in the anesthetized brain. Whenever tested, and data are available from the primary visual cortex of cats and monkeys, the motion-sensitive areas MT and MST in monkeys and infero-temporal cortex of monkeys, the synchronization phenomena were readily demonstrable and showed a dependence on stimulus configuration similar to the synchronization measured under anesthesia (for review see Singer *et al.*[8]).

Of particular interest in this context is the recent finding that response synchronization is especially pronounced when the global EEG desynchronizes and when the animals are attentive. Stimulating the mesencephalic reticular formation in anesthetized animals leads to a transient desynchronization of the EEG, resembling the transition from slow-wave sleep to rapid-eye-movement sleep. Munk *et al.*[34] (1996) and Herculano-Houzel *et al.*[35] (1999) have recently shown that stimulus-specific synchronization of neuronal responses is drastically facilitated when the EEG is in a desynchronized rather than in a synchronized state.

Direct evidence for an attention-related facilitation of synchronization has been obtained from cats that had been trained to perform a visually triggered motor response.[36] Simultaneous recordings from visual, association, somatosensory and motor areas revealed that the cortical areas involved in the execution of the task synchronized their activity, predominantly with zero phase-lag, as soon as the animals prepared themselves for the task and focused their attention on the relevant stimulus. Immediately after the appearance of the visual stimulus, synchronization increased further over the recorded areas, and these coordinated activation patterns were maintained until the task was completed. However, once the reward was available and the animals engaged in consumatory behavior, these coherent patterns collapsed and gave way to low-frequency oscillatory activity that did not exhibit any consistent phase relations. This close correspondence between performance of an attention-demanding visuo-motor task and the occurrence of inter-areal synchroniza-

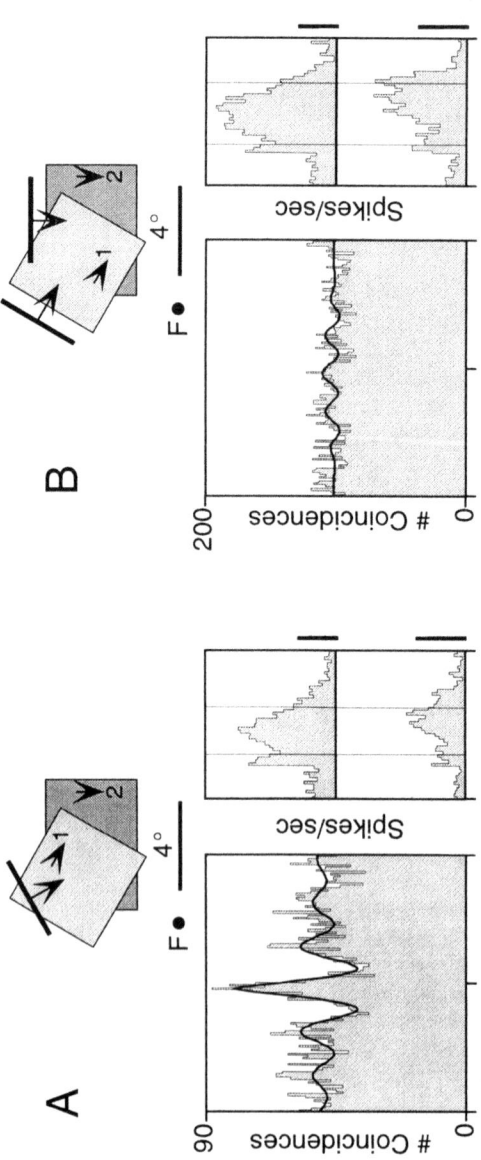

FIGURE 1. Stimulus-dependence of neuronal synchronization in area MT of the visual cortex of a macaque monkey carrying out a fixation task. Neuronal responses were obtained from two cell groups with different directional preferences. The figure shows cross-correlograms and peri-stimulus-time histograms for four different stimulation conditions. The small *insets* indicate the receptive field locations (1,2) with respect to the fixation point (F) and the directional preference of the neurons (small arrows). (**A**) A single moving stimulus bar, whose direction of motion was intermediate between the neurons' preferences, led to a pronounced synchronization of the two cell groups, as indicated by the central maximum in the cross-correlogram. (**B**) Presentation of two stimuli moving in the respective preferred directions of cell group 1 and 2 abolishes synchronization. (**C, D**) The synchronization observed with a single stimulus does not depend on its particular orientation. (**C**) Changing orientation and direction of motion by 15° or (**D**) using one of the bars from the configuration in (**B**) had little influence on synchronization. *Scale bars* for the peri-stimulus-time histograms correspond to 40 spikes/sec. The *continuous line* superimposed on the correlograms represents a damped cosine function that was fitted to the data to assess the significance of the correlogram modulation. (Modified from Kreiter and Singer.[28])

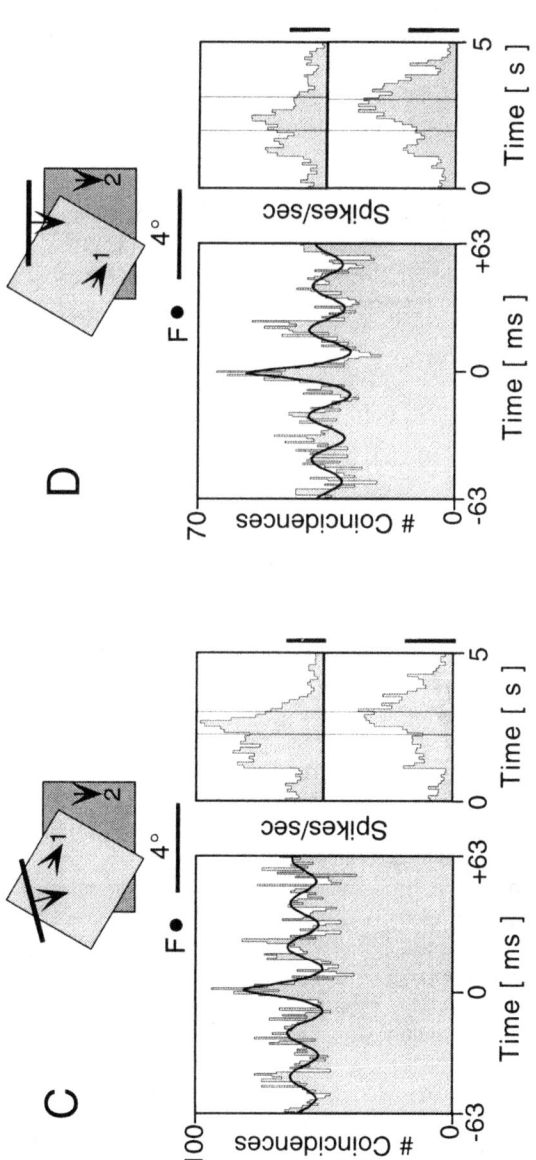

FIGURE 1. *Continued.*

tion suggests a functional role of the temporal patterning of widely distributed neuronal activity. One possibility is that the synchronization observed during the preparatory period reflects an entrainment of activity into a temporal pattern that is common to selected cortical areas in order to facilitate rapid temporal coordination of signals and fast convergence towards points of stability once the stimulus has become available. Attentional mechanisms could impose a coherent subthreshold modulation on neurons in cortical areas that need to participate in the execution of the anticipated task and thereby permit rapid synchronization of selected responses using the synchronizing mechanisms described above. According to this scenario, the attentional mechanisms would induce what one might call a state of expectancy in the respective cortical areas by imposing on them a specific, task-related dynamic activation pattern which then, once stimulus-driven input becomes available, acts like a dynamic filter that causes rapid synchronization of selected responses, thereby accomplishing the required grouping and binding of responses and in addition assuring rapid transmission.

PERCEPTION

In a series of visual experiments attempts have been made to find correlations between perceptual disturbances and abnormalities in neuronal synchronization.

Kittens were made strabismic shortly after eye opening, which results in an inability to group into a coherent percept signals generated by the two eyes. This inability is reflected by the failure of neurons driven by the two eyes to synchronize their responses even if these are evoked by a single object.[32] A likely reason for the disruption of response synchronization is that the tangential intracortical connections between neurons driven by different eyes are lost during early development due to consistent de-correlation of the responses evoked from the two eyes.[31]

A subgroup of the strabismic animals developed, in addition, a syndrome called strabismic amblyopia. Subjects suffering from strabismic amblyopia, and this is true for both animals and humans, have reduced visual acuity in the amblyopic eye. Moreover, they have difficulties in identifying figures if these are embedded in a contour-rich background, suggesting problems with perceptual grouping. In these amblyopic animals there was a close correlation between perceptual deficits and abnormalities in response synchronization, but there was no evidence for abnormalities of the response properties of individual cells. Quite unexpectedly, neurons in the primary visual cortex responded equally well to visual stimuli irrespective of whether these were shown to the normal or to the amblyopic eye. Thus, neurons driven by the amblyopic eye continued to respond vigorously to gratings that the animals had not been able to resolve with this eye during previous behavioral testing. Responses mediated by the normal and the amblyopic eye showed no difference in their amplitude or feature specific tuning irrespective of the spatial frequency of the applied test gratings. The only significant difference was the reduced ability of neurons driven by the amblyopic eye to synchronize their responses, and this difference was particularly pronounced when the spatial frequency of the grating stimuli approached the range beyond which the animals had no longer been able to resolve gratings with the amblyopic eye.[37]

In primary visual cortex, there is, thus, a close correlation between a specific perceptual deficit and alterations in synchronization; and this relation could very well be causal. If synchronization is used to group responses together and to label them for further joint processing, then one expects that disturbances in synchronization should lead to disturbances in perceptual grouping such as occur for interocular binding operations in all strabismic animals and for monocular grouping operations in animals suffering from strabismic amblyopia. Since reduced synchronization is likely to reduce the saliency of responses conveyed by the amblyopic eye, it can also account for the fact that the amblyopic eye consistently loses in interocular competition when both eyes are open. Here, then, is a clear case where the firing of neurons in a cortical area does not correspond to perception, suggesting that the firing of individual neurons is only a necessary but not a sufficient condition to support perception. Additional and, in this case, indispensable information appears to be conveyed by the precise temporal relations among the discharges of simultaneously active neurons.

Another close correlation between response synchronization and perception and a remarkable dissociation between responses of individual neurons and perception has been found in experiments on binocular rivalry. When the two eyes are presented with patterns that cannot be fused into a single coherent percept, the two patterns are perceived in alternation rather than as a superposition of their components. This implies that there is a central gating mechanism which selects in alternation the signals arriving from the two eyes for further processing. Interocular rivalry is thus a suitable paradigm to investigate the neuronal correlates of dynamic response selection, a process closely related to the formation of assemblies.

This paradigm has been applied to investigate how neuronal responses that are selected and perceived differ from those that are suppressed and excluded from supporting perception. Multiunit and field potential responses were recorded with chronically implanted electrodes from up to 30 sites in cat primary visual cortex while the animals were exposed to rivalrous stimulation conditions.[38] Because the animal performs tracking eye movements only for the pattern that is actually perceived, it was possible to infer from the optokinetic tracking response which of the two eyes is selected. The outcome of these experiments was surprising as it turned out that the discharge rate of neurons in primary visual cortex failed to reflect the alternating suppression and selection of input from the two eyes. A close and highly significant correlation existed, however, between changes in the strength of response synchronization and the outcome of rivalry. Cells mediating responses of the eye that won in interocular competition increased the synchronicity of their responses upon introduction of the rivalrous stimulus, while the reverse was true for cells driven by the eye that became suppressed. Thus, in this particular case of competition, selection of responses for further processing appears to be achieved by raising their saliency through synchronization rather than by enhancing discharge frequency. Likewise, suppression is not achieved by inhibiting responses but by desynchronization (FIG. 2). In other terms one could say that only activity exhibiting a sufficient degree of temporal coordination has access to conscious awareness.

As in the amblyopic animals, there is thus a remarkable dissociation, at least in primary visual areas, between perception and the discharge rate of individual neurons. Cells whose responses are not perceived and are excluded from controlling behavior respond as vigorously as cells whose responses are perceived and support

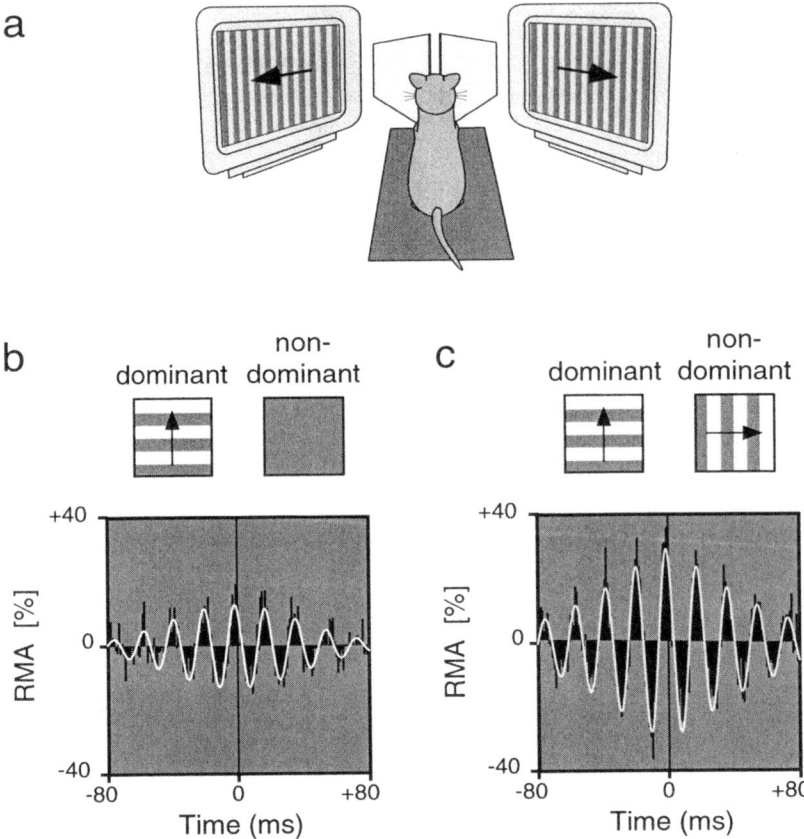

FIGURE 2. Neuronal synchronization under conditions of binocular rivalry. (**a**) Using two mirrors, different patterns were presented to the two eyes of strabismic cats. Panels **b–e** show normalized cross-correlograms for two pairs of recording sites activated by the eye that won (**b,c**) and lost (**d,e**) in interocular competition, respectively. *Insets* above the correlograms indicate stimulation conditions. Under monocular stimulation (**b**), cells driven by the winning eye show a significant correlation which is enhanced after introduction of the rivalrous stimulus to the other eye (**c**). The reverse is the case for cells driven by the losing eye (compare conditions **d** and **e**). The *white continuous line* superimposed on the correlograms represents a damped cosine function fitted to the data. RMA, relative modulation amplitude of the center peak in the correlogram, computed as the ratio of peak amplitude over offset of correlogram modulation. This measure reflects the strength of synchrony. (Modified from Fries *et al.*[38])

behavior. This dissociation is particularly stringent in the case of rivalry because here responses to physically unchanged stimuli were recorded from the same neurons before and after introducing the rivalrous stimulus. Responses could be followed continuously while they passed from a condition where they were readily perceivable to a condition where they either continued to support perception in spite of rivalry or became excluded from perception. Another puzzling result of the rivalry

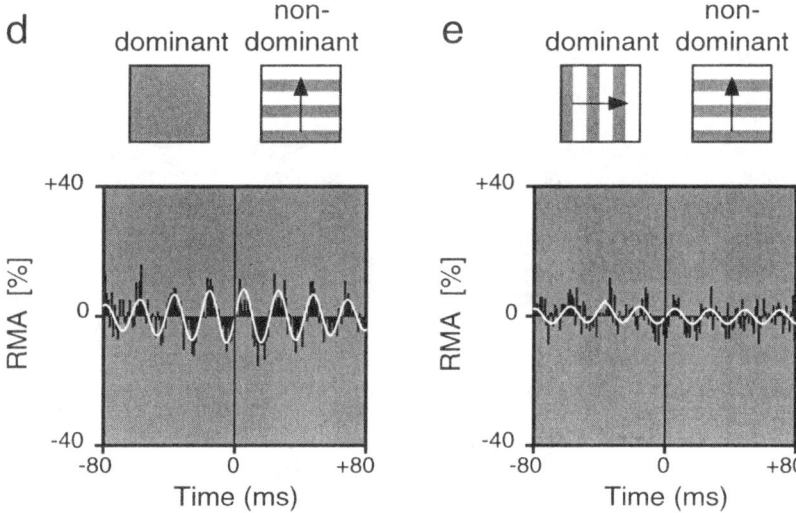

FIGURE 2. *Continued.*

study is that responses that win the competition increase their synchronicity upon presentation of the rivalrous stimulus. This suggests the action of a mechanism that enhances the saliency of the selected responses by improving their synchronicity in order to protect them against the interference caused by the rivalrous stimulus.

These results provide direct support for the hypothesis that precise temporal relations between the discharges of spatially distributed neurons matter in cortical processing and that synchronization may be exploited to jointly raise the saliency of the responses selected for further processing. The important point here is that this selection can obviously be achieved without inhibiting the non-selected responses. Thus, in principle, it should be possible to select a second group of responses by synchronizing them independently of the first. The result would be two coexisting, but functionally distinct, assemblies at the same processing level. The example of rivalry also illustrates how synchronization and rate modulation depend on each other. The signals from the suppressed eye failed to induce tracking eye movements, indicating that eventually the vigorous but poorly synchronized responses in primary visual areas failed to drive the neurons responsible for the execution of eye movements. Direct evidence for the failure of neurons at subsequent processing stages to respond to the input from the respective suppressed eye has been obtained in behaving monkeys trained to indicate which of the two eyes they were actually using.[39,40] This interdependence of discharge rates and synchrony provides the option to use both coding strategies in parallel in order to encode complementary information (see above).

A particularly close correlation between neuronal synchrony and perceptual grouping has recently been observed in experiments with plaid stimuli. These stimuli are well suited for the study of dynamic binding mechanisms because minor changes of the stimulus cause a binary switch in perceptual grouping. Two superimposed gratings moving in different directions (plaid stimuli) may be perceived either as two surfaces, one being transparent and sliding on top of the other (component motion), or as a single surface, consisting of crossed bars, that moves in a direction intermediate to the component vectors (pattern motion).[41,42] Which percept dominates depends on the luminance of grating intersections because this variable defines the degree of transparency.[43] Component (pattern) motion is perceived when luminance conditions are compatible (incompatible) with transparency (FIG. 3A). Here is a case where local changes in stimulus properties cause global changes in perceptual grouping. In the case of component motion, responses evoked by the two gratings must be segregated and only responses evoked by the contours of the same grating must be grouped to represent the two surfaces; in the case of pattern motion, responses to all contours must be bound together to represent a single surface. If this grouping of responses is initiated by selective synchronization, three predictions must hold (FIG. 3B): First, neurons that prefer the direction of motion of one of the two gratings and have colinearly aligned receptive fields should always synchronize their responses because they respond always to contours that belong to the same surface. Second, neurons that are tuned to the respective motion directions of the two gratings should synchronize their responses in case of pattern motion because they then respond to contours of the same surface but they should not synchronize in case of component motion because their responses are then evoked by contours belonging to different surfaces. Third, neurons preferring the direction of pattern motion should also synchronize only in the pattern and not in the component motion condition.

An important aspect of these predictions is that the expected changes in synchrony differ for different cell pairs, depending on the configuration of their receptive fields. Thus, when searching for relations between synchrony and cognitive functions, it is not only crucial to identify the processing stage where one assumes a particular binding function to be accomplished, but also to select the appropriate cell pairs. Averaging data across cell pairs with different receptive field configuration can mask dynamic changes in synchrony and is likely to reveal only the static anisotropies in the network of synchronizing connections. Such a problem may have contributed to the negative results of a recent study which failed to show a relation between perceptual grouping and internal synchronization in monkey striate cortex.[44]

In the case of the plaid stimuli, predictions were tested with multielectrode recordings from areas 18 and PMLS of the visual cortex of lightly anesthetized cats after we had confirmed with eye-movement recordings in awake cats that the ani-

---

FIGURE 3. (**A**) Two superimposed gratings that differ in orientation and drift in different directions are perceived either as two independently moving gratings (component motion) or as a single pattern drifting in the intermediate direction (pattern motion), depending on whether the luminance conditions at the intersections are compatible with transparency. (**B**) Predictions on the synchronization behavior of neurons as a function of their receptive field configuration (*left*) and stimulation conditions (*right*). (**C**) Changes in synchronization behavior of two neurons recorded simultaneously from areas 18 and PMLS that were activated with a plaid stimulus under component (*upper graph*) and pattern motion conditions (*lower graph*). The two neurons preferred gratings with orthogonal orientation (see receptive field configuration [top] and tuning curves obtained with component and pattern, respectively) and synchronized their responses only when activated with the pattern stimulus (compare cross-correlograms on the *right*). (Reproduced by the courtesy of Miguel Castelo-Branco and Sergio Neuenschwander.)

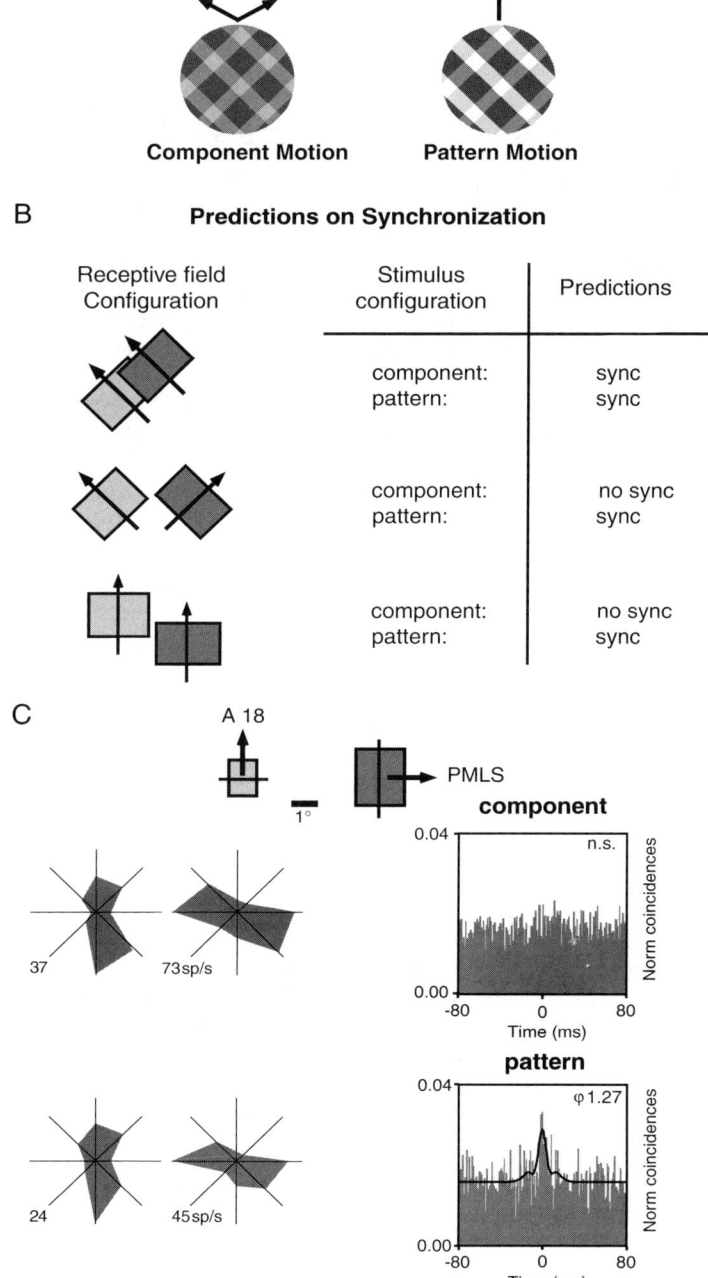

FIGURE 3. *See previous page for caption.*

mals distinguished between component and pattern motion. Cross-correlation analysis of responses from cell pairs distributed either within or across areas 18 and PMLS confirmed all three predictions. Cells synchronized their activity if they responded to contours that are perceived as belonging to the same surface[45] (FIG. 3C). Analysis of the neurons' discharge rate confirmed that most of the cells in these visual areas respond preferentially to the component gratings of the plaids (component-specific cells[46]) and not to the pattern as a whole. However, in contrast to synchrony, variations in response amplitude failed to reflect the transition from component to pattern motion induced by transparency manipulation. Dynamic changes in synchronization could thus serve to encode in a context-dependent way the relations among the simultaneous responses to spatially superimposed contours and thereby bias their association with distinct surfaces. Future investigations have to clarify whether the populations of differentially synchronized neurons already serve as the final representation of the perceived surfaces or whether in case of pattern motion additional assemblies are formed. These would then have to consist of conjunction units tuned to the specific constellations of superimposed gratings, and their responses would have to bind together to signal that they code for the same surface.

In conclusion the data reviewed in this chapter indicate that evaluation of internally generated correlation patterns between responses of simultaneously recorded neurons permits the extraction of information about stimulus configurations, behavioral states and perception that cannot be obtained by analyzing the responses of individual neurons sequentially. The relevant variable containing this additional information is the rather precise synchronization of a fraction of the discharges constituting the respective responses. The data indicate further that responses containing synchronized epochs have a higher probability of being processed further and eventually to be perceived than do responses lacking such synchronized epochs, supporting the hypothesis that synchronization is used as a mechanism for response selection. Since synchronization necessarily involves at least two neurons, it inevitably raises simultaneously the saliency of more then one response. It is thus well suited to select subsets of responses for further joint processing, thereby defining the group of selected responses as related. Thus, synchronization fulfills the requirements postulated for a binding mechanism that selects a subset from a larger number of simultaneously active neurons and labels the responses of this subset in a way that favors joint processing at the subsequent processing stage. The evidence that synchronization probability reflects Gestaltcriteria that guide perceptual grouping supports the hypothesis that synchronization serves as a binding mechanism in the context of assembly formation by jointly raising the saliency of selected subsets of responses. Transient synchronization of distributed responses might thus be considered as the distinguished state to which the assembly forming self-organizing process converges during sensory-motor processing.

THE GENERALITY OF SYNCHRONICITY

Studies in non-visual sensory modalities and in the motor system indicate that synchrony and oscillatory activity may actually be quite ubiquitous in the nervous system. Synchronization in the gamma frequency range occurs in the olfactory system of various vertebrate and invertebrate species, where it has been related to the processing of odor information (for review see Laurent[47]). In the auditory cortex, synchronized gamma oscillations have been described both in humans (for review see Joliot et al.[48]) and in animals.[49,50] In the somatosensory system, synchronized oscillatory activity in this frequency range has recently been described both in the cat[51] and in the monkey.[52] Furthermore, synchronized oscillatory firing has been observed in other systems like the hippocampus[53] and the frontal cortex.[54]

Similar evidence is available for the motor system where neural synchronization in the gamma frequency range has been discovered in cats,[51] monkeys,[52,55] and humans.[56]

Synchrony may also play a role in sensorimotor integration. In awake, behaving monkeys, task-dependent synchronization between units distributed across sensory and motor cortical areas and within motor cortex itself has been reported.[52,55,57–59] Thus, synchrony also seems to play a role in visuomotor coordination and in the programming of motor responses. As proposed previously, it may be instrumental for the flexible channeling (binding) of sensory signals to particular motor programs.[2]

Synchronization also seems to play a role in the linkage between cortical assemblies and subcortical target structures such as the superior colliculus. This possibility is suggested by the existence of precise temporal relationships between the discharges of neurons in areas of the visual cortex and the superior colliculus.[60] In these experiments, it could be shown that cortico-tectal interactions are strongly dependent on the temporal coherence of cortical activity. If cortical neurons engage in synchronous oscillatory activity either with partners within the same cortical area or with cells in other cortical areas, their impact on tectal cells is enhanced, indicating that tectal cells are driven more effectively by synchronous than by asynchronous cortical activity. This finding is consistent with the idea that the temporal organization of activity patterns plays an important role in defining the output of the cortex.

Taken together, available evidence suggests that comparable synchronization phenomena are found in a large number of different functional systems. Thus, it seems justified to generalize the results obtained in the visual cortex and to suggest that temporal coordination of discharges may be of general relevance for neural information processing. Importantly, there is increasing evidence that dynamic synchronization, in particular at frequencies in the gamma band, occurs also in the human brain. EEG studies have provided evidence for precise synchronization of activity in the γ-frequency range in human visual cortex that is related to perception and reflects the subjective coherence of stimulus arrangements.[61–65]

SYNCHRONICITY AS A GENERAL CODE FOR RELATEDNESS

If synchronicity serves as the signature of relatedness, synchronized responses should be interpreted as being related, irrespective of the cause of synchronization. Psychophysical evidence supports this conjecture. It indicates that synchronously presented stimuli are bound perceptually and interpreted as elements of the same figure with greater probability than asynchronously appearing texture elements (Refs. 66–70; but see Ref. 71). Hence, the synchronicity of responses imposed by simultaneously appearing texture elements (stimulus-locked synchronization) seems to be exploited for perceptual grouping. With respect to their strength and temporal precision, the externally induced and internally generated synchrony is virtually indistinguishable. Since the psychophysical results indicate that the former is interpreted as a signature of relatedness, it would be puzzling if this were not the case also for internally generated synchrony. Synchronization could thus serve as a general tag of relatedness, irrespective of whether it results from coincidence of external events or from internal grouping operations.

CONCLUSION

The hypothesis defended here is based on the following assumptions:

(1) phenomenal awareness emerges from an iteration of self-similar cognitive operations;

(2) these are accomplished by cortical networks, and iteration is achieved by the addition of cortical areas of higher order that process the output of lower-order areas in the same way as these process their respective input;

(3) in order to account for the required combinatorial flexibility these cognitive operations are likely to be based on the dynamic, self-organizing association of distributed neurons into functionally coherent assemblies and not solely on the generation of content-specific responses of individual specialized cells;

(4) the binding mechanism that groups neurons into assemblies and labels their responses as related is the transient synchronization of discharges with a precision in the millisecond range; hence brief episodes of synchronized firing may be seen as a signature of the self-organizing dynamic process that leads to the formation of functionally coherent assemblies of spatially distributed neurons; and

(5) the formation of such dynamically associated, synchronized cell assemblies requires activated brain states characterized by "desynchronized" EEG and is facilitated by attentional mechanisms.

The first assumption differs from the others because it is a conceptual premise which by itself does not provide any experimentally testable predictions, but each of the following subordinate assumptions leads to predictions about structural and functional features of brains capable of supporting the cognitive operations that give rise to phenomenal awareness. The data reviewed above illustrate that there is supportive experimental evidence for many of these features. However, we are lacking the proof that the observed features actually serve the function that our theories assign to them. This is the case not only for the more recently discovered functional properties such as the transient synchronization of distributed neuronal responses, but also for the rate-modulated discharges of individual neurons. As long as we have no complete theory on the structure of neuronal codes, it cannot be decided whether a sequence of discharges of a particular unit signifies that this unit participates in an assembly that lasts as long as the sequence of discharges or whether the unit participates in several different, successively organized assemblies, or whether it represents a content on its own. This uncertainty is due to the difficulty in identifying assemblies. Assemblies can only be identified if one succeeds in recording simultaneously from a sufficiently large fraction of neurons actually participating in a particular assembly. For reasons detailed elsewhere[8] this is technically very demanding, and therefore attempts to identify assemblies are still at the very beginning. Thus, if it is the case that the cognitive processes required for consciousness involve the organization of highly distributed assemblies, we are a long way from the direct identification of the neuronal correlates of even the simplest forms of consciousness.

As long as analysis remains confined to the activity of individual neurons it will remain difficult to decide whether a recorded response is only a necessary or whether it is a sufficient condition for consciousness. Obviously, neurons need to discharge in order to convey information; if a group of neurons in a particular transmission chain stops responding, the content conveyed by that group of neurons cannot be perceived. Hence, correlations between perceptual awareness and cellular responses indicate only that the discharges of cells at a particular processing stage are necessary for a particular content to reach the level of awareness. In order to find out whether additional prerequisites have to be fulfilled, such as the binding of these responses into widely distributed assemblies, variables need to be determined that permit assessment of order parameters beyond the level of single units. This can only be achieved with recording techniques that disclose the spatio-temporal activation profile of large numbers of neurons. The fact that the most global of these methods, the EEG, differentiates rather reliably between brain states where consciousness is or is not possible favors the hypothesis that consciousness-supporting cognitive processes require coordination of activity well beyond the level of single-cell firing. Consciousness manifests itself only during brain states characterized by "desynchronized" EEGs. These states, in turn, favor the occurrence of gamma oscillations and long-distance synchronization of neuronal responses with a precision in the millisecond range. It seems not unreasonable, therefore, to pursue the hypothesis that the cognitive operations required for phenomenal awareness to manifest itself consist of the formation of large assemblies of distributed neurons whose signature of relatedness is the internally generated synchronicity of discharges.

REFERENCES

1. KRUBITZER, L. 1998. Constructing the neocortex: influence on the pattern of organization in mammals. *In* Brain and Mind: Evolutionary Perspectives. M.S. Gazzaniga & J.S. Altman, Eds.: 19–34. HFSP. Strasbourg.
2. ROELFSEMA, P.R., A.K. ENGEL, P. KÖNIG & W. SINGER. 1996. The role of neuronal synchronization in response selection: a biologically plausible theory of structured representation in the visual cortex. J. Cogn. Neurosci. **8:** 603–625.
3. BRAITENBERG, V. 1978. Cell assemblies in the cerebral cortex. *In* Architectonics of the Cerebral Cortex. Lecture Notes in Biomathematics 21, Theoretical Approaches in Complex Systems. R. Heim & G. Palm, Eds.: 171–188. Springer-Verlag. Berlin.
4. EDELMAN, G.M. 1987. Neural Darwinism: The Theory of Neuronal Group Selection. Basic Books. New York.
5. PALM, G. 1990. Cell assemblies as a guideline for brain research. Concepts Neurosci. **1:** 133–147.
6. GERSTEIN, G.L. & P.M. GOCHIN. 1992. Neuronal population coding and the elephant. *In* Information Processing in the Cortex, Experiments and Theory. A. Aertsen & V. Braitenberg, Eds.: 139–173. Springer-Verlag. Berlin-Heidelberg-New York.
7. VON DER MALSBURG, C. 1985. Nervous structures with dynamical links. Ber. Bunsenges. Phys. Chem. **89:** 703–710.
8. SINGER, W., A.K. ENGEL, A.K. KREITER, M.H.J. MUNK, S. NEUENSCHWANDER & P.R. ROELFSEMA. 1997. Neuronal assemblies: necessity, signature and detectability. Trends Cog. Sci. **1(7):** 252–261.

9. GRAY, C.M., P. KÖNIG, A.K. ENGEL & W. SINGER. 1989. Oscillatory responses in cat visual cortex exhibit inter-columnar synchronization which reflects global stimulus properties. Nature **338:** 334–337.
10. SINGER, W. & C.M. GRAY. 1995. Visual feature integration and the temporal correlation hypothesis. Annu. Rev. Neurosci. **18:** 555–586.
11. SINGER, W. 1999/2000. Response synchronization: a universal coding strategy for the definition of relations. In The New Cognitive Neurosciences, 2nd ed. M.S. Gazzaniga, Ed.: 325–338. MIT Press. Cambridge, MA.
12. ABELES, M. 1982. Role of the cortical neuron: integrator or coincidence detector? Isr. J. Med. Sci. **18:** 83–92.
13. SOFTKY, W. 1994. Sub-millisecond coincidence detection in active dendritic trees. Neuroscience **58:** 13–41.
14. KÖNIG, P., A.K. ENGEL & W. SINGER. 1996. Integrator or coincidence detector? The role of the cortical neuron revisited. Trends Neurosci. **19:** 130–137.
15. SHADLEN, M.N. & W.T. NEWSOME. 1994. Noise, neural codes and cortical organization. Curr. Opin. Neurobiol. **4:** 569–579.
16. CARR, C.E. 1993. Processing of temporal information in the brain. Annu. Rev. Neurosci. **16:** 223–243.
17. NEUENSCHWANDER, S. & W. SINGER. 1996. Long-range synchronization of oscillatory light responses in the cat retina and lateral geniculate nucleus. Nature **379:** 728–733.
18. CASTELO-BRANCO, M., S. NEUENSCHWANDER & W. SINGER. 1998. Synchronization of visual responses between the cortex, lateral geniculate nucleus, and retina in the anesthetized cat. J. Neurosci. **18:** 6395–6410.
19. KÖNIG, P. & T.B. SCHILLEN. 1991. Stimulus-dependent assembly formation of oscillatory responses: I. Synchronization. Neural Comput. **3:** 155–166.
20. FRIES, P., P.R. ROELFSEMA, W. SINGER & A.K. ENGEL. 1997. Correlated variation of response latencies due to synchronous subthreshold membrane potential fluctuations in cat striate cortex. Soc. Neurosci. Abstr. **23:** 1266.
21. KÖNIG, P., A.K. ENGEL & W. SINGER. 1995. The relation between oscillatory activity and long-range synchronization in cat visual cortex. Proc. Natl. Acad. Sci. USA **92:** 290–294.
22. VOLGUSHEV, M., M. CHISTIAKOVA & W. SINGER. 1998. Modification of discharge patterns of neocortical neurons by induced oscillations of the membrane potential. Neuroscience **83(1):** 15–25.
23. GRAY, C.M. & W. SINGER. 1987. Stimulus-specific neuronal oscillations in the cat visual cortex: a cortical functional unit. Soc. Neurosci. Abstr. **13:** 1449.
24. GRAY, C.M. & W. SINGER. 1989. Stimulus-specific neuronal oscillations in orientation columns of cat visual cortex. Proc. Natl. Acad. Sci. USA **86:** 1698–1702.
25. ENGEL, A.K., A.K. KREITER, P. KÖNIG & W. SINGER. 1991. Synchronization of oscillatory neuronal responses between striate and extrastriate visual cortical areas of the cat. Proc. Natl. Acad. Sci. USA **88:** 6048–6052.
26. ENGEL, A.K., P. KÖNIG & W. SINGER. 1991. Direct physiological evidence for scene segmentation by temporal coding. Proc. Natl. Acad. Sci. USA **88:** 9136–9140.
27. FREIWALD, W.A., A.K. KREITER & W. SINGER. 1995. Stimulus dependent intercolumnar synchronization of single unit responses in cat area 17. Neuroreport **6:** 2348–2352.
28. KREITER, A.K. & W. SINGER. 1996. Stimulus-dependent synchronization of neuronal responses in the visual cortex of awake macaque monkey. J. Neurosci. **16:** 2381–2396.
29. ENGEL, A.K., P. KÖNIG, A.K. KREITER & W. SINGER. 1991. Interhemispheric synchronization of oscillatory neuronal responses in cat visual cortex. Science **252:** 1177–1179.
30. NOWAK, L.G., M.H.J. MUNK, J.I. NELSON & J.A.C. BULLIER. 1995. Structural basis of cortical synchronization. I. Three types of interhemispheric coupling. J. Neurophysiol. **74:** 2379–2400.
31. LÖWEL, S. & W. SINGER. 1992. Selection of intrinsic horizontal connections in the visual cortex by correlated neuronal activity. Science **255:** 209–212.
32. KÖNIG, P., A.K. ENGEL, S. LÖWEL & W. SINGER. 1993. Squint affects synchronization of oscillatory responses in cat visual cortex. Eur. J. Neurosci. **5:** 501–508.
33. SCHMIDT, K.E., R. GOEBEL, S. LÖWEL & W. SINGER. 1997. The perceptual grouping criterion of colinearity is reflected by anisotropies of connections in the primary visual cortex. Eur. J. Neurosci. **9:** 1083–1089.

34. MUNK, M.H.J., P.R. ROELFSEMA, P. KÖNIG, A.K. ENGEL & W. SINGER. 1996. Role of reticular activation in the modulation of intracortical synchronization. Science **272**: 271–274.
35. HERCULANO-HOUZEL S., M.H.J. MUNK, S. NEUENSCHWANDER & W. SINGER. 1999. Precisely synchronized oscillatory firing patterns require electroencephalographic activation. J. Neurosci. **19(10)**: 3992–4010.
36. ROELFSEMA, P.R., A.K. ENGEL, P. KÖNIG & W. SINGER. 1997. Visuomotor integration is associated with zero time-lag synchronization among cortical areas. Nature **385**: 157–161.
37. ROELFSEMA, P.R., P. KÖNIG, A.K. ENGEL, R. SIRETEANU & W. SINGER. 1994. Reduced synchronization in the visual cortex of cats with strabismic amblyopia. Eur. J. Neurosci. **6**: 1645–1655.
38. FRIES, P., P.R. ROELFSEMA, A.K. ENGEL, P. KÖNIG & W. SINGER. 1997. Synchronization of oscillatory responses in visual cortex correlates with perception in interocular rivalry. Proc. Natl. Acad. Sci. USA **94**: 12699–12704.
39. LOGOTHETIS, N.K., D.A. LEOPOLD & D.L. SHEINBERG. 1996. What is rivalling during binocular rivalry? Nature **380**: 621–624.
40. LOGOTHETIS, N.K. & J.D. SCHALL. 1989. Neuronal correlates of subjective visual perception. Science **245**: 761–763.
41. ADELSON E.H. & J.A. MOVSHON. 1982. Phenomenal coherence of moving visual patterns. Nature **300**: 523–525.
42. STONER G.R., T.D. ALBRIGHT & V.S. RAMACHANDRAN. 1990. Transparency and coherence in human motion perception. Nature **344**: 153–155.
43. ALBRIGHT T.D. & G.R. STONER. 1995. Visual motion perception. Proc. Natl. Acad. Sci. USA **92**: 2433–2440.
44. LAMME, V.A.F. & H. SPEKREIJSE. 1999. Neuronal synchrony does not represent texture segregation. Nature **396**: 362–366.
45. CASTELO-BRANCO, M., R. GOEBEL, S. NEUENSCHWANDER & W. SINGER. 1998. Neuronal synchronization in areas A18 and PMLS of the cat reflects the rules of physical and perceptual transparency. Europ. J. Neurosci. Abstr. **10(Suppl. 10)**: 237.
46. GIZZI, M.S., E. KATZ, R.A. SCHUMER & J.A. MOVSHON. 1990. Selectivity for orientation and direction of motion of single neurons in cat striate and extrastriate visual cortex. J. Neurophysiol. **63**: 1529–1543.
47. LAURENT, G. 1996. Dynamical representation of odors by oscillating and evolving neural assemblies. Trends Neurosci. **19**: 489–496.
48. JOLIOT, M., U. RIBARY & R. LLINÁS. 1994. Human oscillatory brain activity near 40 Hz coexists with cognitive temporal binding. Proc. Natl. Acad. Sci. USA **91**: 11748–11751.
49. EGGERMONT, J.J. 1992. Neural interaction in cat primary auditory cortex. Dependence on recording depth, electrode separation, and age. J. Neurophysiol. **68**: 1216–1228.
50. DE CHARMS, R.C. & M.M. MERZENICH. 1996. Primary cortical representation of sounds by the coordination of action-potential timing. Nature **381**: 610–613.
51. STERIADE, M., F. AMZICA & D. CONTRERAS. 1996. Synchronization of fast (30–40 Hz) spontaneous cortical rhythms during brain activtion. J. Neurosci. **16**: 392–417.
52. MURTHY, V.N. & E.E. FETZ. 1996. Synchronization of neurons during local field potential oscillations in sensorimotor cortex of awake monkeys. J. Neurophysiol. **76**: 3968-3982.
53. BUZSÁKI, G. & J.J. CHROBAK. 1995. Temporal structure in spatially organized neuronal ensembles: a role for interneuronal networks. Curr. Opin. Neurobiol. **5**: 504–510.
54. VAADIA, E., I. HAALMAN, M. ABELES, H. BERGMAN, Y. PRUT, H. SLOVIN & A. AERTSEN. 1995. Dynamics of neuronal interactions in monkey cortex in relation to behavioural events. Nature **373**: 515–518.
55. SANES, J.N. & J.P. DONOGHUE. 1993. Oscillations in local field potentials of the primate motor cortex during voluntary movement. Proc. Natl. Acad. Sci. USA **90**: 4470–4474.
56. KRISTEVA-FEIGE, R., B. FEIGE, S. MAKEIG, B. ROSS & T. ELBERT. 1993. Oscillatory brain activity during a motor task. Neuroreport **4**: 1291–1294.
57. HATSOPOULOS, N.G., C.L. OJAKANGAS & J.P. DONOGHUE. 1997. Planning of sequential arm movements from simultaneously recorded motor cortical neurons. Soc. Neurosci. Abstr. **23**: 1400.

58. OJAKANGAS, C.L., N.G. HATSOPOULOS & J.P. DONOGHUE. 1997. Reorganization of neuronal synchrony in M1 during visuomotor adaptation. Soc. Neurosci. Abstr. **23:** 1399.
59. RIEHLE, A., S. GRÜN, M. DIESMANN & A. AERTSEN. 1997. Spike synchronization and rate modulation differentially involved in motor cortical function. Science **278:** 1950–1953.
60. BRECHT, M., W. SINGER & A.K. ENGEL. 1998. Correlation analysis of corticotectal interactions in the cat visual system. J. Neurophysiol. **79:** 2394–2407.
61. TALLON-BAUDRY, C., O. BERTRAND, C. DELPUECH & J. PERNIER. 1996. Stimulus specificity of phase-locked and non-phase-locked 40 Hz visual responses in human. J. Neurosci. **16:** 4240–4249.
62. TALLON-BAUDRY, C., O. BERTRAND, C. DELPUECH & J. PERNIER. 1997. Oscillatory γ-band (30-70 Hz) activity induced by a visual search task in humans. J. Neurosci. **17(2):** 722–734.
63. TALLON-BAUDRY, C., O. BERTRAND, F. PERONNET & J. PERNIER. 1998. Induced γ-band activity during the delay of a visual short-term memory task in humans. J. Neurosci. **18(11):** 4244–4254.
64. RODRIGUEZ, E., N. GEORGE, J.-P. LACHAUX, J. MARTINERIE, B. RENAULT & F.J. VARELA. 1999. Perception's shadow: long-distance synchronization of human brain activity. Nature **397:** 430–433.
65. MILTNER, W.H.R., C. BRAUN, M. ARNOLD, H. WITTE & E. TAUB. 1999. Coherence of gamma-band EEG activity as a basis for associative learning. Nature **397:** 434–436.
66. LEONARDS, U., W. SINGER & M. FAHLE. 1996. The influence of temporal phase differences on texture segmentation. Vision Res. **36(17):** 2689–2697.
67. LEONARDS, U. & W. SINGER. 1997. Selective temporal interactions between processing streams with differential sensitivity for colour and luminance contrast. Vision Res. **37(9):** 1129–1140.
68. LEONARDS, U. & W. SINGER. 1998. Two segmentation mechanisms with differential sensitivity for colour and luminance contrast. Vision Res. **38(1):** 101–109.
69. ALAIS, D., R. BLAKE & S.-H. LEE. 1998. Visual features that vary together over time group together over space. Nature Neurosci. **1(2):** 160–164.
70. USHER, M. & N. DONNELLY. 1998. Visual synchrony affects binding and segmentation in perception. Nature **394:** 179–182.
71. KIPER, D.C., K.R. GEGENFURTNER & J.A. MOVSHON. 1996. Cortical oscillatory responses do not affect visual segmentation. Vision Res. **36:** 539–544.

Cajal on Neurons, Molecules, and Consciousness

JEAN-PIERRE CHANGEUX

Institut Pasteur, Paris, France

ABSTRACT: The discovery of chemical synaptic transmission together with the asymmetric distribution of neurotransmitter release sites and receptors offer an explanation for Cajal's theory on dynamic polarization.

KEYWORDS: Neurotransmitters; Receptors; Synaptic transmission; Consciousness

Cajal's *Textura* was written at a moment that coincided with two major discoveries in the field of brain chemistry: first, the mechanisms of chemical synaptic transmission were described by Elliott,[1] on the basis of his findings about the action of adrenaline (1905), and, second, the concept of a "receptive substance," or receptor, for pharmacological agents was proposed by Langley,[2,3] inspired by his experiments on the effect of nicotine and curare on skeletal muscle (1905–1906). Neither of these authors received the Nobel prize, in contrast to Golgi and Cajal, yet these fundamental discoveries had a dramatic impact on the research of the just-started twentieth century. These studies complemented Cajal's approach to the morphology of the nerve cell and the physiological insight of Sherrington on signal transmission in neural circuits. This dawn of the chemistry of the brain did not cast any shadow on Cajal's remarkable insight and courage in putting forward the *neuron doctrine*. Here, I will briefly explore how this third, chemical, dimension expands and enriches the views of Cajal and permits responses to several of the questions he raised. I will refer to the French version of the *Textura—Histologie du système nerveux de l'homme et des vertébrés*, published in 1909.[4]

CAJAL'S THEORY ON DYNAMIC POLARIZATION

On page 90 of *Histologie*, Cajal wrote that "the neuron doctrine ... is the unity and independence of the nerve cell including all its appendices." This means that the nerve cell is bounded by *one* cytoplasmic membrane without any cellular bridge with any other cell. The axons are "free" at their end without any "anastomosis" (p. 80). There is no continuity between the "terminals of one neuron" and the "protoplasmic expansion or the body of another neuron." Cajal uses the French word *articulation*

Address for correspondence: Institut Pasteur, 25–28 rue du Docteur Roux, 75724 Paris Cedex 15, France.

to specify this kind of contact. Electron microscopy brilliantly confirmed the juxtaposition (rather than the fusion) of cytoplasmic membranes at the level of the synapses, the width of the cleft being larger in "chemical synapses"[5] than in the electrical "gap junctions."[6] Cajal's neuron doctrine, in this respect, is fully valid.

Yet Cajal realized that the neuron doctrine could not immediately explain the "marche des courants [movement of currents]" from one neuron to another. What is the origin of the polarity in the transmission of signals (indicated by his famous arrows) in neuronal circuits? Cajal hesitates. On the one hand, in *Histologie*, he presents and discusses the concept of dynamic polarization of the neuron in considerable detail. "All the currents collected on the dendrites and the cell body are polarized toward the axon" (p. 132); there exists, he continues, an intrinsic "axipetal polarization of the protoplasma." Cajal then goes as far as stating that "the neurofibrils ... are the unique conductors of the nervous excitations" (p. 176). Taking these statements literally would mean that the polarity is built into the structure of the whole cell from the dendrites to the axon. Accordingly, retrograde propagation of the nerve impulse should not be possible, yet it takes place, even under *in vivo* physiological conditions.[7] Cajal did not realize the role of the cytoplasmic membrane in the genesis and propagation of electrical signals. It was again too early, since Bernstein[8] proposed this concept almost simultaneously with Cajal's *Textura* (in 1902–1904). Nevertheless, it would be unjust not to mention one sentence of *Histologie* which illustrates that Cajal hesitated or perhaps complemented his own views on the intrinsic polarization of the nerve cell. He emphasizes the role of the "articulation" between nerve cells, writing "for us, the cause of the dynamic polarization ... is uniquely in the relationship which exists *between* the neurons ... where the seat is the entry of excitation in the neuron" (*Histologie*, p. 135). In any case, Cajal did not (could not) assign the law of dynamic polarization to the polarity of signal transmission at the level of the "articulation" between nerve cells. It was the fundamental observation by Sherrington[9] on the unidirectional transmission of the physiological signals that led to the universally accepted conclusion that the specialized contact between nerve cells, the *synapse*, is indeed responsible for the dynamic polarization of nerve circuits. But Sherrington failed to understand why.

NEUROTRANSMITTERS AND THEIR RECEPTORS AND THE POLARITY OF SYNAPTIC TRANSMISSION

The physiological demonstration that the polarity of signal transmission is intrinsic to the synapse did not illuminate the mechanisms involved. A violent controversy plagued the field, particularly led by the electrophysiologist John Eccles, who for decades opposed the idea that chemicals mediate transmission in the brain. Such a possibility contradicted his dualist views. But, when the data of the biochemists and of the pharmacologists became irrefutably strong, he was forced to a public and spectacular repentance. The chemistry and molecular biology of the synapse inaugurated a new world of knowledge that Eccles and physiologists could not foresee until the 1950s.

First of all, the experimental and theoretical work of Dubois-Reymond, Bernard, and Elliott established that neurons synthesize, store, and release chemical substances, some of them unique to the nervous system, which serve as "first messengers" between nerve cells and between nerve and effector cells (gland, muscle...). Those include classical neurotransmitters: acetylcholine, adrenaline, norepinephrine, glutamate, GABA, and glycine, which either tend to elicit the genesis of a nerve impulse (and are thus *excitatory*) or to inhibit its initiation (and are thus *inhibitory*). Neuropeptides may also serve as neurotransmitters and often coexist in the same neuron with classical neurotransmitters.[10] Pioneered by the characterization of choline acetyltransferase, the first enzyme identified which is involved in neurotransmitter biosynthesis,[11] an important body of enzymes, transporters, vesicle proteins, docking, fusion and endocytosis proteins have been identified in nerve endings, clearly demonstrating the molecular polarity of neurotransmitter release in the presynaptic side of the synapse. On the other, postsynaptic, side are located receptors that recognize the neurotransmitter and convert the chemical signal into an electrical (ion channel opening) or metabolic (interaction with a G protein or activation of a kinase) response. The first neurotransmitter receptor to be isolated, the nicotinic receptor protein,[12] paved the way for the identification of more than 2,000 different receptor species.[13] All of them are membrane proteins which mediate signal transduction. Through conformational changes, structural and functional interactions between the two categories of topographically distinct sites they carry: the neurotransmitter binding site and the biologically active site (ion channel, G protein binding site...). In this respect, they are typical *allosteric proteins*.[13]

In addition to their polarized distribution at the synapse, receptor molecules possess a transmembrane polarity. For instance, application of acetylcholine elicits an ionic response exclusively when applied to the external surface of the postsynaptic membrane.[14,15] Interestingly, this feature results from the transmembrane disposition of the receptor protein: the binding site for acetylcholine is carried by the NH_2-terminal large hydrophilic domain of the subunits, while the small COOH-terminal hydropilic domain faces the cytoplasmic side of the membrane. Moreover, the receptor protein is immobilized and stabilized at the level of the postsynaptic domain through a complex network of interactions with the basal lamina and with cytoskeletal proteins.[16,17] Neurons receive multiple and diverse nerve endings often containing and releasing different neurotransmitters. The neuronal surface thus forms a rather stable patchwork of different species of receptors from the tip of its dendrites up to the ultimate terminations of its axon.

Cajal's pioneering efforts to understand the causes of the dynamic polarization of the nerve cell have today been rewarded by an extensive description of the neuron at the molecular level and by the understanding of the polarity of neuronal intercommunication in chemical and molecular terms.

CAJAL FROM MOLECULES TO CONSCIOUSNESS

Cajal's writings on higher brain function and specifically on consciousness are scarce. He wrote in *Histologie* (p. 879) that "to localize the intellectual activity, the will and self-consciousness...to distinct cortical spheres appears to us as a chimera....," but as he continues, "in fact, they are the result of a combined action of a large number of mnemonic spheres." This, in my opinion, means that Cajal held neither a spiritualist, dualist, view of consciousness, nor a "phrenologist," reductionist one, but adopted what is called today a distributed connectionist approach. It is within this framework that Cajal called the pyramidal cell a "psychic corpuscle" characterized by axon collaterals "more abundant, longer and more ramified" than the other types of nerve cells (*Nouvelles Idées*, p. 77).[18] He further stated that "the [psychic] acts are certainly accompanied by molecular modifications in the nerve cells" (*Histologie* p. 882). The subsequent paper in this volume by Dehaene, Kerszberg and Changeux aims at illustrating this prophetic view of Cajal.

Last but not least, Cajal also adopted a rather modern attitude toward the mechanisms of learning. Unambiguously, he anticipates the most recent selectionist views on the development of the nervous system.[19–22] He writes that "during embryonic development dendrites and axonal ramifications, extend, divide gradually and establish a relationship with an increasingly large number of neurons," but "all these initial connections do not persist." "...[O]ne may say, *trial associations* [are created] destined to subsist or to be destroyed according to undetermined circumstances." (*Histologie* p. 888). In the article by Dehaene *et al.* which follows, the model of the *conscious workspace* presented implements these inspired selectionist views of Cajal on the functional organization of the brain.

REFERENCES

1. ELLIOTT, T.R. 1905. The action of adrenaline. J. Physiol. **32:** 401–467.
2. LANGLEY, J.N. 1905. On the reaction of cells and nerve-endings to certain poisons, chiefly as regards on the reaction of striated muscle to nicotine and to curare. J. Physiol. **33:** 374–413.
3. LANGLEY, J.N. 1906. On nerve endings and special excitable substances in cells. Proc. R. Soc. **78:** 170–194.
4. RAMÓN Y CAJAL, S. 1909–1911. Histologie du système nerveux de l'homme et les vertébrés [2 vols.]. Paris. Maloine. [French translation of Textura del sistema nervioso del hombre y de los vertebrados. 1899–1904. Imprenta N. Moya. Madrid.]
5. PALADE, G. & S. PALAY. 1954. Electron microscopy observations of interneuronal and neuromuscular synapses. Anat. Rec. 118: 335.
6. GRUNDFEST, H. 1959. Synaptic -1 ephatic transmission. *In* Handbook of Physiology, Sect. 1, Vol. 1. J. Field, Ed. :147–197. American Physiological Society. Washington, DC.
7. NEBER, E. & B. SAKMANN. 1976. Single channel currents recorded from membrane and denervated frog muscle fibers. J. Physiol. **258:** 709–729.
8. BERNSTEIN, H. 1902. Untersuchungen zur Thermodynamik der bioelektrischen Ströme. Pflügers Arch., **92:** 521–562.
9. CHANGEUX, J. & S. EDELSTEIN. 1998. Allosteric receptors after 30 years. Neuron **2:** 959–980.
10. HOKFELT, T. *et al.* 1986. Coexistence of neural messengers: an overview. Progr. Brain Res. **68:** 33–70.
11. NACHMANSON, D. 1959. Chemical and Molecular Basis of Nerve Activity. Academic Press. New York.
12. CHANGEUX, J.-P. 1981. The acetylcholine receptor: an "allosteric" membrane protein. Harvey Lectures **75:** 85–254.
13. SHERRINGTON, C.S. 1897. The central nervous system. *In* Textbook of Physiology, Vol. 3, 7th ed. M.A. Foster, Ed. Macmillan. London.
14. DEL CASTILLO, J. & B. KATZ. 1957. A study of curare action with an electrical micromethod. Proc. R. Soc. Lond. (Biol.) **146:** 339–356.
15. DEL CASTILLO, J. & B. KATZ. 1957. Interaction at endplate receptors between different choline derivatives. Proc. R. Soc. Lond. (Biol.) **146:** 369–381.

16. DUCLERT, A. & J.P. CHANGEUX. 1995. Acetylcholine receptor gene expression at the developing neuromuscular junction. Physiol. Rev. **75:** 339–368.
17. SANES, J.R. & J.W. LICHTMAN. 1999. Development of the vertebrate neuromuscular junction. Annu. Rev. Neurosci. **22:** 389–442.
18. RAMÓN Y CAJAL, S. 1894. Les nouvelles idées sur la structure du systeme nerveux chez l'homme et chez les vertebrées. Reinwald. Paris.
19. CHANGEUX, J.-P., P. COURRÈGE & A. DANCHIN. 1973. A theory of the epigenesis of neural networks by selective stabilization of synapses. Proc. Natl. Acad. Sc. USA **70:** 2974–2978.
20. CHANGEUX, J-.P. & A. DANCHIN. 1976. Selective stabilization of developing synapses as a mechanism for the specificication of neuronal networks. Nature **264:** 705–712.
21. EDELMAN, G. 1978. The Mindful Brain. Cortical Organization and the Group-Selective Theory of Higher Brain Function. MIT Press. Cambridge, MA.
22. EDELMAN, G. 2000. This symposium.

A Neuronal Model of a Global Workspace in Effortful Cognitive Tasks

STANISLAS DEHAENE,[a] MICHEL KERSZBERG,[b]
AND JEAN-PIERRE CHANGEUX[b]

[a]*Institut National de la Santé et de la Recherche Médicale, 91401 Orsay, France*

[b]*Centre National de la Recherche Scientifique, Institut Pasteur, 75015 Paris, France*

> ABSTRACT: A minimal hypothesis is proposed concerning the brain processes underlying effortful tasks. It distinguishes two main computational spaces: a unique global workspace composed of distributed and heavily interconnected neurons with long-range axons, and a set of specialized and modular perceptual, motor, memory, evaluative, and attentional processors. Workspace neurons are mobilized in effortful tasks for which the specialized processors do not suffice. They selectively mobilize or suppress, through descending connections, the contribution of specific processor neurons. In the course of task performance, workspace neurons become spontaneously coactivated, forming discrete though variable spatio-temporal patterns subject to modulation by vigilance signals and to selection by reward signals. A computer simulation of the Stroop task shows workspace activation to increase during acquisition of a novel task, effortful execution, and after errors. We outline predictions for spatio-temporal activation patterns during brain imaging, particularly about the contribution of dorsolateral prefrontal cortex and anterior cingulate to the workspace.
>
> KEYWORDS: Consciousness; Mental effort; Prefrontal cortex

We propose a simple hypothesis concerning the neural basis of "making a conscious mental effort." Why are some cognitive tasks performed effortlessly, whereas others require focused attention and conscious control? Mental effort is clearly unrelated to objective measures of computational difficulty: We routinely perform vision and motor control tasks without awareness of the complex underlying information processing, whereas elementary tasks, such as subtracting 9 from 37, call for our attention and conscious effort.

Neurophysiological, anatomical, and brain-imaging studies have revealed that tasks that can be performed effortlessly mobilize well-defined modular cerebral systems specialized for various aspects of sensory-motor processing.[1,2] On the other hand, humans exhibit the capacity to go beyond modularity and flexibly, though ef-

---

Address for correspondence: Dr. Stanislas Dehaene, Institut National de la Santé et de la Recherche Médicale, Unité 334, Service hospitalier Frédéric Joliot, Commissariat à l'énergie atomique, 4 Place du Général Leclerc, 91401 Orsay, France.

dehaene@shfj.cea.fr

ABBREVIATIONS: dlPFC, dorsolateral prefrontal cortex; AC, anterior cingulate.

fortfully, recombine these specialized cerebral processes in novel ways.[3,4] Once we are conscious of an item, we can readily perform a large variety of operations on it, including evaluation, memorization, action guidance, and verbal report. This impressive ability must be reconciled with the neurobiological fact that there is no single "cardinal area" to which all areas project.[5-8]

Here, we propose a formal architecture of distributed neurons with long-distance connectivity that provides a "global workspace" that can potentially interconnect multiple distributed and specialized brain areas in a coordinated, though variable manner, and whose intense mobilization might be associated with a subjective feeling of conscious effort. This minimal scheme extends former attempts to model effortful tasks of delayed response,[9] card-sorting,[10] number-processing,[11] and planning[12] on the basis of plausible molecular, anatomical, and functional features of the brain. Here, we present simulations of another task, the Stroop task, to explicitly specify a common architectural principle underlying the effortful character of all these tasks, thus providing empirically testable predictions.

THEORETICAL PREMISES

Two Main Computational Spaces

We distinguish two main computational spaces within the brain (FIG. 1). The first is a processing network, composed of a set of parallel, distributed, and functionally specialized processors[5] or modular subsystems[6] ranging from primary sensory processors (such as area V1) or unimodal processors (such as area V4), which combine multiple inputs within a given sensory modality, up to heteromodal processors (such as the visuo-tactile neurons in area LIP or the "mirror" neurons in area F5) that extract highly processed categorical or semantic information. Each processor is subsumed by topologically distinct cortical domains with highly specific local or medium-range connections that "encapsulate" information relevant to its function.[13]

The second computational space is a global workspace, consisting of a distributed set of cortical neurons characterized by their ability to receive from and send back to homologous neurons in other cortical areas horizontal projections through long-range excitatory axons (which may impinge on either excitatory or inhibitory neurons). Our view is that this population of neurons does not belong to a distinct set of "cardinal" brain areas but, rather, is distributed among brain areas in variable proportions. It is known that long-range cortico-cortical tangential connections, including callosal connections, mostly originate from the pyramidal cells of layers 2 and 3, which give or receive the so-called "association" efferents and afferents. We therefore propose that the extent to which a given brain area contributes to the global workspace would be simply related to the fraction of its pyramidal neurons contributing to layers 2 and 3, which is particularly elevated in von Economo's type 2 (dorsolateral prefrontal) and type 3 (inferior parietal) cortical structures.[14] In addition, these cortical neurons establish strong vertical and reciprocal connections, via layer 5 neurons, with corresponding thalamic nuclei, thus contributing both to the stability of workspace activity, for instance via self-sustained circuits and to the direct access to the processing networks.[15,16]

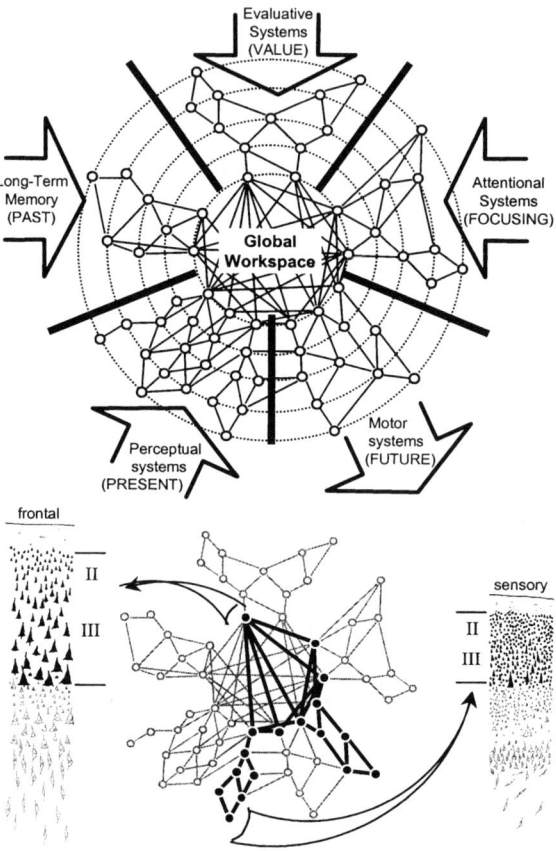

FIGURE 1. *Top*: Schematic representation of the five main types of processors connected to the global workspace (inspired from Ref. 13). *Bottom*: Sample activation during effortful processing; a coherent link between two informationally encapsulated processors is established through the activation of distributed workspace neurons. The long-range workspace connectivity, supported by layer II/III neurons, is more prominent in Van Economo's frontal-type cortex (*left*) than in sensory cortex (*right*).[14]

Selective Gating of Workspace Inputs and Outputs

Although a variety of processor areas project to the interconnected set of neurons composing the global workspace, at any given time only a subset of inputs effectively accesses it. We postulate that this gating is implemented by descending modulatory projections from workspace neurons to more peripheral processor neurons. These projections may selectively amplify or extinguish the ascending inputs from processing neurons, thus mobilizing, at a given time, a specific set of processors in the workspace while suppressing the contribution of others.

Spatio-Temporal Dynamics of Workspace Activity

The global workspace is the seat of a particular kind of "brain-scale" activity state characterized by the spontaneous activation, in a sudden, coherent and exclusive manner, of a subset of workspace neurons, the rest of workspace neurons being inhibited. The entire workspace is globally interconnected in such a way that only one such "workspace representation" can be active at any given time. This all-or-none invasive property distinguishes it from peripheral processors in which, due to local patterns of connections, several representations with different formats may coexist.

A representation that has invaded the workspace may remain active in an autonomous manner and resist changes in peripheral activity. If it is negatively evaluated, or if attention fails, it may, however, be spontaneously and randomly replaced by another discrete combination of workspace neurons. Functionally, this neural property implements an active "generator of diversity," which constantly projects and tests hypotheses (or prerepresentations) on the outside world.[9-12] The dynamics of workspace neuron activity is thus characterized by a constant flow of individual coherent episodes of variable duration.

Content of the Global Workspace

Through their mutual projection to and from workspace neurons, five major categories of processors can be dynamically mobilized and multiply reconfigured (FIG. 1).

Perceptual circuits give the workspace access to the present state of the external world. In humans, perceptual circuits include the object-oriented ventral and lateral areas of the temporal lobes as well as the temporal and inferior parietal areas involved in language comprehension (including Wernicke's area).[13] Thus, the content of any attended object or discourse can access the global workspace.

Motor programming circuits allow the content of the workspace to be used to guide future intentional behavior. A hierarchy of nested circuits implements motor intentions, from the highest level of abstract plans to individual actions, themselves composed of gestures.[12,17] In humans, these circuits include premotor cortex, posterior parietal cortex, supplementary motor area, basal ganglia (notably the caudate nucleus), and cerebellum, as well as the high-level speech production circuits of the left inferior frontal lobe, including Broca's area. Connections of the workspace to motor and language circuits at the higher levels of this hierarchy endow any active representation in the workspace with the property of reportability,[18] namely the fact that it can be described or commented upon using words or gestures.

Long-term memory circuits provide the workspace with an access to past percepts and events. Hippocampal and parahippocampal areas play a special role in mediating the storage in and retrieval from long-term memory stores, which are presumably distributed throughout the cortex according to their original content and modality.[13]

Evaluation circuits[9,10,19,20] allow representations in the workspace to be associated with a positive or negative value. The main anatomical systems in this respect include the orbitofrontal cortex, anterior cingulate (AC), hypothalamus, amygdala, and ventral striatum as well as the mesocortical catecholaminergic and cholinergic projections to prefrontal cortex. Reciprocal projections allow evaluation circuits to be internally activated by the current workspace content (auto-evaluation[10]) and, conversely, to selectively maintain or change workspace activity according to whether its value is predicted to be positive or negative.[9–12,20]

Attention circuits allow the workspace to mobilize its own circuits independently from the external world. Changes in workspace contents need not necessarily lead to changes in overt behavior, but may result in covert attention switches to selectively amplify or attenuate the signals from a subset of processor neurons. Although all descending projections from workspace neurons to peripheral modular processors are important in this selective amplification process, a particular role is played by areas of the parietal lobe in visuo-spatial attention.[7,8,13]

Global Modulation of Workspace Activation

The state of activation of workspace neurons is assumed to be under the control of global vigilance signals, for instance from mesencephalic reticular neurons. Some of these signals are powerful enough to control major transitions between the awake state (workspace active) and slow-wave sleep (workspace inactive). Others provide graded inputs that modulate the amplitude of workspace activation, which is enhanced whenever novel, unpredicted, or emotionally relevant signals occur, and conversely, drops when the organism is involved in a routine activity.

COMPUTER SIMULATION

To specify the above hypotheses in a computationally explicit manner, a minimal computer simulation of the workspace architecture and dynamics is presented. We are aware that it is necessarily partial and incomplete. We restrict it to the learning and execution of the well known Stroop task,[21] which includes both an easy, automatic component and an effortful, attention-demanding component.

Network Architecture and Dynamics

FIGURE 2 schematizes the proposed neuronal architecture, composed of excitatory and inhibitory units grouped into different assemblies: input systems, specialized processors, workspace neurons, vigilance, and reward systems. Each assembly is composed of multiple replicas of a basic element comprising an excitatory unit, a gating inhibitory unit, and a processing inhibitory unit. Gating and processing inhibitory units are classical McCulloch–Pitts units whose activity level S^i_{inh}, ranging from 0 to 1, obeys the update rule $S^i_{\text{inh}} = \text{sigmoid}(\Sigma w^{i,j} S^j)$, where the sigmoid function is defined as $\text{sigmoid}(x) = 1/(1 + e^{-x})$, and the $w^{i,j}$ are the synaptic weights of neurons contacting inhibitory unit i. For simplicity only excitatory units (both local and long-distance) are assumed to make synaptic contact onto inhibitory units.

The activity of excitatory units, S_{EXC}, obeys a modified update rule:

$$S^i_{\text{EXC}} = \text{sigmoid}(\Sigma^i_{\text{asc}} \Phi(\Sigma^i_{\text{desc}}))$$

where $\Sigma^i_{\text{asc}} = \Sigma w^{i,j}_{\text{asc}} S^j$ and $\Sigma^i_{\text{desc}} = \Sigma w^{i,j}_{\text{desc}} S$.

The weights $w^{i,j}_{\text{asc}}$ and $w^{i,j}_{\text{desc}}$ can be positive or negative, because inputs to excitatory units may come from excitatory as well as inhibitory units. The equation separates these inputs into two types: descending connections from hierarchically

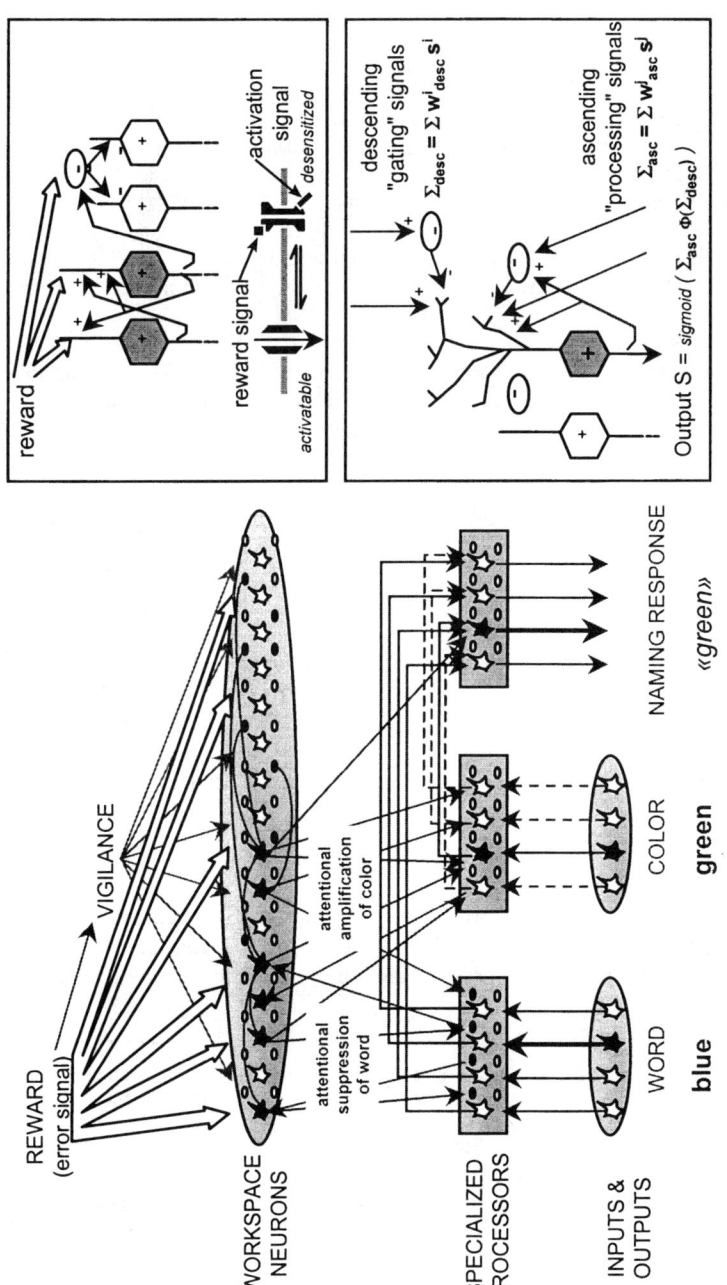

FIGURE 2. See following page for caption.

higher assemblies (subscript desc) and ascending or processing inputs (subscript asc), which represent all the other (nondescending) connections that give the neuron its specific functionality (FIG. 2, lower inset). The monotonic modulating function Φ is chosen as a sigmoid with $\Phi(x)$, when $x \to -\infty$, $\Phi(0) = 1$ and $\Phi(x) \to 2$ when $x \to +\infty$. This equation implies that descending signals have a gating effect on lower-level neuronal activity, with attentional amplification if $\Sigma_{desc} > 0$ normal unattended processing if $\Sigma_{desc} = 0$, and attentional suppression if $\Sigma_{desc} < 0$.

For simplicity, only the synaptic weights between two excitatory units are assumed to be modifiable according to a reward-modulated Hebbian rule $\Delta w^{post,pre} = \varepsilon R S^{pre} (2S^{post} - 1)$, where R is a reward signal provided after each network response ($R = +1$, correct; $R = -1$, incorrect), pre is the presynaptic unit and post the postsynaptic unit.[9] Weights are bounded to remain between 0 and a maximum value (here arbitrarily fixed at 7).

Finally, workspace neuron activity is under the influence of both vigilance and reward signals. The vigilance signal V is treated as having a descending modulatory influence on all workspace neurons according to the above-described gating mechanism. It is updated after each response: if $R > 0$, then $\Delta V = -0.1$ V, otherwise $\Delta V = 0.5 (1 - V)$. This rule has the effect of a slowly decreasing vigilance with sharp increases on error trials. The reward signal R influences the stability of workspace activity through a short-term depression or potentiation of synaptic weights[9,10,12]: if $R < 0$, $S^{pre} > 0.5$ and $S^{post} > 0.5$, then $\Delta w'^{post,pre} = -0.5 \, w'^{post,pre}$, otherwise $\Delta w'^{post,pre} = 0.2 (1 - w'^{post,pre})$, where w' is a short-term multiplier on the excitatory synaptic weight from unit pre to unit post. A plausible molecular implementation of this rule has been proposed in terms of allosteric receptors[9,10] (FIG. 2, *upper inset*). It postulates that the time coincidence of a diffuse reward signal and of a postsynaptic marker of recent neuronal activity transiently shifts the allosteric equilibrium either toward, or from, a desensitized refractory conformation. Through this "chemical Hebb rule," negative reward destabilizes the self-sustaining excitatory connections between currently active workspace neurons, thus initiating a change in workspace activity.

Implementation of the Stroop Tasks

We submitted the network to several versions of the word-color Stroop tasks.[21] For this purpose, four input units were dedicated to encoding four color words, four other input units encoded the color of the ink used to print the word, and four internal

---

FIGURE 2. Architecture of the simulated network. Proposed mechanisms for reward-dependent changes in workspace unit activity *(upper inset)* and for the interaction of ascending and descending connections to a given area *(lower inset)*. Although each unit in the simulation presumably represents ≈100 neurons in an actual brain, our scheme epitomizes the basic organization of a cortical column, with intra-columnar recurrent excitation, intra-areal and mid-range excitatory connections providing excitation or inhibition (via intermediate processing inhibitory interneurons), and descending excitatory connections providing upward or downward modulation of activity (via intermediate gating inhibitory interneurons). The network is depicted in a state of activity typical of a correct trial in the effortful Stroop task. Attentional amplification reverses the relation between conflicting word and color inputs by amplifying the weaker color unit activity and suppressing the stronger word unit activity.

units corresponded to the four naming responses (FIG. 2). Routine task 1 (color-naming) consisted in turning a single color unit on and rewarding the network for turning the corresponding naming unit on. Direct one-to-one connections between color and naming units implemented a minimal version of the color-naming process. Routine task 2 (word-naming with color interference) consisted in turning a word unit on together with another incompatible ink color unit and rewarding the network for turning on the naming unit appropriate to the word, not the ink color. Again, word-naming was implemented by direct one-to-one connections from word to naming units. As in previous models of the Stroop test,[22,23] stronger connections were used in the word-to-name pathway than in the color-to-name pathway, corresponding to the greater frequency of word-naming in everyday use.[21] Finally, the effortful task (color-naming with word interference) consisted in providing conflicting word and color inputs, as in task 2, but rewarding the network for turning on the naming unit appropriate to the ink color, not the word.

Connections to and from workspace units were critical for the latter task. A random, patchy connection scheme was used, so that each processor had a Gaussian probability of contacting units in any given region of the workspace, and a similar Gaussian probability of receiving projections from units in the same region (with random initial weights). Note that ascending and descending connections in the model are reciprocal only in a statistical sense: any two processor and workspace units are generally not connected bidirectionally, but any region of the workspace that receives ascending projections from multiple processor units is highly likely to send back descending projections to the same units.

Simulation Results

When placed in routine task 1 (color-naming, no interfering word) the network performs correctly with only processor unit activation, using the direct one-to-one connections from color units to name units. Although workspace activity is occasionally observed if vigilance is initially set high, it is clearly not needed. Hence, vigilance quickly drops without having an impact on performance (FIG. 3).

Similar results are obtained when the network is submitted to routine task 2 (word naming with color interference). Even though there are now two conflicting inputs, word-to-name connections are stronger than color-to-name connections. Hence, the naming response appropriate to the word is activated faster and more strongly than the one appropriate to the color, which is quickly extinguished by lateral inhibition. Thus, workspace unit activity is not needed for this task either.

When the naive network is then switched to the effortful task (color naming with word interference), an initial series of errors takes place as the network perseverates in applying the routine task 2. The delivery of negative reward leads to an increase in vigilance and to the sudden activation of variable patterns amongst workspace units. The next '30 trials can be described as a "search phase." Workspace activation varies in a partly random manner as various response rules are explored. Workspace activation patterns that lead to activating the incorrect response unit are negatively rewarded and tend not to be repeated in subsequent trials. Eventually, the network settles into a stable activation pattern, with a fringe of variability that slowly disappears in subsequent trials. This stable pattern, which leads to correct performance, is characterized by (i) preferential descending projections to the excitatory units of

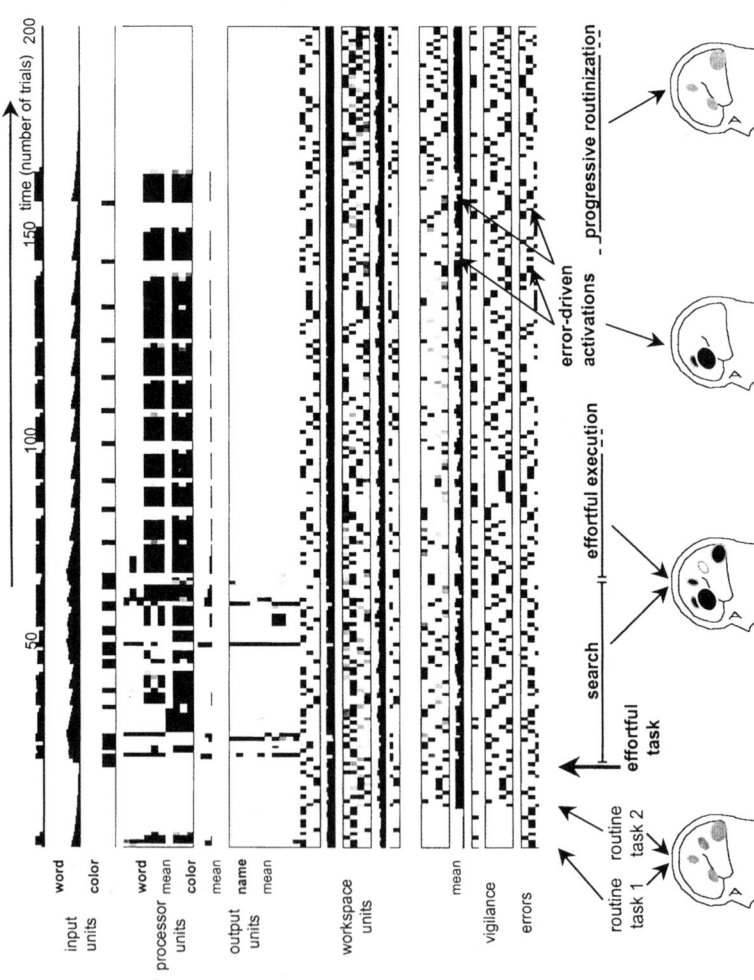

FIGURE 3. Temporal dynamics of the simulation in the course of learning the effortful Stroop task; 200 trials were simulated. The Stroop task was introduced without warning after trial 20. Note the selective activation of workspace units with a simultaneous amplification of color processors and a suppression of word processors. Workspace activity is seen in the initial phase of searching for the appropriate response rule (with considerably inter-trial variability), during the effortful execution of the task, and following each erroneous response. For the purposes of illustration, putative brain-imaging correlates of routine and workspace activation are shown (see Refs. 24 and 25).

the color-processing network, thus causing an amplification of the color input, and its transmission to response units; (ii) preferential descending projections to the inhibitory gating units of the word-processing network, thus causing a suppression of the word input; and (iii) strong long-distance excitatory connections amongst active workspace units maintaining the pattern active in the inter-trial interval. Across multiple simulations with different initial connectivity, an activation pattern with these characteristics was invariably found (after '5–50 trials), although its detailed composition varied. The crucial factor here is the patchy distribution of initial connections to and from the workspace, which ensures that sectors of the workspace with the appropriate preexisting connections do indeed exist in the initial state and can be selectively stabilized.

Following the search phase, the network goes through a phase of "effortful task execution" in which workspace activation remains indispensable to correct performance. During this phase, workspace activity remains high even on occasional trials in which the word and ink color information do not conflict. When performance is correct for a series of consecutive trials, vigilance tends to drop. However, any lapse in workspace activation is immediately sanctioned by an error. Each error is immediately followed by an intense reactivation of the workspace. Progressively though, the task becomes routinized as the Hebbian rule applied to processor units tended to increase the color-to-name connections and to decrease the word-to-name connections. Routinization is characterized by increasingly longer periods of correct performance without accompanying workspace activation. Eventually, workspace activation disappears, as the processor network now handles the routinized task by itself.

An interesting property of the network is its ability to maintain an active, sustained state of workspace and processor unit activity for some delay. This is due to the mutually reinforcing excitatory ascending and descending connections between processor and workspace units, together with the excitatory connections within the workspace itself. Once this self-sustained state of activity is established, the descending attentional amplification is often sufficient to maintain processor units active for some duration, even when input units are turned off. Hence, the network architecture is adequate to pass delayed-response versions of the routine and effortful tasks in which the response must be postponed after the stimulus has been turned off. It is noteworthy that given this additional delayed-response requirement, even the routine task of color-naming now requires workspace activity.

EMPIRICAL TESTS AND PREDICTIONS

Brain Imaging

The key empirical prediction of our hypothesis in the domain of brain imaging is the existence of a strong correlation between cortical areas that are found active in conscious effortful tasks and areas that possess a strong long-distance cortico-cortical connectivity, presumably associated with dense cortical layers 2 and 3. Brain imaging-techniques, once they resolve the transverse laminar distribution of brain activation, might show a differential laminar pattern of activity as a function of whether a given area is recruited for an automatic task or for an effortful task. The global activation of neurons dispersed in multiple cortical areas also might be visualized as a temporary increase in the long-distance coherence of brain activity in electro- and magneto-encephalography[26] or in studies of functional connectivity with functional MRI.[27]

We also predict the conditions under which areas rich in workspace neurons should be seen as "active" by using brain-imaging techniques. In our simulation, workspace unit activation exhibits the following properties: (i) it is absent during routine tasks; (ii) it appears suddenly when a novel, nonroutine task is introduced; (iii) it varies semi-randomly during the initial learning of a novel task; (iv) it is high and stable during execution of a known but not yet routinized effortful task; (v) it decreases during routinization; (vi) it resumes sharply following an error; (vii) it is present during the delay period of a delayed-response task; and (viii) it temporarily mobilizes, in a descending manner, other units involved in specific task components.

Brain-imaging experiments indicate that dorsolateral prefrontal cortex (dlPFC) and AC possess these properties. Both are active in effortful cognitive tasks, including the Stroop test, with a graded level of activation as a function of task difficulty.[28–30] With automatization, activation decreases in dlPFC and AC, but it immediately recovers if a novel, nonroutine situation occurs.[31] AC activates in tight synchrony with subjects' errors.[25,32] In the Wisconsin card-sorting test, dlPFC activates when subjects have to search for a new sorting rule.[33] dlPFC and AC possess the ability to remain active in the absence of external stimulation, such as during the delay period of a delayed-response task,[28] or during internally driven activities such as mental calculation.[34] dlPFC and AC activity also has been found to correlate with subjective conscious perception in various situations in which carefully matched conscious and unconscious conditions were contrasted.[35,36] Finally, concomitant with dlPFC and AC activation, a selective attentional amplification is seen in relevant posterior areas during focused-attention tasks.[7, 37]

Workspace activity in our model is concentrated in distinct, localized subsets of neurons that vary with the peripheral processors that must be amplified or suppressed. This is compatible with the evidence for specialization within subregions of AC and dlPFC.[30,38] Our model also posits that effortless or automatic processing should activate specialized processors throughout the cortex without requiring coordination by global workspace neurons. Recent images of brain activity during unconscious processing support this hypothesis.[35,39,40] In particular, subliminal word stimuli have been shown to cause an entire stream of perceptual, semantic, and motor processes ending up in primary motor cortex.[41]

Anatomy and Physiology

Consistent with a privileged contribution of horizontal, long-distance connections in establishing a coherent workspace, a dense network of connections linking dorso-lateral prefrontal and inferior parietal areas to anterior and posterior cingulate, temporal cortices, and parahippocampal cortices has been identified in the monkey.[38] It may support the interconnection of the workspace to high-level perceptual, motor, memory, attentional, and evaluation circuits.

The model emphasizes the top-down mobilization of processor neurons by workspace neurons via excitatory descending connections. Such selective amplification or reduction of peripheral neuronal activity has been observed experimentally.[42,43] Because the descending projections are excitatory, they exert their modulatory effect in our model via intermediate connections to a special class of "gating" inhibitory interneurons that have a multiplicative effect on postsynaptic neuronal firing during effortful attentional suppression. These neurons differ from standard "processing inhibitory interneurons," which are the main targets of ascending and horizontal connections, have additive effects on postsynaptic firing, and are active during any type of processing in a given area, automatic as well as effortful. The differential behavior of these two categories of neurons could be established by electrophysiological recordings.

Pharmacology and Molecular Biology

Our theory predicts that workspace neurons are the specific targets of projections from neuronal structures that provide reward and vigilance inputs, presumably via specialized neurotransmitter pathways. Mesocortical dopaminergic neurons and cholinergic pathways, in particular, are known to differentially target prefrontal cortex.[13,44] The decoding of such signals by workspace neurons may be effected by specific subtypes of neurotransmitter receptors.[45] Pathological mutations in humans and in genetically modified animals, in which the expression or the physiological properties of a specific subtype of receptor is altered, may thus help decipher the cerebral circuits involved in effortful tasks.[46]

CONCLUSIONS

At variance with previous models,[9,10,22,23] the proposed neuronal architecture successfully allows the Stroop test to be learned without postulating prewired rule-coding units adequate for the task and on the basis of realistic neuronal processes. Our implementation of a global computational workspace operating under conditions of selection by reward does not aim at an exhaustive description of a "conscious workspace."[5] It is limited in scope to features characteristic of effortful tasks, for which it leads to a number of critical predictions, which can be experimentally tested, in particular, with brain-imaging techniques.

The model suffers from shortcomings that should be dealt with in future developments. Although workspace neurons are assumed to be heavily interconnected, they need not be functionally equivalent but rather may be organized in multiple hierarchically nested specialized circuits. An attempt at simulating these nested levels of internal planning was presented in a previous model of the Tower of London task.[12] Other important issues include characterization of the variability in the initial connectivity needed to learn multiple tasks;[47,48] the inclusion of novelty detection mechanisms, presumably implemented in the hippocampus, which may serve as input to workspace units;[49] and the connection to the workspace of self-representations that might allow the simulated organism to reflect on its own internal processes.

ACKNOWLEDGMENTS

This article is reprinted with permission from the *Proceedings of the National Academy of Sciences (USA)* (Vol. 95, pp. 14529–14534, November 1998). We thank M. Posner and M. Zoli for their comments and the Fondation pour la Recherche Médicale, the College de France, the Association contre la Myopathie, and the European Union Biotech program for support.

REFERENCES

1. FELLEMAN, D. J. & D. VAN ESSEN. 1991. Cereb. Cortex **1:** 1–47.
2. CHENG, K. & C.R. GALLISTEL. 1986. Cognition **23:** 149–178.
3. HERMER, L. & E.S. SPELKE. 1994. Nature (London) **370:** 57–59.
4. FODOR, J. A. 1983. The Modularity of Mind. MIT Press. Cambridge ,MA.
5. BAARS, B.J. 1989. A Cognitive Theory of Consciousness. Cambridge University Press. Cambridge, MA.
6. SHALLICE, T. 1988. From Neuropsychology to Mental Structure. Cambridge University Press, Cambridge, MA.
7. POSNER, M.I. & S. DEHAENE. 1994. Trends Neurosci. **17:** 75–79.
8. POSNER, M.I. 1994. Proc. Natl. Acad. Sci. USA **91:** 7398–7403.
9. DEHAENE, S. & J.P. CHANGEUX. 1989. J. Cognit. Neurosci. **1:** 244–261.
10. DEHAENE, S. & J.P. CHANGEUX. 1991. Cereb. Cortex **1:** 62–79.
11. DEHAENE, S. & J.P. CHANGEUX. 1993. J. Cognit. Neurosci. **5:** 390–407.
12. DEHAENE, S. & J.P. CHANGEUX. 1997. Proc. Natl. Acad. Sci. USA **94:** 13293–13298.
13. MESULAM, M.M. 1998. Brain **12:** 1013–1052.
14. VON ECONOMO, C. 1929. The Cytoarchitectonics of the Human Cerebral Cortex. Oxford University Press. London.
15. LLÍNAS, R. R. & D. PARÉ. 1991. Neuroscience **44:** 521–535.
16. MUNK, M. H., P.R. ROELFSEMA, P. KONIG, A. ENGEL & W. SINGER. 1996. Science **272:** 271–274.
17. JEANNEROD, M. 1997. The Cognitive Neuroscience of Action. Blackwell. Oxford.
18. WEISKRANTZ, L. 1997. Consciousness Lost and Found: A Neuro-psychological Exploration. Oxford University Press. New York.
19. FRISTON, K. J., G. TONONI, G.N. REEKE, O. SPORNS & G.M. EDELMAN. 1994. Neuroscience **59:** 229–243.
20. SCHULTZ, W., P. DAYAN & P.R. MONTAGUE. 1997. Science **275:** 1593–1599.
21. MACLEOD, C. M. 1991. Psychol. Bull. **109:** 163–203.
22. COHEN, J. D., K. DUNBAR & J. MCCLELLAND. 1990. Psychol. Rev. **97:** 332–361.
23. KIMBERG, D. Y. & M.J. FARAH. 1993. J. Exp. Psychol. Gen. **122:** 411–428.
24. RAICHLE, M. E., J.A. FIESZ, T.O. VIDEEN & A.K. MACLEOD. 1994. Cereb. Cortex **4:** 8–26.
25. DEHAENE, S., M.I. POSNER & D.M. TUCKER. 1994. Psychol. Sci. **5:** 303–305.
26. TONONI, G., R. SRINIVASAN, D.P. RUSSELL & G.M. EDELMAN. 1998. Proc. Natl. Acad. Sci. USA **95:** 3198–3203.
27. FRISTON, K.J., C.D. FRITH, P. FLETCHER, P.F. LIDDLE & R.S. FRACKOWIAK. 1996. Cereb. Cortex **6:** 156–164.
28. COHEN, J.D., W.M. PERLSTEIN, T.S. BRAVER, L.E. NYSTROM, D.C. NOLL, J. JONIDES & E.E. SMITH. 1997. Nature (London) **386:** 604–608.
29. PARDO, J. V., P.J. PARDO, K.W. JANER & M.E. RAICHLE. 1990. Proc. Natl. Acad. Sci. USA **87:** 256–259.
30. PAUS, T., L. KOSKI, Z. CARAMANOS & C. WESTBURY. 1998. NeuroRep. **9:** R37–R47.
31. RAICHLE, M.E., J.A. FIEZ, T.O. VIDEEN, A.K. MACLEOD, J.V. PARDO, P.T. FOX & PETERSEN. 1994. Cereb. Cortex **4:** 8–26.
32. CARTER, C.S., T.S. BRAVER, D. BARCH, M.M. BOTVINICK, D. NOLL & J.D. COHEN. 1998. Science **280:** 747–749.

33. KONISHI, S., K. NAKAJIMA, I. UCHIDA, M. KAMEYAMA, K. NAKAHARA, K. SEKIHARA & Y. MIYASHITA. 1998. Nat. Neurosci. **1:** 80–84.
34. ROLAND, P.E. & L. FRIBERG. 1985. J. Neurophysiol. **53:** 1219–1243.
35. SAHRAIE, A., L. WEISKRANTZ, J. L. BARBUR, A. SIMMONS, S.C.R. WILLIAMS & M.J. BRAMMER. 1997. Proc. Natl. Acad. Sci. USA **94:** 9406–9411.
36. GRAFTON, S.T., E. HAZELTINE & R. IVRY. 1995. J. Cognit. Neurosci.**7:** 497–510.
37. CORBETTA, M., F.M. MIEZIN, S. DOBMEYER, G.L. SMULMAN & S.E. PETERSEN. 1991. J. Neurosci. **11:** 2383–2402.
38. GOLDMAN-RAKIC, P.S. 1988. Annu. Rev. Neurosci. **11:** 137–156.
39. MORRIS, J.S., A. OHMAN & R.J. DOLAN. 1998. Nature (London) **393:** 467–470.
40. WHALEN, P. J., S.L. RAUCH, N.L. ETCOFF, S.C. MCINERNEY, M.B. LEE & M. JENIKE. 1998. J. Neurosci. **18:** 411–418.
41. DEHAENE, S., L. NACCACHE, L., G. LE CLEC'H, E. KOECHLIN, M. MUELLER, G. DEHAENE-LAMBERTZ, P.F. VAN DE MOORTELE & D. LE BIHAN. 1998. Nature (London) **395:** 597–600.
42. MORAN, J. & R. DESIMONE. 1985. Science **229:** 782–784.
43. MOTTER, B.C. 1994. J. Neurosci. **14:** 2178–2189.
44. DESCARRIES, L., V. GISIGER & M. STERIADE. 1997. Prog. Neurobiol. **53:** 603–625.
45. GRANON, S., B. POUCET, C. THINUS-BLANC, J.P. CHANGEUX & C. VIDAL. 1995. Psychopharmacology **119:** 139–144.
46. PICCIOTTO, M.R., M. ZOLI, R. RIMONDINI, C. LENA, L.M. MARUBIO, E.M. PICH, K. FUXE & J.P. CHANGEUX. 1998. Nature (London) **391:** 173–177.
47. CHANGEUX, J.P., P. COURRÈGE & A. DANCHIN. 1973. Proc. Natl. Acad. Sci. USA **70:** 2974–2978.
48. EDELMAN, G. 1987. Neural Darwinism. Basic Books. New York.
49. GRAY, J.A. 1994. Behav. Brain Sci. **18:** 659–722.

Consciousness and the Brain

The Thalamocortical Dialogue in Health and Disease

RODOLFO LLINÁS AND URS RIBARY

Department of Physiology and Neuroscience, New York University School of Medicine, New York, New York 10016, USA

ABSTRACT: The goal of this paper is to explore the basic assumption that large-scale, temporal coincidence of specific and nonspecific thalamic activity generates the functional states that characterize human cognition.

KEYWORDS: Thalamocortical; Gamma-band activity; Cognition; Functional Brain imaging

INTRODUCTION

I will confine my presentation to experimental data concerning human consciousness, *à la* Cajal. To me this is clearly the most parsimonious manner in which to approach the issue.

In the type of wonderful meeting such as we have had, most of us [and most certainly the speaker] remain awake throughout the presentation, although we understand why, given the complexity of the subject and the nature of jet lag, some of us might fall asleep. If a person falls asleep, especially in a non-REM condition, we may regard that person, during that time, as having ceased to exist as an entity capable of consciousness. The lyric of a well-known old tango tune entitled "Silencio en la Noche" describes the condition in succinct poetic fashion: "el músculo duerme, la ambición descansa [the muscle sleeps, ambition rests]." Indeed, a person does not exist as a cognitive being during dreamless sleep. So, what does this mean? We will rightly infer that consciousness is but one functional state of the brain. The converse is also true: the brain has other equally costly metabolically active states in which cognition is not generated.

The next question to ask, agreeing that a prerequisite for cognition is either wakefulness or dreaming, would be to describe the absolute minimal neuronal machinery required for the support of such functional condition. We can easily agree that in addition to the brain stem and the associated basal ganglia/amygdalar nucleus, we need the brain cortical mantle and the thalamus. Indeed if we lack the thalamus, all that beautiful cortex is useless, and, in the absence of cortex, the thalamus on its own is quite impotent. I have personally seen patients in Dr. Plum's neurology clinic at Cornell Medical School with an intact cortex, but with medial thalamic lesions, in a state close to total coma—in agreement with previous papers on this subject. On the basis

---

Address for correspondence: Rodolfo Llinás, M.D., Ph.D., New York University School of Medicine, Department of Physiology and Neuroscience, 550 First Avenue, New York, NY 10016.
llinar01@popmail.med.nyu.edu

of such cases, as well as on magnetoencephalographic data in humans, I proposed a decade ago that consciousness arises from a continuous "dialogue" between the thalamus and the cortex.

THE BASIC NEURONAL CIRCUIT IN HUMAN CONSCIOUSNESS

Given that sensory inputs generate but a fractured representation of universals, the issue of perceptual unity concerns the mechanisms that allow these different sensory components to be gathered into one global image. In recent years, this has been described as "binding," to be implemented by temporal conjunction.[1-4]

Because the number of possible categories of perceptions is so extensive, their implementation via purely hierarchical connectivity is very unlikely, where a single "grandmother" neuron or a small group of such neurons would represent specific elements of a category. A second problem with the hierarchical proposal is sampling size, that is, a very large number of specific elements in a very large number of categories would make the retrieval problem immense. Thus, even considering that neuronal elements transduce and transmit signals at millisecond rate from the onset of sensory primitives, exhausting all sequential combinations would be awkwardly time-intensive. But at a more familiar level, it takes roughly the same amount of time to recognize that a face is familiar than that it is not. As in any sequential strategy, it takes much longer to conclude nonfamiliarity—as it would require comparing it with "all known faces"—than familiarity, as in the latter the search will proceed for only as long as necessary to match. From a different perspective the grandmother-neuron hypothesis fails to explain how their unique "perceptual insights" (the specific elements in a given category) are communicated to the rest of the nervous system; that is, how do grandmother cells tell the rest of their neurons what they know, given their unique position at the top of a hierarchy?

Alternatively, since categorizations are generated by spatial mapping of the primary sensory cortex and its associated cortical structures, a more dynamic interaction, based on temporal coherence, may generate dissipative functional structures[5] capable of as rapid a change as the perception they generate. Thus, a simultaneity mapping may be envisioned that takes advantage of the parallel and synchronous organization of the brain networks in order to generate perception.

The hypotheses to be discussed below are derived from two areas of research, the first from the investigation of single neuronal elements studied *in vitro* and *in vivo* and the second from measurements made via noninvasive magnetoencephalography in humans. The principal issue to be discussed is the assumption that the intrinsic electrical properties of neurons, and the dynamic events resulting from their connectivity, result in global resonant states which we know as cognition.

INTROSPECTION AND REALITY EMULATION

Several lines of research suggest that the brain is essentially a closed system[5] capable of self-generated activity based on the intrinsic electrical properties of its component neurons and their connectivity. In such a view the CNS is a "reality"-emulating system[6] and the parameters of such "reality" are delineated by the senses.[7] The hypothesis that the brain is a closed system follows from the observation that the thalamic input from the cortex is larger than that from the peripheral sensory system,[8] suggesting that thalamocortical iterative recurrent activity is the basis for consciousness.[7] In addition, neurons with intrinsic oscillatory capabilities that reside in this complex synaptic network allow the brain to self-generate dynamic oscillatory states which shape the functional events elicited by sensory stimuli. In this context, functional states such as wakefulness or REM sleep and other sleep stages are prominent examples of the breadth of variation that self-generated brain activity may yield.

The above hypothesis assumes that, for the most part, the connectivity of the human brain is present at birth, and is "fine-tuned" later on during normal maturation. This view of a neurological *a priori* was suggested in early neurological research,[10,11] with the identification by Broca of a cortical speech center and the discovery of point-to-point somatotopic maps in the motor and sensory cortices[12] and in the thalamus.[13,14]

A second organizing principle may be equally important—one that is based on the temporal rather then the spatial relationships among neurons. This temporal mapping may be viewed as a type of functional geometry.[15] This mechanism has been difficult to study until recently, since it requires the simultaneous measurement of activity from large numbers of neurons and is not an aspect usually considered in neuroscience.

TEMPORAL MAPPING AND COGNITIVE CONJUNCTION

Synchronous neuronal activation during sensory input has recently been studied in the mammalian visual cortical cells when light bars of optimal orientation and displacement rate are presented.[16–18] Furthermore, the components of a visual stimulus corresponding to a singular cognitive object (e.g., a line in a visual field) yield coherent gamma-band oscillations in regions of the cortex that may be as far as 7 mm apart,[17–19] or may even be in the contralateral cortex. In fact, gamma-band oscillatory activity between related cortical columns has a high correlation coefficient under such circumstances. In addition, coherent 40-Hz oscillations throughout the cortical mantle of awake human subjects have been revealed by magnetoencephalography.[20] These oscillations may be reset by sensory stimuli; and phase comparison revealed the presence of a 12- to 13-msec phase shift between the rostral and caudal poles of the brain.[20] These gamma oscillations display a high degree of spatial organization and thus may be a candidate mechanism for the production of temporal conjunction of rhythmic activity over a large ensemble of neurons.

From a neuronal point of view the mechanism by which gamma oscillation may be generated has been studied at the level of single neurons and of neuronal circuits. For example, it has been shown that the membrane potential of sparsely spiny inhibitory neurons in cortical layer IV supports gamma-frequency membrane voltage oscillation (FIG. 1), the mechanism for the oscillation being a sequential activation of a persistent low-threshold sodium current[21] followed by a subsequent potassium conductance.[22] The inhibitory input of these sparsely spinous interneurons onto pyramidal cells projecting to the thalamus can entrain 40-Hz oscillation in the reticular nucleus and so entrain, by rebound activation, the specific and nonspecific thalamus.

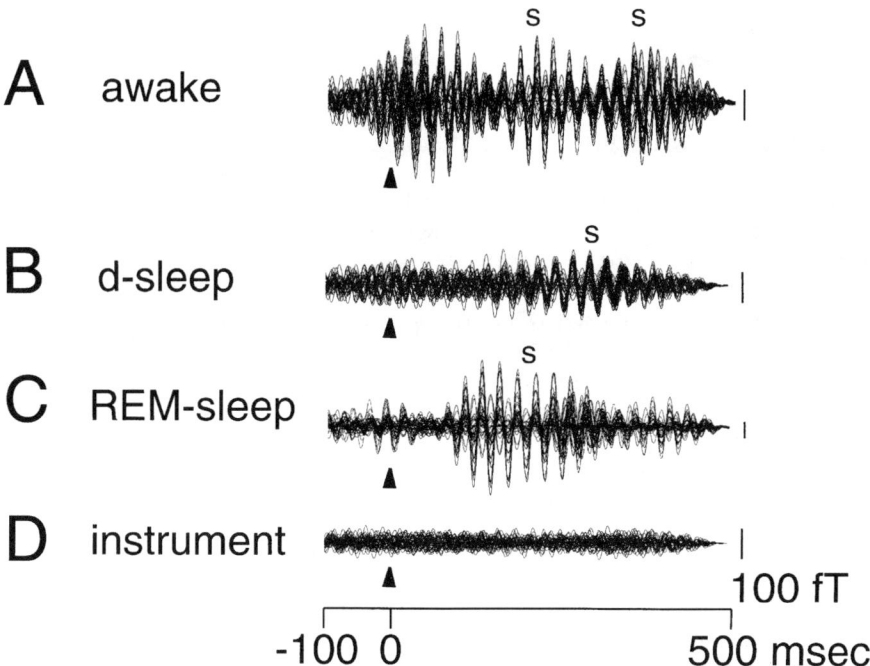

FIGURE 1. 40-Hz oscillation in wakefulness and a lack of 40-Hz reset in delta sleep and REM sleep. Recording using a 37-channel MEG. In (**A–D**) spontaneous oscillatory responses following auditory stimulus. In **A**, the subject is awake and the stimulus is followed by a reset of 40-Hz activity. In **B** and **C**, the stimulus produced no resetting of the rhythm. However, spontaneous 40-Hz oscillations occur in REM sleep independent of the stimulus. (**D**) The noise of the system in femtotesla (fT). (Modified from Llinás and Ribary[28]).

Indeed, since the GABAergic reticular thalamic neurons project to most of the relay nuclei of the thalamus,[23] layer-IV cells would indirectly make a contribution to the 40-Hz resonant oscillation in the thalamocortical network. It has recently been demonstrated that under *in vivo* conditions relay-thalamic and reticular-nucleus neurons and pyramidal cells themselves are capable of close to 40-Hz oscillation on their own, laying out in this manner the possibility for network resonance intrinsically at gamma-band frequency.[24] The ionic mechanisms underlying this oscillation are similar to those of the spiny layer-IV neurons.[25]

When the interconnectivity of these nuclei is combined with the intrinsic properties of the individual neurons, a network for resonant neuronal oscillation emerges in which specific cortico-thalamo-cortical circuits would tend to resonate at gamma frequency. According to this hypothesis, neurons at the different levels, and most particularly those in the reticular nucleus, would be responsible for the synchronization of gamma oscillation in distant thalamic and cortical sites. We will see later that these oscillations may be organized globally over the CNS, especially as it has been shown that neighboring reticular-nucleus cells may be linked by dendro-dendritic and intranuclear axon collaterals.[26]

THALAMOCORTICAL RESONANCE AND CONSCIOUSNESS

On the basis of research about the minimal temporal interval in sensory discrimination we may establish that consciousness is a noncontinuous event determined by synchronous activity in the thalamocortical system.[27] Since this activity is present during REM sleep[28] but is not seen during non-REM sleep, we may postulate further that the resonance is modulated by the brainstem and would be given content by sensory input in the awake state and by intrinsic activity during dreaming. These studies have addressed issues concerning: (*a*) the presence of gamma-band activity during sleep and (*b*) the possible differences between gamma resetting in different sleep/wakefulness states.

Spontaneous magnetic activity was recorded continuously during wakefulness, delta sleep, and REM sleep using a 37-channel sensor array (FIG. 1). Since Fourier analysis of the spontaneous, broadly filtered rhythmicity (1–200 Hz) demonstrated a large peak of activity at 40 Hz over much of the cortex, we decided that it was permissible to filter the data at gamma-band frequency (30–50 Hz). Large coherent signals with a very high signal-to-noise ratio were typically recorded from all 37 sensors, as shown in FIG. 1A for a single 0.6-sec epoch of global spontaneous oscillations in an awake individual.

The second set of experiments examined the responsiveness of the oscillation to an auditory stimulus during wakefulness, delta sleep, and REM sleep. The stimulus comprised frequency-modulated 500-msec tone bins, triggered 100 msec after the onset of the 600-msec recording epoch; recordings were made at random intervals over about 10 minutes. In agreement with previous findings,[28,30,31] auditory stimuli produced well-defined 40-Hz oscillation during wakefulness (FIG. 1A), but no resetting was observed during delta (FIG. 1B) or REM sleep (FIG. 1C) in this or the six other subjects we examined.

The traces in FIGURE 1 are a superposition of the 37 traces recorded during a single 600-msec epoch. Their alignment indicates the high level of coherence of the 40-Hz activity at all the recording points following the auditory stimulus. A high level of coherence is also typical of spontaneous 40-Hz bursts.

These findings indicated that while the awake state and the REM sleep state are electrically similar with respect to the presence of 40-Hz oscillations, a central difference remains in the inability of sensory input to reset the 40-Hz activity during REM sleep. By contrast, during delta sleep the amplitude of these oscillations differs from that of wakefulness and REM sleep, but as in REM sleep there is no 40-Hz sensory response. Another significant finding is that gamma oscillations are not reset by sensory input during REM sleep, although clear evoked-potential responses indicate that the thalamo-neocortical system is accessible to sensory input.[7,33] We consider this to be the central difference between dreaming and wakefulness. These data suggest that we do not perceive the external world during REM sleep because the intrinsic activity of the nervous system does not place sensory input in the context of the functional state being generated by the brain.[7] That is, the dreaming condition is a state of hyperattentiveness to intrinsic activity in which sensory input cannot access the machinery that generates conscious experience.

An attractive possibility in considering the morphophysiological substrate is that the "nonspecific" thalamic system, particularly the intralaminar complex, plays an important part in such coincidence generation. Indeed the neurons of this complex project in a spatially continuous manner to the most superficial layers of all cortical areas, including the primary sensory cortices. This possibility is particularly attractive, given that single neurons burst at 30–40 Hz especially during REM sleep,[24] which is a finding consistent with the macroscopic magnetic recordings observed in this study, and with the fact that damage to the intralaminar system results in lethargy or coma.[34,35]

BINDING OF SPECIFIC AND NONSPECIFIC GAMMA BAND ACTIVITY

A schematic of a neuronal circuit that may subserve temporal binding is presented in the left side of FIGURE 2. Gamma oscillations in neurons in specific thalamic nuclei[19] establish cortical resonance through direct activation of pyramidal cells and feed-forward inhibition through activation of 40-Hz inhibitory interneurons in layer IV.[22] These oscillations re-enter the thalamus via layer-VI pyramidal–cell axon collaterals,[36] producing thalamic feedback inhibition via the reticular nucleus.[23] A second system is illustrated on the right side of FIGURE 2. Here the intralaminar nonspecific thalamic nuclei projection to cortical layers I and V and to the reticular nucleus is illustrated.[28] Layer-V pyramidal cells return oscillations to the reticular nucleus and intralaminar nuclei. The cells in this complex have been shown to oscillate at gamma-band frequency and to be capable of recursive activation.[24]

It is also apparent from the literature that neither of these two circuits alone can generate cognition. Indeed, as stated above, damage of the nonspecific thalamus produces deep disturbances of consciousness, while damage of specific systems produces loss of the particular modality. Although at this early stage it must be quite simple in its formulation, the above suggests a hypothesis regarding the overall organization of brain function. The hypothesis rests on two tenets: First, the "specific" thalamocortical system is viewed as encoding specific sensory and motor activity by the resonant thalamocortical system specialized to receive such inputs (e.g., the LGN and visual cortex); the specific system is understood to comprise those nuclei, whether sensorimotor or associative, that project mainly, if not exclusively, to layer IV in the cortex. And the second tenet is that, following optimal activation, any such thalamocortical loop would tend to oscillate at gamma-band frequency, and activity in the "specific" thalamocortical system could be easily "recognized" over the cortex by this oscillatory characteristic.

In this scheme, areas of cortical sites "peaking" at gamma-band frequency would represent the different components of the cognitive world that have reached optimal activity at that time. The problem now is the conjunction of such a fractured description into a single cognitive event. We propose that this could come about by the concurrent summation of specific and nonspecific 40-Hz activity along the radial dendritic axis of given cortical elements, that is, by coincidence detection. This view

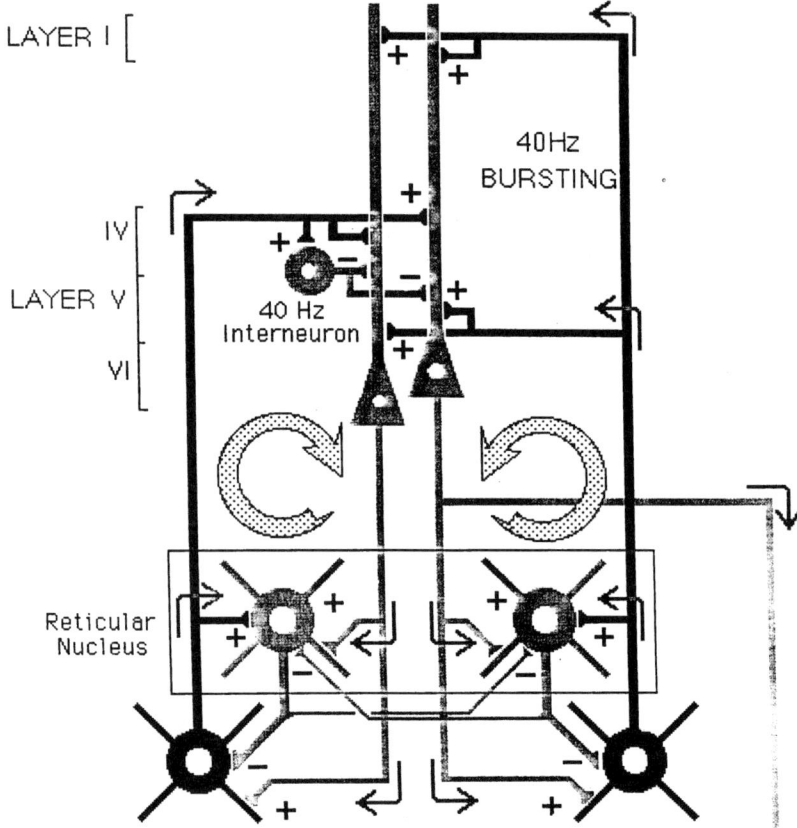

FIGURE 2. Thalamocortical circuits proposed to subserve temporal binding. Diagram of two thalamocortical systems. *Left:* Specific sensory or motor nuclei project to layer IV of the cortex, producing cortical oscillation by direct activation and feed-forward inhibition via 40-Hz inhibitory interneurons. Collaterals of these projections produce thalamic feedback inhibition via the reticular nucleus. The return pathway (circular arrow on the right) re-enters this oscillation to specific- and reticularis-thalamic nuclei via layer-VI pyramidal cells. *Right*: Second loop shows nonspecific intralaminary nuclei projecting to the most superficial layer of the cortex and giving collaterals to the reticular nucleus. Layer-V pyramidal cells return oscillation to the reticular- and the nonspecific-thalamic nuclei, establishing a second resonant loop. The conjunction of the specific and nonspecific loops is proposed to generate temporal binding. (Modified from Llinás and Ribary.[28])

differs from the binding hypothesis proposed by Crick and Koch in which cortical binding is attributed to the activation of cortical V4, pulvinar or claustrum.[3]

THE THALAMOCORTICAL DYSRHYTHMIC SYNDROME

Very recently, a significant corollary to the thalamocortical dialogue hypothesis for consciousness has been encountered concerning several neurological and psychiatric conditions.[37] Indeed spontaneous magnetoencephalography (MEG) activity from patients suffering from neurogenic pain, tinnitus, Parkinson's disease or depression showed increased low-frequency theta rhythmicity, in conjunction with a widespread and marked increase of coherence among high- and low-frequency oscillations.

These data indicate the presence of a *thalamocortical dysrhythmia* which we propose is responsible for all the above-mentioned conditions. The coherent theta activity, which results from a resonant interaction between thalamus and cortex, is due to the generation of low-threshold calcium spike bursts by thalamic cells. The presence of these bursts is directly related to thalamic cell hyperpolarization brought about by either excess inhibition or disfacilitation.[37] The emergence of positive clinical symptoms is viewed as resulting from ectopic gamma-band activation, which we refer to as the "edge effect." This effect is observable as increased coherence between low- and high-frequency oscillations, probably resulting from inhibitory asymmetry between high- and low-frequency thalamocortical modules at the cortical level.

The basic assumption concerning the genesis of this syndrome is that thalamocortical dysrhythmia is a CNS intrinsic property brought about by changes in intrinsic voltage-gated ionic conductances at the level of thalamic relay cells, namely the deinactivation of T channels by cell membrane hyperpolarization.[4] Low-threshold spike bursts are thus produced and lock the related thalamocortical circuits in low-frequency resonance. Low-frequency loops interact at the cortical level with high-frequency ones, giving rise to the edge effect and the generation of a positive symptom. In tinnitus, peripheral neurogenic pain, Parkinson's disease, and some neuropsychiatric disorders with striatal origin, the dysrhythmic mechanism is triggered "bottom up," which means from the thalamus toward the cortex. In other situations like epilepsy, neuropsychiatric conditions of cortical origin, and central cortical neurogenic pain, we may have a "top down" mechanism, triggered by a reduction of the cortico-thalamic input. Both "bottom up" and "top down" situations result in excess inhibition or disfacilitation, generating thalamic cell membrane hyperpolarization and low-frequency oscillation. And so, the same mechanism responsible for the organization of consciousness, when altered in its organization and timing, can be the genesis of neuropsychiatric conditions.

SUMMARY

Cognition, a property of thalamocortical cycling, appears to function on the basis of temporal coherence. Such coherence would be embodied by the simultaneity of neuronal firing based on passive and active dendritic conduction along the apical dendritic core conductors. In this fashion, the time-coherent activity of the specific and nonspecific oscillatory inputs, obtained by summing distal and proximal activity in given dendritic elements, would enhance *de facto* 40-Hz cortical coherence by their multimodal character. And in this way it provides one mechanism for global binding. The "specific" system would supply the *content* that relates to the external world, and the nonspecific system would give rise to the temporal conjunction, or the *context* (on the basis of a more interoceptive context concerned with alertness). Together they would generate a single cognitive experience. Furthermore, when this rhythmicity is altered in particular fashions, neurological and psychiatric conditions ensue.

ACKNOWLEDGMENTS

This work was supported by Grant NS13742 (to R.L.) from the National Institutes of Health (NINCDS) and by the Charles A. Dana Foundation.

REFERENCES

1. BIENENSTOCK, E. & C. VON DER MALSBURG. 1986. Statistical coding and short-term synaptic plasticity: a scheme for knowledge representation in the brain. In Disordered Systems and Biological Organization. E. Bienenstock, F. Fogelman & G. Weisbuch, Eds. :247–272. Springer-Verlag. Les Houches.
2. VON DER MALSBURG, C. 1981. The correlation theory of brain function. Internal report, Max-Planck Institute for Biophysical Chemistry. Goettingen.
3. CRICK, F. & C. KOCH. 1990. Some reflections on visual awareness. Cold Spring Harbor Symp. Quant. Biol. **55**: 953–962.
4. LLINÁS, R. 1990. Intrinsic electrical properties of mammalian neurons and CNS function. In Fidia Research Foundation Neuroscience Award Lectures, Vol. 4 :1–10. Raven Press. New York.
5. LLINÁS, R. & D. PARE. 1996. In The Mind-Brain Countinuum. R. Llinas & P. Churchland, Eds. MIT Press. Cambridge, MA.
6. LLINÁS, R. & U. RIBARY. 1993. Perception as an oneiric-like state modulated by the senses. In Large-Scale Neuronal Theories of the Brain. MIT Press. Cambridge, MA. In press.
7. LLINÁS, R. & D. PARÉ. 1991. Of dreaming and wakefulness. Neuroscience **44**: 521–535.
8. WILSON, J.R., M.J. FRIEDLANDER & S.M. SHERMAN. 1984. Ultrastructural morphology of identified X- and Y-cells in the cat's lateral geniculate nucleus. Proc. R. Soc. **B221**: 411-436.
9. EDELMAN, G.M. 1987. Neuronal Darwinism: The Theory of Neuronal Group Selection. Basic Books. New York.
10. CAJAL, S.R. 1929. Etude sur la Neurogénèse de quelques Vertébrés. Charles C Thomas. Springfield, IL.
11. HARRIS, W A. 1987. Neurogenetics. In Encyclopedia of Neuroscience. G. Adelman, Ed.: 791–793. Birkhäuser. Basel.
12. PENFIELD, W. & T. RASMUSSEN. 1950. The Cerebral Cortex of Man. MacMillan. New York.
13. MOUNTCASTLE, V.B. & E. HENNEMANN. 1949. Pattern of tactile representation in thalamus of cat. J. Neurophysiol. **12**: 85–100.
14. MOUNTCASTLE, V.B. & E. HENNEMANN. 1952. The representation of tactile sensibility in the thalamus of the monkey. J. Comp. Neurol. **97**: 409–440.
15. PELLIONISZ, A. & R.R. LLINÁS. 1982. Space-time representation in the brain: the cerebellum as a predictive space-time metric tensor. Neuroscience **7**: 2949–2970.
16. ECKHORN, R., R. BAUER, W. JORDAN, M. BROSCH, W. KRUSE, M. MUNK & H.J. REITBOCK. 1988. Coherent oscillations: a mechanism of feature linking in the visual cortex? Biol. Cybern. **60**: 121–130.
17. GRAY, C.M., P. KONIG, A.K. ENGEL & W. SINGER. 1989. Oscillatory responses in cat visual cortex exhibit inter-columnar synchronization which reflects global stimulus properties. Nature **338**: 334–337.
18. GRAY, C.M. & W. SINGER. 1989. Stimulus-specific neuronal oscillations in orientation columns of cat visual cortex. Proc. Natl. Acad. Sci. USA **86**: 1698–1702.
19. SINGER, W. 1993. Synchronization of cortical activity and its putative role in information processing and learning. Annu. Rev. Physiol. **55**: 349–374.
20. LLINÁS, R. R. & U. RIBARY. 1992. Rostrocaudal scan in human brain: a global characteristic of the 40-Hz response during sensory input. In Induced Rhythms in the Brain. E. Basar & T. Bullock, Eds. :147–154. Birkhäuser. Boston.
21. LLINÁS, R. & M. SUGIMORI. 1980. Electrophysiological properties of in vitro Purkinje cell somata in mammalian cerebellar slices. J. Physiol. (London) **305**: 171–195.

22. LLINÁS, R.R., A.A. GRACE & Y. YAROM. 1991. In vitro neurons in mammalian cortical layer 4 exhibit intrinsic activity in the 10 to 50 Hz frequency range. Proc. Natl. Acad. Sci. USA. **88:** 897–901.
23. STERIADE, M., A. PARENT & J. HADA. 1984. Thalamic projections of reticular nucleus thalami of cat: a study using retrograde transport of horseradish peroxidase and double fluorescent tracers. J. Comp. Neurol. **229:** 531–547.
24. STERIADE, M., R. CURRÓDOSSI & F. CONTRERAS. 1993. Electrophysiological properties of intralaminar thalamocortical cells discharging rhythmic (^{a}40 hz) spike-bursts at ^{a}1000 Hz during waking and rapid eye movement sleep. Neuroscience **56** : 1–9.
25. SERIADE, M., R. CURRÓDOSSI, D. PARÉ & G. OAKSON. 1991. Fast oscillations (20–40 Hz) in thalamocortical systems and their potentiation by mesopontine cholinergic nuclei in the cat. Proc. Natl. Acad. Sci. USA **88:** 4396–4400.
26. DESCHÊNES, M., A. MADARIAGA-DOMICH & M. STERIADE. 1985. Dendrodendritic synapses in the cat reticularis thalami nucleus: a structural basis for thalamic spindle synchronization. Brain Res. **334:** 165–168.
27. JOLIOT, M., U. RIBARY & R. LLINÁS. 1994. Neuromagnetic oscillatory activity in the vecinity of 40 Hz coexists with cognitive temporal binding in the human brain. Proc. Natl. Acad. Sci. USA **1:**11748–11751
28. LLINÁS, R. & U. RIBARY. 1993. Coherent 40-Hz oscillation characterizes dream state in humans. Proc. Natl. Acad. Sci. USA **90:** 2078–2081.
29. LANDE, R. 1979. Quantitative genetic analysis of multivariate evolution, applied to brain-body size allometry. Evolution. **33:** 400–416.
30. GALAMBOS, R., S. MAKEIG & P.J. TALMACHOFF. 1981. A 40-Hz auditory potential recorded from the human scalp. Proc. Natl. Acad. Sci. USA **78:** 2643–2647.
31. PANTEV, C., S. MAKEIG, M HOKE, R. GALAMBOS, S. HAMPSON & C. GALLEN. 1991. Human auditory evoked gamma-band magnetic fields. Proc. Natl. Acad. Sci. USA **88:** 8996–9000.
32. KRISTOFFERSON, A.B. 1984. Quantal and deterministic timing in human duration discrimination. Ann. N.Y. Acad. Sci. **423:** 3–15
33. SERIADE, M. 1991. In Cerebral Cortex. A. Peters & E.G. Jones, Eds. :279–357. Plenum. New York.
34. FACON, E., M. STERIADE & N. WERTHEIM. 1958. Hypersomnie prolongée engendrée par des lésions bilatérales due systèm activateur médial le syndrome thrombotique de la bifurcation du tronc basilaire. Rev. Neurol. **98:** 117–133.
35. CASTAIGNE, P., A. BUGE, R. ESCOUROLLE & M. MASSON. 1962. Ramollissement pédonculaire médian, tegmento-thalamique avec ophtalmoplégie et hypersomnie. Rev. Neurol. **106:** 357–367.
36. STERIADE, M., E.G. JONES & R. LLINÁS. 1990. Thalamic Oscillations and Signalling. John Wiley. New York.
37. LLINÁS, R., U. RIBARY, D. JEANMONOD, E. KRONBERG & P. P. MITRA. 1999. Thalamocortical dysrhythmia: a neurological and neuropsychiatric syndrome characterized by magnetoencephalography. Proc. Natl. Acad. Sci. USA **96:** 15222–15227.

The Neuroanatomy of Phenomenal Vision: A Psychological Perspective

PETRA STOERIG

Institute of Experimental Psychology II, Heinrich-Heine-University, D-40225 Düsseldorf, Germany

ABSTRACT: Somewhere in the visual system, phenomenal vision—the seeing of colors, brightness, depths, shades, and motion—is generated not only from the distribution of light on the retina, but also when the eyes are closed, in dreams, hallucinations, phosphenes, and (possibly) imagery. Whether these different forms of phenomenal vision share a common substrate although their origins are different (optical, mechanical, electrical, endogenous) is discussed in the light of evidence from neuropsychological and functional imaging studies. Whereas extrastriate visual cortical areas appear to be involved in all types of phenomenal vision that have been studied, the necessity of a contribution from primary visual cortex is demonstrated by the loss of conscious vision that follows its destruction. If both extrastriate and primary cortical activation are needed, the latter may not just provide an indispensable input, but may also need to receive the output of the extrastriate processing via reentrant connections.

KEYWORDS: Veridical vision; Blindsight; Nonveridical vision; Phosphenes; Dreams; Hallucinations; Imagery; Afterimages; V1; extrastriate cortex; Vision

INTRODUCTION

Where in the visual system does the neuronal processing of visual information become conscious? In the past ten years, several suggestions have been put forward: they focus on the extrastriate cortical areas, either in isolation[1,2] or conjointly with the primary visual cortex,[3,4] or on those extrastriate visual areas that form the ventral, occipitotemporal stream of visual cortical processing only,[5] or they include extra-visual areas in the frontal lobes,[6–8] or in the reticular formation.[9] In addition to this already wide range of structures, within the broader discussion of the neuronal basis of consciousness, thalamocorticothalamic loops linking the visual cortical areas with specific and unspecific thalamic nuclei are discussed.[10–12]

Focusing specifically on visual consciousness instead of on the general question of conscious representation restricts the problem to the best-studied of the sensory systems: Whatever mechanisms mediate the mysterious transformation of neural information into sensory awareness in the visual system would, presumably, play a similar role in other sensory systems. Unfortunately, however restricted conscious vision appears when compared to the entirety of conscious experience, it is still very complex. It includes awareness of brightness and darkness, of colors and motion, of

---

Address for correspondence: Institute of Experimental Psychology II, Heinrich-Heine-University, D-40225 Düsseldorf, Germany. Voice: +49.211.81-12265; fax: 49.211.81-14522.
petra.stoerig@uni-duesseldorf.de

depth and shapes and objects; it includes recognition of what one sees and what it may be used for; it includes veridical as well as non-veridical vision as in dreams and hallucinations, and ultimately it includes the conscious organism, a self, who sees, recognizes, and acts upon the visual information. Embedding conscious vision within the full range of the organism's experience requires reference to structures outside of the visual system and, because sensation serves action, requires the use of inclusion of the motor system as well. Nevertheless, while recognizing that conscious vision is something that only a conscious organism has, and that it is there to serve this organism by guiding its actions, I prefer, on heuristic grounds, to restrict the inquiry to the conscious representation of visual information, Moreover, I shall mainly address what I regard as conscious vision's most basic aspect, namely, that of seeing brightness and darkness, colors, and movements. This is phenomenal vision, whose elements are the visual qualia from which objects are constructed. It comes in veridical and nonveridical forms.

ORGANIZATION OF THE VISUAL SYSTEM

Let us first look at the visual process and the neural system which mediates it. Our current scientific paradigm and our immediate apprehension agree that there exists a real, physical world in which we live and whose properties we perceive. The physical reality we visually perceive consists of a small part of the electromagnetic spectrum, which, as light waves or particles emitted from light sources or reflected from surfaces, falls through the eye upon the retina. Here the spatial and spectral distribution of the light is transformed into a physiological code—nerve impulses that carry information about contrast, location, and chromaticity. The nerve impulses are transmitted from the retinal ganglion cells along the optic nerve and via the optic chiasm to the ten brain nuclei known to receive <u>direct</u> retinal input. The lion's share of the information is sent, first, to the dorsal lateral geniculate nucleus (dLGN), and from there on to the primary visual cortex (V1, or striate cortex) on the medial aspect of the occipital lobe. From here, the information is forwarded to the many functionally specialized extrastriate visual cortical areas that together comprise the visual cortex. These areas receive their visual input not only from V1, but also from the various retinorecipient nuclei which project to the visual cortical areas either directly or via other subcortical nuclei. In addition to their lateral connections, the visual areas are interconnected both in serial and in parallel, and in both the forward (caudorostral) and backward (rostrocaudal) directions[13] (FIGS. 1 and 2).

The subcortical visual nuclei are functionally specialized. The nucleus suprachiasmaticus is involved in the entrainment of the circadian rhythms to the light–dark cycle, the pretectum in the pupillary light reflex, the nucleus of the optic tract in optokinetic nystagmus, and the superior colliculus in saccadic eye-movements and attention. Evidence for functional specialization of visual cortex is provided (1) by electrophysiological recording studies, which have shown that neurons in different cortical regions have different receptive field properties, (2) by functional imaging studies which have demonstrated activation of different cortical areas by different types of stimuli, and (3) by clinical (neuropsychological) studies correlating selective impairments of visual functions with lesions in different visual cortical areas. The specialized areas tentatively identified by such studies, may themselves be seg-

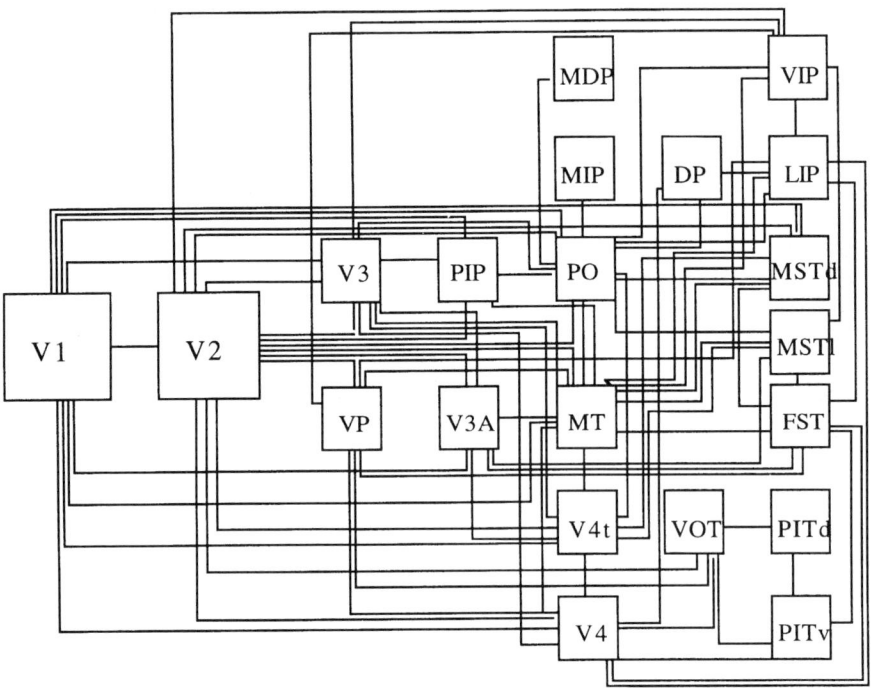

FIGURE 1. A schematic representation of functionally specialized visual cortical areas. Almost all known connections are bidirectional. (Data from Felleman and Van Essen.[13])

regated into still smaller functional compartments, increasing the difficulty of determining how and where vision becomes conscious. Were the visual system organized in a quasi-Cartesian fashion so that all retinal input eventually converged onto a single structure whose destruction abolished all conscious vision, we should happily accept that structure as "the mind's eye." Instead, we find a network of heavily interconnected, functionally specialized structures at both cortical and subcortical levels. Visual signals originating at the same retinal locus will be conveyed along different routes, via differing numbers of relay nuclei, by axons with different conduction velocities, arriving at their destination at different times.

How can perceptual unity arise from such a distributed network? Where in this dense mesh of interconnected visual neurons does the visual neural code get transformed into the phenomenal visual world? After all, qualia do not exist in the physical world, nor are they properties of neuronal processes. Instead, they represent a mental level of reality; their perception by an animal defines its vision as conscious. The construction of qualia may depend uniquely upon a single neuronal processing feature, or a combination of such features, from microtubules, synapses, and neurotransmitters, to neuronal morphology and connectivity, velocity of signal transmission, and the synchronous activity of cell assemblies distributed in cortical and subcortical structures. Several of these possibilities are dealt with in other chapters

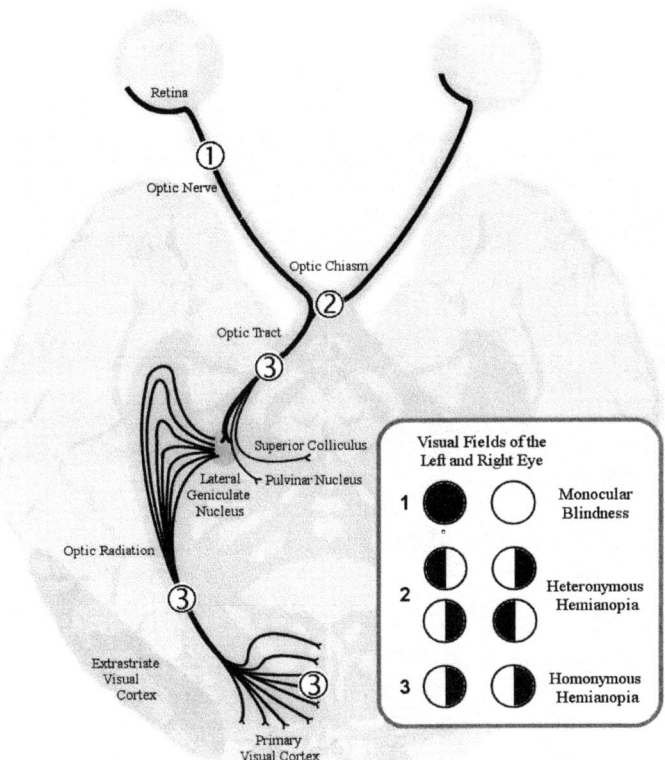

FIGURE 2. The primary visual pathways and (*inset*) the field defects resulting from lesions within this system. While destruction of the eye (1) or the optic nerve causes blindness in one eye, lesions involving the optic chiasm (2) will, depending on their precise location, cause a bitemporal or binasal heteronymous hemianopia. Post-chiasmatic lesions (3), due to the crossing of fibers from the nasal retinae, affect homonymous parts of the visual fields of the two eyes, regardless of whether they involve the optic tract, the radiation, or the primary visual cortex.

of this volume. In this chapter I shall focus on the macroscopic level, that is, the level of structures and networks of structures, and ask: where are visual qualia made?

VERIDICAL PHENOMENAL VISION

Absolute blindness is an absence of all visual qualia. It may result from destruction of one or more of the following visual structures: the eye, the retina, the optic nerve, the optic tract, the dorsal lateral geniculate nucleus (dLGN), the optic radiation, and the primary (V1) and secondary visual cortex (V2). A unilateral lesion will affect the visual field of one eye if it is prechiasmatic, and the visual field of both eyes if it is behind the chiasma (FIG. 2). The more distant it is from the retina, the more fibers projecting to extrageniculate visual nuclei will be spared, and the more visual functions will remain intact. While a retrochiasmatic lesion may spare only the projection to the nucleus suprachiasmaticus, a retrogeniculate lesion will leave intact all retinofugal fibers projecting to extrageniculate nuclei. Visual reflexes such as the pupillary light reflex can then be elicited from the blind visual field, and so can nonreflexive visual functions, provided procedures such as forced-choice guessing are used to circumvent the blindness that the patients experience. The visual functions that have thus far been demonstrated include localization, detection, and discrimination of visual flux, and of the size, orientation, motion, motion direction, wavelength, and shape of stimuli presented in the blind field. These types of visual function, which are demonstrable in a subject's blind field, have been termed *blindsight* (see Weiskrantz et al.,[14] Weiskrantz,[15] and Stoerig and Cowey[16] for reviews). This phenomenon demonstrates that nonreflexive visual processing is possible in the absence of visual *awareness* of the processed information. Since the extrageniculo-striate cortical visual system is undamaged in these patients, we must infer that the extrageniculo-striate system is, by itself, insufficient to mediate visual awareness.

Like destruction of the dLGN, destruction of the primary visual cortex causes a complete loss of phenomenal vision, but only the cortical lesion will permit the various nonreflexive visual functions of blindsight. Destruction of the secondary visual cortical area which surrounds V1 on all sides appears to have similar effects to those of a lesion in V1. Destruction of lower V2 causes a quadrantanopia in the upper contralateral hemifield, and destruction of upper V2 is followed by an anopia of the lower quadrant.[17] Disconnection of the primary visual cortex both from its geniculate input and from the higher visual cortical areas thus causes a loss of visual qualia. However, if the lesion selectively destroys extrastriate visual cortical areas *without* disconnecting V1 from the remaining cortical regions, visual qualia remain. Thus, when the occipitotemporal areas V4/V8 (the so-called "color complex") is selectively affected, color vision is lost, but movement and brightness remain. Conversely, when area MT, which is part of the human motion complex (hMT+), is affected, conscious motion vision is compromised, but color and brightness vision remain. It follows that phenomenal vision depends on the functional integrity of the early visual cortical areas surrounding and including V1/V2, with different areas supporting different qualia.

THE ROLE OF V1

The role that V1 plays in the concerted action mediating visual awareness is unclear. One hypothesis suggests that V1 functions like a cortical retina,[18] providing an input into the array of extrastriate areas without which they are incapacitated and cannot mediate phenomenal vision.[6] Alternatively, V1 could participate in visual awareness directly, supporting a quale of its own; indeed, the mediation of brightness has been suggested as its primary contribution to conscious vision.[19,20] Finally, its role could be to receive the results of extrastriate cortical visual processing via its extensive recurrent fibers, this feedback providing the crucial information necessary to generate qualia.[4,21] The first of these hypotheses affords V1 only a comparatively trivial role, but, like the third, is consistent with the loss of phenomenal vision produced by destruction of V1. The second is based largely upon a body of data suggesting the gradual development of some forms of conscious vision in a hemianopic patient, GY, who suffered unilateral damage to his occipital lobe at age 8. This patient, now in his forties, has participated in a large number of studies of his residual visual functions, which have suggested that he is now aware of visual stimuli provided they have some salient feature, such as movement.[22-25] This visual awareness is phenomenal, or at least that is the conclusion drawn by the authors from GY's ability to find a perceptually satisfactory match in the intact field for a stimulus presented in the impaired field.[26] We have observed a similar slow change from absolute to relative blindness in another patient (FS) whose lesion occurred later in life (age 42), but who, like GY, has extensively used his hemianopic field in numerous blindsight studies.[27-30] In neither patient was any evidence for ipsilesional V1 activation found in functional imaging studies.[1,8,30-32] Within the limits of current technology, this demonstrates that some conscious vision may become possible without ipsilesional V1.

VERIDICAL VISION WITHOUT V1

What evidence suggests that it is specifically brightness that is missing in this kind of V1-less, low-level vision? Morland *et al.,*[19] using a forced-choice procedure, asked GY to try and match colors, motion velocity, and brightness between his normal and impaired hemifield. This involved his manually adjusting the visual properties of the matching stimuli so as to make a stimulus presented in one hemifield resemble another presented in the other field. [As in all forced-choice procedures, guessing was an available option]. While the patient's color and velocity matches were quite successful, his brightness matches bore little resemblance to those of a normal observer, leading the authors to suggest that brightness, rather than color and motion, depended on V1. These results, taken alone, are insufficient to support the hypothesis. Not only may a forced-choice match in a blindsight subject be based on phenomenal properties quite different from those that mediate a match in unimpaired subjects, but also it may reflect isomorphic processes underlying quite different perceptual representations such as conscious and unconscious ones. More importantly, GY strongly denies "seeing" colors, and even his extensively studied motion processing performance[1,22,23] may reflect his inferences about positional information rather than motion perception *per se.*[23,27,32] It is therefore premature to conclude, even in GY's case, that brightness is the only quale dependent upon V1's integrity.

Independently of whether V1 plays a special role in brightness perception, one wonders what the source is of residual conscious vision in the absence of ipsilesional V1? Given the observation that destruction of V1 produces cortical blindness, how can its absence be compensated? One possibility is that qualia may be mediated by extrastriate cortex alone; another that qualia require the joint activation of both extrastriate and extravisual systems. The first alternative is contradicted by the fact that stimulation of the impaired hemifield, although it activates extastriate cortical areas in patients with absolute cortical blindness, does not produce even rudimentary awareness of the stimuli.[33] Extrastriate cortical activation alone is therefore insufficient, even if it involves not just dorsal but also those ventral extrastriate cortical areas[30] that have been implicated in the mediation of conscious vision.[5] But perhaps ipsilesional extrastriate cortical activation, though initially insufficient, could with practice recover to the point of supporting low-level phenomenal vision. Increasing use of the hemianopic field might be the most likely process mediating such recovery, but there may be others.

There is the alternative possibility, that for visual awareness, extrastriate cortical activation needs to be coupled to activation in extravisual structures, that is, structures outside the classically defined visual system. This hypothesis was suggested by the results of two functional magnetic resonance imaging studies on GY. As GY's visual awareness depends on the velocity of a moving stimulus,[24] both studies used a dot stimulus moving at different speed through the patient's impaired field, and compared a condition evoking awareness (fast motion) with one that did not (slow motion). Both studies found activation in the motion complex (hMT+) *which appeared stronger in the aware condition.*[9] In addition, both found differential activation of extravisual structures, the laterodorsal frontal cortex in the first study (Sahraie *et al.*[8]; note numerous additional foci) and the brainstem reticular formation in the second study.[9] The different conclusions of the two studies illustrate some of the problems associated with imaging studies of visual awareness. First, high-resolution images of the entire brain are needed to avoid biasing the findings, and, second, very good quality images are needed to avoid false positives (if the quality is poor, many of the putative foci of activation are probably meaningless). Finally, differences in activation, although often attributed to differences in awareness, may arise from differences in properties of the stimuli themselves;for example, different velocities may themselves trigger differential activation patterns. [Note: Zeki and ffytche [9] attempted an analysis designed to control for stimulus speed].

In view of the divergent results and the problems inherent in this approach, we do not yet know how the low-level conscious vision of patient GY is mediated. It may involve extra-visual structures, as suggested by the studies cited above, or reorganization of the functional connectivity of visual structures. Either way, it appears to be independent of involvement of ipsilesional V1. However, these exceptional cases should not obscure the fact that the vast majority of patients with complete destruction of V1 are cortically blind. Indeed, it is this observation that provides the empirical foundation for the traditional neurologists' view that V1 is the substrate of conscious vision. Finding the neuronal correlate of phenomenal vision in the absence of ipsilesional V1 should tell us something interesting about long-term plasticity in the visual system. Both patients have regained their conscious vision in the course of many years of experiments that forced them to use their hemianopic field. This type of practice has resulted not only in better performance in blindsight tasks and more residual visual functions, but, at least in their case, to the return of some conscious vision. How the recovery of vision in these cases is mediated is an exciting and important question which may have therapeutic implications. However, the neuronal correlate of visual awareness in these individuals is very likely to be different from that of the normal observer, in whom phenomenal vision depends on the integrity of V1.

Early visual cortical areas that include V1, V2, V3, V4, V8, hMT+ and possibly others seem to partake in the mediation of phenomenal vision since their destruction causes a partial or complete loss of visual qualia in the affected part of the visual field. As noted earlier, V1 could function either as an indispensable provider of input to processing mechanisms in higher cortical areas, and/or as the recipient of feedback generated by processing in these areas. The latter hypothesis implicates the very extensive feedback connections among the visual cortical areas whose inactivation, via inactivation of an up-stream visual area, markedly alters the functional tuning of V1 neurons (e.g., Hupé et al.[34]). If the results of processing by higher-order areas were fed back to V1, this could explain the unambiguous positioning of objects in the visual field on the basis of the high spatial resolution of V1, which is in contrast to the much lower resolution in increasingly higher areas. This hypothesis gains support from a number of recent neurophysiological studies that used very different approaches. They have shown that the late response components (80–100 ms) of V1 neurons differ from the early ones in orientation tuning,[35] in preserving figure-ground segregation,[36] and most importantly, in the perceptual interpretation of stimuli.[37] Independent confirmation of this result comes, first, from experiments in binocular rivalry showing that a small percentage of V1 neurons respond according to the monkey's present percept and independent of its visual input,[38] and, second from a study showing that the responses of V1 neurons in cats reflected brightness rather than physical contrast.[39] Additional support for the hypothesis comes from studies of the effects of experimental interventions, such as masks and transcranial magnetic pulses, upon the conscious perception of a stimulus. These psychophysical studies have identified two different time windows for effective disruption of visual awareness. In addition to an early time window (ca. 20–30 ms), which coincides with the arrival of the retinal information in V1, a much later one (ca. 100–120 ms) was particularly effective at suppressing the conscious perception of a visual stimulus. The earlier window coincides with the initial processing of visual inputs, and will prevent those inputs from being forwarded to higher areas. But at 100–120 ms, when the information has long since reached extrastriate cortex, presentation of a masking stimulus still interferes with the after-discharges of V1 neurons,[40] and a magnetic pulse over the occipital pole still suppresses stimulus perception.[41] If visual awareness were indeed dependent upon the reception by V1 of feedback from extrastriate visual processing, V1 would play a more interesting role than that of a visual relay. The "feedback" hypothesis is certainly consistent with the observation that the late-response components of V1 neurons reflect the perceptual rather than the physical properties of a visual stimulus, since these late components are most likely to be affected by the results of feedback from extrastriate areas. Interestingly, lesions in higher visual cortical areas do not abolish or diminish the patient's repertoire of visual qualia, but cause higher-order perceptual deficits.

NONVERIDICAL PHENOMENAL VISION

The previous section dealt with veridical vision—the situation in which light falling onto the retina is transduced into nerve impulses, and eventually transformed into visual qualia. But there are other means to evoke phenomenal vision. Afterimages are seen although the stimulus that induced them has disappeared. Phosphenes are phenomenal events, caused by mechanical, electrical, or magnetic stimulation of the retina or the visual cortex. Visual dreams are phenomenal, and result from involuntary intrinsic neuronal activation, as do hallucinations, while visual imagery may also be phenomenal, and is caused by voluntary intrinsic activation. Do all these kinds of phenomenal vision share a common mechanism? Do they all depend on V1 and its extrastriate partners? Or is the neuronal correlate of phenomenal vision so varied that quite different structures may mediate it under different conditions, so that it is dependent not on a particular structure or set of structures but upon such features as the strength or the temporal patterning of nerve impulses?

Let us begin with the phenomenon of **phosphenes**. Rubbing one's eyes causes visual experiences that can be complexly patterned and colorful, while a bump on the head causes one to "see" the "stars" with which we are familiar from cartoons. Electrical stimulation of the eyes or brain also causes phosphenes, as does the much newer and painless transcranial magnetic stimulation (TMS). Both kinds, electro- and magnetophosphenes, can be evoked in people who have lost their eyesight because of damage to the eye or optic nerve: A retinal input is not needed. But what about cortical areas? In the majority of studies using TMS, the technique has been used to suppress rather than evoke vision[42] (see Walsh and Cowey[43] for recent review). These studies have found that the timing of the magnetic pulse in relation to the presentation of the visual stimulus is critical (see above). However, several studies have also described magnetophosphenes evoked from stimulation over the occipital lobe,[44–46] suggesting that phosphenes were mediated by activity in early visual cortical areas or even the optic radiation. An obvious problem with attempts to infer the site of phosphene production from the location of visual structure most directly stimulated is that the strong TMS pulse may activate a relatively wide network of structures. Nevertheless, the kind of phosphenes—simple arrangements of dots or lines or stars—provide a cue as to the involvement of early visual cortex, because it is direct electrical stimulation of these structures that evokes this type of phosphene.[47] If V1 is necessary for the seeing of phosphenes, its destruction should prevent their appearance. As yet, there is no published study, but in our own tests of three patients with homonymous visual field defects we failed to elicit phosphenes in the blind field. Because we used stimulation parameters optimized for *normal* observers, these data are preliminary; however, they do suggest a critical role for the early visual cortex in the production of magnetophosphenes.

Afterimages are another instance of exogenously induced phenomenal vision. A recent functional magnetic resonance imaging study in normal observers has revealed that both the presentation of a saturated color stimulus, and the long-lasting colored after-image induced by prolonged viewing of the stimulus are accompanied by activation in V1 and in the color complex (V4/V8). In addition to these areas, the motion complex hMT+ was activated during the afterimage phase only, which may account for the observation that the subjective dynamic component was seen only during the after-image.[48] Thus activation in the cortical motion complex area produces a phenomenal motion effect in normal observers even though the stimulus itself is not moving (see Tootell et al.[49] for MT's role in the motion aftereffect). The role of V1 in perception of the afterimage was first explored by Bender and Kahn[50] in patients with V1 lesions using colored figures that they presented entirely or partly in their patient's field defect. Their results showed that afterimages were not reported when the stimulus fell entirely into the blind field, but that it was subject to some perceptual completion upon central fixation, that is, when only part of the figure was invisible to their patient (FIG. 3, top). These findings agree with our own data (FIG. 3, bottom) as well as those of Marcel,[51] demonstrating that information from the cortically blind field may complete or otherwise influence the percept, but that, by

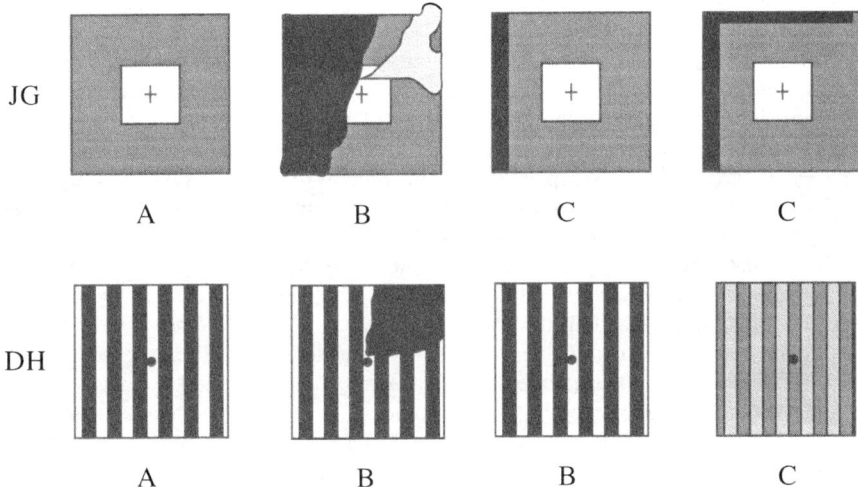

FIGURE 3. Perceptual completion and afterimages in patients with visual field defects from post-geniculate lesions. *Upper row*: Bender and Kahn's[52] patient JG; *lower row*: patient DH (own unpublished data). **A:** The stimulus was a green 5 × 5 cm square superimposed on a red 10 × 10 cm square for JG, and a high-contrast yellow-blue grating for DH. **B:** The patient's rendering of the stimulus when fixation was in the center of the figure. The black region was not seen, and the light gray one appeared blurred to JG. Note that patient DH reported perceptual completion under direct fixation on some trials. **C:** The afterimages drawn by both patients show extensive completion. The opponent colors of the negative afterimage appeared somewhat paler, as indicated by the reduced contrast (*bottom right*).

itself, it is not sufficient to produce a phenomenal image; this also agrees with other experiments on perceptual completion.[26,52,53]

Little agreement exists, however, regarding V1's role in **dreaming**. Functional imaging studies agree in reporting extrastriate cortical activation during rapid eye movement (REM) sleep, with its higher incidence of dream reports. They disagree as to whether or not primary visual cortex is also activated, some studies reporting an absence[54] and others the presence[55] of significant activation. Unfortunately, this controversy cannot be resolved by neuropsychological observations. For normal (i.e., intact) individuals, our visual awareness during dreaming is "projected" upon a perceptual area defined by the borders of the normal visual field—and those borders are not something we perceive "positively." Similarly, patients with visual field defects from V1 lesions report that their blindness is "negative" under normal viewing conditions, that is, the *missing* part of the visual field does not appear black or stand out in any way, any more than do the borders of the *intact* visual field in normal people. Because no one has developed a paradigm for testing the visual field during dreaming, it remains unclear whether patients with visual field defects from V1 lesions have a shrunken "internal screen" for dreaming. In contrast, the involvement of extrastriate cortical areas in dreaming seems clear and is further supported by reports from patients with achromatopsia or prosopaganosia associated with lesions of extrastriate visual cortex who experience an absence of color or recognizable faces not only in their waking life, but in their dreams as well.

Studies on the role of V1 in visual **imagery** are as controversial in their results as they are plentiful in number. Whether the system that mediates veridical vision also mediates visual imagery is the core question of the still unresolved "imagery debate." The available psychophysical, functional imaging, and neuropsychological data are in agreement with respect to the involvement of higher visual cortical areas. This was first shown convincingly by Roland et al.[56] in a positron emission tomography (PET) study on normal observers, and confirmed in numerous subsequent studies. What remains at issue is the involvement of early visual cortex. Several studies have demonstrated activation only in higher visual cortical areas,[56–58] while others have found it to extend all the way down to areas V1/V2[59–61] or even the lateral geniculate nucleus.[62] Kosslyn's psychological investigations of the properties of visual imagery led him to conclude that imagery must be supported by the "normal" visual system including early, topographically organized visual cortex (see Kosslyn[65] for review). He has argued that the failure to find activation in early visual cortex was caused by the lack of experimental control during the subject's "resting" condition, which serves as the control against which activation in the "imagery" condition is compared. If the subjects do not "wipe their screen clean" during the resting condition, but instead imagine something of their own accord, they will generate sufficient activation during the resting condition to minimize the contrast between the resting and imagery conditions. As a result, the study will fail to implicate V1/V2 as part of the visual network activated during visual imagery.

Another complicating factor in imagery studies is the variation in the imagining tasks used. These may range from imagining simple geometric pattern and letters to visualizing complex scenes, or even to imagining walking from home to a familiar place. It is generally accepted that simple visual patterns are processed largely in the early cortical areas, while complex spatial and object recognition tasks involve higher extrastriate cortical processing. In the complex tasks, less activation would be expected in the early cortical areas even if the results of the higher processing were to be fed back to earlier areas, because such feedback should require much less "capacity" than the processing task. Lower activation levels in the early areas would then be more likely to be missed. Finally, the task's demands on spatial resolution may influence the extent of early visual cortical involvement, with higher-resolution tasks requiring more processing by the early areas with their superior spatial maps of the visual field. This hypothesis is consistent with the report that imagining the same object in different sizes and at different positions within the visual field leads to early visual cortical activation.[60–62]

If the extent of top-down activation of the visual cortical areas is task-dependent then the deficits of patients with lesions in different visual cortical areas should reflect the presumed processing capacities of the specific areas. The results of several studies of patients with early visual cortical damage are consistent with this assumption. These patients did not show a deficit in tasks requiring answers to "high imagery content" questions such as "Does a bear have round or pointed ears?" or "Is a grapefruit larger or smaller than an orange?," which despite their referring to concrete objects can be answered on the basis of stored visual information.[64,65] Failure to correctly respond to such questions is more common in patients with visual agno-

FIGURE 4. Farah et al. [68] reported that their patient required approximately twice the distance to imagine an object of a definite size after unilateral occipital lobectomy, indicating a shrinkage of the "field of visual imagery" that reflects the hemianopia induced by the surgery.

sia, suggesting that interference with this type of visual information retrieval reflects a disturbance of higher visual function rather than of cortical blindness. In contrast, in a patient available for testing both pre-and postoperatively, unilateral removal of the occipital lobe did reveal a striking change associated with the lesion and the subsequent hemianopia.[66] The patient was asked to imagine herself walking towards various objects of well-defined size, to stop when the object filled her internal screen to the point of overflow, and then to estimate the imagined distance between herself and the object. On the preoperative test, the patient said, for example, 33 cm for a kitten, and 188 cm for a car. During the postoperative test she more than doubled the distance, as if her internal screen had shrunk to the same extent as the visual field (FIG. 4). Furthermore, by repeating the tests with a ruler that had to be imagined in a horizontal or vertical orientation, this shrinkage was found to affect only the horizontal, but not the vertical extent of the image, as it should if the cortical blindness was responsible. Possibly, this task is more visuo-perceptual in nature, although it too draws on visual memory and could theoretically be solved without phenomenal imagery. An impairment of imagery requiring relatively high spatial resolution was also found in Butter et al.'s[67] study of hemianopic patients. When patients were asked to indicate whether an arrow was pointing at one of the dots in a pattern they had been shown in free vision but that was no longer visible, they were found to make more errors with arrows on the side of their hemianopia. Taken together, studies of imagery have usually reported involvement of higher extrastriate visual cortical areas, while the evidence for participation of early visual areas is much less consistent. The outcomes of these studies will be influenced both by task demands and individual problem-solving strategies, and, in the case of functional imaging studies, the design of the protocol and the analysis will be critical.

The last form of nonveridical vision to be addressed here are **hallucinations.** They may appear to patients with blindness due to (post-) retinal pathology—Charles-Bonnet syndrome[68]—in whom the visual cortex remains excitable, as well as to patients with cortically blind visual fields caused by post-geniculate lesions.[69–72] They can be simple or highly complex, ranging from phosphenes to complex geometric patterns to objects and people that move about. The comparatively simple forms—lines, dots, clouds, stars, triangles—are attributed to irritation within the primary visual pathway up to V1[69]; they closely resemble the magnetophosphenes elicited by TMS over the occipital pole. The complex ones, in contrast, are more likely to originate in temporal cortices, where images of scenes and people can also be evoked by electrical stimulation applied during neurosurgery.[73] Whether the precise content of the hallucinated images reflects the major focus of hyperexcitation, as argued by ffytche et al.[2] for patients with Charles-Bonnet syndrome who underwent fMRI during hallucination, is still uncertain.

The simpler hallucinations that are attributed to the early visual structures are regarded as indicative of some visual recovery,[68,74] while the complex ones may reflect a hyperexcitatory response to the lesion that caused the field defect, and usually disappear within a relatively short time.[71] That they are perceived in the cortically blind field demonstrates that strong endogenously generated activity may produce phenomenal images even in the absence of V1/V2. How this pathological activation differs from that caused by TMS is presently unclear. That it at least temporarily causes phenomenal visual images is uncontroversial (or almost so; see Pollen[20]) so that hallucinations are the only instance of fully conscious phenomenal vision without early visual cortex that is present immediately after the blindness-producing incident. The type of veridical phenomenal vision that may develop over long periods of training in blindsight subjects like GY is very crude and low-level when compared to such complex hallucinations as a series of identical gray–green men strolling through the cortically blind hemifield.[69]

SUMMARY AND OUTLOOK: COMPLEXITY AND UNITY

Phenomenal visual images can be caused by a variety of processes, ranging from exogenous (optical, mechanical, electrical, and magnetic events in the eyes or the visual cortex) to endogenous processes (which may be involuntary, as in visual dreams and hallucinations, or voluntary as in visual imagery). Studies using functional imaging techniques have consistently found that visual images, whether veridical or nonveridical, are associated with activation of extrastriate visual cortical areas. In contrast, activation of early visual cortical areas V1/V2 was reported in some, but not all such studies (see TABLE 1).

Despite their remarkable contribution to the study of functional neuroanatomy, imaging techniques are of limited use in demonstrating causation (that is, in establishing whether or not a particular structure is necessary for a particular function). While imaging studies can identify brain regions activated during performance of a particular task, they do not differentiate between activation necessary for the task and that merely associated with its performance. Moreover, interpretation of the results of imaging studies is always linked to the design of the experimental protocol, which may not always do justice to the physiological reality, as well as to the nature of the data analysis. Methodological problems associated with the former include the definition of the resting state in protocols used in studies of visual imagery, the selection of the specific temporal offset used between stimulus and response, or the control of the subject's psychophysiological state during the measurement. Exam-

TABLE 1. Summary of evidence from functional imaging and neuropsychology regarding the participation of primary and higher visual cortical areas in the mediation of veridical and nonveridical forms of vision

Structures	Extrastriate Areas		Primary Area	
Evidence from	Imaging	Neuropsychology	Imaging	Neuropsychology
Function				
Veridical				
Normal vision	yes	yes	yes	yes
Residual vision	yes	yes	no	no
Blindsight	yes	yes	no	no
Nonveridical				
Phosphenes	?	?	?/yes	yes
Afterimages	yes	?	yes	yes
Dreams	yes	yes	yes/no	?
Imagery	yes	yes	yes/no	yes/no
Hallucinations	yes	?	no	no

NOTE: All results, including those from studies on Blindsight where conscious vision is absent, agree on extrastriate visual cortical activation.
Yes/no reflects controversial results; ? indicates the answer is unknown.

ples of the latter type include the use of data smoothing vs. averaging, or the choice of statistical criteria. Such factors may yield contradictory results from comparable data sets (see Sibersweig et al.[75] and Dierks et al.[76] for an example). While functional imaging studies are undoubtedly exciting, such interpretive considerations make them less than conclusive when considered in isolation. Their results need to be complemented by neuropsychological studies of patients with lesions of circumscribed brain regions, which can provide evidence of the functional significance of the damaged regions.

VISUAL CONSCIOUSNESS AND THE ROLE OF V1/V2

The available data (summarized in TABLE 1) show that striate and extrastriate visual cortical areas need to be activated in all normal, nonpathological forms of veridical or nonveridical phenomenal vision. Patients who have suffered destruction of primary visual cortex are blind. They do not see stimuli presented in the blind field, they do not see afterimages of stimuli that were presented to the blind field, they have not been reported to see phosphenes from magnetic stimulation of the lesioned hemisphere, their imagery appears unaffected when their visual memory is tapped but not when a visuo-perceptual task requiring good spatial resolution is given. Whether these patients have visual dreams involving the cortically blind field is unknown. Only in hallucinations and in the rare cases of low-level vision re-established in former blindsight subjects such as GY and FS is phenomenal vision without ipsilesional V1 known to occur.

Neuropsychology thus strengthens the case for V1, but does not prove its necessity without exception—the hallmark of a good rule. The exceptions, both pathological, may indicate that V1's absence can be compensated for under certain conditions. In the case of hallucinations, the spontaneous extrastriate cortical activation is quite strong, and may therefore spread to other structures, subcortical and cortical, in the ipsi- and contralesional hemisphere. The complexity of this activation pattern is in contrast to the very focal activation observed from visual stimulation of fields of absolute and relative cortical blindness. Stimulation of the normal hemifield results in activation of the normal primary and extrastriate visual cortex, and in ipsilesional extrastriate activation as well, just as in normal observers. Stimulation of the blind field activates ipsilesional extrastriate cortex, but the activation appears quite isolated and focal, involving little if any activation of surrounding ipsilesional or contralesional cortex.[30] These findings make it tempting to speculate that the blind field is blind because the neuronal activation it elicits lacks the capacity to initiate a sufficiently complex pattern of visual cortical activation.[77] Destruction of V1 may prevent the development of such complex patterns, not only by destroying a large part of the input to the extrastriate cortex, but also by interfering with the extrastriate feedback to V1.[78] Unusually strong extrastriate activation, such as present in hallucinations, may allow a phenomenal representation by causing a complex widespread pattern of activation not normally evoked without V1, and extensive training of blindsight may induce processes that to some extent can compensate for the loss of this structure.

If conscious vision is always mediated by widespread striate–extrastriate cortical activation, could the presence of such activation in an organism's brain prove that it is consciously seeing something? Although this is likely to be the case in organisms who are in a conscious state, and not comatose or anesthetized, it is not true in unconscious organisms. Provided the animals were effectively anesthetized, the fact is clearly demonstrated by recent fMRI experiments in monkeys who showed ample cortical activation in response to visual stimulation despite being under general anesthesia.[79] As only conscious organisms can have conscious perception, evidence for strong activation of striate and extrastriate visual cortical areas cannot prove conscious vision and thus cannot prove consciousness in animals whose possible consciousness we cannot yet assess unequivocally. This *caveat* demonstrates the need to eventually account for the substrate of conscious vision, isolated here for simplicity's sake, within the larger context of the neural substrates of conscious (as opposed to unconscious) states in general. Such an account would attempt to explain how the presence of a general state of consciousness—presumably mediated by unspecific systems and temporarily abolished by anesthesia (see Lamme *et al.*[80] for effects of anesthesia on neuronal activity in V1)—transforms the visuo-cortical activation into phenomenal awareness.

Finally, let us consider that while visual processing is modular, its result is a unified percept. Whether the primary visual cortex provides a neural substrate for that perceptual unity remains an open question. The fact that it receives perceptually relevant cortico-cortical feedback, and that its destruction causes blindness despite the availability of extrageniculo-striate input, makes V1 a prime contender for that role. Having a structure at the bottom end of a presumed cortical processing hierarchy turns out to be responsible for the visuo-perceptual unity produced by that processing would add a nice twist, which the great Cajal, who cherished whodunits and who wrote one himself ("A secreto agravio, secreta venganza"), would have appreciated.

REFERENCES

1. BARBUR, J.L., J.D.G. WATSON, R.S.J. FRACKOWIAK & S. ZEKI. 1993. Conscious visual perception without V1. Brain **116:** 1293–1302.
2. FFYTCHE, D.H., R.J. HOWARD, M.J. BRAMMER, A. DAVID, P. WOODRUFF & S. WILLIAMS. 1998. The anatomy of conscious vision: an fMRI study of visual hallucinations. Nature Neurosci. **1:** 738–742.
3. STOERIG, P. 1996. Varieties of vision: from blind processing to conscious recognition. Trends Neurosci. **19:** 401–406.
4. LAMME, V. 2000. Blindsight: the role of feedforward and feedback corticocortical connections. Acta Psych. In press.
5. MILNER, A.D. & M. GOODALE. 1995. The Visual Brain in Action. Oxford University Press. New York.
6. CRICK, F. & C. KOCH. 1995. Are we aware of neural activity in primary visual cortex? Nature **375:** 121–123
7. CRICK, F. & C. KOCH. 1998. Consciousness and neuroscience. Cerebral Cortex **8:** 97–107.
8. SAHRAIE, A., L. WEISKRANTZ, J.L. BARBUR, A. SIMMONS, S.C. WILLIAMS & M.J. BRAMMER. 1997. Pattern of neuronal activity associated with conscious and unconscious processing of visual signals. Proc. Natl. Acad. Sci. USA **94:** 9406–9411.
9. ZEKI, S. & D.H. FFYTCHE. 1998. The Riddoch syndrome: insights into the neurobiology of conscious vision. Brain **121:** 25–45.
10. LLÍNAS, R.R. & D. PARÉ. 1991. Of dreaming and wakefulness. Neuroscience **44:** 521–535.
11. JONES, E.G. 1998. A new view of specific and nonspecific thalamocortical connections. In Consciousness. at the Frontiers of Neuroscience. H.H. Jasper et al., Eds. Advan. Neurol. **77:** 49–71.
12. LLÍNAS, R.R. & U. RIBARY. 1998. Temporal conjunction in thalamocortical transactions. In Consciousness. at the Frontiers of Neuroscience. H.H. Jasper et al., Eds. Advan. Neurol. **77:** 95–102.
13. FELLEMANN, D..J. & D.C. VAN ESSEN. 1991. Distributed hierarchical processing in the primate cerebral cortex. Cerebral Cortex **1:** 1–47.
14. WEISKRANTZ, L., E.K. WARRINGTON, M.D. SANDERS & J. MARSHALL. 1974. Visual capacity in the hemianopic field following a restricted cortical ablation. Brain **97:** 709–728.
15. WEISKRANTZ, L. 1986. Blindsight: A Case Study and Implications. Oxford University Press. New York.
16. STOERIG, P. & A. COWEY. 1997. Blindsight in man and monkey. Brain **120:** 535–559.
17. HORTON, J.C.& W.F. HOYT. 1991. Quadrantic visual field defects: a hallmark of lesions in extrastriate (V2/V3) cortex. Brain **114:** 1703–1718.
18. HENSCHEN, S.E. 1910. Zentrale Sehstörungen. In Handbuch der Neurologie 2. M. Lewandowski, Ed. : 89–98. Springer. Berlin.
19. MORLAND, A.B., S.R. JONES, A.L. FINLAY, D. DEYZAC, S. LE & S. KEMP. 1999. Visual perception of motion, luminance and colour in a human hemianope. Brain **122:** 1183–1198.
20. POLLEN, D.A. 1999. On the neural correlates of visual perception. Cerebral Cortex **9:** 4–19.
21. STOERIG, P. & A. COWEY. 1995. Visual perception and phenomenal consciousness. Behav. Brain Res. **71:** 147–156.
22. BARBUR, J.L., K.H. RUDDOCK & V.A. WATERFIELD. 1980. Human visual responses in the absence of the geniculo-striate projection. Brain **102:** 905–928.
23. BLYTHE, I.M., J.M. BROMLEY, C. KENNARD & K.H. RUDDOCK. 1986. Visual discrimination of target displacement remains after damage to the striate cortex in humans. Nature **320:** 619–621.
24. WEISKRANTZ, L., J.L. BARBUR & A. SAHRAIE. 1995. Parameters affecting conscious versus unconscious visual discrimination in a patient with damage to the visual cortex (V1). Proc. Natl. Acad. Sci. USA **92:** 6122–6126.
25. STOERIG, P. & E. BARTH. Phenomenal vision in the absence of V1. Submitted for publication.

26. PÖPPEL, E. 1986. Long-range colour-generating interactions across the retina. Nature **320:** 523–525
27. PÖPPEL, E. 1985. Bridging a neuronal gap. Naturwissenschaften **72:** 599.
28. STOERIG, P. 1987. Chromaticity and achromaticity: evidence for a functional differentiation in visual field defects. Brain **110:** 869–886.
29. STOERIG, P., A. KLEINSCHMIDT& J. FRAHM. 1998. No visual responses in denervated V1: high-resolution functional magnetic resonance imaging of a blindsight patient. NeuroRep. **9:** 21–25.
30. GOEBEL, R., L. MUCKLI, F.E. ZANELLA, W. SINGER & P. STOERIG. Sustained extrastriate cortical activation without visual awareness revealed by fMRI studies of hemianopic patients. Submitted for publication.
31. KLEISER, R., M. NIEDEGGEN, J. WITTSACK, R. GOEBEL & P. STOERIG. Is V1 necessary for conscious vision in areas of relative cortical blindness? NeuroImage. In press.
32. AZZOPARDI, P. & A. COWEY. 2001. Motion discrimination in cortically blind patients. Brain **124:** 30–46.
33. STOERIG, P., R. GOEBEL, L. MUCKLI, H. HACKER & W. SINGER. 1997. The functional neuroanatomy of blindsight. Soc. Neurosci. Abs. **23:** 845.
34. HUPÉ, J.M., A.C. JAMES, B.R. PAYNE, S.G. LOMBER, P. GIRARD& J. BULLIER. 1998. Cortical feedback improves discrimination between figure and background by V1, V2 and V3 neurons. Nature **394:** 784–787.
35. RINGACH, D.L., M.J. HAWKEN & R. SHAPLEY. 1997. Dynamics of orientation tuning in macaque primary visual cortex. Nature **387:** 281–284.
36. LAMME, V.A.F., V. RODRIGUEZ-RODRIGUEZ & H. SPEKREIJSE. 1999. Separate processing dynamics for texture elements, boundaries and surfaces in primary visual cortex of the macaque monkey. Cerebral Cortex **9:** 406–413.
37. ZIPSER, K., V.A.F. LAMME & P.H. SCHILLER. 1996. Contextual modulation in primary visual cortex. J.Neurosci. **16:** 7376–7389.
38. LOGOTHETIS, N.K. 1998. Single units and conscious vision. Phil. Trans. R. Soc. London B **353:** 1801–1818.
39. ROSSI, A.F., C.D. RITTENHOUSE & M.A. PARADISO. 1996. The representation of brightness in the primary visual cortex. Science **273:** 1104–1107.
40. MACKNICK, S.L. & M.S. LIVINGSTONE. 1998. Neuronal correlates of visibility and invisiblity in the primate visual system. Nature Neurosci. **1:** 144–149.
41. CORTHOUT, E., B. UTTL, V. WALSH, M. HALLETT & A. COWEY. 1999. Timing of activity in early visual cortex as revealed by transcranial magnetic stimulation. NeuroRep. **10:** 2631–2534.
42. AMASSIAN, V.E., R.Q. CRACCO, P.J. MACCABE, J.B. CRACCO, A. RUDELL & L. EBERLE. 1989. Suppression of visual perception by magnetic coil stimulation of human occipital cortex. Electroenceph. Clin. Neurophysiol. **74:** 458–462.
43. WALSH, V. & A. COWEY. 1998. Magnetic stimulation studies of visual cognition. Trends Cogn. Sci. **2:** 103–10.
44. MARG, E. & D. RUDIAK. 1994. Phosphenes induced by magnetic stimulation over the occipital brain: description and probable sites of stimulation. Optom. Vis. Sci. **71:** 301–311.
45. KAMMER, T. 1998. Phosphenes and transient scotomas induced by magnetic stimulation of the occipital lobe: their topographical relationship. Neuropsychologia **37:** 191–198.
46. KASTNER, S., I. DEMMER & U. ZIEMANN. 1998. Transient visual field defects induced by transcranial magnetic stimulation over the occipital pole. Exp. Brain Res. **118:** 199–226.
47. FOERSTER, O. 1937. Motorische Felder und Bahnen. *In* Handbuch der Neurologie 6. O. Bumke & O.Foerster, Eds. Springer. Berlin.
48. KONEN, C., R. KLEISER & P. STOERIG. 2000. Afterimages: an fMRI-study of subjective experience. Soc.. Neurosci. Abs. In press.
49. TOOTELL, R.B.H., J.B. REPPAS, A.M. DALE, R.B. LOOK, T.J. BRADY & B.R. ROSEN. 1995. Visual motion aftereffect in human cortical area MT revealed by functional magnetic resonance imaging. Nature **375:** 139–141.

50. BENDER, M.B. & R.L. KAHN. 1949. After-imagery in defective fields of vision. J. Neurol. Neurosurg. Psychiat. **12**: 196–204.
51. MARCEL, A.J. 1998 Blindsight and shape perception: deficit of visual consciousness or of visual function? Brain **121**: 1565–1588.
52. WARRINGTON, E.K. 1962. The completion of visual forms across hemianopic field defects. J. Neurol. Neurosurg. Psychiatry **25**: 208–217.
53. TORJUSSEN, T. 1976. Residual function in cortically blind hemifields. Scand. J. Psychol. **17**: 320–322.
54. BRAUN, A.R., T.J. BALKI N, N.J. WESENSTEN, F. GWADRY, R.E. CARSON, M. VARGA P. BALDWIN, G. BELENKY & P. HERSCOVITCH. 1998. Dissociated pattern of activity in visual cortices and their projections during human rapid eye movement sleep. Science **279**: 91–95.
55. LÖVBLAD, K.-O., R. THOMAS, P.M. JAKONB, T. SCAMMELL, C. BASSETTI, M. GRISWOLD, J. IVES, J. MATHESON, R.R. EDELMAN & S. WARACH. 1999. Silent functional magnetic resonance imaging demonstrates focal activation in rapid eye movement sleep. Neurology **53**: 2193–2195.
56. ROLAND, P.E., L ERIKSSON, S. STONE-ELANDER & L. WILDEN. 1987. Does mental activity change the oxidative metabolism of the brain? J. Neurosci. **7**: 2373–2389.
57. ROLAND, P.E. & B. GULYAS. 1994. Visual imagery and visual representation. Trends Neurosci. **17**: 291–287.
58. D'ESPOSITO, M., J.A. DETRE, G.K. AGUIRRE, M. STALLCUP, D.C. ALSOP, L.J. TIPPET & M.J. FARAH. 1997. A functional MRI study of mental image generation. Neuropsychologia **35**: 725–730.
59. LEBIHAN, D., R. RURNER, T.A. ZEFFIRO, C.A. CUENOD, P. JEZZARD & V. BONNEROT. 1993. Activation of human primary visual cortex during visual recall: a magnetic resonance imaging study. Proc. Natl. Acad. Sci. USA **90**: 11802–11805.
60. KOSSLYN, S.M., A.M. ALPERT, W.L. THOMPSON, V. MALJKOVIC, S.B. WEISE, C.F. CHABRIS, S.E. HAMILTON, S.L. RAUCH & F.S. BUONANNO. 1993. Visual mental imagery activates topographically organized visual cortex: PET investigations. J. Cogn. Neurosci. **5**:263–287.
61. KOSSLYN, S.M,. W.L. THOMPSON, I.J. KIM & N.M. ALPERT. 1995. Topographical representations of mental images in primary visual cortex. Nature **378**: 496–498.
62. CHEN, W., T. KATO, X.-H. ZHU, S. OGAWA, D.W. TANK & K. UGURBIL. 1998. Human primary visual cortex and lateral geniculate nucleus activation during visual imagery. NeuroRep. **9**: 3669–3674.
63. KOSSLYN, S.M. 1994. Image and Brain. MIT Press. Cambridge, MA.
64. GOLDENBERG, G. & C. ARTNER. 1991. Visual imagery and knowledge about the visual appearance of objects in patients with posterior cerebral artery lesions. Brain Cogn. **15**: 160–186.
65. CHATTERJEE, A. & M.H. SOUTHWOOD. 1995. Cortical blindness and visual imagery. Neurology **45**: 2189–2195.
66. FARAH, M., M.J. SOSO & R.M. DASHEIFF. 1992. Visual angle of the mind's eye before and after unilateral occipital lobectomy. J. Exp. Psychol. Hum. Percept. Perform. **18**: 241–246.
67. BUTTER, C.M., S. KOSSLYN, D. MIJOVIC-PRELEC & A. RIFFLE. 1997. Field-specific deficits in visual imagery following hemianopia due to unilateral occipital infarcts. Brain **120**: 217–228.
68. BONNET, C. 1769. Essai analytique sur les facultes de l'ame. 2. Aufl, Bd.2, Kopenhagen, Genf: Philibert.
69. GLONING, I., K. GLONING & H. HOFF. 1967. Über optische Halluzinationen. Wien. Z. Nervenheil. **25**: 1–19.
70. KÖLMEL, H.W. 1985. Complex visual hallucinations in the hemianopic field. J. Neurol. Neurosurg. Psychiat. **48**: 29–38
71. KÖLMEL, H.W. 1988. The Homonymen Hemianopsien. Springer. Berlin
72. LEPORE, F.E. 1990. Spontaneous visual phenomena with visual loss: 104 patients with lesions of retinal and neural afferent pathways. Neurology **40**: 444–447.
73. PENFIELD, W. & P. PEROT. 1963) The brains's record of auditory and visual experience. Brain **86**: 595–696.

74. WUNDERLICH, G., B. SUCHAN, J. VOLKMANN, H. HERZOG, V. HŠMBERG & R.J. SEITZ. 2000. Visual hallucinations in recovery from cortical blindness. Arch. Neurol. **57:** 561–565.
75. SILBERSWEIG, D.A., E. STERN, C. FRITH, C. CAHILL, A. HOLMES, S. GROOTOONK, J. SEAWARD. P. MCKENNA, S.E. CHUA & L. SCHNORR. 1995. A functional neuroanatomy of hallucinations in schizophrenia. Nature **378:** 176–179.
76. DIERKS, T., D.E.J. LINDEN, M. JANDL, E. FORMISANO, R. GOEBEL, H. LANFERMANN & W. SINGER. 1999. Activation of Heschl's gyrus during auditory hallucinations. Neuron **22:** 615–621.
77. TONONI, G. & G.M. EDELMAN. 1998. Consciousness and complexity. Science **282:** 1846–1851.
78. BULLIER, J., P. GIRARD & P.-A. SALIN. 1994. The role of area 17 in the transfer of information to extrastriate visual cortex. *In* Primary Visual Cortex in Primates. A. Peters & K.S. Rockland, Eds. :301–330. Plenum. New York.
79. LOGOTHETIS, N.K., H. GUGGENBERGER, S. PELED & J. PAULS. 1999. Functional imaging of the monkey brain. Nature Neurosci. **2:** 555–562.
80. LAMME, V.A.F., K. ZIPSER & H. SPEKREIJSE. 1998. Figure-ground activity in primary visual cortex is suppressed by anesthesia. Proc. Natl. Acad. Sci. USA **95:** 3263–3268.

Co-Evolution of Human Consciousness and Language

MICHAEL A. ARBIB

Computer Science Department and USC Brain Project, University of Southern California at Los Angeles, Los Angeles California 90089-2520, USA

> ABSTRACT: This article recalls Cajal's brief mention of consciousness in the *Textura* as a function of the human brain quite distinct from reflex action, and discusses the view that human consciousness may share aspects of "animal awareness" with other species, but has its unique form because humans possess language. Three ingredients of a theory of the evolution of human consciousness are offered: the view that a précis of intended activity is necessarily formed in the brain of a human that communicates in a human way; the notion that such a précis constitutes consciousness; and a new theory of the evolution of human language based on the mirror system of monkeys and the role of communication by means of hand gestures as a stepping-stone to speech.
>
> KEYWORDS: Brain; Cajal; Consciousness; Evolution; Language; Mirror neurons

SANTIAGO RAMÓN Y CAJAL AND THE NATURE OF CONSCIOUSNESS

We remember Santiago Ramón y Cajal for his wonderful ability to observe the minute peculiarities of neurons, to draw them in a scientifically accurate yet aesthetically pleasing way, and to combine his neuroanatomy with the insightful speculation on neural function, all of which continue to inspire us today. Ramón y Cajal was, and is, Spain's greatest scientist and we assembled in Zaragoza, site of his early achievements, to celebrate his greatness. Yet this conference was in English instead of Spanish! How could that be? I was comforted to find the following quote from Cajal's *Recuerdos de Mi Vida* which justifies our behavior:

> There are only three peoples who enjoy the enviable privilege of using their native tongues in their scientific communications: the English, the French, and the Germans. Educated people of other countries have no choice, if they wish to make public their ideas, than to understand these three languages and to write in one of them. What right has Spain, a country of slender intellectual production, to try to impose the study of Spanish upon the Japanese, the Swedish, the Polish, the Russian, the Slovak, the Hungarian, the Dutch, the Rumanian, and the others who already spend most of their youth in mastering the three or four learned languages and write in them? [1]

Indeed, Cajal chose French as his medium of international communication. Today, however, those three language choices have shrunk to just one, English, and so Cajal would indeed approve of its use at the symposium.

Address for correspondence: USC Brain Project, University of Southern California, Hedco Neuroscience Building, Room 5, 3614 Watt Way, Los Angeles, California 90089-2520. Voice: 213-740-1176.
arbib@pollux.usc.edu; http://www-hbp.usc.edu/

Elsewhere in the same autobiography, I find Cajal talking in a way that may seem inconsistent with the theme of evolution by natural selection that runs through many of the talks at this symposium:

> The subject [of the retina] always fascinated me because, to my idea, life never succeeded in constructing a machine so subtilely [sic] devised and so perfectly adapted to an end as the visual apparatus. It is one of the rare cases, nevertheless, in which nature has deigned to employ physical means which are accessible to our present knowledge. I must not conceal the fact that in the study of this membrane I for the first time felt my faith in Darwinism (hypothesis of natural selection) weakened, being amazed and confounded by the supreme constructive ingenuity revealed not only in the retina and in the dioptric apparatus of the vertebrates but even in the meanest insect eye. There, in fine, I felt more profoundly than in any other subject of study the shuddering sensation of the unfathomable mystery of life.[1]

Cajal reminds us that evolution can operate at many levels, and that when we see the incredible variety of neural forms and connections in even so *a priori* (but not *a posteriori*) restricted a system as the insect retina, we can no longer view natural selection as a straightforward "magic key" to form and function. Natural selection can operate on the macromolecular building blocks of cells, on crucial cellular subsystems, and on the morphology of cells themselves, as well as the connectivity of these cells and their formation into diverse nuclei. What is selected about a subsystem, then, may be the impact of some change on a larger system or on a smaller detail, rather than the immediate change in the subsystem itself. Moreover, we understand that the genetic code may not specify adult forms so much as the processes of self-organization in cell-assemblies which can yield "normal" connectivity in the adult raised in a normal environment. Further, the environment which fosters adaptive self-organization may be as much social as physical in nature.

Nicholas Strausfeld is one modern investigator who has taken up Cajal's challenge by confronting the anatomy of the invertebrate nervous system and the results of a multitude of observations of insects in their natural environment with the cladistic analysis that yields a relatively fine-grained evolutionary tree as the basis for more informed hypotheses about visual system evolution.

My favorite neuron is the Purkinje cell of the cerebellum as portrayed by Ramón y Cajal, and one might expect a conference in honor of the 100th anniversary of the publication of *Textura del sistema nervioso del hombre y los vertebrados* to concentrate, indeed, on intimate details of Cajal's portrayal of the texture of nervous systems in the light of 100 years of research in functional neuroanatomy. However, the chosen theme for this conference is entitled *Cajal and Consciousness*. Alas, the word "consciousness" seems to appear very rarely in Cajal's writings. In preparation for this symposium, I searched the few volumes of Cajal on my bookshelf for the word "consciousness" and found only one place there where consciousness is discussed, namely in Chapter 36, "Structure-Function Relationships in the Cortex" of the English translation of Cajal's *Histologie du systeme nerveux*[2]—itself the (expanded) French translation of the *Textura* whose centenary we are celebrating. The following brief extracts will "set the level" for our discussion of consciousness, showing that Cajal distinguished conscious activity from reflexes, but not from other mental processes:

> [I hypothesize] that the entire cerebral cortex is formed by various types of perception and memory areas. [Strangely, he did not mention motor areas here. MA].... [I] suggest that attempts to localize intellectual activity, volition, and self-consciousness amount to pursuing a chimera. In our view, cognitive or intellectual operations are not

elaborated by a privileged area, but result from the combined activity in a great many first and second-order mnemonic areas.... [I]n humans and other animals many reflex actions take place that are appropriate for a given situation, and yet are not accompanied by...conscious epiphenomena....Thus, we do not propose to equate reflex activity and instinct with intellectual activity.... Some have suggested that cortical activity may be conscious or unconscious depending on the extent to which vital force is depleted or not depleted as neural impulses traverse a series of neurons; such depletion may be greater in shorter, less active pathways.

In the last sentence, Cajal is reacting to the vitalism which was rampant at that time, particularly in Europe. Cajal himself was a staunch "mechanistic" as can be seen from the preamble to the *Textura*. However, it is not clear to me why vitalists should think that the depletion of "vital force" would be greater in shorter pathways, or that shorter pathways would be less active?

...Functional theories based on the localization of different cortical areas, no matter how good, fail completely to explain mechanisms underlying cognitive activity, which is almost certainly accompanied by molecular changes in neurons, as well as by very complex changes in relationships between neurons. Therefore, to understand cognitive activity, it will be necessary to understand these molecular and connectional changes, not to mention the exact histology of each cortical area and all of their pathways. However, this is still not enough; we also will need to understand the properties of neural impulses: What energy transformations are required for their initiation, spread, and involvement in the phenomena accompanying perception and thought, namely, consciousness, volition, and emotion?

...Lugaro believed that neuronal impulses invariably are transmitted by way of chemical phenomena. For example, the environmental stimulus first produces a chemical modification in a nerve ending, and this modification in turn acts as a physicochemical stimulus on the cytoplasm of other neurons, thus leading to the generation of additional neuronal currents.... We find it difficult to discuss a theory that is not based on any physiological evidence, and thus does not fall within the realm of straightforward possibilities.

It appears that in this case Lugaro was ahead of his time. Cajal seemed to accept the idea that exercise could narrow the gap between presynaptic and postsynaptic elements, and that this decreased synaptic width increased the functional strength of neurons:

...Tanzi's Hypothesis about the Hypertrophy of Neuronal Pathways with Use. "An increased frequency of neuronal currents passing across a synapse will lead to increased metabolism in the affected pathway, and this in turn will lead to hypertrophy, as in well-exercised muscle....As a result, exercise, which in essence decreases synaptic width, is able to increase the functional strength of neurons."...This hypothesis is based on established observations [and] has the added advantage of showing how habitual actions become easier and more automatic, as well as how actions that we refer to as conscious and voluntary (as opposed to reflex) may depend on the amount of resistance encountered by neuronal impulses in their physicochemical stage.

Cajal offers his own theory on the rapid growth of interneuronal connections as a mechanism for refining neural processes and psychological aptitudes.

Is it not true that, in addition to favorable biological conditions, many years of physical and mental gymnastics are required to become a pianist, orator, mathematician, or intellectual? How can this slow transformation be explained? First by acknowledging that preexisting biological pathways are reinforced by use, and then by assuming that new pathways are established through continued branching and growth of dendritic and axonal arborizations. If this is indeed the case, then talents can be acquired only on the underlying condition that abundant, complex relationships are established by continued use between cell groups in primary and secondary mnemonic or association areas that are poorly if at all interconnected in the uncultivated individual.

In short, Cajal offers no particular guidance as to the nature of consciousness. Rather, he seems to advance an associations theory (one might almost say a "Pre-

Hebbian" theory) in which ideas are encoded by groups of neurons, and thought is based on association of ideas as encoded in the brain by strengthened synapses between corresponding groups of neurons. We can agree with Cajal that many functions of the organism involve no single circuit but the "cooperative computation" of many regions of the brain, with these depending on the body in which the brain is located, and the environment in which the organism is situated. However, Cajal lacked our modern database of neurophysiology, either to characterize the contribution of cells to ongoing patterns of perception, memory, or action, or to offer a modern theory of neural computation in which inhibition plays as crucial a role as excitation, and in which many other more subtle processes are brought into play. Thanks to Wilfrid Rall,[4] neuroscientists have begun to build models of neural networks that link the physiology to some of the beautiful details of neuron morphology delineated by Cajal. However, in what follows I shall focus on data and models which treat neurons as single compartments rather than subtle structures, and show that even at this level and above, we can do much to illuminate the search for neural correlates of consciousness. Indeed, I shall argue that it is not the details of morphology or neurochemistry that distinguish the neurons of a "conscious" from an "unconscious" mode of operation so much as the larger circuits and systems of which they are part."'

"BRAIN STATE" VERSUS "MENTAL STATE"

A human brain may be characterized in terms of hundreds of regions which may be distinguished, for example, by the types of neurons they contain, the chemical properties of those neurons, the arrangement of the neurons into layers or other structures, as well as by the patterns of connections they may have with receptors, effectors, and other regions of the brain. Each region in turn may contain millions, or even hundreds of millions of neurons. Current models of the brain focus, in particular, on two properties of neurons in a network:

(i) the current "output" of each neuron (the pattern of electric signaling on its *axon*, the output fiber that may branch again and again to connect it to hundreds or thousands of other neurons); and

(ii) the "strength" or "weight" (plus or minus, excitatory or inhibitory) of each *synapse*, i.e., each point where the axon of one neuron impinges upon another neuron. This *synaptic weight* measures the extent to which the signal in the first neuron's axon will affect the activity of the second neuron.

A great deal of work on learning and memory holds that the learning process changes the synaptic weights of the brain in such a way that on a later occasion the activity of the network will be changed to allow recall of a specific memory or exhibition of an acquired skill. The upshot of all this it that we can describe the state of the brain at two levels (and this is still only a partial approximation—for example, some synapses may play a neuromodulatory role, rather than being excitatory or inhibitory):

(1) *The activity state:* the current output of each individual neuron. The dynamic interaction of these "firing patterns" determine the brain's "computations"

that underlie perception, thought and action, including those processes that in humans involve language.

(2) *The synaptic state:* the current synaptic weight of each synapse. These "connection strengths" crucially determine the dynamic fate of a specific firing pattern—the same activity which might have faded without trace yesterday, might today trigger a strong emotional interaction because some intervening traumatic event has been encoded in the brain's synapses.

These states are of overwhelming complexity, with perhaps 10^{11} neurons and 10^{15} synapses in the human brain. How do these then relate to mental state? Put simply, the mental state is a gross abstraction of the brain state which is at *approximately* the same level as language. The locution "at approximately the same level as language" is meant to convey two things: (i) that a mental state may *or may not* be expressible in words, while asserting (ii) that the level of detail that we ascribe to a mental state is far, far cruder than a brain state.

For example, I may see a face without being able to place it. The words "I've seen that person before—but where?" do not exhaust the mental state, for the latter includes the experience of facial features that we cannot put into words. If and when I recall the face, "Oh yes, during intermission at the opera last Saturday," the transition may be inexplicable at the "mental level," involving subtle neural processes that retrieved a memory of the scene involving that face, a representation rich enough to ground recognition of the context, with the subsequent return to the "mental level." The point here is that brain states are immensely complicated and causally complete, whereas mental states are relatively simple and thus only sometimes causally efficacious. In this regard logic is not the essence of the mental, but is rather a crystallization of the limiting case where decisions and inferences can be made via inferential chains at the mental level without recourse to the brain's greater patternings.

Again, if we admire a sunset, our mental state involves our awareness and aesthetic appreciation of the rich patterning of red, orange and purple in the cloud formations banked above the horizon. The words "Look at that!" may then suffice to help a friend share aspects of that mental state without in any way reducing that state to those three neutral words. But the extent of that aesthetic appreciation does not begin to exhaust the complexity of the brain states which flash through the brain millisecond by millisecond as we enjoy the scene.

The relation of words to the above two vignettes is interesting. In the first case, the words are parts of our own thoughts, not tools for communication, and act as a précis of the current mental state that is itself a précis of the much more complex (and temporally extended) brain state. In the second case, the words we use for communication have nothing to do with the scene—but they convey the expectation that the friend too will appreciate the view of that sunset, an expectation that may be based either on one's knowledge of the friend's aesthetic preferences or on two more general propositions: "Most people enjoy watching a good sunset," and "It's good to increase the enjoyment of others." However, I again emphasize that logic is not "the essence of the mental," and it would in general not be the case that any form of inference based on these two propositions was involved in your coming to say "Look at that!" I reiterate that causality is at the level of brain states, not mental states.

It should also be stressed that much of the brain state is irrelevant to one's mental state. For example, the state of the neural networks involved in the regulation of breathing does not affect our mental state save in times of crisis, and even then the effect on our mental state may be based on awareness of our overt pattern of breathing, rather than on any monitoring of the relevant neural activity. But beware of that word "monitoring". We are *not* offering a dualist theory in which mind and brain are separate, with the mind monitoring the activity of the brain to extract highlights. Rather, we hold that the mental state is itself captured within the activity of the brain, forming some sort of précis of the broader neural activity *and* memory structures.

CONSCIOUSNESS, LANGUAGE, AND DISTRIBUTED SCHEMAS

Butler and Hodos[4] show that the course of brain evolution among vertebrates has been determined in great part by:

(*a*) Formation of multiple new nuclei through elaboration or duplication;

(*b*) Regionally specific increases in cell proliferation in different parts of the brain; and

(*c*) Gain of some new connections and loss of some established connections

These changes can be accompanied by the kinds of exquisite variations in neural morphology observed by Cajal in the invertebrate retina. These phenomena can be influenced by relatively simple mutational events that can thus become established in a population as the result of random variation. However, contrary to Cajal's apparent doubts on the powers of natural selection, neuroscience proceeds on the basis that selective pressures determine whether the behavioral phenotypes expressive of the central nervous system organization produced by these random mutations increase their proportional representation within the population and eventually become normal for a new species. What needs stressing here is that the genome does not come neatly packaged in terms of separate sets of genes for separate nuclei of the brain, nor does each nucleus control its own set of behaviors. At the lowest levels, the specification of a brain region can call on generic hierarchies of gene regulation and expression for the formation of boundaries amongst generic precursors of, for example, neurons and glia. At a higher level, late structural genes that typify a taxon may elaborate on these (as in Cajal's invertebrate retinas) in multifarious and marvelous ways. At the highest levels, an overt behavior may reflect (*a*) the interactions of multiple brain regions and (*b*) the organization of low-level sensory filters, as exemplified by taxon-specific arrangements of the optic lobes in different insects. Cajal, it should be recalled, was also impressed by the cellular organization in the retinas of birds, which have to solve similar computational problems to those that challenge the insect visual system.

Moreover, and of great relevance to our later analysis of the evolution of language, *behavioral phenotypes* are not the result of "brain genes" alone; rather, they express both the brain's inherent organization, and the learning that has shaped it through the experiences of the individual organism, and these are determined in great part by the social milieu in which the organism is raised. For many species, this "social milieu" is hard to disentangle from the biology, but for primates we can discern a variety of "rituals," "practices," and "tribal customs" that constitute a body of culture constrained by, but in no sense determined by, the biological make-up of the social group. Thus as we come to analyze the evolution of the hominids, culture comes to play an important role even in biological evolution, as well as being itself subject to change and selection.

It should also be noted that certain genes seem to control the coordinated development of "brain systems" involving many brain regions, rather than being "specialists" for some local neural structures. From the work of Holmes,[5] we view the cerebellum's role as crucial to the graceful adaptation and coordination of movements, while conceding that the plan of movement is elaborated elsewhere. In mammals, cerebral cortex and cerebellum seem to be coupled in a genetically controlled system in such a way that they can co-evolve so that it now appears that lateral cerebellum can contribute to even the highly cognitive aspects of neural function. Yet the role of cerebellum in refining motor control has been a persistent feature of vertebrates. It is of great interest that genes in the fruit fly may similarly control the co-ordinated development and final structure of an analogous set of brain systems (midline neuropils) called the central complex. As shown by Roland Strauss and colleagues at the University of Würzburg, this center plays a pivotal role in the supervision of locomotion. Other studies (by Strausfeld) identify a fascinating relationship between the elaboration of subunit organization in the central complex of different insects and their different motor abilities, such as agility and dexterity.

Without wishing to equate consciousness with motor control—far from it—I would suggest that consciousness, too, may be a system function that involves networks including but not necessarily limited to cerebral cortex, and that as cerebral cortex evolves, so too does consciousness. But just as cerebellar adaptation for eye movements is a far cry from cerebellar adaptation for, say, piano playing or speech, so may we expect the quality of consciousness to vary from species to species. In particular, I would speculate that consciousness ranges from an almost reflex awareness of basic motor, sensory (which may include awareness of subtle social cues), and motivational states (so that even "simple" mammals may be aware of the difference between feeling maternal and feeling enraged) up to the subtle consciousness that slips in and out of elaborate verbal arguments. We are not then to seek a magic transition from totally non-conscious other species to conscious humans, but rather to seek an evolutionary path which renders plausible the emergence of consciousness in its human form.

I argue that we are conscious in a fully human sense only because we have language, that is, that as awareness piggy-backs on all manner of neural functions, so too must it piggy-back on language, thus reaching a subtlety and complexity that would otherwise be impossible. However, I strongly deny that consciousness is merely a function of language. For example, as already noted in the previous section, one can be aware of the shape and shading and coloration of a face in great subtlety, and be totally unable to put one's vivid, conscious perception of that face into words. This point is well illustrated by Georgia O'Keeffe's statement, painted on the foyer wall of the Georgia O'Keeffe Museum in Santa Fe, that "The meaning of a word to me is not as exact as the meaning of a color. Colors and shapes make a more definite statement than words. I am often amazed at the spoken and written words telling me what I have painted." As R. Shattuck observes in his review[a] of Nathalie Sarraute's book *Childhood*, Sarraute says,

> For me...there is something prior to language: a sensation, a perception, something in search of its language, which cannot exist without language.... Scarcely does this formless [feeling], all timid, and trembling try to show its face than all powerful language, always ready to intervene so as to re-establish order—its own order—jumps on it and crushes it.

What are we to make of that phrase, "which cannot exist without language?" Sarraute sees language as both expressive and destructive, and that tension between the verbal and non-verbal is surely the hallmark of our consciousness, setting it apart from whatever form of consciousness may be experienced by other creatures. The problem is that the writer, and of course the speaker, must try to express within words that which goes beyond words. When Sarraute recalls a particular childhood moment, she cannot accept the terms "happiness" or "ecstasy":

> [Even the simple word "joy"] cannot gather up what fills me, brims over in me, disperses, dissolves, melts into the pink bricks, the blossom-covered espaliers, the lawn, the pink and white petals, the air vibrating with barely perceptible tremors, with waves...waves of life, quite simply of life, what other word?...of life in its pure state....[6]

From this excursion it is a shock to return to neuroscience, but even here the point is related—what we may capture in correlates of a phenomenon within a limited account of one brain region pales before the richness of multi-level interactions playing out over tens, possibly hundreds of brain regions. (In the previous section, I was contrasting our mental states with the far richer complexity of brain states. Here, I am contrasting the neuroscientists' representation of brain states with the full richness of those states.) The relation of visual cortex to superior colliculus in our later exposition of blindsight will exemplify the view of the British 19th century neurologist Hughlings Jackson of the brain in terms of levels of increasing evolutionary complexity.[7] Jackson was very much influenced, as many people were at that time, by Darwinian concepts of evolution. Jackson argued that damage to a "higher" level of the brain disinhibited "older" brain regions from controls evolved later, to reveal evolutionarily more primitive behaviors.

Elsewhere,[8] I have developed a theory of schemas as functional, as distinct from structural, units in a hierarchical analysis of the brain. The starting point was to describe perceptual structures and distributed motor control in terms of functional units called schemas which may be combined to form new schemas as coordinated control programs linking simpler (perceptual and motor) schemas,[b] but these schemas provide the basis for the more abstract schemas that underlie thought and language more generally. Thinking in terms of schemas reminds us that the behavioral phenotype of an organism is not necessarily linked to a localized structure of the brain, but may involve subtle patterns of "cooperative computation" between brain regions which form a schema. Selection may thus act as much on schemas and hence through neural systems as it does on localized neural structures. Developing this view, Arbib and Liaw[10,11] argue that evolution not only yields new *schemas* connected to the old, but yields reciprocal connections that modify those older schemas. Three principles summarize and extend the key points of the above discussion:

---

[a]Shattuck, R. 1984. Life before language. New York Times Book Review 1 April: 1, 31.

[b]Jeannerod et al.[9] provide a recent application of schema theory to the study of neural mechanisms of grasping.

Principle 1. Cooperative computation: The functions of perceptual-motor behavior and intelligent action of animals situated in the world can be expressed as a network of interacting schemas. Each schema itself involves the integrated activity of multiple brain regions. The method of interaction of schemas is "cooperative computation" (competition/cooperation) so that "computations," which are often seen as the province of traditional symbol-based processing, are carried out by distributed "neuron-like" methods which do not involve explicit symbolic control. Cooperative computation not only serves as a basis for coordinated motor actions, but even for reactive planning, and intelligent behavior, including the use of language.

Principle 2. Evolution and modulation: New schemas and brain regions often arise as "modulators" of existing schemas or brain regions, rather than as new systems with independent functional roles.

Principle 3: Interaction of partial representations: A multiplicity of different representations—whether they be partial representations on a retinotopic basis, abstract representations of knowledge about types of object in the world, or more abstract "planning spaces"—must be linked into an integrated whole. Such linkage, however, may be mediated by distributed processes of competition and cooperation. There is no one place in the brain where an integrated representation of space plays the sole executive role in linking perception of the current environment to action.

NEUROLOGY AND CONSCIOUSNESS

I now offer a few examples from the neurological literature to suggest some subtleties in linking consciousness to the brain. First is the phenomenon of blindsight, which demonstrates that neural activity can effectively link perception and action without intervention of consciousness. Neurologists long held that a monkey (or human) without a visual cortex was blind. However, Humphrey[12] argued that a monkey without visual cortex should have at least as much visual ability as a frog, since the role of tectum in directing whole-body movements in frog, such as those studied in earlier sections, is analogous to the role of superior colliculus (the mammalian homologue of tectum) in directing orienting movements in cat and monkey. After two years, a monkey without visual cortex, but taught to pay attention to available visual cues, was able to use these cues to grab at moving objects, and to use changes in luminance—such as an open door or obstacles with high luminance contrast from the background—for navigation, even though delicate processes of pattern recognition were never regained. Moreover, it was discovered that humans without visual cortex could also "see" in this action-oriented sense, but, remarkably, they were not conscious of the visual stimuli for their actions.[13] This phenomenon of "blindsight" is further explored by Stroeger (in the same volume), who offers more insight into the pathways that may be involved. The lesson is that even schemas that we think of as normally under conscious control can in fact proceed without our being conscious of their activity.

Moreover, consciousness is not a direct property of having neurons of a particular structure or complexity because the same data can be represented in two networks of comparable neural complexity, yet be accessible to consciousness only when one of the networks rather than the other is intact. In particular, clinical studies show a double dissociation between the "declarative" ability to communicate the size of an object, whether verbally or by pantomime, and the "procedural" ability to act upon objects. Goodale et al.[14] studied a patient (DF) who had developed a profound visual form of agnosia following a bilateral lesion of occipitotemporal cortex. The pathways from occipital lobe toward the parietal lobe appeared to be intact. When the patient was asked to indicate the width of any one of a set of blocks, either verbally or by means of her index finger and thumb, her finger separation bore no relationship to the dimensions of the object and showed considerable trial-to-trial variability. Yet, when she was asked simply to reach out and pick up the block, the peak aperture between her index finger and thumb (prior to contact with the object) changed systematically with the width of the object, as in normal controls. A similar dissociation was seen in her responses to the orientation of stimuli. In other words, DF could preshape her hand accurately, even though she appeared to have no conscious appreciation (either verbal or by pantomime) of the visual parameters that guided the preshape.

Jeannerod et al.[15] reported the case of a woman (AT) who was the "opposite" of DF. Patient AT had a lesion of the occipitoparietal region that interrupted the dorsal route of visual processing, but left the inferotemporal lobe and the occipitotemporal pathways intact. AT could verbalize the diameter of a cylinder and could use her hand to pantomime its size, but could not preshape appropriately when asked to grasp it. Instead of an adaptive preshape, she would open her hand to its fullest, and only began to close her hand when the cylinder hit the "web" between index finger and thumb. But there was a surprise! When the stimulus used for the grasp was not a cylinder (for which the "semantics" contains no information about expected size), but rather a familiar object—such as a spool of thread or a lipstick—for which the "usual" size is part of the subject's knowledge, AT showed a relatively adaptive preshape. This suggests that the inferotemporal-parietal pathways provide the parietal areas with "default values" of action-related parameters, that is, values that can serve in place of actual sensory data to, for example, represent the approximate size of a known object to help the parietofrontal system.

It could be argued that the blindsight patient or DF is perfectly conscious of the visual cues they use to guide action, but either cannot or will not give verbal expression to their consciousness, but I discount this possibility and suggest that the above examples support a critique of some of the other views of consciousness presented in this volume. For one, since there are no data whatsoever suggesting that the damaged portions of DF's brain contain microtubules different from those of the regions that support successful "non-declarative" hand movements, there seems to be no evidence for the role of microtubules in consciousness espoused by Hameroff and Penrose in this volume. Again, since thalamocortical oscillations are equally important for the functioning of these "conscious" and "unconscious" regions of cerebral cortex, we must treat Llinás's view of the role of thalamocortical oscillations with care. Perhaps we can compare the role of the electricity supply of a computer—if there is no electricity, then there is no computation, but the power supply does not explain which particular computations will be undertaken. Similarly, we may see thalamocortical oscillations as the sign that cerebral cortex is "powered up" into the waking state, without regarding the oscillations *per se*—as distinct from the detailed neural traffic of some but not all cerebral and other neural systems—as the "carriers" of consciousness.

Even the most exquisite human sensibility cannot support more states of finely discriminated consciousness than there are physical states of the brain. We have a growing understanding of how these brain states support perception, memory, and the control of movement. This essay offers some preliminary contributions to the extension of such insights to the neural mechanisms of language and consciousness.

FROM SOCIAL COOPERATION TO CONSCIOUSNESS

Primitive communication subserves primitive coordination of the members of a social group, but processes that coordinate a group need not involve consciousness. Indeed, the social insects demonstrate a subtlety of group coordination that is in no way a precursor to consciousness. Here, we speculate about a "mammalian scenario" in which group coordination may indeed lay the basis for the co-evolution of consciousness and language.[16,17]

We each have only one body to act with and thus have a limited set of actions available to us at any one time. Thus, as we move towards the actual commitment of the organism to action, there would have to be a channeling from the richness of understanding to the well-focused choice, not necessarily conscious, of a course of action. Large ensembles of schemas in some sense interact, compete, cooperate to constitute a relatively well-focused plan of action that will commit the organism. This combination of many schemas with one body suggests a continuity of behavior by the one individual in similar situations, but also, as this repertoire builds up over time, the possibility that the schemas may eventually cohere in new ways, so that what had been an expected behavior in a certain set of situations may eventually give way, through new patterns of schema interaction, to new courses of behavior. Each individual has sets of schemas with some sort of coherence between them (this is not to claim that all of an individual's schemes are coherent); and the style of such a set of schemas can change over time to provide some sort of unity. I speculate that there are perhaps hundreds of thousands of schemas corresponding to the totality of what a human knows, with perhaps hundreds of these active at any time to subserve the current interaction of the organism with its environment. By contrast, consciousness seems to be rather focused. But what is the role of consciousness? Wouldn't these schemas do their jobs just as well if there were no such thing as consciousness? I cannot make a case for why we must *be* conscious. I think I can make a case for why we have patterns of schema activity that *correlate* with consciousness very well, and I will leave it to the phenomenologists to take the matter further. But first, I do want to stress that our common sense about consciousness can be misleading, that there are many things that we think require our conscious thought that do not, as we saw in our discussion of blindsight and DF.

As we have seen, Hughlings Jackson viewed the brain in terms of levels of increasing evolutionary complexity. He argued that damage to a "higher" level of the brain disinhibited "older" brain regions from controls evolved later, to reveal evolutionarily more primitive behaviors. After the addition of a new "hierarchical level," evolutionary regression may then be exhibited under certain lesions. But the crucial point, and this is very much part of Jackson's analysis, is that once new regions are in place or new schemas are available, they provide an enriched environment for the older parts of the brain. These now have new possibilities for further evolution, whether evolution of brain regions over a biological time scale or the evolution of schemas over an individual time scale. If you compare, for example, the brain of a frog with the brain of a cat, we find that the corresponding regions of the visual midbrain are much richer in the cat, not so much in terms of retinal input, but because there are so many descending pathways whereby the richness of cerebral cortex can influence what goes on in these more classical brain regions. In the terminology of schema theory, *evolution not only yields new schemas connected to the old, but yields reciprocal connections which modify those older schemas.*

Perhaps the development of animal and human communication may also be seen in terms of such evolutionary interaction to give us some insight into how consciousness might have evolved. One of the very striking features about human ability is that we come to incorporate tools into our body schema. When we use a screwdriver our body ends at the end of the screwdriver, not at the end of the hand; when we drive a car, our body ends at the rear bumper, not at our buttocks. Analogously, as creatures developed as social animals (and this account is not restricted to humans), the body might end not at the extremities of the physical body, but extend to incorporate aspects of other members of the group. However, coordinating others is a more subtle matter than just directing an arm or slightly adapting the hand to control a tool. The social animal has to find a way of expressing some précis of its mental state, of its richness of schema activity, so that it may then impinge upon others so that their behavior may be coordinated. With increasing richness of social interactions, though still at a prelinguistic stage in our evolutionary story, there would come the ability to form a précis of schema activity that is not necessarily relevant to deciding what to do next, but is relevant in terms of coordination with others.

Primitive communication subserves primitive coordination of the members of a social group. As in blindsight, processes that coordinate group members need not involve consciousness. As communication evolves (by mechanisms we do not yet understand), the "instructions" that can be given to other members of the group increase in subtlety. Communication evolves at first purely as a way of coordinating the actions of a group. For this to succeed, the brain of each group member must be able not only to generate such signals, but also to integrate signals from other members of the group into its own ongoing motor planning.

We suggest that the key transition in going from the limited set of vocalizations used in communication by, say, vervet monkeys, to the richness of human language came with a *migration in time* from:

(i) an execution/observation matching system enabling an individual to recognize the action (as distinct from the mere movement) that another individual is making, to

(ii) the individual's becoming able to pantomime "this is the action I am about to take."

In the earliest stages of the evolution of this second ability, communication may have involved the accidental release of a motor plan from inhibition, thus allowing a brief prefix of the movement to be exhibited before the full action was released—but this "warning gesture" may have sufficed to alert others in time to bias their action, yielding benefits of adaptive value for groups that could both offer "signals of intention" and make use of them. This yields positive reinforcement to the individual accidentally releasing prefixes of actions, serving in turn as the basis for group selection, favoring the reproduction of those groups that can learn to emit and interpret such signals. This marks, at both the individual and species levels, the beginning of real communication, as distinct from the release of signals.

However, Arbib and Hesse[16,17] do not emphasize this external process of "group selection" in the population as a whole, but rather the changes within the individual brain made possible by the availability of a "précis"—a gesturable representation—of intended future movements (as distinct from current movements). They use the term *communication plexus* for the circuits involved in generating this representation. The Jacksonian element of their analysis is that the evolution of the communication plexus provides an environment for the further evolution of older systems. They suggest that once the brain has such a communication plexus, then a new process of evolution begins whereby the précis comes to serve not only as a basis for communication between the members of a group, but also as a resource for planning and coordination within the brain itself. This "communication plexus" thus evolves a crucial role in schema coordination. The thesis is that it is the activity of this co-evolved process that constitutes consciousness. As such it will progress in richness along with the increased richness of communication that culminates as language in the human line.

There are occasions on which "older" schemas can be better coordinated if they coordinate via the précis than if they coordinate by themselves. We then have a subnetwork of the schema network which provides a précis that may often have no directive role, and yet may evolve to have a role that is sometimes but not always directive. Since lower-level schema activity can often proceed successfully without this highest-level coordination, consciousness may sometimes be active, if active at all, as a monitor rather than as a director of action. In other cases: the précis of schema activity plays the crucial role in determining the future course of schema activity, and thus of action.

This evolutionary process, which occurs with subhuman species, then sets the stage, I would suggest, both for human consciousness and also for the evolution of language to express this rather coarse précis of the richness of the underlying schema activity. In summary, this pretheory sees consciousness as a précis of schema activity, evolving in such a way that it can elaborate certain mental processes at the level of language and logic and is related in part, but not entirely, to communication.

Arbib and Hesse's thesis, then, is that it is the activity of this communication plexus that constitutes consciousness, that is, that "consciousness" is defined by a neurally represented précis of potential behavior. Such a view does not explain the phenomenology of consciousness (that is, the way consciousness "feels" to each of us), but it does accord well with this phenomenology. The fact that lower-level schema activity can often proceed successfully without the high-level coordination afforded by the communication plexus explains why consciousness may sometimes be active as a monitor rather than as a director of action. In other cases, the formation of the précis of schema activity plays the crucial role in determining the future course of schema activity, and thus of action, and this accords with those occasions in which we experience a conscious effort in weighing a number of courses of action before we commit ourselves to behave in a specific way. The reader may consult Arbib and Hesse[17] for an articulation of the philosophical debate between those who, in line with the above argument, see the "self" as embodied within the neural circuitry and the body that contains it, and those dualists who view the self as in some sense separable from brain and body.[18]

A MIRROR SYSTEM FOR GRASPING IN MONKEY AND HUMAN

Grasping

The neurophysiological findings of the Sakata group on parietal cortex and the Rizzolatti group on premotor cortex indicate that parietal area AIP (the anterior intraparietal sulcus) and ventral premotor area F5 in monkey form key elements in a cortical circuit which transforms visual information on intrinsic properties of objects into hand movements that allow the animal to grasp the objects appropriately.[9,19,20] The FARS (Fagg–Arbib–Rizzolatti–Sakata) model[21] provides a computational account of what we shall call the canonical system, centered on the AIP → F5 pathway, showing how it can account for basic phenomena of grasping. Our basic view is that AIP computes "affordances" for grasping from the visual stream and sends (neural codes for) these on to area F5: *affordances* are features of the object relevant to action, in this case to grasping. Motor information is then transferred to the primary motor cortex (denoted F1 or M1), to which F5 is directly connected, as well as to various subcortical centers for movement execution.

F5 neurons discharge during active hand and/or mouth movements.[22,23,24] Moreover, discharge in most F5 neurons correlates with an action rather than with the individual movements that form it, so that one may classify F5 neurons into various categories corresponding to the action associated with their discharge. The most common are: "grasping-with-the-hand" neurons, "grasping-with-the-hand-and-the-mouth" neurons, "holding" neurons, "manipulating" neurons, and "tearing" neurons.

A Mirror System for Grasping

Further study of F5 revealed a class of F5 neurons that discharge not only when the monkey grasped or manipulated objects, but also when the monkey observed the experimenter make a gesture similar to the one that, when actively performed by the monkey, involved activity of the neuron (FIG. 1).[24] Neurons with this property are called "mirror neurons." The majority of mirror neurons are selective for one type of action, and for almost all mirror neurons there is a link between the effective observed movement and the effective executed movement. The actions most represented are: grasp, manipulate, tear, put an object on a plate. Mirror neurons also have (by definition) motor properties. However, not all F5 neurons respond to action observation. We thus distinguish mirror neurons, which are active both when the monkey performs certain actions and when the monkey observes them performed by others, from canonical neurons, which are active when the monkey performs certain actions but not when the monkey observes actions performed by others.

In summary, the properties of mirror neurons suggest that area F5 is endowed with an *observation/execution matching system*: When the monkey observes a motor act that resembles one in its movement repertoire, a neural code for this action is au-

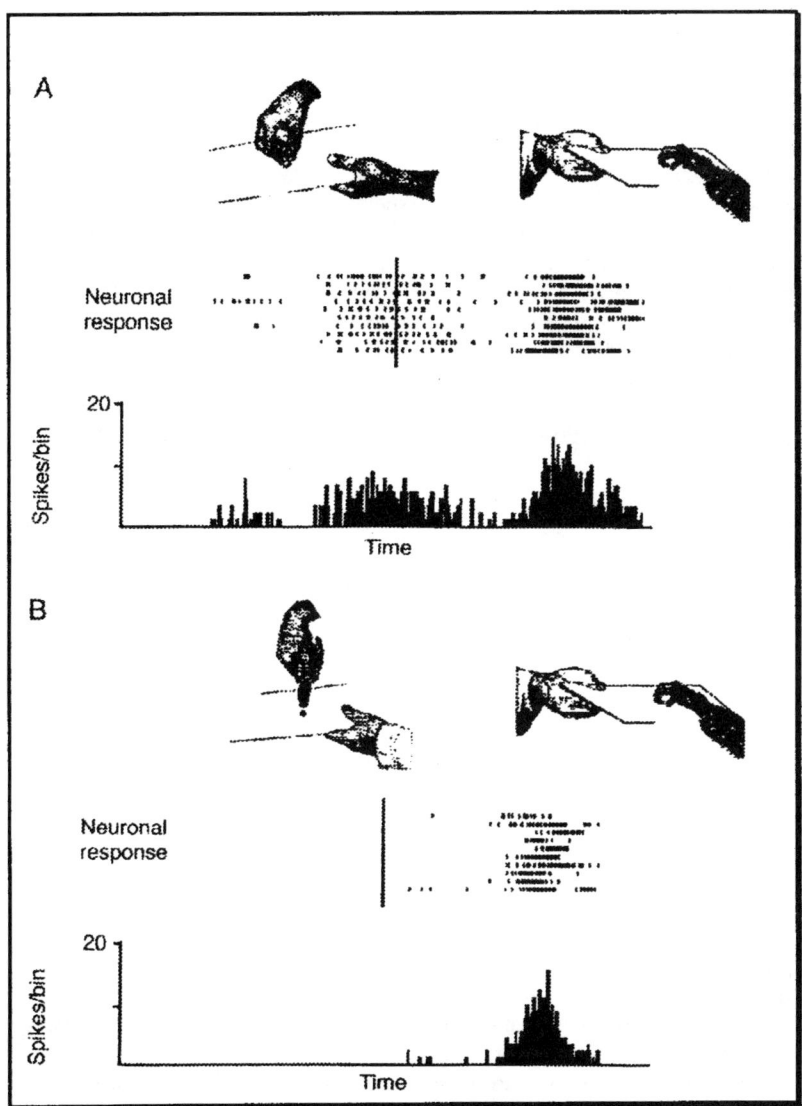

FIGURE 1. Example of a mirror neuron. *Upper part of each panel*: behavioral situations. *Lower part*: neuron's responses. The firing pattern of the neuron on each of a series of consecutive trials is shown above the histogram which sums the response from each trial. **A** (*left*): The experimenter grasps a piece of food with his hand, then moves it toward the monkey, who, at the end of the trial, grasps it. The neuron discharges during observation of the experimenter's grasp, ceases to fire when the food is given to the monkey, and discharges again when the monkey grasps it. **B** (*left*): When the experimenter grasps the food with an unfamiliar tool, the neuron does not respond, but the neuron again discharges when the monkey grasps the food. The rasters are aligned with the moment when the food is grasped by the experimenter (*vertical line*). Each small vertical line in the rasters corresponds to a spike. Histogram bin width: 20 ms. Ordinates, spikes/bin; abscissae, time.

tomatically retrieved. This code consists in the activation of a subset, the mirror neurons, of the F5 neurons which discharge when the observed act is executed by the monkey itself.

Bringing in Broca's Area

Two PET experiments[25,26] were then designed to seek mirror systems in humans. The two experiments differed in many aspects, but both had a condition in which subjects observed the experimenter grasping a 3-D object. Object observation was used as a control situation. (This condition also controlled for verbalization.) Grasp observation significantly activated the superior temporal sulcus (STS), the inferior parietal lobule, and the inferior frontal gyrus (area 45). All activations were in the left hemisphere. The last area is of especial interest: areas 44 and 45 in left hemisphere of the human constitute Broca's area, a major component of the human brain's language mechanisms. Indeed, F5 is generally considered to be the homologue of Broca's area (see Rizzolatti and Arbib[27] for the details). Thus, the cortical areas active during action-observation in humans and monkeys correspond very well. Taken together, human and monkey data indicate that in primates there is a fundamental mechanism for action-recognition: we argue that individuals recognize actions made by others because the neural pattern elicited in their pre-motor areas (in a broad sense) during action-observation is similar to a part of that internally generated to produce that action. This mechanism in humans is circumscribed to the left hemisphere. These findings will lead us (in the next section) to explore the hypothesis that the mirror system provided the basis for the evolution of human language.

THE MIRROR SYSTEM APPROACH TO LANGUAGE EVOLUTION

The mirror system approach to language evolution hypothesizes seven stages in the evolution of human language: (1) grasping, (2) a mirror system for grasping, (3) a "simple" imitation system, (4) a "complex" imitation system, (5) a manual-based communication system, (6) speech, and (7) language. Stages 1 and 2 follow from the work of Rizzolatti and his colleagues and have been described earlier. The transition from Stages 1 and 2 to Stages 5 and 6 was hypothesized by Rizzolatti and Arbib.[25,28] The insertion of Stages 3 and 4 is due to Arbib[29]—our quest to explore the hypothesis that the mirror system provided the basis for the evolution of human language will lead us to argue that "imitation" takes us beyond the "basic" mirror system for grasping, and that the ability to acquire novel sequences if the sequences are not too long and the components are relatively familiar took the hominid line beyond the level of imitation that humans share with other extant primates. Arbib[29] also introduces the notion that stages 6 and 7 are separate, characterizing *speech* as being the open-ended production and perception of sequences of vocal gestures, without implying that these sequences constitute a language. In this regard, we must discuss "language-readiness" to better delineate what it is that biological evolution yielded in humans.

Language-Readiness

Biological evolution may not so much have yielded a human brain "equipped with" language so much as a human brain "ready for" language. The corollary to this is that even though an early *Homo sapiens* infant raised (after some miracle of time travel or cloning) in a human home in today's world would be completely human, an adult *Homo sapiens* of 200,000 years ago would have a consciousness in many ways limited with respect to a modern human. Perhaps his awareness of the sights and sounds and smells around him would be more intense than most modern humans experience, but it would lack the subtle overlays that the modern mind possesses precisely because of the recursive properties opened up by language. Consciousness is shaped by the interaction of our biology (brain and body) with our environment (physical and social) and thus, I claim, has developed drastically since the human brain and body achieved its present form. In this regard we may note Penny Lee's observation[30] that Whorf[31] contrasts a "universe" of "conscious thinking abstracted from experience" with a "universe as unconscious thinking projected upon experience " and refers to "the organization of raw experience into a consistent and readily communicable universe of ideas though the medium of linguistic patterns." She suggests that in referring to "conscious thinking" what Whorf had in mind was the elements of language that allow that experience to be organized and reflected upon in shareable form:

> These elements are what he was later to refer to as "isolates of meaning"; linguistic representations of perceptual invariants drawn from the universally available store generated through structural coupling with the environment....Once established in language, isolates of meaning participate in and significantly help to generate secondary elaborations upon primary experiential data. They also help to consolidate habits of attention to experiential particularities in culture-specific ways.... And although the system develops only in the course of socialization, it is in essence idiolectal, as Hockett (1987) emphasizes. The utility of our own internalized system as a basis for communicating with other people depends on the degree to which its configurations coincide with theirs. It is in the negotiation of this overlap that the linguistic calibration of agreement...occurs. [Idiosyncratic meanings] add richness to concepts held by individuals and may interfere with communication if they diverge too far from the most commonly shared connotations.... [T]he human 'mind/brain' is physically altered in the course of linguistic enculturation as various linkages are strengthened and others weaken over time. New patterns of linkage and configuration are introduced into the complex of neural connections that provide the basis for interpreting physical, verbal, and social information and for making sense of the data of memory and imagination.[30]

I emphasize that ease of acquisition of a skill does not imply genetic encoding of the skill *per se:* The human genome does not encode strategies for exploring the Internet or playing video games. But *computer technology has evolved to match the preadaptations of the human brain and body*. The human brain and body evolved in such a way that we have hands, larynx, and facial mobility suited for generating gestures that can be used in language, and the brain mechanisms needed to produce and perceive rapidly generated sequences of such gestures. In this sense, the human brain and body is *language-ready*. This leads us to the questions:

What were the biological changes supporting language-readiness?

What were the cultural changes extending the utility of language as a socially transmitted vehicle for communication *and* representation?

How did biological and cultural change interact "in a spiral" prior to the emergence of *Homo sapiens*?

Primate Calls are not the Direct Precursors of Human Language

For want of better data, we will assume that the common ancestor of humans and monkeys shared with monkeys a primate call system (a limited set of species-specific calls) and an orofacial gesture system (a limited set of gestures expressive of emotion and related social indicators). Communication is inherently multi-modal, and body posture also plays a role in social communication, though I shall not emphasize this here. What is to be stressed here is that:

(1) Combinatorial properties for the openness of communication are virtually absent in basic primate calls and orofacial communication, even though individual calls may be graded.

(2) The neural substrate for primate calls is in a region of cingulate cortex distinct from F5, which we have seen to be the monkey homologue of Broca's area in the human.

Our challenge in charting the evolution of human language, which for most humans is so heavily intertwined with speech, is thus to understand why it is F5, rather than the area already involved in vocalization, which provided the evolutionary substrate for language.

Stage 3: A "Simple" Imitation System

Twenty million years separate monkeys and humans from their common ancestor, while five million years separate chimps and humans from their common ancestor (see Figure 4.2 in Gamble[33]).

How have the mirror systems of monkey and human diverged from that of their common ancestor?

How have the mirror systems of chimp and human diverged from that of their common ancestor?

Since language played no role in the evolution of monkey or chimp or the common ancestors we share with them, any changes we chart prior to the hominid line should be shown to be adaptive in their own right, rather than as precursors of language. It is clear that mirror neurons may well be fundamental to *imitation*, so that the utility of the mirror system in the common ancestor of human and monkey may have resided in simple forms of imitation as well as in the infant's learning how to observe its own motor behavior, and in learning how to relate its own actions to those of others. In any case, we make the following hypothesis (see Arbib[29] for further discussion): *Extension of the mirror system from single actions to compound actions* was a key innovation in the brain's evolution relevant to the emergence of language-readiness.

The Mirror-System Hypothesis

We will soon proceed to Stage 4 (a manual-based communication system) in our evolutionary progress. Before proceeding further, we need to observe that we are not the first to posit this stage in language evolution. Hewes,[34] Corballis,[35,36] Kimura,[37] and Armstrong *et al.*[38] are among those who argue that gestural communication played a crucial role in human language evolution. In this regard, we stress that the "generativity" which some see as the hallmark of language (i.e., its openness to new constructions, as distinct from having a fixed repertoire like that of monkey vocalizations) is present in motor behavior, which can thus supply the evolutionary substrate for its appearance in language. Our novel tenet is that the *parity requirement* for language in humans—what counts for the speaker must count for the hearer—is met because of the mirror-system hypothesis, namely that "Language evolved from a basic mechanism *not* originally related to communication: the *mirror system for grasping* with its capacity to generate *and* recognize a set of actions." However, the mirror-system hypothesis does *not* say that having a mirror system is equivalent to having language. Monkeys have mirror systems but do not have language, and we expect that many species have mirror systems for varied socially relevant behaviors.

Stage 4: A "Complex" Imitation System

Imprints in the cranial cavity of endocasts indicate that the enlargement of frontal cortex that we would relate to "speech areas" in the human brain were already under way in early hominids such as *H. habilis* long before the larynx reached the modern "speech-optimal" configuration, but there is a debate over whether such areas were already present in australopithecines. This leads us to a related hypothesis: The transition from australopithecines to early *Homo* coincided with the transition from a mirror system used only for action recognition and "simple" imitation to more elaborate forms of imitation that depended on/provided evolutionary pressure for the elaboration of a whole complex of systems that integrated the F5 mirror system for execution/observation of single actions into a far larger system for the execution/observation of complex behaviors. Putting this another way, I argue that what marks hominids as distinct from their common ancestors with chimpanzees is the ability to rapidly exploit novel sequences as the basis for immediate imitation or for the immediate construction of an appropriate response, as well as contributing to the longer-term enrichment of experience. Of course, even this human ability requires that the sequences be not too long and the components be relatively familiar,

Stage 5: A Manual-Based Communication System

We then hypothesize that this ability for "complex" imitation formed the basis for an increasingly human-like mirror system used for intentional communication. However, I want to stress again the thesis that biological evolution created a "language-ready" brain, and that it took a long period of cultural evolution for humans to extend their basic capability for communication to symbol systems with the complexity that characterizes all known human languages. Our hypothetical sequence (Rizzolatti and Arbib[27]) for manual gesture is then

(i) pragmatic action directed towards a goal object;

(ii) imitation of such actions;

(iii) pantomime in which similar actions are produced in the absence of a goal object;

(iv) abstract gestures divorced from their pragmatic origins (if such existed). In pantomime it might be hard to distinguish a grasping movement signifying "grasping" from one meaning "a [graspable] raisin," thus providing an "incentive" for coming up with an arbitrary gesture to distinguish the two meanings.

(v) the use of such elements for the formation of compounds which can be paired with meanings in more or less arbitrary fashion.

My current hypothesis is that stages (iii) and (iv) were present in pre-human hominids, that (v) was present in a rather limited form in *Homo erectus*, and that the "explosive" development of (v) that we know as language depended on "cultural evolution" well after biological evolution had formed modern *Homo sapiens*. This remains speculative, and one should note that biological evolution may have continued to reshape the human genome and brain even after the skeletal form of *Homo sapiens* was essentially stabilized.

Stage 6: Speech

We earlier noted that the neural substrate for primate calls is in a region of cingulate cortex distinct from F5, which we have seen to be the monkey homologue of Broca's area in the human. We thus need to explain why F5, rather than the *a priori* more likely "primate call area," provided the evolutionary substrate for speech in particular, and language in general. Rizzolatti and Arbib[27] answer this by suggesting two evolutionary stages going beyond basic vocalization and orofacial gesture, the first of which is really stage (v) in the above list:

(v) A *distinct* manuo-brachial communication system evolved to complement the primate calls/orofacial communication system. The "speech-like" areas of early hominids (that is, not only the areas homologous to monkey F5 and human Broca's area, but the larger system mediating "complex" imitation of which they were part) mediated orofacial and manuo-brachial communication, but not speech.

(vi) The manual-orofacial symbolic system then "recruited" vocalization. Association of vocalization with manual gestures allowed them to assume a more open referential character, and exploit the capacity for imitation of the underlying brachio-manual system. I stress again that the form of speech reached at this stage involved the open-ended production and perception of sequences of vocal gestures. One can have speech in this sense without the constituent sequences constituting a language in the sense of a modern human language like Swahili or Korean.

Thus, we answer the question "Why did F5, rather than the primate call area provide the evolutionary substrate for speech and language?" by saying that the primate call area could not of itself access the combinatorial properties inherent in the manuo-brachial system.

Lieberman[39] views the descent of the larynx seen in *Homo sapiens* as being crucial in enabling the wide articulatory range exploited in human speech. Clearly, some level of language-readiness and *vocal* communication preceded this: A core of proto-speech was needed to provide pressures for laryngeal evolution. However, as I shall further argue below, it is quite possible that early humans and their *H. erectus* precursors may have had complex vocal communication without having languages akin to modern languages.

Having shown why speech did not evolve "simply" by extending the classic primate vocalization system, we must note that the language and vocalization systems are nonetheless linked. Lesions centered in the anterior cingulate cortex and supplementary motor areas of the brain can also cause mutism in humans, similar to the effects produced in muting monkey vocalizations. Conversely, a patient with a Broca's area lesion may nonetheless swear when provoked. But note that "emitting an imprecation" is more like a monkey vocalization than like the syntactically structured use of language. Lieberman suggests that the primate call made by an infant separated from its mother not only survives in the human infant, but in humans develops into the breath group, the single intake and output of breath (inspiration and expiration) that provides the contour for each continuous sequence of an utterance. I thus hypothesize that the evolution of speech yielded the pathways for cooperative computation between cingulate cortex and Broca's area, with cingulate cortex involved in breath groups and emotional shading, and Broca's area providing the motor control for rapid production and interweaving of elements of an utterance.

The Transition to Homo sapiens

I have argued that the *biological* evolution of *Homo sapiens* yielded a mirror system embedded in a far larger system for execution, observation, and imitation of compound behaviors composed from orofacial, manual, and vocal gestures. I also accept that this system supported communication in *Homo erectus*, since otherwise it is hard to see what selective pressure could have brought about the lowering of the larynx, which, as Lieberman observes, makes humans able to articulate more precisely than other primates, but at the increased risk of choking. However, I do not accept that this means that the earliest *Homo sapiens* was endowed with language in anything like its modern human richness. Rather, biological evolution equipped early humans with "language-ready brains" which proved rich enough to support the *cultural evolution* of human languages in all their commonalities and diversities. The divergence of the Romance languages took about one thousand years. The divergence of the Indo-European languages to form the immense diversity of Hindi, German, Italian, English, etc., took about 6,000 years. How can we imagine what has changed since the emergence of *Homo sapiens* some 200,000 years ago? Or in 5,000,000 years of prior hominid evolution? Here I need to make two crucial points:

1. There is a danger, typified by Chomsky's notion of universal grammar,[40] of thinking that there is some set of basic characteristics typical of all language and "hard-wired" into the human genome and thus the human infant's brain. I disagree, arguing that we can each know one or a few languages, but there is no such thing as Language-with-a-big-L that we all know, let alone "know in our genes." It is difficult to learn a foreign language because languages can be inherently different, but more-or-less adequate translations between languages are possible because languages have been shaped both by the need to express a range of basic human experiences, and by cultural diffusion.

2. Bickerton[41] has spoken of *proto-language* as being language restricted, basically, to two-word utterances (generally comprising a verb and a noun in some order), and suggests that it is common to chimps trained to exhibit some form of language-like use of symbols, two-year old humans, and persons speaking pidgins. He then argues that proto-language was possessed by the hominid precursors of humans. However, I note that proto-language is only observed in creatures (chimps or

humans) exposed to human language. I thus argue (with equally little proof, but as a counter-hypothesis to Bickerton's) that early *Homo sapiens* did not have proto-language in this sense. Rather, I shall argue that what they possessed was the ability to name events with novel sequences of (manual and/or vocal) gestures, but that this capability does not imply the ability to separately name the objects and actions that comprised those events. I then claim that the latter ability was a momentous discovery made by humans perhaps 100,000 to 50,000 years ago, rather than a biological heritage from earlier hominids.

The reader should be warned of the dangerous methodology that I employ here. My work is anchored in a rigorous knowledge of modern neuroscience, but when I assert that *Homo sapiens* was not endowed with language in anything like its modern human richness, I am not appealing to hard data, but rather forwarding a hypothesis based on, but in no sense implied by, a variety of evidence. However, I do not (nor should the reader) accept my hypotheses uncritically. Rather, each new hypothesis is confronted with new data and competing hypotheses as my reading progresses. The hypotheses presented in this article have thus survived a great deal of "cross-examination", and have been refined in the process. For example, while my reading of historical linguistics impressed me with the rapidity with which languages change (and I view human language as the sum of human languages, not as some abstract entity above and beyond these bio-cultural products) and thus to distinguish the notion of a "language-ready" brain from a "language-equipped" brain, further reading and reflection leads me to accept that the dichotomy here is not as sharp as I may have believed earlier.

The ability for visual scene perception that must underlie the ability to employ verb-argument structures—the perception of *Action-Object Frames* in which an actor, an action, and related role players can be perceived in relationship—was well established in the primate line, supporting a variety of complex behaviors and social relations. I thus hypothesize that the ability to communicate a fair number of such frames was established in the hominid line prior to the emergence of *Homo sapiens*. Indeed, consideration of the spatial basis for "prepositions" may help show how visuomotor coordination underlies some aspects of language. However, the basic semantic-syntactic correspondences have been overlaid by a multitude of later innovations and borrowings.

The transition to *Homo sapiens* may then have involved "language amplification" through increased speech capability, yielding an increased ability to name actions and objects to create an unlimited set of verb-argument structures, and the ability to compound those structures in diverse ways. I would suggest that many ways of expressing these relationships were the *discovery* of *Homo sapiens*. That is, many grammatical structures like adjectives or conjunctions such as *but*, *and*, or *or* and *that*, *unless*, or *because* might well have been "post-biological" in their origin.

A Multi-Modal System

Our use of writing as a record of speech has long since created the mistaken impression that language is a speech-based system. However, McNeill[42] has analyzed videotapes to show the crucial use that people make of gestures synchronized with speech. Even blind people use manual gestures when speaking. As deaf people have always known, but linguists have only relatively recently discovered,[43] sign lan-

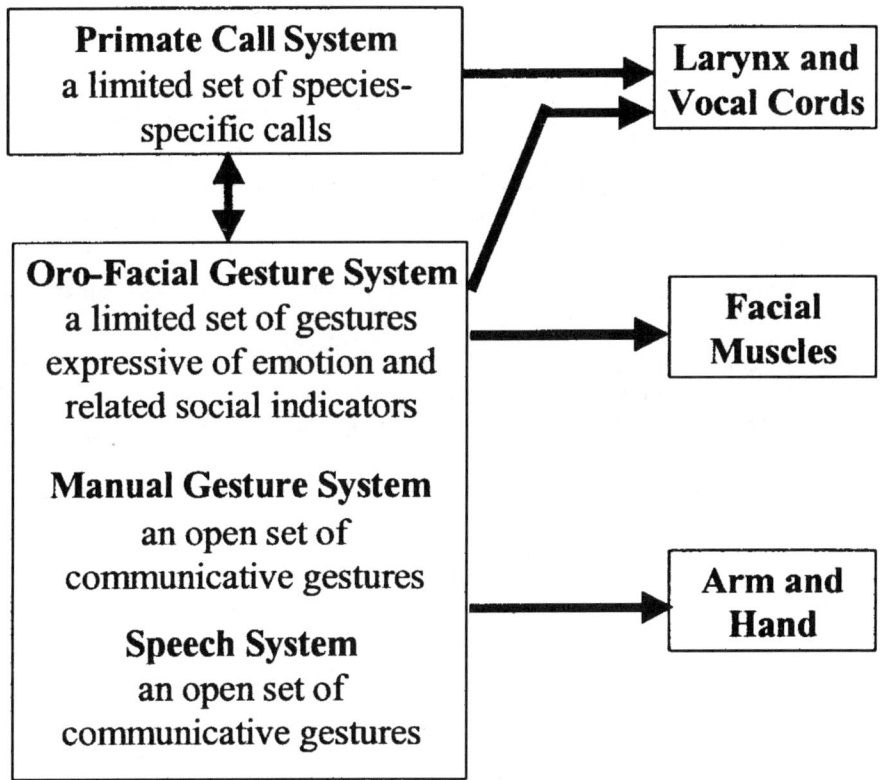

FIGURE 2. The fruit of evolution: Not three separate communication systems, but a single system operating in at least three motor modalities and at least two sensory modalities.

guages are full human languages, rich in lexicon, syntax, and semantics. Moreover, not only deaf people use sign language—so too do some aboriginal Australian tribes, and some native populations in North America. These studies suggest that we locate language-readiness in a speech-manual-orofacial gesture complex. I then hypothesize that during language acquisition a normal person shifts the major information load of language—but by no means all of it—into the speech domain, whereas for a deaf person the major information load is removed from speech and taken over by hand and orofacial gestures. On this basis, I show in FIGURE 2 a single communication system, but stress that it involves many brain regions, each with its own evolutionary story. See Arbib[29] for more details.

CONCLUDING CLAIMS ABOUT CONSCIOUSNESS

To conclude briefly, my argument about consciousness has the following ingredients.

(i) Human consciousness as we normally experience it is a property of the brain, rather than some separate "mind stuff";

(ii) Consciousness is a distributed property that has little access to many brain regions, and provides a précis based on the state of other brain regions that is only partially verbalizable;

(iii) It is possible that portions of our brain can support forms of "animal awareness" that may enrich human consciousness but seem qualitatively different in nature; but

(iv) What makes human consciousness so different is that it includes expression of our thoughts in language;

(v) The *communication plexus* underlying language has (by a process of "Jacksonian evolution") restructured the brain in such a way that consciousness may seem to be sometimes observer and sometimes controller.

The first two would seem to be in agreement with our quotations from Cajal's view in the *Textura* (as translated into English from the French of the *Histologie*); the third acknowledges a possible evolutionary continuity in consciousness, while the fourth stresses that the consciousness of humans who possess language is qualitatively different from that of other creatures; and the last ascribes a specific role to the evolution of a "communication plexus" for the communication of intended action in the emergence of human consciousness.

The last part of the paper takes us part-way back to Cajal by offering a more "brain-based" approach to the evolution of human language, tracing it through seven stages: (1) grasping, (2) a mirror system for grasping, (3) a "simple" imitation system, (4) a "complex" imitation system, (5) a manual-based communication system, (6) speech, and (7) language. Stages 1 and 2 are present in the monkey; stage 3 is posited to be more fully developed in the common ancestor of human and chimpanzee; stages 4, 5 and 6 are posited to occur along the hominid line. However, we do not argue that the "speech" of the first *Homo sapiens* was a human language in anything like the modern sense. Rather, the development of human languages and the attendant enrichment of human consciousness was, I argue, a process that took many tens of millennia. I would thus argue that those brain mechanisms discussed at this conference that we share with other animals—such as those based on thalamo-cortical oscillations, 40 Hz oscillations, or "re-entrant processes"—can, in and of themselves, at best support "animal awareness." They are necessary but not sufficient for consciousness in its full human sense.

REFERENCES

1. RAMÓN Y CAJAL, S. 1937. Recollections of My Life [Volume 8 of Memoirs of the American Philosophical Society, reprinted by the MIT Press]. (English translation of Recuerdos de Mi Vida by E.H. Craigie , Madrid, 1901–1917).
2. RAMÓN Y CAJAL, S. 1911. Histologie du systeme nerveux. A. Maloine. Paris. (This is the second edition, in French, of the Textura del sistema nervioso del hombre y los vertebrados of 1899. Quotations here are from the English translation by N. and L. Swanson, Oxford University Press, 1995.)

3. RALL, W. 1964. Theoretical significance of dendritic trees for neuronal input-output relations. *In* Neural Theory and Modeling. R. F. Reiss, Ed. :73-97. Stanford University Press. Stanford, CA.
4. BUTLER, A.B. & W. HODOS. 1996. Comparative Vertebrate Neuroanatomy: Evolution and Adaptation. John Wiley & Sons. New York.
5. HOLMES, G. 1939. The cerebellum of man. Brain **62**: 1–30.
6. SARRAUTE, N. 1984. Childhood. (Translated by Barbara Wright in consultation with the author). George Braziller. NewYork.
7. JACKSON, J.H. 1878–79. On affections of speech from disease of the brain. Brain **1**: 304–330; **2**: 203–222, 323–356.
8. ARBIB, M.A. 1981. Perceptual Structures and Distributed Motor Control. *In* Handbook of Physiology, Section 2: The Nervous System, Vol. II, Motor Control, Part 1. V.B. Brooks, Ed. :1449–1480. American Physiological Society.
9. JEANNEROD, M., M.A. ARBIB, G. RIZZOLATTI, G. & H. SAKATA. 1995. Grasping objects: the cortical mechanisms of visuomotor transformation. Trends Neurosci. **18**: 314–320.
10. ARBIB, M.A. & J.-S. LIAW. 1995. Sensorimotor transformations in the worlds of frogs and robots. Artificial Intelligence **72**: 53–79.
11. ARBIB, M.A., P. ÉRDI & J. SZENTÁGOTHAI. 1997. Neural Organization: Structure, Function, and Dynamics. MIT Press. Cambridge, MA.
12. HUMPHREY, N.K. 1970. What the frog's eye tells the monkey's brain. Brain Behav. Evol. **3**: 324–337.
13. WEISKRANTZ, L. 1974. The interaction between occipital and temporal cortex in vision: an overview. *In* The Neurosciences: Third Study Program. F.O. Schmitt and F.G. Worden, Eds. :89–204. MIT Press. Cambridge, MA.
14. GOODALE, M. A., A.D. MILNER, L.S. JAKOBSON & D.P. CAREY. 1991. A neurological dissociation between perceiving objects and grasping them. Nature **349**: 154–156.
15. JEANNEROD, M., J. DECETY & F. MICHEL. 1994. Impairment of grasping following a bilateral posterior parietal lesion. Neurophysiologia **32**: 369–380.
16. ARBIB, M.A. 1985. In Search of the Person: Philosophical Explorations in Cognitive Science. University of Massachusetts Press. Amherst, MA.
17. ARBIB, M.A. & M.B. HESSE. 1986. The Construction of Reality. Cambridge University Press. Cambridge, England.
18. ECCLES, J.C. 1977. The Understanding of the Brain, 2nd ed. McGraw-Hill. New York.
19. TAIRA, M., S. MINE, A.P. GEORGOPOULOS, A. MURATA & H. SAKATA. 1990. Parietal cortex neurons of the monkey related to the visual guidance of hand movement. Exp. Brain Res. **83**: 29–36.
20. RIZZOLATTI, G., R. CAMARDA, L. FOGASSI, M. GENTILUCCI, G. LUPPINO & M. MATELLI. M. l988. Functional organization of inferior area 6 in the macaque monkey II. Area F5 and the control of distal movements. Exp. Brain Res. **71**: 491–507.
21. FAGG, A. H. & M.A. ARBIB. 1998. Modeling parietal-premotor interactions in primate control of grasping. Neural Networks **11**: 1277–1303.
22. DI PELLEGRINO, G., L. FADIGA, L. FOGASSI, V. GALLESE & G. RIZZOLATTI. 1992. Understanding motor events: a neurophysiological study. Exp. Brain Res. **91**: 176–180.
23. RIZZOLATTI, G., L. FADIGA, V. GALLESE& L. FOGASSI. 1996. Premotor cortex and the recognition of motor actions. Cogn. Brain Res. **3**: 131–141.
24. GALLESE, V., L. FADIGA, L. FOGASSI & G. RIZZOLATTI. 1996. Action recognition in the premotor cortex. Brain **119**: 593–609.
25. RIZZOLATTI, G., L. FADIGA, M. MATELLI, V. BETTINARDI, D. PERANI & F. FAZIO. 1996. Localization of grasp representations in humans by positron emission tomography: 1. Observation versus execution. Exp. Brain Res. **111**: 246–252.
26. GRAFTON, S.T., M.A. ARBIB, L. FADIGA & G. RIZZOLATTI. 1996. Localization of grasp representations in humans by PET: 2. Observation compared with imagination. Exp. Brain Res. **112**: 103–111.
27. RIZZOLATTI, G. & M.A. ARBIB. 1998, Language within our grasp. Trends Neurosci. **21(5)**: 188–194.
28. ARBIB, M. & G. RIZZOLATTI. 1997. Neural expectations: a possible evolutionary path from manual skills to language. Commun. Cogn. **29**: 393–424.

29. ARBIB, M.A. 2000. The mirror system, imitation, and the evolution of language. *In* Imitation in Animals and Artifacts. Chrystopher Nehaniv & Kerstin Dautenhahn, Eds. MIT Press. Cambridge, MA. In press.
30. LEE, P. 1999. When is "linguistic relativity" Whorf's linguistic relativity? *In* Explorations in Linguistic Relativity, Vol. 1. M. Pütz & M. Verspoor, Eds. John Benjamins. Amsterdam & Philadelphia. In press.
31. WHORF, B.L. 1937, Discussion of Hopi linguistics. *In* Language, Thought, and Reality: Selected Writings of Benjamin Lee Whorf. J.B. Carroll, Ed. :102–111. MIT Press. Cambridge, MA.
32. HOCKETT, C.F. 1987. Refurbishing Our Foundations: Elementary Linguistics from an Advanced Point of View. John Benjamins. Amsterdam and Philadelphia.
33. GAMBLE, C. 1994. Timewalkers: The Prehistory of Global Colonization. Harvard University Press. Cambridge, MA.
34. HEWES, G. 1973. Primate communication and the gestural origin of language. Curr. Anthropol. **14:** 5–24.
35. CORBALLIS, M.C. 1991. The lopsided ape: evolution of the generative mind. Oxford University Press. New York.
36. CORBALLIS, M.C. 1992. On the evolution of language and generativity. Cognition **44:** 197–226.
37. KIMURA, D. 1993. Neuromotor Mechanisms in Human Communication. (Oxford Psychology Series No. 20.) Oxford University Press/Clarendon Press. Oxford, England.
38. ARMSTRONG, D., W. STOKOE & S. WILCOX. 1995. Gesture and the Nature of Language. Cambridge University Press. Cambridge, MA.
39. LIEBERMAN, P. 1991. Uniquely Human: The Evolution of Speech, Thought, and Selfless Behavior. Harvard University Press. Cambridge, MA.
40. CHOMSKY, N. 1980. Rules and Representations. Columbia University Press. New York.
41. BICKERTON, D. 1995. Language and Human Behavior. University of Washington Press. Seattle, WA.
42. MCNEILL, D. 1992. Hand and Mind: What Gestures Reveal about Thought. The University of Chicago Press. Chicago, IL.
43. KLIMA, E.S. & U. BELLUGI. 1979. The Signs of Language. Harvard University Press. Cambridge MA.

From Computing with Numbers to Computing with Words

From Manipulation of Measurements to Manipulation of Perceptions

LOTFI A. ZADEH

University of California at Berkeley Graduate School, and Berkeley Initiative in Soft Computing (BISC), and Computer Science Division and the Electronics Research Laboratory, Department of EECS, University of California, Berkeley, Berkeley, California 94720-1776, USA

ABSTRACT: Interest in issues relating to consciousness has grown markedly during the last several years. And yet, nobody can claim that consciousness is a well-understood concept that lends itself to precise analysis. It may be argued that, as a concept, consciousness is much too complex to fit into the conceptual structure of existing theories based on Aristotelian logic and probability theory.

An approach suggested in this paper links consciousness to perceptions and perceptions to their descriptors in a natural language. In this way, those aspects of consciousness which relate to reasoning and concept formation are linked to what is referred to as the methodology of *computing with words* (CW).

Computing, in its usual sense, is centered on manipulation of numbers and symbols. In contrast, computing with words, or CW for short, is a methodology in which the objects of computation are words and propositions drawn from a natural language (e.g., *small, large, far, heavy, not very likely, the price of gas is low and declining, Berkeley is near San Francisco, it is very unlikely that there will be a significant increase in the price of oil in the near future*, etc.). Computing with words is inspired by the remarkable human capability to perform a wide variety of physical and mental tasks without any measurements and any computations. Familiar examples of such tasks are parking a car, driving in heavy traffic, playing golf, riding a bicycle, understanding speech, and summarizing a story. Underlying this remarkable capability is the brain's crucial ability to manipulate perceptions—perceptions of distance, size, weight, color, speed, time, direction, force, number, truth, likelihood, and other characteristics of physical and mental objects. Manipulation of perceptions plays a key role in human recognition, decision and execution processes. As a methodology, computing with words provides a foundation for a computational theory of perceptions: a theory which may have an important bearing on how humans make—and machines might make—perception-based rational decisions in an environment of imprecision, uncertainty, and partial truth.

A basic difference between perceptions and measurements is that, in general, measurements are crisp, whereas perceptions are fuzzy. One of the funda-

Address for correspondence: Dr. Lotfi Zadeh, Director, Berkeley Initiative in Soft Computing, University of California, Berkeley, California 94720-1776. Voice: 510-642-4959; fax: 510-642-1712.

zadeh@cs.berkeley.edu

mental aims of science has been and continues to be that of progressing from perceptions to measurements. Pursuit of this aim has led to brilliant successes. We have sent men to the moon; we can build computers that are capable of performing billions of computations per second; we have constructed telescopes that can explore the far reaches of the universe; and we can date the age of rocks that are millions of years old. But alongside the brilliant successes stand conspicuous underachievements and outright failures. We cannot build robots that can move with the agility of animals or humans; we cannot automate driving in heavy traffic; we cannot translate from one language to another at the level of a human interpreter; we cannot create programs that can summarize nontrivial stories; our ability to model the behavior of economic systems leaves much to be desired; and we cannot build machines that can compete with children in the performance of a wide variety of physical and cognitive tasks.

It may be argued that underlying the underachievements and failures is the unavailability of a methodology for reasoning and computing with perceptions rather than measurements. An outline of such a methodology—referred to as a computational theory of perceptions—is presented in this paper. The computational theory of perceptions (CTP) is based on the methodology of CW. In CTP, words play the role of labels of perceptions, and, more generally, perceptions are expressed as propositions in a natural language. CW-based techniques are employed to translate propositions expressed in a natural language into what is called the Generalized Constraint Language (GCL). In this language, the meaning of a proposition is expressed as a generalized constraint, X isr R, where X is the constrained variable, R is the constraining relation, and isr is a variable copula in which r is an indexing variable whose value defines the way in which R constrains X. Among the basic types of constraints are possibilistic, veristic, probabilistic, random set, Pawlak set, fuzzy graph, and usuality. The wide variety of constraints in GCL makes GCL a much more expressive language than the language of predicate logic.

In CW, the initial and terminal data sets, IDS and TDS, are assumed to consist of propositions expressed in a natural language. These propositions are translated, respectively, into antecedent and consequent constraints. Consequent constraints are derived from antecedent constraints through the use of rules of constraint propagation. The principal constraint propagation rule is the generalized extension principle. The derived constraints are re-translated into a natural language, yielding the terminal data set (TDS). The rules of constraint propagation in CW coincide with the rules of inference in fuzzy logic. A basic problem in CW is that of explicitation of X, R and r in a generalized constraint, X isr R, which represents the meaning of a proposition, p, in a natural language.

There are two major imperatives for computing with words. First, computing with words is a necessity when the available information is too imprecise to justify the use of numbers; and second, when there is a tolerance for imprecision which can be exploited to achieve tractability, robustness, low solution cost and better rapport with reality. Exploitation of the tolerance for imprecision is an issue of central importance in CW and CTP. At this juncture, the computational theory of perceptions—which is based on CW—is in its initial stages of development. In time, it may come to play an important role in the conception, design and utilization of information/intelligent systems. Furthermore, it may contribute to a better understanding of those aspects of consciousness that relate to reasoning and concept formation. The role model for CW and CTP is the human mind.

KEYWORDS: Consciousness; Intelligent systems; Theory of perceptions; tolerance; Robustness; Fuzzy logic; Constraint propagation; Computing with words

INTRODUCTION

During the past several years, consciousness and related facets of human cognition have become objects of intense interest. The literature on consciousness is growing at a geometric rate. And yet nobody can claim that consciousness is a well-understood concept that lends itself to precise analysis.

Actually, a stronger statement can be made. More specifically, it may be argued that the concept of consciousness does not fit the conceptual structure of existing scientific theories. The point of departure for this argument is that consciousness may be viewed as the ability to form, manipulate, and reason with perceptions. Now, perceptions have a dual structure. In one respect, they relate to the complex neural processes that take place in the human brain. But in another respect, which is much simpler, perception can be described in a natural language. In a sense, then, perceptions can be equated to their descriptors in a natural language. This, in essence, is the basis for the approach described in this paper.

Human perceptions of time, speed, direction, force, shape, likelihood, possibility, truth and other attributes of physical and mental objects are intrinsically imprecise, reflecting a fundamental limitation on the cognitive ability of the human brain to resolve detail and store information. In more specific terms, perceptions are, for the most part, f-granular, in the sense that (*a*) the values of attributes are granulated, with a granule being a clump of attribute-values which are drawn together by indistinguishability, similarity or proximity; and (*b*) the granules have unsharp (fuzzy) boundaries. For example, when a perception is described as "Michelle is young," then Age is an f-granular variable, with the granules of Age being very young, young, middle-aged, old, very old, etc.

F-granularity of perceptions puts them well beyond the expressive power of conventional meaning-representation languages. For this reason, existing theories, among them probability theory, control theory, and system theory, do not have a capability to operate on perception-based information. As an illustration, probability theory lacks the ability to come up with answers to the questions:

(*a*) Usually Robert returns from work at about 6 pm. What is the probability that Robert is home at 6:30 pm?

(*b*) A box contains twenty balls of various sizes. Several are large and a few are small. What is the probability that a ball drawn at random is neither large nor small?

(*c*) X is a random variable with a small mean and small variance. What is the probability that X is not small?

Let T denote a theory, e.g., probability theory. To enable T to operate on perception-based information it is necessary to generalize T in three stages labeled: f-generalization; f.g-generalization; and nl-generalization. More concretely, f-generalization involves fuzzification, that is, progression from crisp sets in T to fuzzy sets in T, leading to an f.g-generalization of T which is denoted as T^+. For example, if T is probability theory, then in T^+ probabilities, functions, relations, intervals and everything else are allowed to have fuzzy denotations. In particular, probabilities described as low, high, not very high, etc., are interpreted as fuzzy subsets of the unit interval, or, equivalently, as possibility distributions of their numerical values.

F.g-generalization involves f-granulation (fuzzy granulation) of variables, functions, relations, etc., in T, leading to a generalization which is denoted as T^{++}. For example, f-granulation of an interval [1,3] in T leads to an f-granulated interval in which the f-granules are labeled about 1, about 2, and about 3. Membership functions of such granules are usually assumed to be triangular or trapezoidal. Basically, f-granulation may be viewed as a form of fuzzy quantization.

Nl-granulation involves an addition to T^{++} of a capacity to represent the meaning of a proposition which describes a perception in a form that lends itself to computation. Nl-generalization of T^{++} leads to what may be called p-generalization of T denoted as T^p. Basically, this generalization adds to T a capability to operate on perception-based information.

In relation to consciousness, a theory which is of direct relevance is probability theory. Let PT denote standard probability theory of the kind taught in university-level courses. Then PT^+, PT^{++} and PT^p are, respectively, f-generalization, f.g-generalization and p-generalization of PT. Earlier in our discussion it was asserted that PT cannot answer questions (*a*), (*b*) and (*c*). What can be asserted now is that what is needed to answer these questions and, more generally, questions in which the given information is perception-based, is PT^p.

If perceptions are equated to their descriptions in a natural language, then operating on perceptions reduces to manipulation of propositions drawn from a natural language. In our approach, this is done through the use of a fuzzy-logic-cased methodology referred to as computing with words (CW).

Linkage of consciousness to perceptions and linkage of perceptions to computing with words suggest that the methodology of CW could play a significant role in the development of a better understanding of those facets of consciousness which relate to reasoning and concept formation. This remains to be done. The present paper has a much more limited objective of developing the methodology of CW and using it as a formulation for what is called a *computational theory of perceptions* (CTP).

In addition to serving as a foundation for the computation theory of perceptions (FIG. 1), CW serves, more basically, as a way of adding to any measurement-based theory, T, the capabilit yto operate on perception-based information. In essence, there are four principal rationales for the use of CW.

(a) The don't-know rationale. In this case, the values of variables and/or parameters are not known with sufficient precision to justify the use of conventional methods of numerical computing. An example is decision-making with poorly defined probabilities and utilities.

(b) The don't-need rationale. In this case, there is a tolerance for imprecision which can be exploited to achieve tractability, robustness, low solution cost, and better rapport with reality. An example is the problem of parking a car.

(c) The can't-solve rationale. In this case, the problem cannot be solved through the use of numerical computing. An example is the problem of automation of driving in city traffic.

(d) The can't-define rationale. In this case, a concept that we wish to define is too complex to admit of definition in terms of a set of numerical criteria. A case in point is the concept of causality. Causality is an instance of what may be called an amorphic concept.

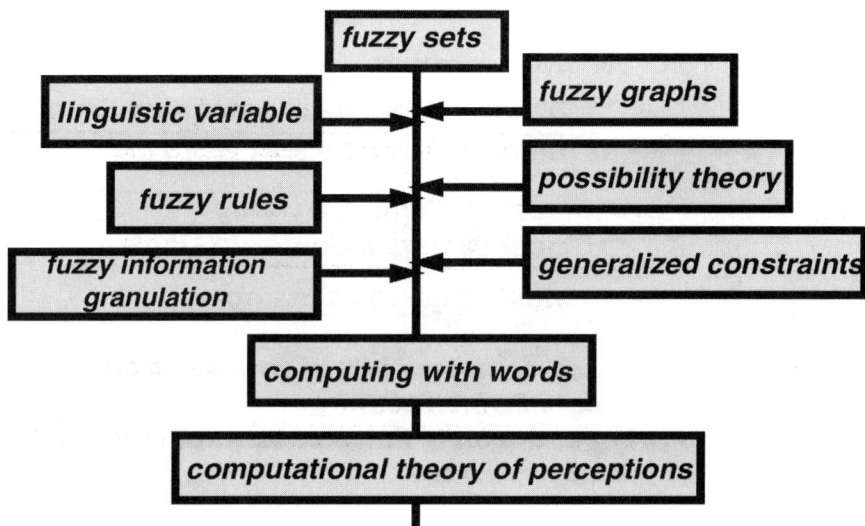

FIGURE 1. Conceptual structure of computational theory of perceptions.

The basic idea underlying the relationship between CW and CTP is conceptually simple.

More specifically, in CTP perceptions and queries are expressed as propositions in a natural language. Then, propositions and queries are processed by CW-based methods to yield answers to queries. Simple examples of linguistic characterization of perceptions drawn from everyday experiences are:

Robert is highly intelligent
Carol is very attractive
Hans loves wine
Overeating causes obesity
Most Swedes are tall
Berkeley is more lively than Palo Alto
It is likely to rain tomorrow
It is very unlikely that there will be a significant increase in the price of oil in the near future

Examples of correct conclusions drawn from perceptions through the use of CW-based methods are shown in FIGURE 2a. Examples of incorrect conclusions are shown in FIGURE 2b.

Perceptions have long been an object of study in psychology. However, the idea of linking perceptions to computing with words is in a different spirit. An interesting system-theoretic approach to perceptions is described in a recent work of R. Vallee.[31] A logic of perceptions has been described by H. Rasiowa.[26] These approaches are not related to the approach described in our paper.

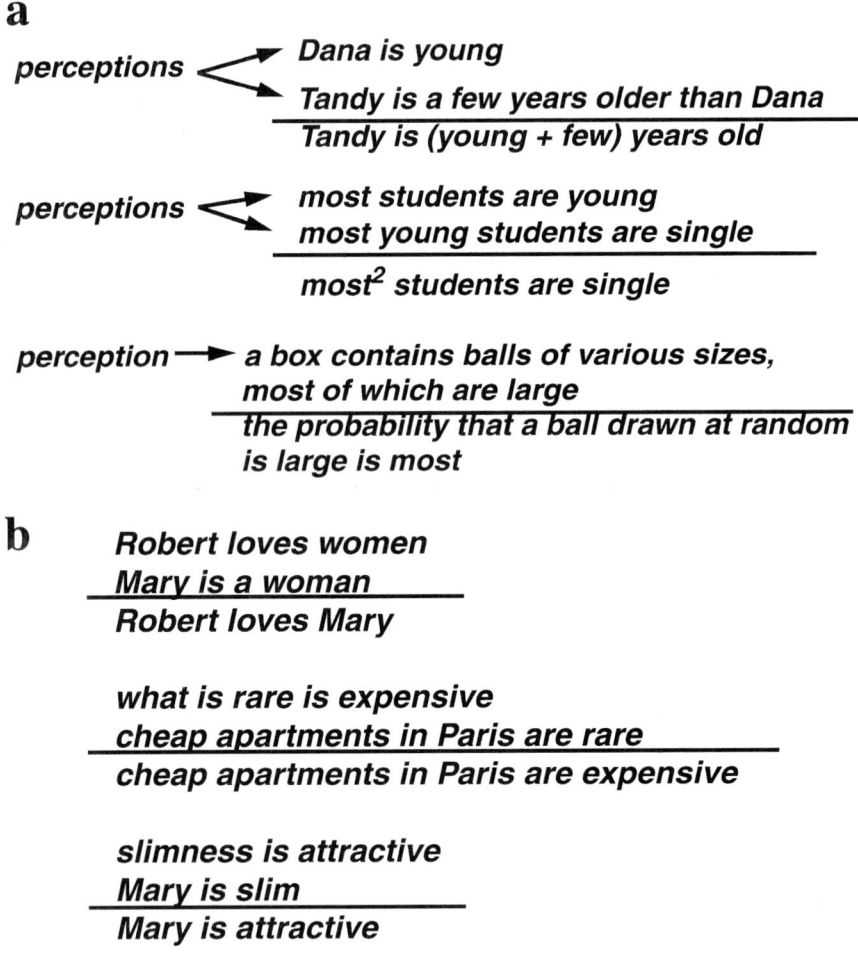

FIGURE 2. (a) Examples of reasoning with perceptions; (b) Examples of incorrect reasoning.

An important point that should be noted is that classical logical systems such as propositional logic, predical, logic and modal logic, as well as AI-based techniques for natural language processing and knowledge representation, are concerned in a fundamental way with propositions expressed in a natural language. The main difference between such approaches and CW is that the methodology of CW—which is based on fuzzy logic—provides a much more expressive language for knowledge representation and much more versatile machinery for reasoning and computation.

In the final analysis, the role model for computing with words is the human mind and its remarkable ability to manipulate both measurements and perceptions. What should be stressed, however, is that although words are less precise than numbers, the methodology of computing with words rests on a mathematical foundation. An exposition of the basic concepts and techniques of computing with words is presented in the following sections. The linkage of CW and CTP is discussed very briefly because the computational theory of perceptions is still in its early stages of development. The linkage of CW to consciousness is a direction that is suggested but not explored.

WHAT IS CW?

In its traditional sense, computing involves for the most part manipulation of numbers and symbols. By contrast, humans employ mostly words in computing and reasoning, arriving at conclusions expressed as words from premises expressed in a natural language or having the form of mental perceptions. As used by humans, words have fuzzy denotations. The same applies to the role played by words in CW.

The concept of CW is rooted in several papers, starting with my 1973 paper "Outline of a New Approach to the Analysis of Complex Systems and Decision Processes,"[37] in which the concepts of a linguistic variable and granulation were introduced. The concepts of a fuzzy constraint and fuzzy constraint propagation were introduced in "Calculus of Fuzzy Restrictions,"[39] and developed more fully in "A Theory of Approximate Reasoning"[45] and "Outline of a Computational Approach to Meaning and Knowledge Representation Based on a Concept of a Generalized Assignment Statement."[49] Application of fuzzy logic to meaning representation and its role in test-score semantics are discussed in "PRUF—A Meaning Representation Language for Natural Languages"[43] and "Test-Score Semantics for Natural Languages and Meaning-Representation via PRUF."[46] The close relationship between CW and fuzzy information granulation is discussed in "Toward a Theory of Fuzzy Information Granulation and its Centrality in Human Reasoning and Fuzzy Logic."[53]

Although the foundations of computing with words were laid some time ago, its evolution into a distinct methodology in its own right reflects many advances in our understanding of fuzzy logic and soft computing—advances which took place within the past few years (see REFERENCES AND RELATED PAPERS.) A key aspect of CW is that it involves a fusion of natural languages and computation with fuzzy variables. It is this fusion that is likely to result in an evolution of CW into a basic methodology in its own right, with wide-ranging ramifications and applications.

We begin our exposition of CW with a few definitions. It should be understood that the definitions are dispositional, that is, admit of exceptions.

As was stated earlier, a concept which plays a pivotal role in CW is that of a granule. Typically, a granule is a fuzzy set of points drawn together by similarity. A word may be atomic, as in *young*, or composite, as in *not very young* (FIG. 3). Unless stated to the contrary, a word will be assumed to be composite. The denotation of a word may be a higher-order predicate, as in Montague grammar.[12,23]

In CW, a granule, g, which is the denotation of a word, w, is viewed as a fuzzy constraint on a variable. A pivotal role in CW is played by fuzzy constraint propagation from premises to conclusions. It should be noted that, as a basic technique, constraint propagation plays important roles in many methodologies, especially in mathematical programming, constraint programming, and logic programming (see REFERENCES AND RELATED PAPERS.)

As a simple illustration, consider the proposition *Mary is young*, which may be a linguistic characterization of a perception. In this case, *young* is the label of a gran-

- *a word is a label of a fuzzy set*

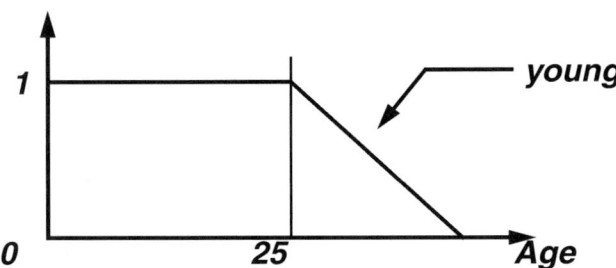

- *a string of words is a label of a function of fuzzy sets*
  - *not very young* ⟶ *(^{2}young)'*
- *a word is a description of a constraint on a variable*
  - *Mary is young* ⟶ *Age(Mary) is young*

FIGURE 3. Words as labels of fuzzy sets.

ule *young*. (Note that for simplicity the same symbol is used both for a word and its denotation.) The fuzzy set *young* plays the role of a fuzzy constraint on the age of Mary (FIG. 3).

As a further example consider the propositions

$$p_1 = \text{Carol lives near Mary}$$

and

$$p_2 = \text{Mary lives near Pat.}$$

In this case, the words *lives near* in p_1 and p_2 play the role of fuzzy constraints on the distances between the residences of Carol and Mary, and Mary and Pat, respectively. If the query is: How far is Carol from Pat?, an answer yielded by fuzzy constraint propagation might be expressed as p_3, where

$$p_3 = \text{Carol lives not far from Pat.}$$

More about fuzzy constraint propagation will be said at a later point.

A basic assumption in CW is that information is conveyed by constraining the values of variables. Furthermore, information is assumed to consist of a collection of propositions expressed in natural or synthetic language. Typically, such propositions play the role of linguistic characterization of perceptions.

A basic generic problem in CW is the following:

We are given a collection of propositions expressed in a natural language which constitute the *initial data set*, or IDS for short.

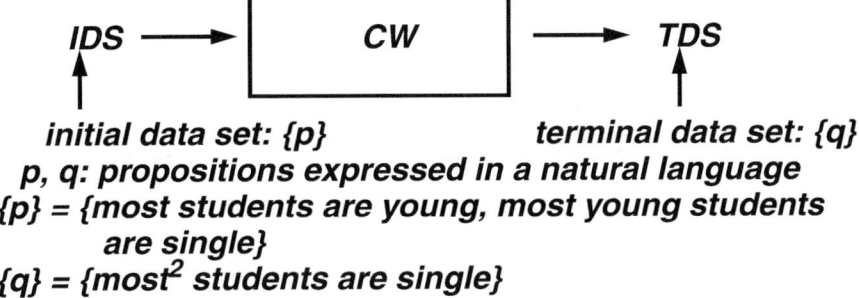

FIGURE 4. Computing with words as a transformation of an initial data set (IDS) into a terminal data set (TDS).

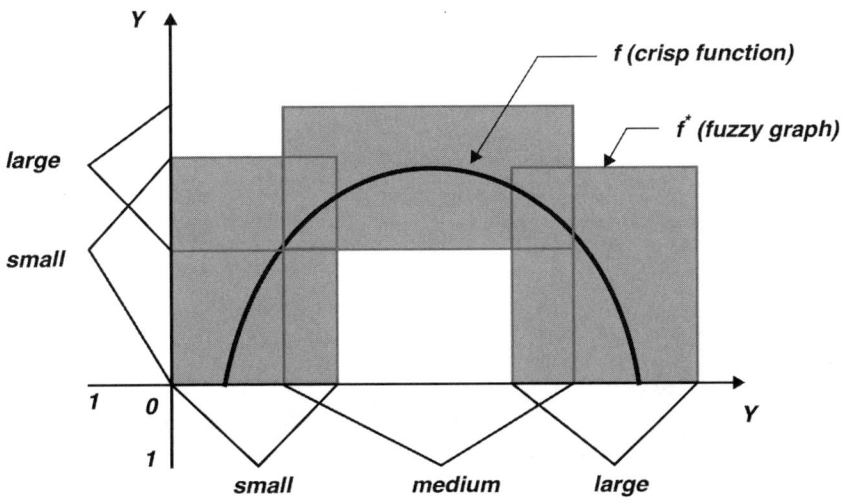

FIGURE 5. Fuzzy graph of a function.

From the initial data set we wish to infer an answer to a query expressed in a natural language. The answer, also expressed in a natural language, is referred to as the *terminal data set*, or TDS for short. The problem is to derive TDS from IDS (FIG. 4).

A few problems will serve to illustrate these concepts. At this juncture, the problems will be formulated but not solved.

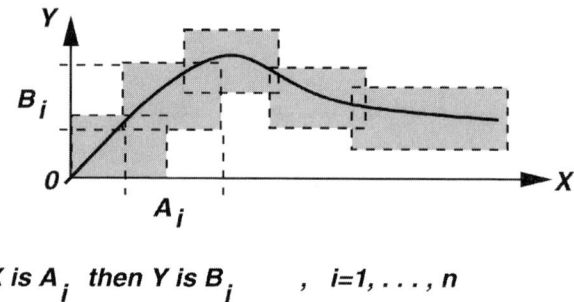

FIGURE 6. A fuzzy graph of a function represented by a rule-set.

1. Assume that a function, f, $f: U \to V$, X is described in words by the fuzzy if-then rules What this implies is that is approximated to by a fuzzy graph (FIG. 5),

f: if X is *small* then Y is *small*
if X is *medium* then Y is *large*
if X is *large* then Y is *small*.

What this implies is that f is approximated to by a fuzzy graph f^* (FIG. 5), where

$f^* = small \times small +$
$medium \times large +$
$large \times small.$

In f^*, + and × denote, respectively, the disjunction and cartesian product. An expression of the form $A \times B$, where A and B are words, will be referred to as a *cartesian granule*. In this sense, a fuzzy graph may be viewed as a disjunction of cartesian granules. In essence, a fuzzy graph serves as an approximation to a function or a relation.[38,51] Equivalently, it may be viewed as a linguistic characterization of a perception of f (FIG. 6).

In the example under consideration, the IDS consists of the fuzzy rule-set f. The query is: What is the maximum value of f (FIG. 7)? More broadly, the problem is: How can one compute an attribute of a function, f (e.g., its maximum value or its area or its roots), if f is described in words as a collection of fuzzy if-then rules? Determination of the maximum value will be discussed in greater detail at a later point.

2. A box contains ten balls of various sizes of which several are large and a few are small. What is the probability that a ball drawn at random is neither large nor small? In this case, the IDS is a verbal description of the contents of the box; the TDS is the desired probability.

3. A less simple example of computing with words is the following:

Let X and Y be independent random variables taking values in a finite set $V = \{v_1, ..., v_n\}$ with probabilities $p_1, ..., p_n$ and $q_1, ..., q_n$, respectively. For simplicity of notation, the same symbols will be used to denote X and Y and and their generic values, with p and q denoting the probabilities of X and Y, respectively.

***f*: if *X* is small then *Y* is small**
if *X* is medium then *Y* is large
if *X* is large then *Y* is small

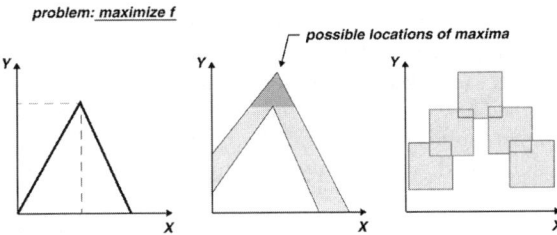

FIGURE 7. Fuzzy graph of a function defined by a fuzzy rule-set.

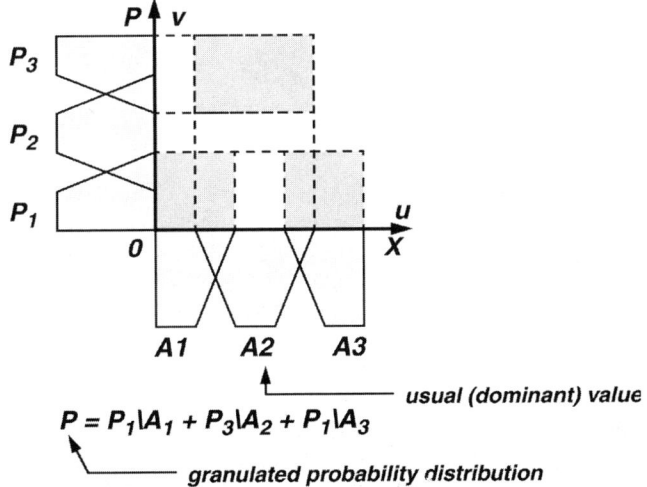

FIGURE 8. A fuzzy graph representation of a granulated probability distribution.

Assume that the probability distributions of X and Y are described in words through the fuzzy if-then rules (FIG. 8):

P: if X is *small* then p is *small*
  if X is *medium* then p is *large*
  if X is *large* then p is *small*

and

Q: if Y is *small* then q is *large*
if Y is *medium* then q is *small*
if Y is *large* then q is *large*

where granules *small, medium,* and *large* are values of linguistic variables X and Y and in their respective universes of discourse. In the example under consideration, these rule-sets constitute the IDS. Note that *small* in P need not have the same meaning as small in Q, and likewise for *medium* and *large*.

The query is: How can we describe in words the joint probability distribution of X and Y? This probability distribution is the TDS.

For convenience, the probability distributions of X and Y and may be represented as fuzzy graphs:

P: *small* × *small* + *medium* × *large* + *large* × *small*
Q: *small* × *large* + *medium* × *large* + *large* × *large*

with the understanding that the underlying numerical probabilities must add up to unity.

Since X and Y are independent random variables, their joint probability distribution (P,Q) is the product of P and Q. In words, the product may be expressed as[51]:

(P,Q): *small* × *small* × (*small*∗*large*) + *small* × *medium* × (*small*∗*small*) +
small × *large* × (*small*∗*large*) + ... + *large* × *large* × (*small*∗*large*)

where ∗ is the arithmetic product in fuzzy arithmetic.[14] In this example, what we have done, in effect, amounts to a derivation of a linguistic characterization of the joint probability distribution of X and Y starting with linguistic characterizations of the probability distribution of X and the probability distribution of Y.

A few comments are in order. In linguistic characterizations of variables and their dependencies, words serve as values of variables and play the role of fuzzy constraints. In this perspective, the use of words may be viewed as a form of granulation, which in turn may be regarded as a form of fuzzy quantization.

Granulation plays a key role in human cognition. For humans, it serves as a way of achieving data compression. This is one of the pivotal advantages accruing through the use of words in human, machine, and man–machine communication.

The point of departure in CW is the premise that the meaning of a proposition, p, in a natural language may be represented as an implicit constraint on an implicit variable. Such a representation is referred to as a *canonical form* of p, denoted as $C,F(p)$ (FIG. 9). Thus, a canonical form serves to make explicit the implicit constraint which resides in p. The concept of a canonical form is described in greater detail in the following section.

As a first step in the derivation of TDS from IDS, propositions in IDS are translated into their canonical forms, which collectively represent *antecedent* constraints. Through the use of rules for constraint propagation, antecedent constraints are transformed into *consequent* constraints. Finally, consequent constraints are translated into a natural language through the use of *linguistic approximation,*[10,18] yielding the terminal data set TDS. This process is schematized in FIGURE 10.

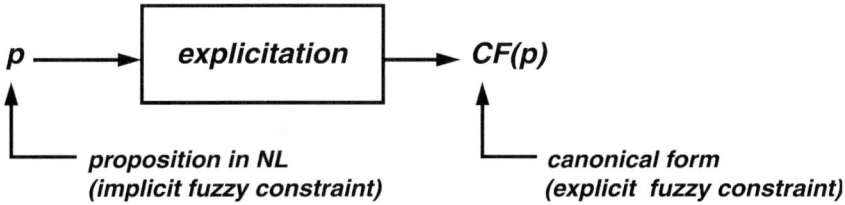

FIGURE 9. Canonical form of a proposition.

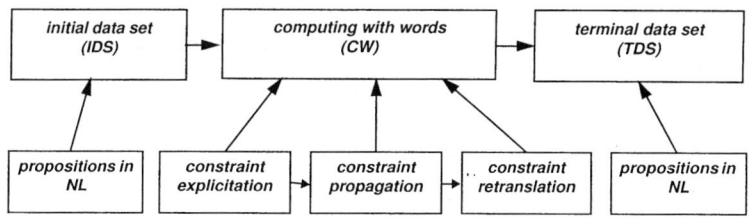

FIGURE 10. Conceptual structure of computing with words.

In essence, the rationale for computing with words rests on two major imperatives. First, computing with words is a necessity when the available information is too imprecise to justify the use of numbers. And second, it is necessary when there is a tolerance for imprecision which can be exploited to achieve tractability, robustness, low solution cost, and better rapport with reality.

In computing with words, two core issues arise. First is the issue of representation of fuzzy constraints. (More specifically, the question is: How can the fuzzy constraints that are implicit in propositions expressed in a natural language be made explicit?) And second is the issue of fuzzy constraint propagation, that is, the question of how fuzzy constraints in premises (i.e., antecedent constraints) can be propagated to conclusions (i.e., consequent constraints).

These are the issues which are addressed in the following sections.

REPRESENTATION OF FUZZY CONSTRAINTS, CANONICAL FORMS, AND GENERALIZED CONSTRAINTS

Our approach to the representation of fuzzy constraints is based on test-score semantics.[46,47] In outline, in this semantics, a proposition, p, in a natural language is viewed as a network of fuzzy (elastic) constraints. Upon aggregation, the constraints which are embodied in p result in an overall fuzzy constraint which can be represented as an expression of the form

$$X \text{ is } R$$

where R is a constraining fuzzy relation and X is the constrained variable. The expression in question is the canonical form of p. Basically, the function of a canonical form is to place in evidence the fuzzy constraint which is implicit in p. This is represented schematically as

$$p \to X \text{ is } R$$

in which the arrow $\to$ denotes explicitation. The variable X may be vector-valued and/or conditioned.

In this perspective, the meaning of p is defined by two procedures. The first procedure acts on a so-called explanatory database, ED, and returns the constrained variable, X. The second procedure acts on ED and returns the constraining relation, R.

An explanatory database is a collection of relations in terms of which the meaning of p is defined. The relations are empty, that is, they consist of relation names, relations attributes and attribute domains, with no entries in the relations. When there are entries in ED, ED is said to be *instantiated* and is denoted EDI. EDI may be viewed as a description of a possible world in possible world semantics,[6] while ED defines a collection of possible worlds, with each possible world in the collection corresponding to a particular instantiation of ED.[47]

As a simple illustration, consider the proposition

$$p = \text{Mary is not young.}$$

Assume that the explanatory database is chosen to be

$$ED = POPULATION[\text{Name; Age}] + YOUNG[\text{Age}; \mu]$$

in which POPULATION is a relation with arguments Name and Age; YOUNG is a relation with arguments Age and μ; and + is the disjunction. In this case, the constrained variable is the age of Mary, which in terms of ED may be expressed as

$$X = \text{Age(Mary)} = {}_{\text{Age}}POPULATION[\text{Name} = \text{Mary}].$$

This expression specifies the procedure which acts on ED and returns X. More specifically, in this procedure, Name is instantiated to Mary and the resulting relation is projected on Age, yielding the age of Mary.

The constraining relation, R, is given by

$$R = ({}^2YOUNG),$$

which implies that the intensifier *very* is interpreted as a squaring operation, and the negation *not* as the operation of complementation.[36]

Equivalently, R may be expressed as

$$R = YOUNG[\text{Age}; 1 - \mu^2].$$

As a further example, consider the proposition

$$p = \text{Carol lives in a small city near San Francisco}$$

and assume that the explanatory database is:

$$\begin{aligned}ED = &\ POPULATION[\text{Name;Residence}] + \\ &\ SMALL[\text{City}; \mu] + \\ &\ NEAR[\text{City1; City2}; \mu]\end{aligned}$$

In this case,
$$X = \text{Residence}(\text{Carol}) = {}_{\text{Residence}}\text{POPULATION}[\text{Name} = \text{Carol}]$$
and
$$R = SMALL[City; \mu] \cap{}_{City1} NEAR[City2 = \text{San\_Francisco}]$$

In R, the first constituent is the fuzzy set of small cities; the second constituent is the fuzzy set of cities that are near San Francisco; and $\cap$ denotes the intersection of these sets.

So far we have confined our attention to constraints of the form
$$X \text{ is } R.$$
In fact, constraints can have a variety of forms. In particular, a constraint—expressed as a canonical form—may be conditional, that is, of the form
$$\text{if } X \text{ is } R \text{ then } Y \text{ is } S,$$
which may also be written as
$$Y \text{ is } S \text{ if } X \text{ is } R.$$
The constraints in question will be referred to as *basic*.

For purposes of meaning representation, the richness of natural languages necessitates a wide variety of constraints in relation to which the basic constraints form an important though special class. The so-called generalized constraints[49] contain the basic constraints as a special case and are defined as follows. The need for generalized constraints becomes obvious when one attempts to represent the meaning of simple propositions such as

Robert loves women
John is very honest
Checkout time is 11 AM
Slimness is attractive

in the language of standard logical systems.

A generalized constraint is represented as
$$X \text{ isr } R$$
where isr, pronounced "ezar," is a variable copula which defines the way in which R constrains X. More specifically, the role of R in relation to X is defined by the value of the discrete variable r. The values of r and their interpretations are defined below.

e : equal (abbreviated to =)
d : disjunctive (possibilistic) (abbreviated to blank)
v : veristic
p : probabilistic
λ : probability value
u : usuality
rs : random set
rfs : random fuzzy set
fg : fuzzy graph
ps : rough set (Pawlak set)
. : ...

As an illustration, when $r = e$, the constraint is an equality constraint and is abbreviated to =. When r takes the value d, the constraint is *disjunctive* (possibilistic) and isd abbreviated to is, leading to the expression

$$X \text{ is } R$$

in which R is a fuzzy relation which constrains X by playing the role of the possibility distribution of X. More specifically, if X takes values in a universe of discourse, $U = \{u\}$ then $Poss\{X = u\} = \mu_R(u)$, where μ_R is the membership function of R, and Π_X is the possibility distribution of X, that is, the fuzzy set of its possible values.[42] In schematic form:

$$X \text{ is } R \quad \begin{array}{l} \longrightarrow \Pi_X = R \\ \longrightarrow Poss\{X = u\} = \mu_R(u). \end{array}$$

Similarly, when r takes the value v, the constraint is *veristic*. In the case,

$$X \text{ isv } R$$

means that if the grade of membership of u in R is μ, then $X = u$ has truth value μ. For example, a canonical form of the proposition

$$p = \textit{John is proficient in English, French, and German}$$

may be expressed as

Proficiency(John) isv (1|English + 0.7|French + 0.6|German)

in which 1.0, 0.7 and 0.6 represent, respectively, the truth values of the propositions *John is proficient in English*, *John is proficient in French,* and *John is proficient in German*. In a similar vein, the veristic constraint

Ethnicity(John) isv (0.5|German + 0.25|French + 0.25|Italian)

represents the meaning of the proposition *John is half German, quarter French and quarter Italian.*

When $r = p$, the constraint is *probabilistic*. In this case,

$$X \text{ isp } R$$

means that R is the probability distribution of X. For example,

$$X \text{ isp } N(m, \sigma^2)$$

means that X is normally distributed with mean m and variance σ^2. Similarly,

$$X \text{ isp } (0.2\backslash a + 0.5\backslash b + 0.3\backslash c)$$

means that X is a random variable which takes the values, a, b, and c with respective probabilities 0.2, 0.5, and 0.3.

The constraint

$$X \text{ isu } R$$

is an abbreviation for

basic premises

- *information is conveyed by constraining -- in one way or another -- the values which a variable can take*

- *when information is conveyed by propositions in a natural language, a proposition represents an implicit constraint on a variable*

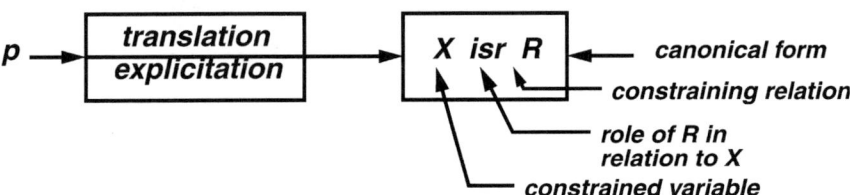

- *the meaning of p is defined by two procedures*

(a) a procedure which identifies X
(b) a procedure which identifies R and r

the procedure act on an explanatory database

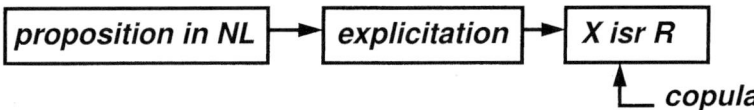

FIGURE 11. Representation of meaning in test-score semantics.

$$usually(X \text{ is } R)$$

which in turn means that

$$Prob\{X \text{ is } R\} \text{ is } usually.$$

In this expression X is R is a fuzzy event and *usually* is its fuzzy probability, that is, the possibility distribution of its crisp probability. The constraint

$$X \text{ isrs } P$$

is a random set constraint. This constraint is a combination of probabilistic and possibilistic constraints. More specifically, in a schematic form, it is expressed as

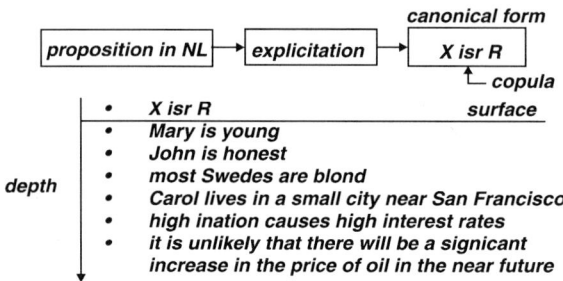

FIGURE 12. Depth of explicitation.

$$X \text{ isp } P$$
$$\frac{(X, Y) \text{ is } Q}{Y \text{ isrs } R}$$

where Q is a joint possibilitistic constraint on X and Y, and R is a random set. It is of interest to note that the Dempster–Shafer theory of evidence[29] is, in essence, a theory of random set constraints.

In computing with words, the starting point is a collection of propositions which play the role of premises. In many cases, the canonical forms of these propositions are constraints of the basic, possibilistic type. In a more general setting, the constraints are of the generalized type, implying that explicitation of a proposition, p, may be represented as

$$p \to X \text{ isr } R$$

where X isr R is the canonical form of p (FIG. 11).

As in the case of basic constraints, the canonical form of a proposition may be derived through the use of test-score semantics. In this context, the depth of p is, roughly, a measure of the effort that is needed to explicitate p, that is, to translate p into its canonical form. In this sense, the proposition X isr R is a surface constraint (depth = zero), with the depth of explicitation increasing in the downward direction (FIG. 12). Thus a proposition such as *Mary is young* is shallow, whereas *it is unlikely that there will be a substantial increase in the price of oil in the near future*, is not.

Once the propositions in the initial data set are expressed in their canonical forms, the groundwork is laid for fuzzy constraint propagation. This is a basic part of CW which is discussed in the following section.

FUZZY CONSTRAINT PROPAGATION AND THE RULES OF INFERENCE IN FUZZY LOGIC

The rules governing fuzzy constraint propagation are, in effect, the rules of inference in fuzzy logic. In addition to these rules, it is helpful to have rules governing fuzzy constraint modification. The latter rules will be discussed at a later point in this section.

In a summarized form, the rules governing fuzzy constraint propagation are the following[51]: (A and B are fuzzy relations. Disjunction and conjunction are defined, respectively, as max and min, with the understanding that, more generally, they could be defined via t-norms and s-norms.[15,24] The antecedent and consequent constraints are separated by a horizontal line.)

conjunctive rule 1

$$\frac{X \text{ is } A \\ X \text{ is } B}{X \text{ is } A \cap B}$$

conjunctive rule 2 $(X \in U, Y \in B, A \subset U, B \subset V)$

$$\frac{X \text{ is } A \\ Y \text{ is } B}{(X, Y) \text{ is } A \times B}$$

disjunctive rule 1

$$\text{or} \quad \frac{X \text{ is } A \\ X \text{ is } B}{X \text{ is } A \cup B}$$

disjunctive rule 2 $(A \subset U, B \subset V)$

$$\frac{X \text{ is } A \\ Y \text{ is } B}{(X, Y) \text{ is } A \times V \cup U \times B}$$

where $A \times V$ and $U \times B$ are cylindrical extensions of A and B, respectively.

conjunctive rule for isv

$$\frac{X \text{ isv } A \\ X \text{ isv } B}{X \text{ isv } A \cup B}$$

projective rule

$$\frac{(X, Y) \text{ is } A}{Y \text{ is proj}_v A}$$

where $\text{proj}_v A = \sup_u A$

surjective rule

$$\frac{X \text{ is } A}{(X, Y) \text{ is } A \times V}$$

derived rules

compositional rule

$$\frac{\begin{array}{c} X \text{ is } A \\ (X, Y) \text{ is } B \end{array}}{Y \text{ is } A \circ B}$$

where $A \circ B$ denotes the composition of A and B.

extension principle (mapping rule)[34,40]

$$\frac{X \text{ is } A}{f(X) \text{ is } f(A)}$$

where $f: U \to U$, and $f(A)$ is defined by

$$\mu_{f(A)}(v) = \sup_{u|v = f(u)} \mu_A(u)$$

inverse mapping rule

$$\frac{f(X) \text{ is } A}{X \text{ is } f^{-1}(A)}$$

where $\mu_{f^{-1}(A)}(u) = \mu_A(f(u))$

generalized modus ponens

$$\frac{\begin{array}{c} X \text{ is } A \\ \text{if } X \text{ is } B \text{ then } Y \text{ is } C \end{array}}{Y \text{ is } A \circ ((\neg B) \oplus C)}$$

where the bounded sum $\neg B \oplus C$ represents Lukasiewicz's definition of implication.

generalized extension principle

$$\frac{f(X) \text{ is } A}{q(X) \text{ is } q(f^{-1}(A))}$$

where

$$\mu_q(v) = \sup_{u|v = f(u)} \mu_A(q(u)).$$

The generalized extension principle plays a pivotal role in fuzzy constraint propagation. However, what is used most frequently in practical applications of fuzzy logic is the *basic interpolative rule*, which is a special case of the compositional rule of inference applied to a function which is defined by a fuzzy graph.[38,51] More specifically, if f is defined by a fuzzy rule set

$$f: \text{if } X \text{ is } A_i \text{ then } X \text{ is } B_i, i = 1, \ldots, n$$

or equivalently, by a fuzzy graph

$$f \text{ is } \Sigma_i A_i \times B_i,$$

and its argument, X, is defined by the antecedent constraint

$$X \text{ is } A,$$

then the consequent constraint on Y may be expressed as

$$Y \text{ is } \Sigma_i m_i \wedge B_i$$

where m_i is a matching coefficient,

$$m_i = \sup(A_i \cap A),$$

which serves as a measure of the degree to which A matches A_i.

syllogistic rule[48]

$$\frac{Q_1 \quad A\text{'s are } B\text{'s}}{Q_2 \quad (A \text{ and } B)\text{'s are } C\text{'s}}$$
$$(Q_1 \otimes Q_2) \, A\text{'s are } (B \text{ and } C)\text{'s}$$

where Q_1 and Q_2 are fuzzy quantifiers; A, B, and C, are fuzzy relations; and $Q_1 \otimes Q_2$ is the product of Q_1 and Q_2 in fuzzy arithmetic.

constraint modification rules[36,43]

$$X \text{ is } mA \rightarrow X \text{ is } f(A)$$

where m is a modifier such as *not*, *very*, *more or less*, and $f(A)$ defines the way in which m modifies A. Specifically,

$$\text{if } m = not \text{ then } f(A) = A' \text{ (complement)}$$

$$\text{if } m = very \text{ then } f(A) = {}^2A \text{ (left square)}$$

where $\mu_{{}^2A}(u) = (\mu_A(u))^2$. This rule is a convention and should not be construed as a realistic approximation to the way in which the modifier *very* functions in a natural language.

probability qualification rule[45]

$$(X \text{ is } A) \text{ is } \Lambda \rightarrow P \text{ is } \Lambda$$

where X is a random variable taking values in U with probability density $p(u)$; Λ is a linguistic probability expressed in words like *likely*, *not very likely*, etc.; and P is the probability of the fuzzy event X is A, expressed as

$$P = \int_U \mu_A(u)p(u)du.$$

The primary purpose of this summary is to underscore the coincidence of the principal rules governing fuzzy constraint propagation with the principal values of inference in fuzzy logic. Of necessity, the summary is not complete and there are many specialized rules which are not included. Furthermore, most of the rules in the summary apply to constraints which are of the basic, possibilistic type. Further development of the rules governing fuzzy constraint propagation will require an extension of the rules of inference to generalized constraints.

As was alluded to in the summary, the principal rule governing constraint propagation is the generalized extension principle, which in a schematic form may be represented as

$$\frac{f(X_1, ..., X_n) \text{ is } A}{}$$

In this expression, $X_1, ..., X_n$ are database variables; the term above the line represents the constraint induced by the IDS; and the term below the line is the TDS expressed as a constraint on the query $q(X_1, ..., X_n)$. In the latter constraint, $f^{-1}(A)$ denotes the preimage of the fuzzy relation A under the mapping $f: U \to V$, where A is a fuzzy subset of V and U is the domain of $f(X_1, ..., X_n)$.

Expressed in terms of the membership functions of A and $q(f^{-1}(A))$, the generalized extension principle reduces the derivation of the TDS to the solution of the constrained maximization problem

$$\mu_{q(X_1, ..., X_n)}(v) = sup_{(u_1, ..., u_n)}(\mu_A(f(u_1, ..., u_n)))$$

in which $u_1, ..., u_n$ are constrained by

$$v = q(u_1, ..., u_n).$$

The generalized extension principle is simpler than it appears. An illustration of its use is provided by the following example.

The IDS is:

most Swedes are tall

The query is: *What is the average height of Swedes?*

The explanatory database consists of a population of N Swedes, $Name_1 ..., Name_N$.

The database variables are $h_1, ..., h_N$, where h_i is the height of $Name_i$, and the grade of membership of $Name_i$ in *tall* is $\mu_{tall}(h_i)$, $i = 1, ..., n$.

The proportion of Swedes who are tall is given by the sigma-count[43]

$$\sum Count\ (tall.Swedes/Swedes) = \frac{1}{N}\sum_i \mu_{tall}(h_i)$$

from which it follows that the constraint on the database variables induced by the IDS is

$$\frac{1}{N}\sum_i \mu_{tall}(h_i) \text{ is } most.$$

In terms of the database variables $h_1, \ldots, h_N$, the average height of Swedes is given by

$$h_{ave} = \frac{1}{N}\sum_i h_i.$$

Since the IDS is a fuzzy proposition, h_{ave} is a fuzzy set whose determination reduces to the constrained maximization problem

$$\mu_{h_{ave}}(v) = sup_{h_1, \ldots, h_N}\left(\mu_{most}\left(\frac{1}{N}\sum_i \mu_{tall}(h_i)\right)\right)$$

subject to the constraint

$$v = \frac{1}{N}\sum_i h_i.$$

It is possible that approximate solutions to problems of this type might be obtainable through the use of neurocomputing or evolutionary-computing-based methods.

As a further example, we will return to a problem stated in an earlier section, namely, maximization of a function, f, which is described in words by its fuzzy graph, f^* (FIG. 7). More specifically, consider the standard problem of maximization of an objective function in decision analysis. Let us assume—as is frequently the case in real-world problems—that the objective function, f, is not well-defined and that what we know about f can be expressed as a fuzzy rule set

$$f: \quad \text{if } X \text{ is } A_1 \text{ then } Y \text{ is } B_1$$
$$\text{if } X \text{ is } A_2 \text{ then } Y \text{ is } B_2$$
$$\text{if } X \text{ is } A_n \text{ then } Y \text{ is } B_n$$

or, equivalently, as a fuzzy graph

$$f \text{ is } \sum_i A_i \times B_i.$$

The question is: What is the point or, more generally, the maximizing set[54] at which f is maximized, and what is the maximum value of f?

The problem can be solved by employing the technique of α-*cuts*.[34,40] With reference to FIGURE 13, if A_{i_α} and B_{i_α} are α-cuts of A_i and B_i, respectively, then the corresponding α-cut of f^* is given by

$$f^*_\alpha = \Sigma_i A_{i_\alpha} \times B_{i_\alpha}.$$

From this expression, the maximizing fuzzy set, the maximum fuzzy set, and maximum value fuzzy set can readily be derived, as shown in FIGURES 13 and 14.

A key point which is brought out by these examples and the preceding discussion is that explicitation and constraint propagation play pivotal roles in CW. This role can

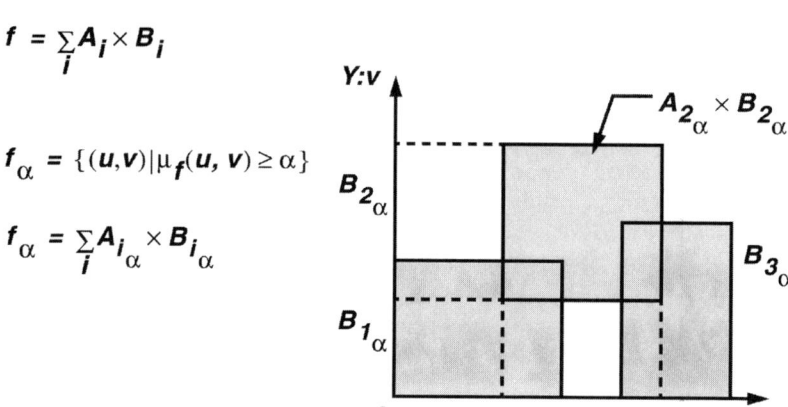

FIGURE 13. Cuts of a function described by a fuzzy graph.

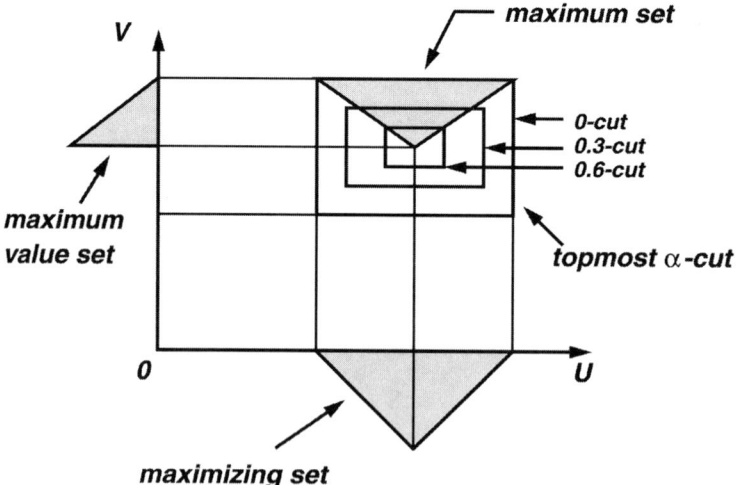

FIGURE 14. Computation of maximizing set, maximum set, and maximum value set.

be concretized by viewing explicitation and constraint propagation as translation of propositions expressed in a natural language into what might be called the *generalized constraint language* (GCL) and applying rules of constraint propagation to expressions in this language—expressions which are typically canonical forms of propositions expressed in a natural language. This process is schematized in FIGURE 15.

The conceptual framework of GCL is substantively differently from that of conventional logical systems, e.g., predicate logic. But what matters most is that the ex-

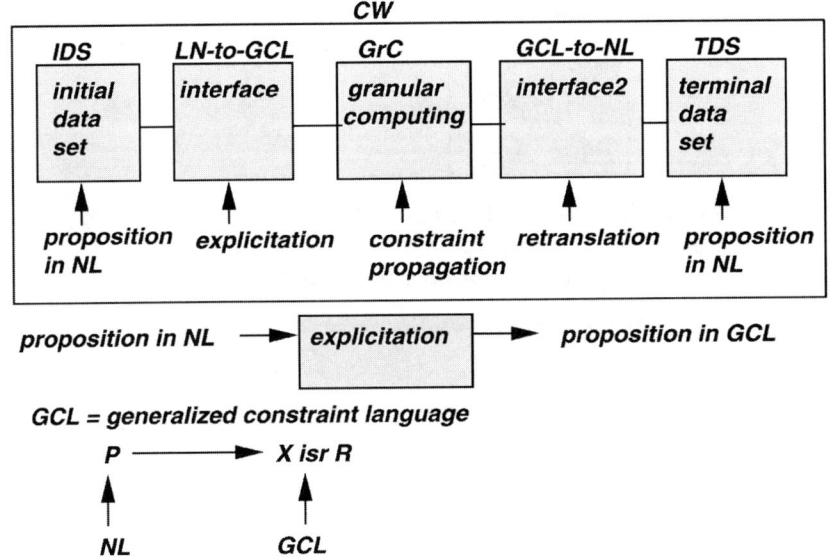

FIGURE 15. Conceptual structure of computing with words.

pressive power of GCL—which is based on fuzzy logic—is much greater than that of standard logical calculi. As an illustration of this point, consider the following problem.

A box contains ten balls of various sizes of which several are large and a few are small. What is the probability that a ball drawn at random is neither large nor small?

To be able to answer this question it is necessary to be able to define the meanings of *large, small, several large balls, few small balls,* and *neither large nor small.* This is a problem in semantics which falls outside of probability theory, neurocomputing, and other methodologies.

An important application area for computing with words and manipulation of perceptions is decision analysis since in most realistic settings the underlying probabilities and utilities are not known with sufficient precision to justify the use of numerical valuations. There exists an extensive literature on the use of fuzzy probabilities and fuzzy utilities in decision analysis. In what follows, we shall restrict our discussion to two very simple examples which illustrate the use of perceptions.

First, consider a box that contains black balls and white balls (FIG. 16). If we could count the number of black balls and white balls, the probability of picking a black ball at random would be equal to the proportion, r, of black balls in the box.

Now suppose that we cannot count the number of black balls in the box but our perception is that most of the balls are black. What, then, is the probability, p, that a ball drawn at random is black?

Assume that *most* is characterized by its possibility distribution (FIG. 17). In this case, p is a fuzzy number whose possibility distribution is *most*, that is,

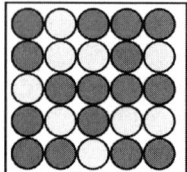

perception : most balls are black
question: what is the probability, P, that a ball drawn at random is black?

FIGURE 16. A box with black and white balls.

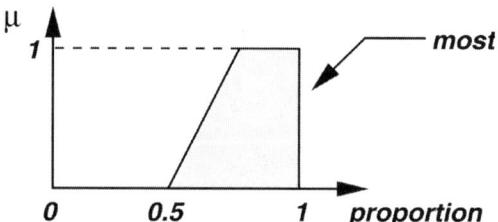

FIGURE 17. Membership function of *most*.

p is *most*.

Next, assume that there is a reward of dollars if the ball drawn at random is black and a penalty of dollars if the ball is white. In this case, if p were known as a number, the expected value of the gain would be:

$$e = ap - b(1 - p).$$

Since we know not p but its possibility distribution, the problem is to compute the value of e when p is *most*. For this purpose, we can employ the extension principle,[34,40] which implies that the possibility distribution, E, of e is a fuzzy number which may be expressed as

$$E = a \, most - b(1 - most).$$

For simplicity, assume that *most* has a trapezoidal possibility distribution (FIG. 17). In this case, the trapezoidal possibility distribution of E can be computed as shown in FIGURE 18.

It is of interest to observe that if the support of E is an interval $[\alpha, \beta]$ which straddles O (FIG. 19), then there is no noncontroversial decision principle which can be employed to answer the question: Would it be advantageous to play a game in which a ball is picked at random from a box in which most balls are black, and a and b are such that the support of E contains O?

Next, consider a box in which the balls $b_1, \ldots, b_n$ have the same color, but vary in size, with b_i, $i = 1, \ldots, n$ having the grade of membership μ_1 in the fuzzy set of

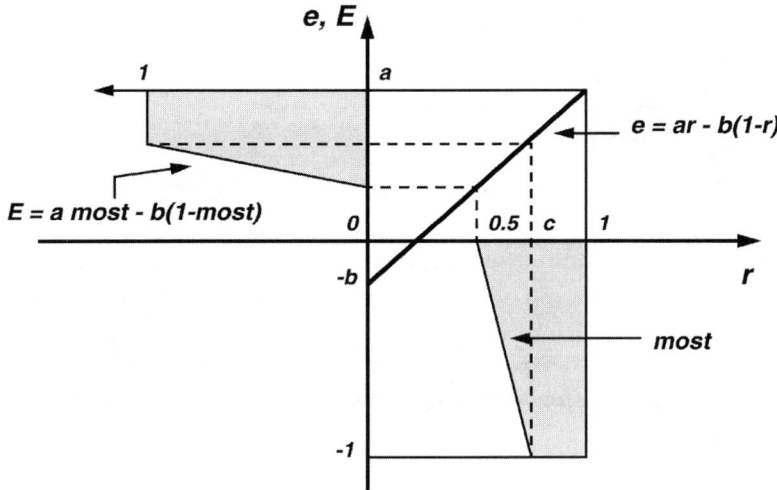

FIGURE 18. Computation of expectation through use of the extension principle.

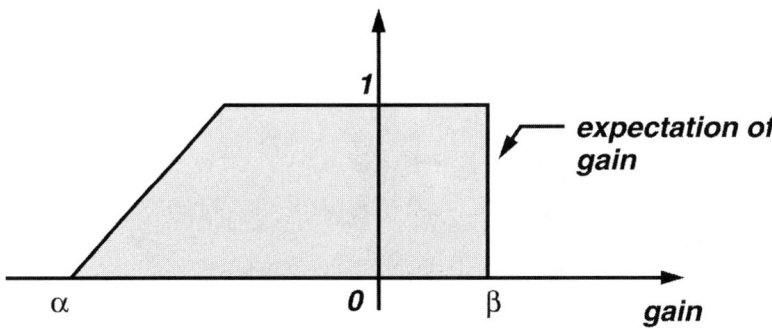

FIGURE 19. Expectation of gain.

large balls (FIG. 20). The question is: What is the probability that a ball drawn at random is large, given the perception that most balls are large?

The difference between this example and the preceding one is that the event *the ball drawn at random is large* is a fuzzy event, in contrast to the crisp event *the ball drawn at random is black*.

The probability of drawing b_i is $1/n$. Since the grade of membership of b_i in the fuzzy set of large balls is μ_i, the probability of the fuzzy event *the ball drawn at random is large* is given by[35]

$$P = \frac{1}{n}\sum \mu_i$$

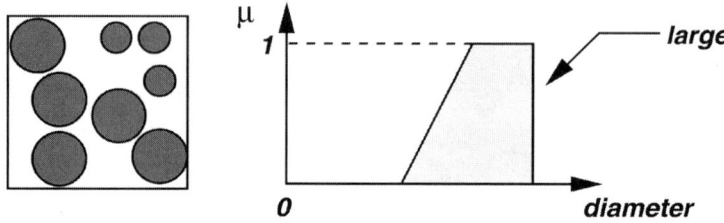

FIGURE 20. A box with balls of various sizes and a definition of large ball.

On the other hand, the proportion of large balls in the box is given by the relative sigma-count[40,43]

$$\sum Count\,(large.balls/balls.in.box) = \frac{1}{n}\sum \mu_i$$

Consequently, the canonical form of the perception *most balls are large* may be expressed as

$$\frac{1}{n}\sum \mu_i \text{ is } most$$

which leads to the conclusion that

$$P \text{ is } most.$$

It is of interest to observe that the possibility distribution of P is the same as in the preceding example.

If the question was: What is the probability that a ball drawn at random is *small?*, the answer would be

$$P \text{ is } \frac{1}{n}\sum v_i$$

where v_i, $i = 1, \ldots, n$, is the grade of membership of b_i in the fuzzy set of small balls, given that

$$\frac{1}{n}\sum \mu_i \text{ is } most.$$

What is involved in this case is constraint propagation from the antecedent constraint on the μ_i to a consequent constraint on the v_i. This problem reduces to the solution of a nonlinear program.

What this example points to is that in using fuzzy constraint propagation rules, application of the extension principle reduces, in general, to the solution of a nonlinear program. What we need—and do not have at present—are approximate methods of solving such programs which are capable of exploiting the tolerance for imprecision. Without such methods, the cost of solutions may be excessive in relation to the imprecision that is intrinsic in the use of words. In this connection, an intriguing possibility is to use neurocomputing and evolutionary computing techniques to arrive at approximate solutions to constrained maximization problems. The use of such techniques may provide a closer approximation to the ways in which humans manipulate perceptions.

CONCLUDING REMARKS

In our quest for machines that have a high degree of machine intelligence (high MIQ), we are developing a better understanding of the fundamental importance of the remarkable human capacity to perform a wide variety of physical and mental tasks without any measurements and any computations. Underlying this remarkable capability is the brain's crucial ability to manipulate perceptions—perceptions of distance, size, weight, force, color, numbers, likelihood, truth and other characteristics of physical and mental objects. A basic difference between perception and measurements is that, in general, measurements are crisp, whereas perceptions are fuzzy. In a fundamental way, this is the reason why to deal with perceptions it is necessary to employ a logical system that is fuzzy rather than crisp.

Humans employ words to describe perceptions. It is this obvious observation that is the point of departure for the theory outlined in the preceding sections.

When perceptions are described in words, manipulation of perceptions is reduced to computing with words (CW). In CW, the objects of computation are words or, more generally, propositions drawn from a natural language. A basic premise in CW is that the meaning of a proposition, p, may be expressed as a generalized constraint in which the constrained variable and the constraining relation are, in general, implicit in p.

In coming years, computing with words and perceptions is likely to emerge as an important direction in science and technology. In a reversal of long-standing attitudes, manipulation of perceptions and words which describe them is destined to gain in respectability. This is certain to happen because it is becoming increasingly clear that in dealing with real-world problems there is much to be gained by exploiting the tolerance for imprecision, uncertainty, and partial truth. This is the primary motivation for the methodology of computing with words (CW) and the computational theory of perceptions (CTP) that are outlined in this paper.

And finally, computing with words will also contribute to a better understanding of those aspects of consciousness which ultimately relate to reasoning and concept formation by the human mind.

ACKNOWLEDGMENTS

This research was supported in part by NASA Grant NAC2-1177, ONR Grant N00014-96-1-0556, ONR Grant FDN0014991035, ARO Grant DAAH 04-961-0341, and the BISC Program of UC Berkeley. This paper is a revised version of a paper under the same title which appeared in the *IEEE Transactions on Circuits and Systems* (Vol. 45: 105–119 [1999]).

REFERENCES AND RELATED READINGS

1. BERENJI, H.R. 1994. Fuzzy reinforcement learning and dynamic programming. *In* Fuzzy Logic in Artificial Intelligence. Proceedings of the IJCAI '93 Workshop. A.L. Ralescu, Ed. :1–9. Springer-Verlag. Berlin.
2. BLACK, M. 1963. Reasoning with loose concepts. Dialog **2:** 1–12.
3. BOSCH, P. 1978. Vagueness, ambiguity and all the rest. *In* Sprachstruktur, Individuum und Gesselschaft. M. Van de Velde and W. Vandeweghe, Eds. Niemeyer. Tubingen.
4. BOWEN, J., R. LAI & D. BAHLER. 1992. Fuzzy semantics and fuzzy constraint networks. *In* Proceedings of the 1st IEEE Conference on Fuzzy Systems (San Francisco) :1009–1016.
5. BOWEN, J., R. LAI & D. BAHLER. 1992. Lexical imprecision in fuzzy constraint networks. *In* Proceedings of the National Conference on Artificial Intelligence. :616–620.
6. CRESSWELL, M.J. 1973. Logic and Languages. Methuen. London.
7. DUBOIS, D., H. FARGIER & H. PRADE. 1994. Propagation and satisfaction of flexible constraints. *In* Fuzzy Sets, Neural Networks, and Soft Computing. R.R. Yager & L.A. Zadeh, Eds. Von Nostrand Reinhold. New York.
8. DUBOIS, D., H. FARGIER & H. PRADE. 2001. Possibility theory in constraint satisfaction problems: handling priority, preference and uncertainty. Applied Intelligence J. In press.
9. DUBOIS, D., H. FARGIER & H. PRADE. 1993. The calculus of fuzzy restrictions as a basis for flexible constraint satisfaction. *In* Proceedings of the 2nd IEEE International Conference on Fuzzy Systems (San Francisco). :1131–1136.
10. FREUDER, E.C. & P. SNOW. 1990. Improved relaxation and search methods for approximate constraint satisfaction with a maximin criterion. *In* Proceedings of the 8th Biennial Conference on the Canadian Society for Computational Studies of Intelligence (Ontario) :227–230.
11. GOGUEN, J.A. 1969. The logic of inexact concepts. Synthese **19:** 325–373.
12. HOBBS, J.R. 1978. Making computation sense of Montague's intensional logic. Artif. Intel. **9:** 287–306.
13. KATAI, O., S. MATSUBARA, H. MASUICHI, M. IDA, *et al.* 1992. Synergetic computation for constraint satisfaction problems involving continuous and fuzzy variables by using Occam. *In* Transputer/Occam: Proceedings of the 4th Transputer/Occam International Conference. S. Noguchi & H. Umeo, Eds. :146–160. IOS Press. Amsterdam.
14. KAUFMANN, A. & M.M. GUPTA. 1985. Introduction to Fuzzy Arithmetic: Theory and Applications. Van Nostrand. New York.
15. KLIR, G. & B. YUAN. 1995. Fuzzy Sets and Fuzzy Logic. Prentice Hall. Englewood Cliffs, NJ.
16. LANO, K. 1991. A constraint-based fuzzy inference system. *In* EPIA 91: 5th Portuguese Conference on Artificial Intelligence. P. Barahona, L.M. Pereira & A. Porto, Eds. :15–26. Springer-Verlag. Berlin.
17. LODWICK, W.A. 1990. Analysis of structure in fuzzy linear programs. Fuzzy Sets and Systems **38(1):** 15–26.
18. MAMDANI, E.H. & B.R. GAINES, Eds. 1981. Fuzzy Reasoning and Its Applications. London.
19. MARES, M. 1994. Computation Over Fuzzy Quantities. CRC Press. Boca Raton, FL.
20. NOVAK, V. 1991. Fuzzy logic, fuzzy sets, and natural languages. Int. J. Gen. Systems **20(1):** 83–97.
21. NOVAK, V., M. RAMIK, M. CERNY & J. NEKOLA, Eds. 1992. Fuzzy Approach to Reasoning and Decision-Making. Kluwer. Boston.
22. OSHAN, M.S., O.M. SAAD & A.G. HASSAN. 1995. On the solution of fuzzy multiobjective integer linear programming problems with a parametric study. Advan. Model. Anal. A **24(2):** 49-64.
23. PARTEE, B. 1976. Montague Grammar. Academic Press. New York.
24. PEDRYCZ, W. & F. GOMIDE. 1998. Introduction to Fuzzy Sets. MIT Press. Cambridge, MA.
25. QI, G. & G. FRIEDRICH. 1992. Extending constraint satisfaction problem solving in structural design. *In* Industrial and Engineering Applications of Artificial Intelli-

gence and Expert Systems: 5th International Conference, IEA/AIE-92. F. Belli & F.J. Radermacher, Eds. 341–350. Springer-Verlag. Berlin.
26. RASIOWA, H. & M. MAREK. 1989. On reaching consensus by groups of intelligent agents. *In* Methodologies for Intelligent Systems. Z.W. Ras, Ed. :234–243. North-Holland. Amsterdam.
27. ROSENFELD, A., R.A. HUMMEL & S.W. ZUCKER. 1976. Scene labeling by relaxation operations. IEEE Transactions on Systems, Man and Cybernetics **6:** 420–433.
28. SAKAWA, M., K. SAWADA & M. INUIGUCHI. 1995. A fuzzy satisficing method for large-scale linear programming problems with block angular structure. Eur. J. Op. Res. **81(2):** 399–409.
29. SHAFER, G. 1976. A Mathematical Theory of Evidence. Princeton University Press. Princeton, NJ.
30. TONG, S.C. 1994. Interval number and fuzzy number linear programming. Advan. Model. Anal. A. **20(2):** 51–56.
31. VALLEE, R. 1995. Cognition et Systeme. l'Interdisciplinaire Systeme(s). Paris.
32. YAGER, R.R. 1989. Some extensions of constraint propagation of label sets. Int. J. Approx. Reasoning **3:** 417–435.
33. ZADEH, L.A. From circuit theory to system theory. Proc. IRE **50:** 856–865.
34. ZADEH, L.A. 1965. Fuzzy sets. Inf. Control **8:** 338–353.
35. ZADEH, L.A. 1968. Probability measures of fuzzy events. J. Math. Anal. Appl. **23:** 421–427.
36. ZADEH, L.A. 1972. A fuzzy-set-theoretic interpretation of linguistic hedges. J. Cybernetics **2:** 4–34.
37. ZADEH, L.A. 1973. Outline of a new approach to the analysis of complex system and decision processes. IEEE Trans. Systems, Man & Cybernetics, **SMC-3:** 28–44.
38. ZADEH, L.A. 1974. On the analysis of large scale systems. *In* Systems Approaches and Environment Problems. H. Gottinger, Ed. :23–37. Vandenhoeck and Ruprecht. Gottingen.
39. ZADEH, L.A. 1975. Calculus of fuzzy restrictions. *In* Fuzzy Sets and Their Applications to Cognitive and Decision Processes. L.A. Zadeh, K.S. Fu & M. Shimura, Eds. :1–39. Academic Press. New York.
40. ZADEH, L.A. 1975. The concept of a linguistic variable and its application to approximate reasoning. Inf. Sci. 8: 199–249 [part I]; 301–357 [part II]; **9:** 43–80 [part III].
41. ZADEH, L.A. 1976. A fuzzy-algorithmic approach to the definition of complex or imprecise concepts. Int. J. Man-Machine Stud. **8:** 249–291.
42. ZADEH, L.A. 1978. Fuzzy sets as a basis for a theory of possibility. Fuzzy Sets & Systems **1:** 3–28.
43. ZADEH, L.A. PRUF—a meaning representation language for natural languages. Int. J. Man-Machines Stud. **10:** 395–460.
44. ZADEH, L.A. 1979. Fuzzy sets and information granularity. *In* Advances in Fuzzy Set Theory and Applications. M. Gupta, R. Ragade & R. Yager, Eds. :3–18. North-Holland. Amsterdam.
45. ZADEH, L.A. 1979. A theory of approximate reasoning. *In* Machine Intelligence, Vol. 9. J. Hayes, D. Michie & L.I. Mikulich, Eds. :149–194. Halstead Press. New York.
46. ZADEH, L.A. 1981. Test-score semantics for natural languages and meaning representation via PRUF. *In* Empirical Semantics. B. Rieger, Ed. :281–349. Brockmeyer. West Germany. [Also Technical Report Memorandum 246, AI Center, SRI International, Menlo Park, CA, 1981.]
47. ZADEH, L.A. 1982. Test-score semantics for natural languages. *In* Proceedings of the Ninth International Conference on Computational Linguistics (Prague) :425–430.
48. ZADEH, L.A. 1984. Syllogistic reasoning in fuzzy logic and its application to reasoning with dispositions. *In* Proceedings of the 1984 International Symposium on Multiple-Valued Logic (Winnipeg, Canada) :148–153.
49. ZADEH, L.A. 1986. Outline of a computational approach to meaning and knowledge representation based on a concept of a generalized assignment statement. *In* Proceedings of the International Seminar on Artificial Intelligence and Man-Machine Systems. M. Thoma & A. Wyner, Eds. :198–211. Springer-Verlag. Heidelberg.

50. ZADEH, L.A. 1994. Fuzzy logic, neural networks and soft computing. Commun. ACM **37(3):** 77–84.
51. ZADEH, L.A. 1996. Fuzzy logic and the calculi of fuzzy rules and fuzzy graphs: a precis. *In* Multiple Valued Logic 1: 1–38. Gordon and Breach. New York.
52. ZADEH, L.A. 1996. Fuzzy logic = computing with words. IEEE Trans. Fuzzy Systems **4:** 103–111.
53. ZADEH, L.A. 1997. Toward a theory of fuzzy information granulation and its centrality in human reasoning and fuzzy logic. *In* Fuzzy Sets and Systems 90: 111–127.
54. ZADEH, L.A. 1998. Maximizing sets and fuzzy markoff algorithms. IEEE Trans. Systems, Man & Cybernetics (Part C: Applications and Reviews) **28:** 9–15.

Who Was Cajal?

ALBERTO PORTERA-SÁNCHEZ

Professor Emeritus of Neurology, Complutense University of Madrid, Madrid, Spain

ABSTRACT: After a brief introduction, a series of Cajal's own thoughts and recollections of his difficult childhood and adolescence are literally transcribed. They clearly represent the astonishing achievements of an equally astonishing child who was born in a tiny village of the Pyrenees mountains. Even today, visitors find it very difficult to understand how it was possible for a child to free himself from a medieval atmosphere and climb to the highest scientific level: to be awarded with the Nobel Prize in Medicine.

KEYWORDS: Ramón y Cajal, life of; Aragón (Spain), as cradle of art and science; Childhood travails and their overcoming; Paternal conflict

INTRODUCTION

Studying Don Santiago's writings shows that his colossal energy and intelligence were already developed as a child. Later in life these qualities allowed him to discover what had remained occult to so many scientists and for such a long time.

The following paragraphs that I am going to read are selected fragments, translated by me, of his autobiography *Recuerdos de mi Vida: Infancia y Juventud*, published in 1901.[1] Cajal describes in great detail the places where he lived as well as the profound transformation of his personality that took place during his childhood and adolescence. This transformation was not easy—rather, it was the consequence of the continual, hard confrontation between the existing rules of society and his family and his own cherished way of life, a way that emanated from the depths of himself, from his still child-like self.

In the first phase of his life three forces were constantly in collision: the firm paternal determination to control his education, the rigid systems of education that prevailed at the time, and his inflexible, passionate desire to become an artist.

Despite losing the many battles that emerged during his school years, Cajal was able to obtain the final victory. Paradoxically, in submitting to his authoritarian father, he was able to reach, later in life, the greatest success. His future would have been totally different had he been the victor in the earlier smaller skirmishes.

From Don Santiago's writings it may be learned that the path he was forced to follow to integrate his natural qualities with his paternal objectives was not an easy one. On many occasions he chose isolation and solitude as a means to be free.

His mood was frequently invaded by melancholy and religious doubts, although his rich imagination gave him intense moments of satisfaction. As a child he was able to feel awe in contemplating natural phenomena and to feel intense desire to un-

Address for correspondence: Fundacion General U.C.M., Donoso Cortés 63, 28015 Madrid, Spain. Voice: 91 394 61 30; fax: 91 391 61 30.

derstand them. In such situations we can appreciate the exquisite qualities that would help him, first to admire and later to understand, the fascinating scenery observed under his microscope throughout his entire life.

WHO WAS CAJAL?

The remainder of this paper consists of Cajal's own words.

Cajal Initiates His Autobiography

I was born on the 1st May of 1852 in Petilla de Aragón....Due to the changing fortune of the medical profession my father, Don Justo Ramón Casadesus, of pure Aragonese extraction and a modest surgeon..., came to work in this insignificant village...in which I spent my two first years of life.

My father was of energetic character...laborious...and full of noble ambition. My mother was...a young, beautiful and robust mountain girl.

Despite the Frequent Confrontations between Father and Son, Cajal Recognized His Enormous Debt to His Father

I cannot complain about my paternal biological inheritance...with his blood he willed me the moral principles to which I owe all that I am: strong will power; faith in work; the conviction that diligent efforts...are capable of modeling and organizing the muscle as well as the brain.

From him I learned...the beautiful ambitions of becoming something...not to spare sacrifice to achieve my goals...nor to allow secondary events to bend my path.

At the Age of 40, He Visited Petilla de Aragón, Where He Had Lived the First Two Years of His Life

More than once I had felt strong desires to visit the humble village where I was born.

I regret not having seen the light for the first time in a great city...I had to content myself with my sad and humble small town. Following the natural feelings of returning home, I undertook a trip to Petilla.

Mounted on a mule...I started my way on a certain day of August...before me appeared the typical, desolate and sad Spanish land...mountains bare of trees.

Petilla is one of the poorest and most abandoned villages in the highlands of Aragón, lacking roads...only rough and narrow trails to reach the humble village.

A great mountain, rough and rocky...massively fills the entire horizon...colossal rocks...seeming cyclopean walls which had emerged from the impulse of a geological cataclysm.

At the Age of Four He Began His Schooling

My education and instruction began in Valpalmas when I was four years old...in the modest school...I began the first steps of understanding letters...but...my true teacher was my father, who decided to teach me how to read and write and to introduce me to the notions of geography, physics, arithmetic and grammar... for him, ignorance was the greatest of disgraces and teaching the noblest of duties.

Thanks to his care... at 6 years of age I was able to write correctly... and knew some concepts of geography, French and arithmetic.

Among my natural inclinations included... the curiosity for and contemplation of natural phenomena and a certain dislike for social interaction.

Cajal's Admiration of Natural Phenomena Evoked a Clear Feeling of Satisfaction but, at the Same Time, a Need to Withdraw from Society

During my childhood I was a restless and mysterious creature, withdrawn and antisocial.... Still, some of this brisk anti-sociability so often censured by my parents and friends lasts in me today.

There is a special egoism in recapitulating one's own ideas. This brings a certain pleasure.... Far from others, we create the illusion of being completely free. Solitude produces something like self-control.

The admiration of Nature was one of the powerful tendencies of my spirit... the splendor of the sun, the magic of sunsets. The varied and picturesque decoration of the mountains. A passion for animals was aroused in me specially for birds.... I watched the marvelous process of incubation and followed the metamorphosis of the new born.

At Age Seven He Noted His First Philosophical and Religious Doubts as a Consequence of a Deep Impression Felt While Watching Someone Dying

One day, while in school, the skies were suddenly darkened when an instantaneous and horrible explosion froze the blood in our veins... terrified we madly searched for our way out....

A loud voice directed our attention towards a strange and blackish figure hanging from the bell tower... there, under the bell the body of the unfortunate priest remained immobile... he died a few days later.

Lightning had hit the tower and partially melting the bell had electrocuted the priest. For the first time the concepts of disorder and chaos penetrated my mind.

For a child Nature represents a perpetual miracle as learned from the catechism.... a God exists on high, who piously makes vigil over the great cosmic machinery and maintains the order among its elements.

... Suddenly such a beautiful conception started to waiver. The cheerful palette of the sublime Artist darkened and converted into tragedy. My spirit floated in a sea of confusion and all my anxious questions failed to find a satisfactory response.

His Natural Ability for Drawing and Painting Was Going to Be the Cause of Persistent Conflicts with His Father

It was then at the age eight or nine that a strong artistic sensibility emerged in me.

A white wall always exerted irresistible fascination upon me... but since I was not permitted to draw at home because my parents considered painting an unproductive distraction, I went to the fields and sketched carriages, horses, peasants and whatever scenery seemed interesting to me.

Discontented with the world I found refuge within myself. Within the theater of my febrile fantasy I substituted ordinary people for idealized characters with no other occupation than the serene contemplation of truth and beauty.

Observing my intense vocation for painting my father decided that I renounce my whims for drawing and that I prepare myself for the study of medicine...thus emerged the rigid opposition to my strongly felt vocation.

When I was almost 10 years old my father decided to send me to study in Jaca...to a school famous for taming unruly and defiant youths.

In 1862 He Traveled to Jaca

A certain beautiful September morning I started my way towards the border city. This was the first time that I was away from home...I was invaded by melancholy.

In Jaca my father handed me over to the Escolapian Fathers and advised them to rigidly supervise me and punish me without remorse for any behavioral deviation.

Each Day His Vocation for the World of Art Grows—As a Consequence His School Failure Is More Apparent

My artistic fantasies vigorously resurged...I disliked Latin, grammar, and a relentless physical and moral struggle between my brain and books commenced.

I frankly confess that I am solely responsible for my poor success in school. My body was undoubtedly sitting in the classroom but my spirit was continuously wandering about imaginary spaces...the written pages slipped through my head without entering in to my brain.

The Observation of the Natural World Became a Continuous Need

I was fortunate to find great comfort in art and in the contemplation of Nature. Facing the formidable mountains surrounding Jaca, the historical Aragonese city, I was able to forget my own sadness.

The city itself charmed me. I enjoyed savoring the beauty of the ancient cathedral, exploring its towers and climbing the city walls. My foremost aspiration was to walk up the river and reach the peaks of the Pyrenees. What will there be behind these gigantic, white, silent and immutable peaks? Will it be possible to see France with its green mountains, its fertile valleys, and its beautiful cities?

The Punishments in School Constantly Increased

Facing the failure of the traditional systems of punishment the holy fathers experimented upon me the techniques of fasting. Each day I was kept in the classroom without food until dark. Finally I stopped going to school and wrote to my father about what was occurring.

Due to His Persistence a Drastic Decision Was Made

In 1865 my schooling was interrupted because my father considered that I lacked maturity...this was my third high school year, the most agitated and hazardous of my life as a student.

As a punishment I had to accept a job in a barbershop...my father was trying to rein in my freedom and teach me a skill with which some day I might earn a living.

At 14 I interpreted my slavery as an excessive punishment. Precisely when waves of romanticism were coursing my soul, I was forced to wield the dirty and soapy barber brush.

His Reintegration to School Did Not Yield Satisfactory Results

After what has been noted, it is superfluous to say that my scientific and literary instruction did not progress during 1866. But I could have passed the exams if my professor of Greek had not converted me into the target of his bad humor.

I was certain of my failure so decided not to present myself for examinations... my father was furious and punished me again. Before finishing the school year he put me to work as an apprentice to a shoemaker. One year as a "shoe-repair" boy passed when my father, satisfied with his educational experiment, decided to send me back to school....

A Short Time after, Cajal Began to Study Medicine in Zaragoza...

CONCLUSION

Cajal's fundamental discoveries permit us, without any doubt, to grant him the paternity of most of we know about the structure of the nervous system and to consider him as one of the most important scientists in the history of neuroscience.

In view of his natural abilities and his endurance and imagination, Cajal could have well become an acceptable barber or might even have founded a magnificent barbershop. He could also have been an excellent shoe designer. He was close to becoming a family doctor like his father. But it was his first encounter with the microscope that can be considered the most important moment in the history of neuroscience. Many renowned scientists had previously used the microscope, but no one had been able to obtain the enormous amount of information that Cajal was able to accumulate.

Cajal, using the microscope as a tool, was able to open the magic door through which he could use his avid mind to discover and interpret the marvelous complex structures and functions of the most perfected system towards which life has evolved in the Universe: the human brain.

REFERENCE

1. RAMÓN Y CAJAL, S. 1901. Recuerdos de mi Vida: Infancia y Juventud.

Index of Contributors

Albright, T.D., 11–40
Arbib, M.A., 195–220

Changeux, J.-P., 147–151, 152–165

Dehaene, S., 152–165

Edelman, G., 111–122

Gell-Mann, M., 41–49

Hameroff, S., 74–104

Jacob, F., 71–73
Jessell, T.M., 11–40

Kandel, E.R., 11–40

Kerszberg, M., 152–165

Llinás, R., 166–175

Margulis, L., 55–70
Marijuán, P.C., 1–10
Morowitz, H.J., 50–54

Penrose, R., 105–110
Portera-Sánchez, A., 253–257
Posner, M.I., 11–40

Ribary, U., 166–175

Singer, W., 123–146
Stoerig, P., 176–194

Zadeh, L.A., 221–252

Subject Index

Afterimages, 184–185
Alerting function, localization of [fig.], 33
Anatomists' early view of neurons, 11–12
Aragón (Spain), as cradle of learning, 8–9, 253–257
Assemblies, coding of, 127–129
Awareness, 29–31, 124–125

Behavioral states and response synchronization, 131–134
Binding problem, 21–23, 105-110,
Biological complexity, 4–5
Biological information processing, 51–53
Bionts [fig.], 62
Blindsight, 176–190
Borrelia, 65
Brain
   and consciousness, 166–173
   and spacetime geometry, 74–100, 105–110
   what Cajal would find now, 75–77
Brain economy, 3–8
Brain imaging, 161–162
Brain state vs. mental state, 198–200
Broca's area, 210

Canonical forms, 233–249
Cerebral cortex, 123–143
Childhood travails of Ramón y Cajal, 253–257
Cingulate cortex
   and cognition and emotion, 31–35
   and volition, 31–35
Cladonia cristatella (British-soldier lichens) [fig.], 61
Cognition and anterior cingulate, 31–35
Cognitive conjunction and temporal mapping, 168–170
Cognitive process, organization of, 126–127

Cognitive tasks, global workspace in, 152–163
Communication systems, 213–217
Complexity, 41–49
   cosmic growth of, 51
Computation in information processing, 17–18
Computational theory of perceptions [fig.], 225
Computer simulation of global workspace, 156–161
Computing with words, 221–249
Connection specificity, 15
Conscious cell, 55–70
Consciousness
   and binding problem, 123–143
   and neurology, 203–205
   and spacetime geometry 74–100, 105–110
   analysis of, 28–35
   basic neuronal circuit in, 167
   characterizing, 43–44
   co-evolution of, and language, 195–218
   interdisciplinary view of, 3
   primary and higher-order, 5–8, 111–122
   remembered present, 111–122
   visual, and V1/V2, 189–190
Curved spacetime superpositions, 81–84

Decoherence, 74–100
   and quantum state in brain, 92–96
Decoherence, 74–100
Decohering histories, 41–49
Dendrites, 74–100 (*passim*)
Distributed schemas and language, 200–203
Doctrine of the neuron, 6, 11–13
Dreaming, 185–186
Duplication, 71–73
Dynamic polarization, principle of, 12–14

Emergence and physical laws, 46–47
Emotion and anterior cingulate, 31–35
Emotional function, localization of [fig.], 33
Epistemology of mind and matter, 50–54
Eukaryosis, 65–69
Eukaryotic cells, evolution of, 56–59
Evolution of consciousness, 97–99
 of nervous system, 53–54
Evolutionary novelties, 55–69, 71–73
Explicitation, depth of [fig.], 237
Extrastriate cortex, 176–190

Fuzzy constraints, 233–249
Fuzzy graphs (figs.), 229–231

Gamma band activity
 binding of, 171–172
 during sleep [fig.], 169
Gap junctions, 74–100 (*passim*)
 connecting dendrites [fig.], 92
General relativity, 74–100
Global workspace
 neuronal model of, 152–163
 processors connected to [fig.], 154
Grasping, 208–210
Gratings, superimposed [fig.], 139

Hallucinations, 187–188
Higher-order consciousness, 111–110
Hippocampus, neural circuitry of [fig.], 13

Imagery, 186–187
Imitation system, 212, 213
Information processing
 biological, 51–53
 mechanisms of, 17
Introspection, 167–168

James, William, 111–112

Karyomastigonts, 55–69
 history of [fig.], 67

Language
 and co-evolution of consciousness, 195–218
 and distributed schemas, 200–203
 mirror system approach to, 210–217
Language-readiness, 210–211
Laws of nature, 41–49
Life, geological time scale of [fig.], 58
London forces, 74–100 (*passim*)

Maximum set [fig.], 244
Measurement problem, 105–110
Memory, 111–122
Mental effort, 152–163
Mental state vs. brain state, 198–200
Microtubule automaton simulations (figs.), 88, 89
Microtubule structure [fig.], 87
Microtubules
 in axons and dendrites [fig.], 85
 Orch-OR model in, 74–100, 105–110
 quantum computation in, 85–91
Mind and matter, 50
Minimal cell [fig.], 59
Mirror neuron [fig.], 209
Mirror system
 and language evolution, 210–217
 for grasping, 208–210
Mixotricha, 66-69
 individual cell of [fig.], 68
Molecular recognition, 71–73

Nature, laws of, 41–49
Nervous systems, evolution of, 53–54
Network architecture of global workspace, 156–161
Neural systems, 15–18
Neuroanatomy, 16–17
Neurodynamic optimization, 7, 8
Neurology and consciousness, 203–205
Neuronal plasticity and perception, 23–25

SUBJECT INDEX

Neuronal science, future breakthroughs in, 36–37
Neuronal synchronization [fig.], 132–133
  under binocular rivalry [fig.], 136–137
Neurons
  anatomists' early view of, 11–12
  cortical, and attention, [fig.], 27
Neurophysiology, 17, 19
Neuropsychology, 16
Neurosciences, progress in, 4–5
Neurotransmitters, Cajal on, 147–150
Non-computability, 105–110
Non-veridical phenomenal vision, 183–188
Nuclear origins, 55–69

Objective reduction (OR), orchestrated (Orch), 74–100, 105–110
Orch OR event [fig.], 90, 98
Orch-OR model, 87–100, 105–110

Pauli exclusion principle, 51
Penrose-Hameroff Orch OR model in microtubules, 87–91
Perception (*see also* Visual perception)
Perception
  and neuronal plasticity, 23–25
  and neuronal synchronization, 134-140
  and volition, 96–100
Perceptions, computing with, 221–249
Perceptual categorization, 111–122
Phenomenal vision, psychological perspective on, 176–190
Phosphenes, 184
Physical laws and emergence, 46–47
Prefrontal cortex and cognitive tasks, 152–163
Primary consciousness, 111–122
  model of [fig.], 120
Primate calls, 211–212
Proposition, canonical form of [fig.], 233

Protein conformation, 74–100 (*passim*)
Protoctista, evolutionary origins of, 62–65
Psychophysics, 17

Qualia, mental [fig.], 97
Quantum coherent superposition [fig.], 83
Quantum interpretations, 41–49
Quantum non-locality, 41–49, 105–110
Quantum superposition in microtubules [fig.], 91
Quantum theory, 74–100
Quantum-classical borderline, 105–110

Ramón y Cajal, Santiago
  and consciousness, introduction to, 1–10
  and dynamic polarization, 147–148
  and nature of consciousness, 195–198
  appreciation of work of, 105–107
  figure of, 8–9
  from molecules to consciousness, 149–150
  life of, 253–257
  statue of [fig.], 57
Reality emulation, 167–168
Reasoning with perceptions [fig.], 226
Receptors, Cajal on, 147–150
Reductionism, 41–49
Reentrant connections, 111–122
Reshuffling, 71–73
Response synchronization, 130–134

Self-consciousness, 125–126
Self-selection, 77–79
Self-similarity in nature, 44–46
Semantics, test-score [fig.], 238
Social cooperation and consciousness, 205–208
Speech, 214–215
Spirochete and thermoplasma merger, 65–69
Spirosymplokos, 65, 66

Stroop task
  and global workspace, 156–161
  temporal dynamics in learning [fig.], 160
Subjective experience, 96–100
Symbiogenesis, antecedents of, 60
Symbiosis, 55–69
Synaptic transmission, Cajal on, 147–150
Synchronization, 123–143

Temporal mapping and cognitive conjunction, 168–170
Textura, 1–2
Thalamocortical circuits [fig.], 172
Thalamocortical dialogue, 166–173
Thalamocortical dysrhythmic syndrome, 172–173
Thermoplasma and spirochete merger, 65–69
Time granularity, 5
Tinkering, 71–73

Tubulin, 74–100 (*passim*)

V1, role of, 180–181
Van der Waals forces, 74–100 (*passim*)
Veridical phenomenal vision, 179–183
Visual cortical areas [fig.], 178
Vision linked with other brain systems, 25–28
Visual pathways, primary [fig.], 179
Visual perception, 123–143
  and sensory context [fig.], 20
Visual system
  fundamental themes in, 18–25
  organization of, 177–179
Volition, 31–35
  and perception, 96–100

Words
  as labels of fuzzy sets [fig.], 228
  computing with, 221–249

OHIO UNIVERSITY LIBRARY
Please return this book as soon as you have finished with it. In order to avoid a fine it must be returned by the latest date stamped below. All books are subject to recall after two weeks or immediately if needed for reserve.

CF